The international handbook of addiction behaviour

'Helping people with substance problems is a difficult business . . . the common sense and vision which this text offers will . . . help the helping professions to make that business better informed, more effective and a little more humane.'

Professor Griffith Edwards in the *Foreword*

International in its scope and multidisciplinary in its approach, *The International Handbook of Addiction Behaviour* gives authoritative coverage of current issues in the addiction field in an easy reference form. It brings together the full variety of scientific approaches to addiction behaviour and provides a sound theoretical grounding to the clinical situation.

Written by experts and based on clinical and teaching experience, the *Handbook* proposes a way forward towards integrated treatment interventions. It covers a wide range of licit and illicit drugs including alcohol, nicotine, heroin and cannabis, and deals with gambling as an example of a non-drug dependence. It discusses many aspects of treatment, training, prevention and policy formation in an international perspective.

The International Handbook of Addiction Behaviour breaks new ground by highlighting the links between clinical work, training and research and sets an agenda for a new approach in the addictions field. It will be an invaluable guide for students, trainers and professionals.

The international handbook of addiction behaviour

Edited by
Ilana Belle Glass

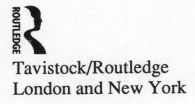

Tavistock/Routledge
London and New York

This book is for
Peter Crome
Griffith and Sue Edwards
Yette and Boris Glass

First published in 1991
by Routledge
11 New Fetter Lane, London EC4P 4EE

Simultaneously published in the USA and Canada
by Routledge
a division of Routledge, Chapman and Hall Inc.
29 West 35th Street, New York, NY 10001

©1991 The collection as a whole: Ilana Belle Glass; individual chapters: the contributors

Typeset by LaserScript Limited, Mitcham, Surrey
Printed and bound in Great Britain by
Mackays of Chatham PLC, Chatham, Kent

British Library Cataloguing in Publication Data
The international handbook of addiction behaviour
1. Drug addiction
I. Glass, Ilana Belle, *1951–*
362.293

Library of Congress Cataloging in Publication Data
The international handbook of addiction behaviour/edited by Ilana Belle Glass.
p. cm.
Includes bibliographical references and index.
1. Substance abuse. 2. Compulsive behavior. I. Glass, Ilana Belle, 1951–
[DNLM: 1. Substance – Abuse handbooks. WM 34 1608]
RC564.I585 1991
616.86–dc20
DNLM/DLC
for Library of Congress
90–9106
CIP

ISBN 0-415-06189-X
      0-415-04127-9 (pbk)

Contents

Contributors

Dr Adityanjee
Registrar
Maudsley Hospital
Denmark Hill
London SE5 8AF
(Tel. 071 703 5411)

Dr Robert M. Anthenelli
Research Fellow
Department of Psychiatry
University of California-San Diego
    (UCSD)
School of Medicine and Alcohol Research
Department of Veterans Affairs Medical
    Center
San Diego
California 92161
USA
(Tel. 619 552 8585)

Dr Keith Ball
Vice President, Action on Smoking
    and Health
Central Middlesex Hospital
Horace Joules Hall
London NW10 7NS
(Tel. 081 965 6393)

Dr Trevor Bennett
University Lecturer
Institute of Criminology
University of Cambridge
7 West Road
Cambridge CB3 9DT
(Tel. 0223 337733)

Dr Ian Bennun
District Psychologist
Torbay Health Authority
Newton Abbot Hospital
East Street
Newton Abbot
Devon
TQ12 4PT
(Tel. 0626 54321)

Dr Morris Bernadt
Honorary Senior Lecturer
Academic Department of Psychological
    Medicine
King's College Hospital
Denmark Hill
London SE5 9RS
(Tel. 071 274 6222)

Dr Sheila Blume
Director
The South Oaks Institute of Alcoholism
    and Addictive Behaviour Studies
Amityville
New York 11701
USA
(Tel. 516 264 4000)
and
Clinical Professor of Psychiatry
SUNY at Stoney Brook
New York 11701
USA

Dr Deborah Brooke
Clinical Lecturer in Addictive Behaviour
Department of Addictive Behaviour
St George's Hospital Medical School
Cranmer Terrace
London SW17 0RE
(Tel. 081 672 9944)

Ms Cheryl Brown
Formerly Clinical Nurse Specialist
Addiction Research Unit
Institute of Psychiatry
101 Denmark Hill
London SE5 8AF
(Tel. 071 703 5411)

Dr Michael Bury
Senior Lecturer
Royal Holloway and Bedford New College
Department of Medical Sociology
11 Bedford Square
London WC1B 3RA
(Tel. 071 580 7112)

Dr Anna Rose Childress
Associate Professor of Psychology in
    Psychiatry
University of Pennsylvania
School of Medicine
Addiction Research Center
3910 Chestnut St/6178
Philadelphia
PA 19104
USA
(Tel. 215 222 3200)

Ms Jo Coupe
Rugby Probation Office
The Courthouse
Newbold Road
Rugby CV21 2LH
Warwickshire
(Tel. 0788 74814)

Dr Peter Crome
Consultant Physician
George Stamp Unit
Orpington Hospital
Orpington
Kent BR6 9JU
(Tel. 0689 27050)

Dr D. Colin Drummond
Research Psychiatrist
Addiction Research Unit
Institute of Psychiatry
101 Denmark Hill
London SE5 8AF
(Tel. 071 703 5411)

Professor Griffith Edwards
Director
National Addiction Centre
Institute of Psychiatry
De Crespigny Park
London SE5 8AF
(Tel. 071 703 5411)

Dr W. Falkowski
Consultant Psychiatrist and Honorary
    Senior Lecturer
Springfield Hospital
61 Glenburnie Road
London SW17 7DJ
(Tel. 081 672 9911)

Dr Michael Farrell
Senior Research Registrar
Addiction Research Unit
Institute of Psychiatry
De Crespigny Park
London SE5 8AF
(Tel. 071 703 5411)

Dr Marian W. Fischman
Professor
The Johns Hopkins University School of
    Medicine
Houck Building, East-2
600 North Wolfe Street
Baltimore
Maryland 21205
USA
(Tel. 301 955 7036)

Dr R.J. Flanagan
Principal Biochemist
Poisons Unit
New Cross Hospital
Avonley Road
London SE14 5ER
(Tel. 071 635 0858)

Dr Richard W. Foltin
Assistant Professor of Behavioral Biology
Department of Psychiatry and Behavioral
    Sciences
The Johns Hopkins University School of
    Medicine
Houck Building, East-2
600 North Wolfe Street
Baltimore
Maryland 21205
USA
(Tel. 301 955 7036)

Dr John Gabe
Lecturer
Department of Social Policy and Social
    Science
Royal Holloway and Bedford New College
Egham Hill
Egham
Surrey TW20 0EX
(Tel. 0784 434455)
and
Department of Community Medicine
University College and Middlesex School
    of Medicine
66–72 Gower Street
London
WC1E 6EA
(Tel. 071 387 7050)

Dr Ilana Belle Glass
Senior Lecturer
National Addiction Centre
Institute of Psychiatry
De Crespigny Park
London SE5 8AF
(Tel. 071 703 5411)

Mr Marcus Grant
Scientist
Programme on Substance Abuse
The World Health Organization
Division of Mental Health
CH-1211 Geneva 27
Switzerland
(Tel. 791 2111)

Dr Petr Hajek
Senior Lecturer and Hon. Principal Clinical
    Psychologist
Imperial Cancer Research Fund Health
    Behaviour Unit
National Addiction Centre
Institute of Psychiatry
De Crespigny Park
London SE5 8AF
(Tel. 071 703 5411)

Dr Jerome H. Jaffe
Associate Director for Treatment Policy
Office for Treatment Improvement
Rockwall II Building, 10th Floor
5600 Fishers Lane
Rockville
Maryland 20857
USA
(Tel. 301 443 6549)

Mr Martin J. Jarvis
Senior Lecturer
Imperial Cancer Research Fund Health
    Behaviour Unit
National Addiction Centre
Institute of Psychiatry
De Crespigny Park
Denmark Hill
London SE5 8AF
(Tel. 071 703 5411)

Dr Bankole A. Johnson
Senior Registrar in Psychiatry
The Warneford Hospital
Warneford Lane
Oxford OX3 7JX
(Tel. 0865 245651)

Dr Michael D. Kopelman
Senior Lecturer in Neuropsychiatry and
    Hon. Consultant Psychiatrist
Academic Unit of Psychiatry
St Thomas' Hospital
Lambeth Palace Road
London SE1 7EH
(Tel. 071 928 9292)

Professor Malcolm Lader
Professor of Clinical Psycho-
    pharmacology
University of London
Institute of Psychiatry
De Crespigny Park
Denmark Hill
London SE5 8AF
(Tel. 071 703 5411)

Professor John Littleton
Department of Pharmacology
King's College
The Strand
London WC2R 2LS
(Tel. 071 836 5454)

Professor James McEwen
Henry Mechan Professor of Public Health
Department of Public Health
University of Glasgow
2 Lilybank Gardens
Glasgow G12 8RZ
(Tel. 041 339 8855)

Dr J. Spencer Madden
Consultant Psychiatrist
The Countess of Chester Hospital
Priority & Community Services Unit
Liverpool Road
Chester CH2 1BQ
(Tel. 0244 365000)

Dr Jane Marshall
Senior Registrar
Alcohol Unit
The Maudsley Hospital
Denmark Hill
London SE5 8AZ
(Tel. 071 703 6333)

Professor Alan Maynard
Professor of Economics and Director of the
    Centre for Health Economics
University of York
Centre for Health Economics
York YO1 5DD
(Tel. 0904 430000)

Dr T.J. Meredith
Senior Medical Officer
Division of Toxicology and Environmental
    Health
Department of Health
London SE1 6TE
(Tel. 071 972 2000)

Mrs Joy Moser
Formerly Senior Scientist
Mental Health Division
World Health Organization
Geneva

Professor Robin Murray
Professor of Psychological Medicine
Institute of Psychiatry
De Crespigny Park
Denmark Hill
London SE5 8AF
(Tel. 071 703 5411)

Professor Charles P. O'Brien
Professor of Psychiatry
University of Pennsylvania
School of Medicine
Addiction Research Center
3900 Chestnut St/6178
Philadelphia
PA 19104
USA
(Tel. 215 898 2301)

Dr P.T. d'Orban
Formerly Consultant Forensic Psychiatrist
Department of Psychiatry
The Royal Free Hospital
Pond Street
London NW3 2QG
(Tel. 071 794 0500)

Dr John B. Peachey
Head
Psychiatry Program
Clinical Institute
Addiction Research Foundation
33 Russell Street
Toronto
Ontario
Canada M5S 2S1
(Tel. 416 595 6000)

Dr Duncan S. Raistrick
Leeds Western Health Authority
Leeds Addiction Unit
19 Springfield Mount
Leeds LS2 9NG
(Tel. 0532 316920)

Dr John Ramsey
Lecturer in Toxicology
St George's Hospital Medical School
Cranmer Terrace
London SW17 0RE
(Tel. 081 672 9944)

Dr Bruce Ritson
Consultant, Senior Lecturer
University Department of Psychiatry
The Kennedy Tower
Royal Edinburgh Hospital
Morningside Park
Edinburgh EH10 5HF
(Tel. 031 447 2011)

Dr Mitchell S. Rosenthal
Director
Phoenix House Foundation
164 West 74 Street
New York 10023
USA
(Tel. 212 595 5810)

Dr Martha Sanchez-Craig
Senior Scientist
Addiction Research Foundation
33 Russell Street
Toronto
Ontario
Canada M5S 2S1
(Tel. 416 595 6000)

Professor John B. Saunders
Royal Prince Alfred Hospital
Missenden Road
Camperdown
NSW 2050
Australia
(Tel. 02 516 6111)

Professor Marc A. Schuckit
Professor of Psychiatry
University of California–San Diego
  (UCSD)
School of Medicine
and
Director
Department of Psychiatry (116)
Veterans Administration Hospital
3350 La Jolla Village Drive
San Diego
California 92161
USA
(Tel. 619 552 8585)

Mr Harry Shapiro
Publications Manager
Institute for the Study of Drug
  Dependence
18 Hatton Place
Hatton Garden
London EC1
(Tel. 071 430 1961)

Ms Margaret Sheehan
Formerly Research Worker
Addiction Research Unit
Institute of Psychiatry
101 Denmark Hill
London SE5 8AF
(Tel. 071 703 5411)

Mr David Simpson
Formerly Director
Action on Smoking and Health
5–11 Mortimer Street
London W1N 7RH
(Tel. 071 637 9843)

Dr Ian Stolerman
Reader in Behavioural Pharmacology
Institute of Psychiatry
De Crespigny Park
Denmark Hill
London SE5 8AF
(Tel. 071 703 5411)

Dr John Strang
Consultant Psychiatrist
Drug Dependence Clinical Research and
    Treatment Unit
Maudsley and Bethlem Royal Hospital
Denmark Hill
London SE5 8AF
(Tel. 071 703 6333)

Dr Harith Swadi
Department of Child & Family
    Consultation
118 Maidstone Road
Chatham
Kent ME4 6DL
(Tel. 0634 813661)

Professor George E. Vaillant
Remsen 7
Dartmouth Medical School
Hanover
NH 03756
USA
(Tel. 603 646 7560)

Ms Margaret Weir
The World Health Organization
Division of Mental Health
Ch-1211 Geneva 27
Switzerland
(Tel. 791 21 11)

Dr Brian Wells
Consultant Psychiatrist
Riverside Health Authority
Riverside Substance Misuse Services
St Mary Abbots Hospital
Marloes Road
London W8 5LQ
(Tel. 081 846 1234)

Dr Robert West
Senior Lecturer
University of London
Royal Holloway and Bedford New College
Egham Hill
Egham
Surrey TW20 0EX
(Tel. 0784 34455)

Dr Adrian Wilkinson
Consultant Psychologist
Addiction Research Foundation
33 Russell Street
Toronto
Ontario
Canada M5S 2S1
(Tel. 416 595 6000)

Dr Alex Wodak
Director
Alcohol and Drug Service
St Vincent's Hospital
Darlinghurst
NSW 2010
Australia
(Tel. 02 331 4344)

Dr Harry Zeitlin
Consultant Child Psychiatrist
Riverside Health Authority
Westminster Children's Hospital
Vincent Square
London SW1P 2NS
(Tel. 081 746 8000)

Foreword

This book derives from Dr Ilana Glass's substantial personal teaching experience in the addictions field. She played a key role in designing and setting up the Institute of Psychiatry's Diploma in Addiction Behaviour. She then went on to supervise and run that course during its first year and has since been closely engaged in its further development as well as continuing with responsibilities as a course teacher. The background to her teaching is a research appointment in the Addiction Research Unit, clinical responsibilities at the Maudsley Hospital, work for the World Health Organization and many other international activities. There can, therefore, be no doubt that the book which she has now edited is need-led and student-led. It is not one of those books which foist a remote and academic view on an audience for which the author has no real sympathy.

In particular the shape of this book reflects Dr Glass's awareness that the substance problem world is, at the clinical front line, highly multidisciplinary. Clinicians need to understand the scientific basis of their work but there is, for instance, no profit in a biological scientist lecturing or writing about his or her subject in a way which will be opaque and alienating for a nurse or social worker. By the same token there is no merit in a sociologist pretending that the biological dimension of understanding is to be dismissed as 'medicalization'. This is a field in which we need to learn from and respect each other's scientific disciplines and clinical perspectives, and this book serves that aim.

The setting in which Dr Glass has been personally engaged as a teacher has also been marked by an extraordinary degree of internationalism. She has often had in the same seminar room students from Africa, Asia, South America and Europe. That experience too is reflected in the texture of this book. Another aspect of the book's structure which must be immediately evident from the contents list is the sweep of the mind-acting substances which it takes as within its remit – it deals with illicit as well as licit drugs, with alcohol, with nicotine and then with gambling as an example of a non-drug dependence. Today's heroin addicts may today or tomorrow be misusing alcohol. A patient-led view of what the helpers should properly be learning can no longer support a definition of the drug expert as someone who does not know how to take a drinking history or a definition of the alcohol specialist as a professional who introduces his patients to benzodiazepines. Neither can patient needs be met by continuing to train a whole galaxy of experts who never take cigarette smoking seriously. Cured of your heroin or alcohol addiction? Tough luck the lung cancer.

In summary, what stands out is the capacity of this text to join together a student-led view of what needs to be taught with a vision which invites multidisciplinarity, which challenges us to take a world view, and which insists that 'the drug problem' can only be understood and taught about as a continuum which transcends chemical boundaries.

The imperative which so often besets the person invited to write a foreword to any book is the need to pretend the work in question is the ticket to the promised land. This book deserves a more respectful and honest welcome. Helping people with substance problems is a difficult business but the common sense and vision which this text offers will in modest but important ways help the helping professions to make that business better informed, more effective and a little more humane. And that is a ticket worth having.

Griffith Edwards
March 1991

Introduction

Ilana Belle Glass

In 1986 the Addiction Research Unit at the Institute of Psychiatry, University of London, ran the first Diploma in Addiction Behaviour course. It is now in its fifth year.

Successive groups of students have indicated that a course book drawing together the course contents would be useful. Other workers and students in the field expressed considerable interest in such a venture.

The book, like the course, is designed in the knowledge that the audience is a multidisciplinary and international one. The challenge remains that of how to address relevant issues in a style which is engaging and appropriate to a variety of disciplines, professions, cultures and countries.

Since our main aim is to train trainers, a central objective is to provide a sound grounding theoretically. Section I harnesses a range of scientific approaches in the addictions field which have application to those working at the front-line.

Clinical issues of diagnosis and management are the lynch-pin of the book. Sections II to V deal with different aspects of the treatment process. From the description of syndromes, to the special complications and health risks, early intervention and principles of management, these emphasize that no professional seriously involved in addiction behaviour can be unaware and unskilled in treatment interventions.

While these clinical problems must be embedded in the provision of services and prevention at a local and national level, international policy plays a decisive role as reflected by the World Health Organization. Sections VI and VII illustrate addiction problems as a community, national and international issue. In most countries the effective use of valuable clinical assets requires as much consideration as training in leadership skills: the interface of implementation of policy, management and education.

Students have come from Zimbabwe, Zambia, Tanzania, Germany, Ecuador, Venezuela, Britain, India, Egypt and Bolivia. Two distinction students, Adityanjee and Jo Coupe, have contributed to this book. Community psychiatric nurses, doctors, specialist psychiatrists, psychologists, a probation officer, a social worker and a physician have participated.

Over the years we have retained a flexibility in the running of the course, which has allowed us to respond to a variety of suggestions and needs. This book is one such response.

We have been constantly amazed by the richness of the student group and their experiences. We have learnt that an academic and hospital-based orientation must be attuned to a practical and community-oriented response. We have learnt that training for leadership is vital, for many of our students will return to their countries, playing a key role in service planning, policy and development, as well as in the clinical arena.

The authors have responded to my brief with generosity and enthusiasm. Since most of the local contributors have run seminars on the course, they were well aware of the problems and potential as they set about their task. Some of the overseas contributors are well acquainted with the Addiction Research Unit and some have lectured on the course during their visits to our centre. They willingly provided enriching reflections from the other side of the Atlantic, from Australia, or from Geneva.

It is, of course, impossible to cover every relevant topic in a handbook. What I hope we have been able to do is to provide an overall perspective which focuses on the application of various approaches to the clinical situation and policy. I hope it constructively debates established views and new opinion, and shows a way forward.

Although this book is the product of the active support of many colleagues, friends and students, several people deserve special thanks. Griffith Edwards was constantly available for 'maintenance encouragement' with invaluable inspired comments. This probably prevented me from abstaining from the process of editing at any stage. John Strang's natural inclination seems to have been to provide me with rapid relevant radical alternatives whenever they were required. Discussions with Michael Farrell dissolved discrepancies and catalysed ideas. Sue Edwards and Cheryl Brown administered and organized the course with admirable efficiency. Peter Crome participated in the enterprise with good humoured resilience, and this made it all the more enjoyable. Working with Gill Davies has, at all times, been a pleasant and positive experience. Ester Lee, Christine Potts, Ann Bugden and Sheila Garnett provided exceptional secretarial assistance.

Section I

Scientific approaches to addiction

Chapter 1

Dependence on psychoactive drugs: finding a common language

D. Colin Drummond

The study of addiction provides a veritable semantic minefield through which clinicians and researchers must tread carefully. Descriptive terms such as 'alcoholic' or 'drug addict' may represent a useful shorthand to describe certain people who take psychoactive substances. They are also sufficiently imprecise as to mean different things to different people and are therefore subject to misinterpretation and futile argument.

The 'inebriate' and the 'opium sot' were once common parlance to describe the habitually intoxicated. Although now mere historical curiosities, they did represent more precise terms than either 'alcoholic' or 'drug addict'. They can be defined simply in terms of consumption of greater than a given quantity of a drug per unit time. This definition, however, makes no reference to the adverse consequences of drug use which are often seen in the clinical setting and does not take account of the mediating effect of drug tolerance.

The 'problem drinker' and 'problem drug taker' currently enjoy popularity as descriptive labels. In practice, there are several difficulties in defining what does or does not constitute a problem, not least of which is the bias of the observer: the patient may have a view which is very different from his wife or doctor. Further, it is often difficult to establish whether drug taking caused a problem or whether a drug is taken as an adaptive response to a problem. Problems must be seen as developing from a complex interaction between the drug, the drug taker and the social environment.

The concept of dependence includes more specific psychophysiological consequences of drug taking, namely the elements of the dependence syndrome. This concept has now been adopted by several international diagnostic classification systems including ICD-10 (WHO, 1987) and DSM-III-R (APA, 1988). Whereas different drugs may be associated with very specific kinds of social, psychological or physical adverse consequences, they often share many common features of dependence.

Given that there are many different ways to describe the phenomena associated with the use of psychoactive drugs, how can the beleaguered clinician or researcher proceed without stepping on the awaiting mines? In 1977, a World Health Organization scientific group (Edwards *et al.*, 1977) proposed the bi-axial concept in which dependence and alcohol-related problems are seen as lying on separate dimensions. Further, in contrast to earlier typological views of alcoholism and drug addiction, dependence and problems are viewed as representing continua of severity rather than all-or-nothing phenomena. Level of consumption can be viewed as a third dimension.

Of course, a multidimensional approach does not circumvent the problem of finding agreement on definitions, but it does provide a more sophisticated conceptualization of addiction for both researchers and clinicians. This chapter aims to describe the nature and clinical utility of the dependence dimension. The foregoing, however, should alert the reader to the danger of viewing addiction in terms of only one dimension.

THE DEPENDENCE SYNDROME

The original description of the alcohol dependence syndrome (Edwards and Gross, 1976) emphasized that the observable phenomena were often, but not always, clustered together. Further, this empirical description did not imply any particular underlying cause. Although the original description referred specifically to alcohol dependence, this has subsequently been expanded to include other drugs. Seven elements of the syndrome were identified, each of which may be subject to pathoplastic influences. In other words, their expression may be coloured by personality and cultural factors. Some later commentators have made a distinction between 'physical' and 'psychological' dependence. This arbitrary distinction was not made in the original description of the syndrome and underestimates the frequent co-occurrence of physical and psychological symptoms.

Increased tolerance to the drug   This refers to the observation that with repeated doses the drug produces less effect or, alternatively, that increased quantities of the drug are required to produce the same effect. The mechanisms which underlie tolerance will be described in greater detail in later chapters, but it may be best regarded as a form of homeostatic response. Clinically an escalation in the quantity of drug consumed per unit time is evidence of such a reduced sensitivity. The severely dependent person is able to tolerate doses of the drug often greater than that which would cause death in the non-dependent. Different drugs vary widely in the rate at which tolerance develops. Significant tolerance to alcohol may take many years to develop, compared to a more rapid development in the case of opiates and cocaine. Tolerance generally continues to increase over time, but in the case of alcohol, tolerance can decline in the later stages of the syndrome.

Repeated withdrawal symptoms   Associated with tolerance is the phenomenon of withdrawal. The onset of these symptoms occurs following a period of abstinence from the drug. The timing of onset and severity of the symptoms depends on the type of drug. Alcohol withdrawal symptoms generally occur on waking, although in the case of severe dependence, symptoms may cause waking during the night or occur between drinks during the day. With all drugs the symptoms show a wide range of severity.

Withdrawal from drugs will be discussed in detail in Section II. Both psychological and physical symptoms result. The nature of the symptoms again depends on the type of drug: in broad terms CNS (Central Nervous System) depressants such as alcohol, opiates and barbiturates lead to a withdrawal syndrome characterized by CNS hyperexcitability. Evidence of this includes anxiety, tremor, sweating, nausea and vomiting and in the case of barbiturates and alcohol, fits and delirium may occur, which can be life-threatening in severe and untreated cases. Stimulant drugs on the other hand such as amphetamines and cocaine produce a withdrawal syndrome characterized by depression, lethargy and somnolence.

Subjective awareness of compulsion to take the drug   Often associated with a withdrawal state is a psychological state, sometimes referred to as 'craving' for the drug. This term does little justice to what is a complex, personal and often intensely unpleasant experience. Rumination about the drug, its likely effects, and the possible methods of its procurement preoccupy the person's thoughts. This may be particularly so when the drug is unavailable and following a small 'priming dose' or appetizer. Sometimes the experience is described in terms of pleasurable anticipation. While this remains an ill-understood phenomenon it is observed in dependence on a wide range of different substances.

Salience of drug-seeking behaviour   As dependence develops, simply obtaining the drug assumes increasing importance in the person's life. Initially this may involve the neglect of social responsibilities such as arriving on time for work or meals at home. Later, obtaining the next drink or injection of a drug may assume more importance than the threatened break-up of a marriage. In some cases this may reach the stage where theft or physical violence are seen by the individual as a necessary means to obtain a drug.

Relief or avoidance of withdrawal symptoms   It may take some time after the first experience of withdrawal symptoms before the sufferer recognizes or begins to make use of the alleviating effect of the drug during withdrawal. Once learned, this approach becomes increasingly important to the extent that, for example, the severely dependent drinker will ensure that sufficient alcohol is left to relieve withdrawal symptoms in the morning, even if this means curtailing his drinking the night before. This may even reach the stage of taking regular and frequent doses of alcohol throughout the day and night to stave off impending withdrawal.

Narrowing of the repertoire of drug taking   The pattern of drug taking becomes increasingly stereotypic with increasing dependence. Whereas once, the person may have taken a drug on one or two occasions per week or only at weekends, gradually this becomes an everyday activity. An increasingly strict daily routine develops. The individual may begin to favour a particular presentation or brand of the drug, such as a particular beer rather than spirits, wine or other beers. Sometimes, paradoxically, in severe dependence the repertoire may appear to increase as the drive to obtain the drug supervenes. In this situation ease of availability and potency of the drug become the priorities.

Reinstatement following a period of abstinence   Withdrawal symptoms generally subside after a week or so of abstinence, although this period varies from drug to drug. Tolerance may also decrease to some extent during abstinence. After a period of abstinence, even if the dependent person begins to take the drug in a controlled manner, the dose will quickly escalate to a pre-abstinence level. Tolerance and withdrawal symptoms will reappear within a few days.

How do the symptoms of dependence relate to each other?

The provisional description of the alcohol dependence syndrome emphasized that all the elements need not be present simultaneously. Indeed from the above account it should be clear that each symptom may be present to a different degree. One recent classification system (ICD-10) has given as an operational definition of dependence the presence of three or more symptoms during the preceding twelve months. But in practice, if one symptom is present how likely are other symptoms to be present also?

A variety of questionnaires have been developed to measure both alcohol and opiate dependence. The Severity of Alcohol Dependence Questionnaire (SADQ) has been the most widely studied (Stockwell *et al.*, 1979). This questionnaire does not attempt to measure all aspects of the alcohol dependence syndrome (ADS) because of difficulties in operationalizing certain elements such as narrowing of drinking repertoire. Nevertheless, it consists of twenty questions which cover most elements of the syndrome. The symptoms are rated in terms of frequency and severity of occurrence. A total score of greater than 30 (out of a maximum possible score of 60) can be regarded as an indication of severe dependence.

A variety of statistical methods has established that all the symptoms are highly positively correlated with each other. In other words if a person experiences severe tremor he is also likely to have severe anxiety and strong craving for alcohol, to take morning drinks and to reinstate the symptoms following abstinence. A similar questionnaire designed to measure opiate dependence, the Severity of Opiate Dependence Questionnaire (SODQ), had broadly similar findings in a group of heroin takers (Sutherland *et al.*, 1987).

How does dependence relate to other dimensions?

The bi-axial concept suggests that problems and dependence lie on conceptually separate dimensions. In other words, a person can experience problems due to the use of a drug without necessarily being dependent. An example of this is the relatively high rate of accidents due to drunk driving in young, inexperienced drinkers. On the other hand, it is theoretically possible to be dependent on a drug without experiencing many significant drug-related problems. The therapeutic use of opiates and nicotine chewing gum is associated with considerably less harm than illicit heroin injecting or cigarette smoking.

The development of instruments to measure dependence has allowed these relationships to be explored statistically. Dependence, as measured by both the SADQ and the SODQ, is highly correlated with the quantity of drug consumed. This is an indication of the effects of tolerance.

Until recently little research attention has been paid to the relationship between dependence and problems. Responses to the Alcohol Problems Questionnaire (APQ) were compared with the SADQ in a group of problem drinkers (Drummond, 1990). The APQ measures a wide range of social, psychological and physical problems related to drinking. The overall number of problems was found to be highly correlated with both dependence and quantity of alcohol consumed. When dependence was controlled for, however, the relationship between problems and consumption was not significant, suggesting that the quantity of alcohol consumed does not in itself determine problems, and that dependence may be an important mediating factor.

THE CLINICAL SIGNIFICANCE OF THE DEPENDENCE CONCEPT

Dependence as a common language

As explained earlier, clinicians and researchers require a common language to ensure that they are talking about the same phenomena. The dependence concept has helped considerably in sharpening up diagnostic precision, just as an internationally agreed unit of alcohol consumption has increased the comparability of studies carried out in different countries.

The dependence concept also provides a means of making experiences intelligible to the afflicted sufferer. The alcoholism concept provides enormous room for fruitless debates about whether one is or is not an alcoholic, based on one's personal view of the archetypal alcoholic, which may be seen as carrying an unfavourable social stigma. Dependence, on the other hand, does not imply any particular aetiology or antisocial consequences and encompasses a range of severity.

Dependence as a predictor

Several studies have demonstrated the usefulness of the dependence concept in predicting treatment needs. Such knowledge can potentially have a real impact on clinical practice. For example, the severity of alcohol dependence as measured by the SADQ has been found to predict the severity of withdrawal symptoms during detoxification and, hence, medication requirements.

Several follow-up studies have found that the severely alcohol dependent are highly unlikely to be able to return to normal drinking. With the problem of reinstatement, resumption of even a small amount of drinking after detoxification in this group quickly results in escalation to a pre-abstinence level of consumption. This has important implications for the choice of treatment goal. While there is considerable debate on this issue, the current evidence points to abstinence as the necessary goal for the severely dependent.

In terms of predicting the likelihood of relapse following treatment the evidence is less clear. Some research has found a positive relationship between dependence and the likelihood of relapse and other work has not. Clearly relapse is a complex process which is subject to many influences other than dependence.

Some experimental laboratory evidence, however, has shown that more severely dependent drinkers report a stronger desire for alcohol and drink more quickly after a small priming dose of alcohol. Further, severely dependent drinkers have stronger physiological responses to cues associated with drinking, such as the sight and smell of a favourite drink, than their less dependent counterparts. While these responses have yet to be examined in a prospective study of relapse, the suggestion is that the severely dependent drinkers will be more responsive and have greater difficulty in resisting alcohol in a potential relapse situation. There may be some value, therefore, in attempting to modify these responses during treatment with behavioural techniques such as cue exposure (see Chapter 32 by Wilkinson and Sanchez-Craig and Chapter 33 by O'Brien and Childress).

CONCLUSIONS

The dependence concept has brought with it a number of important consequences. First, the population of drug takers who are of potential concern to health services is considerably greater than before. Compared to the earlier typological view of the alcoholic as the drinker who has reached a significant level of deterioration both physically and socially, the dependence and problems concepts recognize a spectrum of severity and harm. Early detection and treatment of dependent drug takers has important health implications. The dependence concept provides health professionals with the necessary framework to recognize those at risk of developing more severe difficulties at an early stage in their drug taking career.

With the development of methods of measuring dependence we are beginning to recognize the utility of the concept in clinical and research terms. Refinement of measurement techniques – including the development of methods of scaling the more subtle elements of the syndrome and identification of the behavioural and physiological correlates of dependence – may have tangible consequences for clinical practice.

Most importantly, this concept provides an opportunity for us to be more accurate in describing clinical phenomena. It is no longer adequate to describe someone as an alcoholic or drug addict and assume others will know what we mean. While dependence does not provide all the answers to the complexities of addiction, it provides an essential framework within which we can study the behaviour of drug takers. Without such a framework, important commonalities between different substances may be masked by the enormous diversity of drug-related problems.

REFERENCES

American Psychiatric Association (1988) *Diagnostic and Statistical Manual III Revised*, Washington, D.C.: APA.
Drummond, D.C. (1990) 'The relationship between alcohol dependence and alcohol related problems in a clinical population', *British Journal of Addiction 85: 357–66*.
Edwards, G. and Gross, M.M. (1976) 'Alcohol dependence: provisional description of a clinical syndrome', *British Medical Journal* 1: 1058–61.
Edwards, G., Gross, M.M., Keller, M., Moser, J. and Room, R. (1977) *Alcohol Related Disabilities, WHO Offset Publication No. 32*, Geneva: WHO.
Stockwell, T., Hodgson, R., Edwards, G., Taylor, C. and Rankin, H. (1979) 'The development of a questionnaire to measure severity of alcohol dependence', *British Journal of Addiction* 74: 79–87.
Sutherland, G., Edwards, G., Taylor, C., Phillips, G., Gossop, M. and Brady, R. (1987) 'The measurement of opiate dependence', *British Journal of Addiction* 81: 485–94.
World Health Organization (1987) *Tenth Revision of the International Classification of Diseases. Chapter V(F): Mental, Behavioural and Developmental Disorders*, Geneva: WHO.

CROSS REFERENCES

Chapter 2

Drug dependence as pharmacological adaptation

John Littleton

Everybody knows about drug tolerance. The more you drink, the more alcohol you need to get drunk; the more heroin you take, the more drug you need to get high. But what has this got to do with drug dependence? Why should the continued taking of a drug lead to a state where you cannot do without the drug either mentally or physically? The answer probably lies in the way our brains have evolved to control their functioning in the face of alterations in the internal or external environment. The nerve cells which make up the brain are highly capable of adapting to novel situations and the presence of an addictive drug in the brain is just such a novel situation. Faced with an addictive drug, nerve cells gradually compensate for its presence so that they return to relatively normal functioning, even in the presence of the drug. This is what underlies drug tolerance – the ability of the brain to function at higher and higher concentrations of the drug.

On its own this adaptation is not necessarily harmful. If, however, the drug is withdrawn rapidly, there is a time lag between the removal of the drug and the return-to-normal of the nerve cells. For this period the system is out of balance: nerve cells are compensating for something which has ceased to be present. The consequence is an alteration in function which is opposite to that which the drug caused originally. This is what we call the withdrawal syndrome. It can be mainly psychological or mainly physical, mild or severe, short or prolonged and depends on the drug, the individual, and the individual's psychological make-up, environment and social circumstances. The implications of this concept of adaptation of the brain for the development of drug tolerance and dependence, and for the treatment of these conditions, form the basis of this chapter.

DIFFERENT KINDS OF ADAPTATION

At first sight the above explanation seems quite logical and it can explain both drug tolerance and drug dependence. But is it correct? Most people's personal experience would suggest not. Not everybody who drinks alcohol regularly and who can 'take his drink' shows a withdrawal syndrome when he stops. In other words, someone can be tolerant to a particular drug without also being dependent on it. In order to find out why this can happen, we need to consider a little more how drugs act to produce their effects in the first place.

In general, drugs act on nerve cells to alter their excitability. The 'depressant' drugs like alcohol, tranquillizers and opiates produce an overall decrease in electrical excitability, whereas stimulant drugs such as amphetamines and cocaine cause an overall increase. Nerve cells probably have a whole repertoire of adaptive responses to alterations in their natural excitability, and which one they choose may determine whether the system shows tolerance alone, or tolerance *and* dependence.

Let us take the example of a depressant drug like morphine. This drug produces its depressant effect by acting on specific receptor proteins on the surface of nerve cells. Normally these receptor proteins are acted upon by transmitter substances in the brain which are necessary for the normal functioning of these nerve pathways. What morphine does is to augment the effect of the natural substances in inhibiting the nerves. The question is how can these nerves escape from this extra inhibition caused by morphine? There are two basic strategies. The nerves can either simply lessen the effect of morphine by preventing morphine from reacting with the receptor protein, for example – or the nerves can become intrinsically more excitable so that even in the presence of morphine they continue at their normal level of activity. The first mechanism simply *decreases* the effect of the drug, whereas the second *opposes* its effect. There are several potential molecular mechanisms which could explain these different forms of adaptation, but they are beyond the scope of this chapter. I have described some of them in a previous review (Littleton, 1983) where I coined the terms 'decremental' and 'oppositional' adaptation to describe the two forms.

Now let us consider how these two adaptive mechanisms relate to tolerance and dependence. First, both can obviously explain tolerance in the intact animal. In both cases the presence of morphine produces less of a change in behaviour than it would in an animal or man which showed neither form of adaptation. However, in the case of adaptation where the effect of morphine on the nerve cells is reduced (i.e. 'decremental' adaptation) this does not necessarily have any effect on the excitability of the nerve cells when morphine is removed. There are alterations which could occur on the nerve cell's membrane which would make it more difficult for morphine to produce its effect, but would not affect the ability of the natural transmitters to produce their response. This kind of adaptation could therefore produce a 'pure' kind of tolerance. The effect of the drug is lessened without any detrimental consequences on its removal.

The 'oppositional' kind of adaptation is obviously different. While morphine is present the nerve cells maintain the semblance of normal activity by being intrinsically more excitable. They are balancing the effect of morphine by an opposing force. Removal of morphine from nerves in this adapted state will *inevitably* lead to a functional imbalance, the withdrawal syndrome, until the normal level of excitability in the affected nerve cells can be restored. The adaptation produces both tolerance *and* dependence.

In real life both forms of adaptation probably co-exist with one being predominant, depending on a variety of different factors. Of particular interest here are the relationship of drug-taking behaviour and genetic influences to the kind of adaptation which occurs. These will be the next focus.

WHICH KIND OF ADAPTATION?

We can predict what nerve cells might prefer to do given different patterns of presentation of a drug, from just a simple consideration of decremental and oppositional adaptation. If a drug is presented intermittently, with long gaps between each presentation, it is going to require a lot of energy for the nerve cell to keep initiating an adaptive response and then removing it, as it has to do with oppositional adaptation. Decremental adaptation has a big advantage here in that it does not have to be removed rapidly when the nerve cells are 'between drugs'. Since there is no functional disturbance on removal of the drug the nerve cell can keep the adaptation until it is needed the next time. Perhaps for this reason intermittent drug administration is very likely to lead to tolerance, but is much less likely to lead to dependence than is continuous drug administration (Goldstein, 1972).

In contrast to the above situation, the continuous presence of a drug in the brain is just as likely to produce 'oppositional' adaptation as 'decremental' adaptation. If the drug is always present, then oppositional adaptation does not have to be removed and so requires no more energy than decremental adaptation. It is as though the 'drug present' state becomes recognized as 'normality', so that the nerve cells are capable of making an adaptive response which is semi-permanent and has severe consequences until it is reversed. Continuous drug administration therefore produces a mixture of adaptive responses which is much more likely to lead to dependence than intermittent administration.

This is only a small part of the story of course: all kinds of other factors conspire to make one individual more likely to develop dependence than another. I am being deliberately 'mechanistic' to counterbalance the psychological and sociological approaches later in the book. While on this tack, there is another very important 'mechanistic' determinant of what kind of adaptation an individual may show, and that is the genetic complement.

In human studies it is very difficult to assess the role of genetics in determining susceptibility to drug dependence because so many other variables get in the way. However, in animal studies, it is much easier to establish that some animals become dependent more easily than others, and that this is because of inherited characteristics. An example of this kind of work is that by Goldstein (1973) who showed that susceptibility to physical dependence on alcohol in mice was genetically determined. It may well be that the propensity for either 'decremental' or 'oppositional' adaptation is determined by the genes which control neuronal excitability.

TREATMENT OF DEPENDENCE

If the mechanism of drug dependence really is a consequence of adaptation in nerve cells in the brain, then this has obvious implications for our treatment of dependence. Our aim should be either to allow oppositional adaptation to dissipate slowly at the same pace as the drug is removed from the brain, or to replace oppositional adaptation with decremental adaptation while the drug is present in the brain.

Let us take the first objective. It is possible, for example, to 'cover' the alcohol withdrawal syndrome by giving alcohol in diminishing concentrations by intravenous infusion (Sellers, 1982). This prevents the onset of the alcohol physical withdrawal syndrome and within 48 hours or so the individual is drug-free. Substitution therapy using benzodiazepines for alcohol (or indeed methadone for heroin) to prevent a withdrawal syndrome while the original drug is removed and then to remove the substituted drug has a similar rationale. The removal of the drug effect is controlled rather than precipitate, and the pains of withdrawal are thereby diminished. Or are they? This approach really does little except extend the duration of the withdrawal syndrome or substitute one drug of dependence for another. Not surprisingly, both relapse into drug dependence and multi-drug dependence are common sequelae of these kinds of treatment regimes.

The second objective – removal of oppositional adaptation while the drug is still present – is theoretically interesting, but is it possible? Well no, but it might be if we knew what caused 'oppositional' adaptation for a specific drug. Given that knowledge, removal of the mechanism for dependence might be possible. Whether that would be an advance on current therapies can only be guessed at. A brief discussion of research in the area of prevention of alcohol dependence is provided in my review (Littleton, 1989).

CONCLUSION

This brief account of how brain cells adapt to drugs has been deliberately simplistic. Despite this, I believe it introduces a number of concepts which will be relevant to later contributions. Tolerance and dependence are not identical, but can be related. Drugs given intermittently often produce tolerance only, whereas drugs given continuously produce both tolerance and dependence. Genetics is a factor which influences dependence liability. Treatment of drug dependence is unsatisfactory, but could be made less so if we understood the mechanisms of neuronal adaptation. All these ideas plus much more information on individual drugs are to be found in Jerry Jaffe's chapter on drug dependence (Jaffe, 1988), which I recommend to anyone with an interest in the pharmacology of drug dependence.

REFERENCES

Goldstein, D.B. (1972) 'Relationship of alcohol dose to intensity of withdrawal signs in mice', Journal of Pharmacology and Experimental Therapeutics 180: 203–15.
——(1973) 'Inherited differences in intensity of alcohol withdrawal reactions in mice', Nature 245: 154–6.
Jaffe, J.H. (1988) 'Drug addiction and drug abuse', in A.S. Gilman, L.S. Goodman, T.W. Rall and F. Murad (eds) The Pharmacological Basis of Therapeutics, New York: Macmillan, pp. 532–81.
Littleton, J.M. (1983) 'Tolerance and physical dependence on alcohol at the level of synaptic membranes: a review', Journal of the Royal Society of Medicine 76: 593–601.
——(1989) 'Alcohol intoxication and physical dependence: a molecular mystery tour', British Journal of Addiction 84: 267–76.
Sellers, E.M. (1982) 'Alcohol and drug dependence: application of pharmacodynamics and pharmacokinetics to improve the treatment of withdrawal', Trends in Pharmacological Sciences 3: 450–2.

CROSS REFERENCES

Chapter 3

Behavioural pharmacology of addiction

I. P. Stolerman

GENERAL PRINCIPLES

Behavioural pharmacologists have approached the problem of addiction by integrating pharmacological knowledge with principles of conditioning, learning and motivation derived from studies in experimental psychology. The aim has been to identify general principles that determine how behavioural processes control drug taking, principles that transcend the specific pharmacological actions of individual drugs. For the most part, this has entailed studying how drugs influence behaviour by serving as internal stimuli. Evidence from such studies shows that drugs can serve as positively reinforcing, cueing and punishing stimuli, and it has been possible to show that the behavioural control of drug-taking behaviour follows many of the same rules that govern other patterns of learned behaviour that do not involve drugs. Much has been learned from studying the development and analysis of actual drug-taking behaviour, and by measuring directly the amounts of drugs taken. The results of these studies sometimes, but not always, support conclusions reached by studying responses that are indirect predictors of drug taking, such as self-reported drug use, expressed motives, craving, subjective reports of drug effects and drug withdrawal syndromes.

This behavioural approach may be contrasted with the purely pharmacological attack on the problem, which has emphasized the effects of repeated and long-term administration of drugs, such as the development of tolerance and withdrawal syndromes. Traditionally, acquired tolerance to the effects sought by users was considered to lead to progressive increases in the dose taken, which in turn exacerbated the withdrawal reaction. Avoidance of or escape from withdrawal syndromes was seen as the major motive for continuing drug use. However, withdrawal is only one aspect of a complex situation and focusing on it alone would have prevented almost all the major advances made in the last twenty years in the understanding of addiction to drugs such as amphetamine, cocaine and nicotine.

The core of the behavioural approach has been the finding that addictive drugs can serve as positive reinforcers (rewards) in conditioning experiments, in much the same way as conventional rewards such as food or money. The reward value of a drug is defined empirically by its effectiveness in maintaining drug-taking behaviour, rather than in terms of subjective states such as euphoria. The main findings are presented in some depth in a collection of review articles (Goldberg and Stolerman, 1986). Most of the work has been carried out in animal subjects although recent studies of human drug self-administration have validated some of the basic concepts.

Animals readily learn to make responses (e.g. press a lever) to self-administer, through previously implanted catheters, many drugs misused by humans, and the drugs may thereby be defined as having positive reinforcing effects. The substances taken include opioid analgesics, psychomotor stimulants, nicotine, barbiturates, some benzodiazepines, alcohol and phencyclidine. With few exceptions, psycho-active drugs not associated with problems of abuse are not taken. Of the major classes of misused drugs, only cannabis and the LSD-type of hallucinogen have not been found to have reinforcing effects to date. The main characteristics of self-administration behaviour have now been studied extensively with a wide range of compounds. Other studies have examined the control of drug-taking by aversive stimuli associated with withdrawal syndromes, and aversive effects of the drugs themselves; the latter may set upper limits to drug intake and may be important as regulating factors. Self-administration procedures and other techniques that measure related stimulus effects of drugs can therefore generate valid and reliable models for human drug misuse, and can be used to study the neurobiological basis of addiction. It is notable that additional highly addictive narcotic analgesics have not been marketed since self-administration became a standard procedure for evaluating abuse liability.

One important development has been the analysis of the brain sites and mechanisms through which drugs exert their rewarding effects. Such work was not feasible until recently because of the need to develop and validate the behavioural procedures, to study the behavioural variables affecting drug self-administration, and because of the formidable technical difficulties of studies in which it is often necessary to administer drugs directly into extremely small regions of the brain.

IMPLICATIONS OF DRUGS AS REINFORCERS

Most misused drugs can serve as positive reinforcers (rewards) and thus have the ability to maintain long chains of behaviour over prolonged periods of time. These are particularly powerful effects of drugs that have been demonstrated across a wide range of conditions. Many of the factors which influence behaviour maintained by drug rewards are much the same as those which influence behaviour maintained by conventional rewards. The same behavioural processes of instrumental and classical conditioning, secondary reinforcement, satiation and extinction are involved. Learning processes are crucially important at all stages of the addiction cycle. However, the reinforcing effects of drugs are not immutable properties, but malleable effects that covary with environmental factors, and there is considerable scope for further investigation. Strong genetic influences on reinforcing efficacy remain to be demonstrated, but have been rarely sought (George and Goldberg, 1989). The general psychopharmacological principles that govern the intake of substances that have been socially acceptable, such as ethanol and nicotine, are much the same as those governing the intake of illegal drugs such as heroin.

Drugs can serve as reinforcers in the absence of any need to induce models of putative underlying psychiatric disturbances and without deliberately imposed stress. However, the data do not preclude the possibility that such manipulations may have a facilitating influence although most attempts to demonstrate such effects have been unsuccessful. Drug-taking seems to be a basic characteristic of drug-organism interactions under conditions where there is a ready availability of drugs. The laboratory studies confirm that the schedule of availability has a profound influence on the amounts of drug taken and their toxic consequences.

Drug-taking behaviour cannot be explained adequately by avoidance of or escape from withdrawal symptoms. Drug-taking behaviour in experimental subjects has been shown to develop in test sessions of no more than one hour's duration, in the absence of any prior exposure to the drug. Subjects have also maintained stable intakes of drugs over lengthy periods of time, at such doses and frequencies of intake that withdrawal symptoms have been undetectable. However, because withdrawal is not necessary for drugs to serve as reinforcers, it does not mean that it has no bearing on intake, and there are clear indications that withdrawal symptoms may enhance the positively reinforcing efficacy of opioid drugs.

DISCRIMINATIVE STIMULUS EFFECTS

The ability to recognize the effects of available substances may play an important role in the initiation of bouts of drug taking. Before a substance is used repeatedly, it has to be identified as one that has appropriate effects. Experienced drug users have been found to be very reliable identifiers of drugs. Animals too have this capability; many addictive drugs produce characteristic cues (discriminative stimuli) that can be used to influence behaviour. For example, animals trained to identify the effects of morphine will only identify other opioid drugs of the morphine type as 'drug-like', and it is only such drugs that produce characteristic morphine-like subjective effects in humans. Understanding how abused drugs can serve as discriminative stimuli may therefore make an important contribution to knowledge of factors controlling the initiation of drug intake.

After periods of abstinence or extinction, relapse to drug self-administration may be facilitated by a few priming injections of a drug. In such situations, the effects of the drug may act as discriminative stimuli (cues) indicating that further supplies of drug may be available. Experiments suggest that this effect may show specificity for the type of drug that maintained the original addiction and it is therefore different from simple positive reinforcing effects that do not show such specificity. These findings imply that the relapse process is more related to the carry-over of learned patterns of drug-seeking behaviour than to long-term withdrawal effects; the latter would be minimized rather than enhanced by priming injections of drugs. This type of experiment identifies a specific psychopharmacological mechanism that militates against attempts to resume drug use in a controlled manner. Similar considerations may apply to the much debated controlled resumption of alcohol use, although direct experimental data are lacking.

IMPORTANCE OF DRUG-ASSOCIATED STIMULI

Environmental stimuli that are associated with drugs are often critical. Such stimuli may serve as secondary (conditioned) reinforcers of behaviour as a result of classical, associative conditioning to effects of the drugs; they can maintain drug-seeking behaviour over prolonged periods of time when drugs themselves are not available, and they may retain their efficacy for periods of months, thus contributing greatly to the relapse process in animal models (Goldberg, 1976). Symptoms of withdrawal from opioid analgesic drugs can also be elicited by environmental stimuli present when withdrawal had occurred previously; this type of conditioning has been firmly established in experimental situations, but its frequency and importance clinically remain to be demonstrated.

Tolerance to the effects of an addictive drug is sometimes shown to a greater extent in an environment where a drug was given previously than in a different environment; studies of this effect suggest the classical conditioning (to environmental stimuli present at the time of drug administration) of responses opposing drug actions (Siegel, 1988). In some of these experiments, there is evidence that the withdrawal reaction itself may be a classically-conditioned compensatory response. The development of tolerance is also enhanced or more likely when the behavioural effects of drugs reduce exposure to rewarding environmental stimuli (Demellweek and Goudie, 1983). The data clearly establish the importance of environmental influences in tolerance, but many aspects of the matter including the nature of the conditioning processes involved are not adequately understood.

There is little evidence that tolerance develops to the positive reinforcing effects of drugs and some studies suggest the opposite (sensitization upon repeated exposure). These results do not support the notion that doses escalate to compensate for tolerance; the notion seems to have developed mainly from self-reports of addicts and not from studies under controlled conditions (Falk *et al.*, 1983). The lack of evidence for tolerance to such effects may in part reflect the limited number of attempts to find it, and more work is needed.

BRAIN MECHANISMS OF REINFORCEMENT

Studies have attempted to determine the brain structures and chemicals through which the positive reinforcing effects of drugs are mediated. Recent progress in this area has been reviewed by Koob and Goeders (1989). It has become clear that the neurotransmitter dopamine is of great importance in the case of psychomotor stimulants such as amphetamine and cocaine, and that mesolimbic and mesocortical dopamine systems are involved. Similar brain regions also seem to play a role in the reinforcing effects of opioids such as heroin, although whether dopamine plays the central role is controversial. These are important findings since other evidence suggests that the analgesic effects of opiates and the opiate withdrawal reaction involve different brain structures. It opens possibilities for much more precise targeting of new drugs and it shows the importance of studying those effects that are directly relevant to drug taking (such as the reinforcing effect). Evidence has also linked the mesolimbic dopamine system to the reinforcing effects of nicotine and some workers have gone so far as to suggest that this brain system represents the final common pathway mediating the positive reinforcing effects of the majority of addictive drugs. This view has yet to find general acceptance and multiple brain regions and neurotransmitters may well be involved.

CONCLUSIONS

Behavioural pharmacology has played a major role in prevention of drug abuse through its contributions to the scientific data available to regulatory authorities. It has also had a very significant influence on the current understanding of addiction as the result of interactions of drug action with conditioning and learning processes. It has contributed substantively to evidence that tobacco use is fundamentally based on addiction to nicotine. Inevitably, many questions remain unresolved. Why have the classical hallucinogens and cannabis not been found to have positive reinforcing effects in controlled studies? What is the precise nature and role of the conditioning of drug effects to environmental stimuli? What is the extent of tolerance to positive reinforcing effects of drugs? Is there a psychopharmacological basis for polydrug abuse? Can specific brain regions and chemicals be linked selectively to addictive behaviours? Upon the answers to these and other questions will depend the potential future contribution of behavioural pharmacology to improved methods of treatment.

REFERENCES

Demellweek, C. and Goudie, A.J. (1983) 'Behavioural tolerance to amphetamine and other psychostimulants: the case for considering behavioural mechanisms', *Psychopharmacology* 80: 287–307.
Falk, J.L., Dews, P.B. and Schuster, C.R. (1983) 'Commonalities in the environmental control of behavior', in P.K. Levison, D.R. Gerstein and D.R. Maloff (eds) *Commonalities in Substance Abuse and Habitual Behavior*, Lexington: Lexington Books, pp. 47–110.
George, F.R. and Goldberg, S.R. (1989) 'Genetic approaches to the analysis of addiction procesess', *Trends in Pharmacological Sciences* 10: 78–83.
Goldberg, S.R. (1976) 'Stimuli associated with drug injections as events that control behavior', *Pharmacological Review* 27: 325–40.
Goldberg, S.R. and Stolerman, I.P. (eds) (1986) *Behavioral Analysis of Drug Dependence*, New York: Academic Press.
Koob, G.F. and Goeders, N.E. (1989) 'Neuroanatomical basis of drug self-administration', in J.M. Liebman and S.J. Cooper (eds) *Neuropharmacological Basis of Reward*, Oxford: Clarendon, pp. 214–63.
Siegel, S. (1988) 'Drug anticipation and drug tolerance', in M. Lader (ed.) *The Psychopharmacology of Addiction*, Oxford: Oxford University Press, pp. 73–96.

CROSS REFERENCES

Chapter 4

Psychological theories of addiction

Robert West

The term 'addiction' relates to the difficulty an individual has in managing to go without something. In this chapter it will be used synonymously with 'dependence'. Addiction becomes manifest when individuals continue to engage in a behaviour which is patently damaging and/or despite repeated attempts to stop. Individuals who are highly addicted report feeling a compulsion to engage in the behaviour. Certain drugs, or drug preparations are known to produce addiction in a significant proportion of users. In addition, it is apparent that a behaviour such as gambling can become compulsive. It has been argued that other behaviours, including exercise and using arcade games, are also potentially addictive.

This chapter will not examine individual theories. Excellent reviews can be found in Edwards, 1989; Marlatt *et al.*, 1988; Peele, 1985; Wilson, 1987. Instead it will describe the three main theoretical orientations. These emphasize:

1 the aversive consequences of abstinence (withdrawal avoidance theories);
2 the positive attributes of the behaviour (appetitive theories);
3 distortion of the motivational process itself (motivational distortion theories).

WITHDRAWAL AVOIDANCE THEORIES OF ADDICTION

These theories apply mainly to pharmacological dependencies. Under this view, drug use is initiated by curiosity, social pressure, medical need or desire for pleasurable or beneficial effects. As discussed by John Littleton in Chapter 2, prolonged drug use results in acquired tolerance to the effects of the drug so that larger and larger doses are required to achieve the same effect. This tolerance results from adaptation arising from a mechanism designed to restore equilibrium. This same adaptation means that absence of the drug leads to overcompensation by the adaptive response. The result is a withdrawal syndrome which can be aversive and even life-threatening. Section II of this volume covers the clinical withdrawal states.

Once adaptation has occurred individuals need to continue drug use merely to maintain normal functioning. Thus in terms of the withdrawal avoidance theory, an addict is someone who needs to use a drug in order to stave off aversive withdrawal symptoms.

There are many theories as to how tolerance may be acquired. One way may involve changes in the functioning of the synaptic connections between neurones; chronic exposure to a drug which mimics the action of a neurotransmitter may desensitize the receptor for that neurotransmitter. Another possibility is that changes in associated neural or hormonal systems actively compensate for a drug's action. A third notion is that of behavioural tolerance. According to this view, individuals may adjust their expectations about what constitutes a normal level of functioning, their lifestyle and/or coping mechanisms to take account of a drug. They then find it difficult to readjust to life without the drug. A fourth proposal is that physiological responses antagonistic to drug actions come to be elicited to the cues surrounding drug use by a process of classical (Pavlovian) conditioning. This theory postulates that the body mobilizes antagonistic responses to a drug's action in order to maintain homeostasis. With repeated drug use, these antagonistic or compensatory responses come to be elicited prior to drug ingestion by the cues associated with drug taking, such as the physical setting or the sight of the drug paraphernalia. This results in a decreased response to the drug and an overcompensation when cues for drug taking are present but the drug is not actually ingested. Although there is some evidence of situation-specific tolerance, there have as yet been no convincing demonstrations of conditioned compensatory drug responses in the presence of drug cues.

There are several difficulties with theories of dependence based solely on need to avoid aversive withdrawal symptoms. First, there is often a dissociation between withdrawal symptoms and the difficulty individuals have in abstaining from addictive behaviours. One can detoxify alcoholics or heroin addicts in special treatment centres, but well after the acute withdrawal symptoms have gone, relapses and bouts of craving occur. Cigarette smokers' reports of difficulty in not smoking are largely unrelated to withdrawal symptoms such as irritability, hunger and difficulty in concentrating. There are also many cases of individuals who have become physically dependent on morphine initially administered for pain relief but who experience no difficulty going without the drug when it is stopped, despite the fact that they experience withdrawal symptoms. A second problem is that there are individuals who are addicted to gambling even though there is no drug-induced tolerance. Behavioural tolerance or even neurochemical adaptation to a behavioural phenomenon provides a possible explanation but it remains to be seen whether convincing evidence of these phenomena can be found. A third problem with a simple withdrawal avoidance theory of dependence is the observation that relapse is often associated with particular situations. These include situations where the behaviour has been enacted in the past, or situations involving stress. The conditioning theory of tolerance can be invoked as a possible explanation for the former situation though in the latter case the connection is more tenuous.

APPETITIVE THEORIES OF ADDICTION

Inadequacies in withdrawal avoidance theories of addiction have led to the idea that individuals become dependent on the positive effects of the drug or behaviour. These 'appetitive' theories of addiction vary from drug to drug. In some cases, as with cocaine for example, the theory is that the drug-induced euphoria is so pleasant that it becomes more important to individuals than their own health or diet. Alcohol, it is argued, provides a means of coping with stress by increasing feelings of self-efficacy, deadening sensation, preventing coherent thought or releasing inhibition. Since psychomotor stimulants such as amphetamine affect arousal, it has been proposed that they improve performance on tasks requiring sustained attention in addition to producing euphoriant effects. Smokers claim that cigarettes can calm them down as well as pep them up. The basis for these effects and the extent to which they are attributable to nicotine are still not clear despite considerable research effort. Even more obscure is the mechanism by which gambling provides satisfaction. There is some evidence that the thrill of winning is important.

The dissociation between appetitive and withdrawal of avoidance mechanisms in dependence has received support from studies showing that blocking the action of morphine in one part of the brain stops animals responding to obtain the drug, whereas blocking its action in another part results in the onset of withdrawal symptoms. Thus the neural pathways underlying the opiate withdrawal syndrome and those underlying responding to obtain the drug are quite separate.

Whereas the perceived benefits of addictive behaviours help to explain why people should experience difficulty in abstaining in the absence of withdrawal discomfort, these cannot fully explain addiction. Appetitive theories do not explain, for example, why it should take time for individuals to become addicted. The positive benefits of a drug are apparent to the user relatively early in his or her drug-taking career. In fact, they would be expected, if anything, to decline over time as tolerance develops.

MOTIVATIONAL DISTORTION THEORIES

The third kind of theory proposes that chronic drug ingestion or repetition of a behaviour changes the motivational system underlying that behaviour. At a psychological level there is the concept of 'habit strength'. Habit strength refers to the causal association between a stimulus which is a cue to action and the subsequent action. The mechanism by which repetition of an action in the presence of the cue stimulus strengthens this link is not clear. It has been argued that it may involve the enhancement of synaptic connections in the neural circuitry involved. It is akin to the automation of psychomotor skills. Another distortion of motivation might result from the actions of the drugs concerned. An example is the proposal that nicotine ingestion influences the process of glucoregulation so that termination of nicotine intake is associated with increased appetite for both food and cigarettes.

Motivational distortion theories can explain why relapse and craving can occur in the absence of aversive withdrawal symptoms and also why it takes time and continued exposure to the addictive behaviour for addiction to take hold. However, they have more difficulty with the fact that relapse and craving can be influenced by stress and/or particular cues and situations previously associated with the addictive behaviour. It may be that situational effects modulate the motivational system which has been distorted by the addiction.

INDIVIDUAL DIFFERENCES IN SUSCEPTIBILITY TO ADDICTION

Any theory of addiction has to account for the fact that given apparently the same exposure to a drug or addictive behaviour, some people go on to become addicted whereas others do not. It also has to account for the fact that individuals who have tried to throw off the addiction many times and failed, can on a subsequent attempt succeed. Thus there is inter-individual and intra-individual variation in addictive liability.

Withdrawal avoidance theories of addiction offer several possible explanations of differences in addictive liability. One is that there may be constitutional differences in the development of tolerance to some drug effects. Individuals who develop tolerance more readily may be more likely to become addicted. It may also be the case that individuals who have a lower ability or propensity to tolerate discomfort are more susceptible to addiction because they find it harder to put up with the withdrawal symptoms.

Appetitive theories of addiction suggest other sources of individual variation in susceptibility to addiction. A greater need for the kind of benefit which a drug or behaviour might provide is one such source. For example, individuals who are more susceptible to stress or who are more exposed to stressful life events may be more likely to become addicted to drugs which help them to cope with that stress or at least escape from it mentally. Individuals who are more hedonistic may be more susceptible to pleasurable euphoriant effects of drugs. There is evidence of greater illicit drug use among those with higher scores on sociopathy and sensation seeking scales. However, it is not clear whether this is because of greater initial interest in the drugs leading to greater exposure, or greater addictive liability once exposed.

Motivational distortion theories of addiction would suggest that individual differences in addictive liability may be related to physiological reactivity to drugs or characteristics of the motivational systems prior to exposure to the drugs.

Common to all theories of addiction is the concept that individuals who have greater coping resources or 'willpower' should be more able to resist addiction. The coping skills might help specifically with craving and involve engaging in activities incompatible with the addictive behaviour, or they might involve ways of dealing with any of the possible factors which predispose towards relapse. An individual's perception of his or her ability to cope ('self-efficacy') may also play a role in its own right. The concept of willpower is difficult to pin down but probably involves a propensity to persevere with intentions which have been consciously formulated in the face of adversity or short-term set backs. While one would expect individuals with greater willpower to be more resistant to addiction, there have been few empirical tests of the utility of this concept.

CONCLUSIONS

Three kinds of theory have been discussed: withdrawal avoidance, appetitive and motivational distortion. All three can account for some, though not all, features of addiction. It is possible to expand each kind of theory and so increase its explanatory power. The withdrawal avoidance theory can be made to explain relapse after the acute withdrawal phase by suggesting that there is temporary reinstatement of withdrawal symptoms as a result of conditioning of these to certain situational cues. The presence of craving and the occurrence of relapse in the absence of withdrawal symptoms can be explained by postulating the occurrence of incipient withdrawal symptoms which are not obvious to the addict but are powerful enough to promote craving and relapse. The fact that relapse can often be associated with stress could be explained by arguing that stress can lead to relapse in many kinds of difficult enterprise – there may be no specific link with addiction.

Appetitive theories of addiction can be supplemented by postulating an 'opponent process'. This is a variant of the neuroadaptation view in which a positive affective response to a stimulus is followed by a rebound. With repetition of the stimulus the negative aspect of the response becomes accentuated and becomes superimposed on the positive response.

Motivational distortion theories can be elaborated by defining particular situational factors which would alter the underlying motivational state and/or the psychological interpretation of that state in much the same way as has been postulated for primary drives such as hunger.

It is also possible that addiction involves more than one of the three mechanisms proposed. It may be that relapse can occur in one individual because of aversive withdrawal symptoms and in another because of desire for positive aspects of the addiction. Similarly, relapse early in an attempt at abstinence may occur primarily because of aversive withdrawal symptoms or later because of remembered positive effects of a drug.

Despite relatively detailed knowledge of the characteristics of addictive behaviours gleaned from clinical observation and systematic investigation, a coherent unified theory of addiction has not yet emerged. Most clinicians and researchers in addiction recognize that it is a multifaceted problem, that there is considerable heterogeneity within and across forms of addictive behaviour, and many or all of the theoretical viewpoints described in this chapter may be applicable to varying degrees.

REFERENCES

Edwards, G. (1989) Psychiatry and the Addictions. *Special Issue of International Review of Psychiatry* 1, No 1/2.

Marlatt, A., Baer, J.S., Donovan, D.M. and Kivlahan, D.R. (1988) 'Addictive behaviors: etiology and treatment', *Annual Review of Psychology* 39: 223–52.

Peele, S. (1985) *The Meaning of Addiction*, Lexington: D.C. Heath.

Wilson, T.G. (1987) 'Cognitive processes in addiction', *British Journal of Addiction* 82: 343–53.

CROSS REFERENCES

Chapter 1   Dependence on psychoactive drugs: finding a common language
            D. Colin Drummond
Chapter 2   Drug dependence as pharmacological adaptation
            John M. Littleton
Chapter 3   Behavioural pharmacology of addiction
            I.P. Stolerman
Chapter 17 Pathological gambling: addiction without a drug
            Sheila B. Blume
Chapter 32 Behavioural treatments for alcohol problems
            D. Adrian Wilkinson and Martha Sanchez-Craig
Chapter 33 Behaviour therapy of drug dependence
            Charles P. O'Brien and Anna Rose Childress
Chapter 40 Treatments for smokers
            Petr Hajek

Chapter 5

Drug use and dependence as a social problem: sociological approaches

Jonathan Gabe and Michael Bury

Editor's note
This chapter sets out to deal with drug use and dependence explicitly as a social process. It makes no claim to present a theoretical overview of addiction from a sociological perspective. However, sociological approaches are relevant not only to drug use as a social problem but also to the systematic analysis of addiction in a wider range of social contexts. Hence, this chapter may serve as a useful example for understanding substance abuse as this is manifest with respect to such social issues as ethnicity, gender, social mobility and cultural pluralism.

INTRODUCTION

Illicit drug use is frequently regarded as a social problem by both professionals and the public alike. Recently, some forms of licit drug use have also been taken as problematic, and the distinction between the two has become a matter of public debate. Sociologists have played an important part in the development of such an understanding of both forms of drug use, although they differ in the way they conceptualize and explain the problem's genesis. In this chapter we review critically the different theoretical approaches to the sociological study of drug use and dependence as a social problem. This provides a basis for outlining our own 'developmental approach', which is then illustrated through a brief account of the social problem 'career' of one category of prescribed drugs – benzodiazepine tranquillizers and hypnotics. Focusing on a legally prescribed drug and claims about its 'excessive' use is, we believe, of value because it highlights the equivocal status of those who use it (being on the margins between deviance and normality) and the activities of those concerned to establish or deny the claim that its use represents a social problem.

THEORETICAL APPROACHES

It is possible to identify three broad sociological approaches to the study of social problems: functionalist; conflict; and interactionist/constructionist.[1] Below, we review critically the concerns and core assumptions of each of these approaches and highlight the consequences for the study of drugs. 'Drugs' at this point refers to illicit drugs which, until now, have been the main concern of social problem analysts. This classification of approaches is of course no more than an analytic aid and should not be taken as implying that such approaches are internally homogeneous and coherent, or that individual researchers restrict themselves only to one approach.

Functionalist approaches

Functionalist approaches have dominated the social problems field for most of this century (Horton, 1966; Spector and Kitsuse, 1977). Functionalism in the field of social problems has also been known by other names, including 'social pathology' and 'social disorganization'. Although these names signify differing concerns,[2] they reflect a common core: a belief that a social problem can be defined in functional terms as a form of behaviour or as a condition that impedes the fulfilment of societal goals, interferes with the smooth functioning of society and throws society into disequilibrium (Spector and Kitsuse, 1977: 23). Functionalists believe that the soci-ologist is well placed to define what is or is not a social problem, on the grounds of his or her expert knowledge of the structure of society (Westhues, 1974: 421). They acknowledge that ordinary members of society may share this definition, but also that they may not (Etzioni, 1976). At the level of the social system, they attribute the origins of a social problem to a breakdown in the usually dynamic equilibrium of the parts of the system due to social change, or see it as an unintended consequence of institutional arrangements (Merton, 1971). At the individual level, the origins of problematic behaviour are attributed to ineffective or inappropriate socialization, or the disjuncture between goals and the opportunity to attain them (Merton, 1971). If the problem is identified as systemic, the solution proposed is to bring back into equilibrium those parts of the system that are out of phase. If the focus is on individual 'misbehaviour' the solution offered is moral education.

In the drugs field the functionalist approach is illustrated by Clausen's (1971) discussion of addiction. For him the social problem of addiction to illicit drugs stems both from the failure of American cities to integrate deprived migrants into the social fabric and opportunity structure (systemic level), and from the rejection of the value consensus by those living in the run-down areas of these cities (the individual level).

Over the years there have been many criticisms of functionalist approaches which have challenged their core assumptions and highlighted their limited explanatory value. For us the three most important are the following. First, functionalism has rightly been criticized for failing to take seriously societal members' subjective definitions of social problems and the processes by which they come to define such behaviour as problematic (Fuller and Myers, 1941; Blumer, 1971; Spector and Kitsuse, 1977). Second, while functionalism recognizes stresses or strains within a social system its emphasis on a normative and value consensus has ignored the extent to which norms and values are bound up with the differing material interests of distinctive social groups. Third, by taking as its starting point social problems defined from the point of view of the existing order and by advocating that these problems are best resolved through education, proponents of this approach may be seen as uncritically supporting the maintenance of the *status quo* (Mills, 1943; Westhues, 1974).

Conflict approaches

Although most clearly identified with Marxism, the conflict school also encompasses non-Marxists interested in alienation. Both camps see society in terms of diverse groups with unequal access to wealth and economic and political power, and regard those with the least wealth and power as alienated and discontented. It is this alienation which is seen as the catalyst for the generation of social problems (Horton, 1966). Marxists, however, go further by relating this discontent to the underlying contradictions of the capitalist social system. They are also more likely to see social problems as disguised political issues and argue that the most powerful often have a vested interest in *not* solving social problems, or suggest that the solution of social problems is part and parcel of the problem of social control (Box, 1980; Scull, 1984). From this perspective such problems can only be eradicated if the structure of capitalist society is radically altered.

When the conflict approach is applied to the drugs field it encourages attention to be focused on whether the use of illicit drugs is a form of escape, or resistance, for members of subordinate social groups such as working-class youth. Dorn (1980), for example, has argued that youths have used illicit drugs in this way and considers that the control agencies, seeing such behaviour as a threat to the reproduction of labour power, have responded within a treatment framework.

We have some sympathy with this conflict approach in so far as it emphasizes the role of structural factors in the generation of social problems and stresses the significance of conflicts of interest between social groups with differing amounts of power. However, to the extent that the proponents of a conflict approach fail to take seriously the role of social processes in the development of social problems and treat cultural and symbolic aspects of drug use as marginal, they weaken the explanatory potential of their contributions.

Interactionist and constructionist approaches

These approaches both take the actor's perspective rather than 'objective' conditions as the starting point for an analysis of social problems, and focus on how actors define situations, persons or events as problematic. They also share the assumption that social problems emerge through social interaction, and that the natural history of such problems is uncertain and contingent (Blumer, 1971; Spector and Kitsuse, 1977). They are thus concerned with process rather than structure and meaning rather than causality.

Despite these similarities there are also important differences between interactionist and constructionist views. First, there is the question of scale. Symbolic interactionists tend to focus on small-scale settings (e.g. neighbourhoods, courtrooms) and the interaction between individuals, whereas constructionists generally take a broader view and analyse the relationship between expert discourse and bureaucratic institutions. Second, interactionists tend to operate with a more explicit notion of objective reality (e.g. Becker, 1967). The constructionists' approach, on the other hand, suggests that sociologists should set aside the issue of objective reality and should focus solely on the claims-making activities of those alleging that a particular behaviour is problematic (Spector and Kitsuse, 1977).

In the drugs literature the interactionist approach is illustrated by Becker's (1963) and Young's (1971, 1973) work on marijuana use. They note the growth of this drug's usage and the specific processes involved in becoming a marijuana user. Then, taking the growth in the consumption of the drug as the objective condition, they consider societal reaction to it and the way in which this may amplify the original problem. The constructionist approach is best exemplified by Lidz and Walker's (1980) analysis of the claims-making activities of those who have alleged that there was an epidemic increase in heroin use in the United States during the 1960s and early 1970s. They argue that this epidemic was constructed as a smoke screen for the repression of political and cultural groups.

The value of the interactionist and constructionist approaches is that they draw attention to the emergent nature of social problems and the role of social interaction in such a process. Neither approach is entirely satisfactory, however. Interactionism's contribution to the study of social problems has been limited by its failure to take account of the broader setting and the part played by competing social groups in the generation of a social problem; while constructionism's impact has been reduced as a result of an unwillingness to tackle the question of relativism and to take seriously the experience of social problems. The charge of relativism arises because constructionists have argued that social problems are nothing more than definitional activities or fabrications. To make such a statement, however, begs the question about the status of these analysts' own claims about claims-making activities. For if there is no role for independent evidence, or no broader concern with 'generative' structures, then identifying the 'conditions of possibility' for the development of social problems becomes a never-ending and circular argument.

The second problem of ignoring the experiential dimension (be it harm done through crime or suffering experienced through illness) seems to stem from a view of definitional processes as being largely arbitrary in character, with a meaning only located in relation to the power of interest groups. This leads to an 'aloof' form of social analysis, as if the analyst is at pains to maintain a considerable social distance from the social relations of which he or she is a part. Gusfield (1984), for example, talks of striking an 'Olympian' pose with regard to providing useful knowledge about social problems. Taken to extremes it actually casts doubt on the value of any form of empirical social science and its use (Bury, 1986).

The developmental perspective: a synthesis

In the light of the foregoing remarks there would seem to be a need for a new perspective which combines the strengths of the conflict and interactionist/ constructionist approaches while avoiding the pitfalls. We now sketch out the elements of such an approach and then illustrate its value by applying it to the area of tranquillizer use and dependence. Our starting point is the developmental perspective first outlined by Fuller and Myers (1941) and subsequently developed by Blumer (1971) and Spector and Kitsuse (1977). These authors have attempted to identify various stages in the history of a social problem, beginning with its emergence and ending with its resolution. The stages outlined by Blumer (1971), for example, comprise (1) the emergence of a social problem, (2) the legitimation of the problem, (3) the mobilization of action, (4) the formation of an official plan and (5) the implementation of that plan. One of the merits of this approach is that it highlights the dynamic nature of the history of a social problem. As developed by Blumer and Spector and Kitsuse it also emphasizes the contingent nature of this process, as the movement between stages is seen as highly problematic. The emphasis on contingency is a response to early critics of the developmental view who objected to its 'law-like' connotations (Lemert, 1951).

Our approach differs from earlier formulations, however, in certain important respects. First, we suggest that it is insufficient simply to focus on the claims-making activities of various interest groups. For a social problem to emerge, certain objective conditions need to be met, an issue that has bedevilled the social problems literature from the outset. We note these with regard to tranquillizer use and dependence.

Second, we feel that greater attention needs to be given to explaining why certain claims resonate with the 'general public' while others fail to do so, in the movement between the emergence and legitimation of the problem; why there is, in other words, an 'elective affinity' between the development of social problems and the social contexts in which they occur (Rock, 1977). This requires a cultural analysis of the role of the symbolic in social life. With regard to tranquillizers it means that attention needs to be focused on the social and symbolic meaning of these drugs to particular social groups, and the extent to which these meanings resonate with contemporary concerns about licit and illicit drug taking and the maintenance of health.

Third, we agree with Manning (1985) that there is a need to develop more fully a detailed analysis of how claims are registered and become legitimate, and the reasons for the state's response to such claims. To answer the former point, attention needs to be focused on the role of the mass media as a key link between claims-makers and the state. As we shall see this has been an important vehicle for and influence over the claims made by various groups. It has most certainly added its own particular twist to the tranquillizer story. As regards the analysis of the state's reaction to these claims-making activities this has been largely absent from constructionist accounts, yet what determines the state's response and its nature is central to any understanding of the fate of a social problem. One needs to ask, for example, to what extent the state's response is influenced by the claims-making activities of those concerned about a particular social problem and to what degree it is influenced by other interests and policy considerations. Likewise there is a need to consider whether claims-making is more likely to attract financial resources or encourage legislative changes if the solution demanded is in line with the prevailing ideological climate. Clearly the media and the modern state are both key social institutions in contemporary society (we would argue that it is difficult to imagine a social problem gaining legitimacy without attention from both) and, as we indicate below, both of these institutions are important in the issue of tranquillizer use.

THE CASE STUDY: TRANQUILLIZERS AS A SOCIAL PROBLEM

In this section we sketch out the development of tranquillizers as a social problem in terms of the following stages: emergence; legitimation and mobilization of public opinion; and recognition by the state. A further, more empirically grounded analysis can be found in Gabe and Bury (1988).

Starting with *emergence* we suggest that long-term tranquillizer use has emerged as a problem in Britain for two reasons. First, objective evidence has been accumulated about the real harm and distress caused by long-term use at therapeutic dose and its incidence. Since the early 1980s a growing number of studies have reported that patients agreeing to or requesting withdrawal from long-term tranquillizer use at therapeutic dose have experienced symptoms of physical dependence on withdrawal and that these symptoms can last a year or more. Furthermore, studies which have used representative samples and control groups have found that between 27 per cent and 45 per cent of long-term users are dependent on their drugs.

Second, scientific experts and representatives of mental health pressure groups have claimed in public that benzodiazepines (a) are being overused and misused and (b) have the potential to cause physical dependence at normal therapeutic dosage. Claims about overuse and misuse in Britain were made in the 1970s in response to the growth in tranquillizer prescriptions. Since the early 1980s these have been superseded by claims about benzodiazepines' dependence potential and the existence of a 'withdrawal syndrome', in line with current clinical and epidemiological research.

The next stage in the process involves the media. There is evidence that the media have played a major part in *legitimating* tranquillizer dependence as a social problem and *mobilizing public opinion* around the issue. For example, *That's Life*, the popular British television consumer programme with an audience of around 10 million people at peak viewing time on Sunday evening, considered the subject on at least four occasions between 1983 and 1985. An analysis of the transcripts of these programmes reveals that the programmes offered a platform for the competing claims of medical experts and pressure group representatives about the prevalence of tranquillizer dependence, with the estimates escalating from programme to programme. For example, in the first programme 5 million people were said to be taking one form of tranquillizer or another, and a quarter of a million were said to be unable to get off them. In a later programme, however, 10 million people were said to have taken tranquillizers and 50 per cent of current users were considered to be unable to come off them.

Clearly, as far as the media are concerned, the bigger the estimates the more dramatic the problem and the more newsworthy the coverage. The result, however, is that tranquillizer dependence has been portrayed as being of epidemic proportions.

That's Life, in common with other programmes, also presented a particular image of long-term tranquillizer users as people who had been 'completely taken over' by the drug. Individual users, usually women, were portrayed as victims of a menacing force over which they had little or no control. Such imagery provided little chance for the variable nature of benzodiazepine use to come across, alongside issues of dependence. For instance, no mention was made of tranquillizers used only as sleeping pills, or of their intermittent or sporadic use in managing personal crises. Besides providing a terrain for claims-making activity it can be argued that the media have also played an essential role in mobilizing public opinion, as the huge postbag to *That's Life* following their programmes on tranquillizers demonstrated.

Two reasons suggest themselves as to why programmes like this have 'worked' with the public. First is the ambivalent attitudes of many who take tranquillizers. Such ambivalence creates a receptiveness to the issue amongst specific social groups, especially middle-aged women, and even 'demands' that the media should attend to the problem. Second is the revival of concern about illegal drug use. The climate in Britain in recent years has been one of extreme concern, if not outright panic over the use of illegal drugs, especially amongst the young, with politicians being pressed to state what they intend to do to combat 'this greatest menace in peace time' (Home Affairs Committee, 1985). This greater sensitivity to the damaging effects of illicit drug use can be seen as informing responses to licit drug taking, even in the face of limited evidence of dependence.

Finally, the extent to which long-term tranquillizer use is seen as a social problem is determined by the *response of the state*. The evidence here suggests that the government has been equivocal. While it has made several statutory changes, committed certain monies to support voluntary organizations providing services for those on tranquillizers and issued advice to all doctors about the dependence potential of benzodiazepines, an analysis of the motives behind these actions suggests that the state does not at present see long-term tranquillizer use as a full blown social problem. For example, its decision to introduce the 'limited list' in 1984 was arguably motivated more by the need to reduce the NHS drugs bill in line with general cuts in welfare spending, rather than as a way of tackling long-term tranquillizer use. Likewise, drafting legislation in 1985 to bring benzodiazepines under the Misuse of Drugs Act 1971 and make them controlled drugs seems to have been motivated by the need to ratify the United Nations Convention on Psychotropic Substances of which it is a signatory. In 1984 the UN voted to accept the World Health Organization's recommendation to control 33 benzodiazepines under the Psychotropic Convention. To implement this convention Britain had to duplicate the UN's decision in its domestic legislation. If the state had been more concerned about benzodiazepines it would surely have put them in a schedule that imposed more than minimal controls.

The state's reluctance to accept tranquillizers wholeheartedly as a social problem may in part be because these drugs are not taken in the main by social groups like working-class youths who are seen as a threat to law and order, but by otherwise respectable middle-aged women (and to a lesser extent men). It may also reflect a reluctance to challenge the professional autonomy of doctors. Whatever the reason it would seem that long-term tranquillizer use is currently relatively low on the policy agenda despite the public debate that has occurred on this topic.

CONCLUSION

In this chapter we have reviewed various sociological approaches to drug use and dependence as a social problem, before focusing on one in particular – the developmental approach. Taking tranquillizers as a case study, we have described briefly the stages through which it must pass before full social problem status is conferred. As far as tranquillizers are concerned such a status is still to be achieved. Whether the stages identified here constitute a model of the 'natural history' of drug dependence as a social problem is an open question and can only be answered if further analysis of a more comparative kind is undertaken.

NOTES

1 We do not claim that these approaches encompass all that has been written in this area. They simply represent the most common conceptual models that have been drawn upon.
2 Social pathology focuses on the violation of moral expectations due to faulty socialization, whereas social disorganization emphasizes the maladjustment of parts of the social system as a result of social change. See Rubington and Weinberg, 1981.

REFERENCES

Becker, H. (1963) *Outsiders*, New York: The Free Press.
— (1967) *Social Problems: a Modern Approach*, New York: J. Wiley & Co.
Blumer, H. (1971) 'Social problems as collective behaviour', *Social Problems* 18: 298–306.
Box, S. (1980) 'Where have all the naughty children gone?', in National Deviancy Conference (ed.) *Permissiveness and Control: the Fate of the Sixties Legislation*, London: Macmillan Press.
Bury, M.R. (1986) 'Social constructionism and the development of medical sociology', *Sociology of Health and Illness* 8: 137–69.
Clausen, J.A. (1971) 'Drug use', in R.K. Merton and R. Nisbet (eds) *Contemporary Social Problems* (Third Edition), New York: Harcourt Brace Jovanovich.
Dorn, N. (1980) 'The conservatism of the cannabis debate', in National Deviancy Conference (ed.) *Permissiveness and Control: the Fate of the Sixties Legislation*, London: Macmillan Press.
Etzioni, A. (1976) *Social Problems*, Englewood Cliffs, New Jersey: Prentice-Hall.
Fuller, R.C. and Myers, R.R. (1941) 'The natural history of a social problem', *American Sociological Review* 6: 320–9.
Gabe, J. and Bury, M. (1988) 'Tranquillisers as a social problem', *The Sociological Review* 36: 320–52.
Gusfield, J.R. (1984) 'On the side: practical action and social constructivism in social problems theory', in J.W. Schneider and J.I. Kitsuse (eds) *Studies in the Sociology of Social Problems*, Norwood, New Jersey: Ablex Publishing Company.
Home Affairs Committee (1985) *Interim Report on Drug Misuse*, London: HMSO.
Horton, J. (1966) 'Order and conflict theories of social problems as competing ideologies', *American Journal of Sociology* 71: 701–13.
Lemert, E.M. (1951) 'Is there a natural history of social problems?', *American Sociological Review* 16: 217–23.
Lidz, C.W. and Walker, A.L. (1980) *Heroin, Deviance and Morality*, Beverly Hills: Sage Publications.
Manning, N. (1985) 'Constructing social problems', in N. Manning (ed.) *Social Problems and Welfare Ideology*, Aldershot: Gower Press.
Merton, R.K. (1971) 'Social problems and sociological theory', in R.K. Merton and R. Nisbet (eds) *Contemporary Social Problems* (Third Edition), New York: Harcourt Brace Jovanovich.
Mills, C. Wright (1943) 'The professional ideology of social pathologists', *American Journal of Sociology* 49. Reprinted in I.L. Horowitz (ed.) *Power, Politics and People*, New York: Ballantine Books.
Rock, P. (1977) 'Introduction', in P. Rock (ed.) *Drugs and Politics*, New Brunswick, N.J.: Transaction Books.
Rubington, E. and Weinberg, M.S. (1981) *The Study of Social Problems: Five Perspectives* (Third Edition), New York: Oxford University Press.

Scull, A. (1984) *Decarceration: Community, Treatment and the Deviant: a Radical View* (Second Edition), Cambridge: Polity Press.
Spector, M. and Kitsuse, J. (1977) *Constructing Social Problems*, Menlo Park, California: Cummings Publishing Company.
Westhues, K. (1974) 'Social problems as systemic costs', *Social Problems* 20: 419–31.
Young, J. (1971) *The Drugtakers*, London: MacGibbon and Kee.
— (1973) 'The amplification of drug use', in S. Cohen and J. Young (eds) *The Manufacture of News: Social Problems, Deviance and the Mass Media*, London: Constable.

CROSS REFERENCES

Chapter 6

Career and natural history

Duncan Raistrick

TERMINOLOGY

What do we mean when we say that someone has a 'successful *career* as a footballer' and what does this have to do with addictive behaviour? First, being a footballer defines a particular *role*, one of the many roles making up an individual's life. Second, career characterizes a progression of *behaviour* which develops against a backdrop of an expected norm or some template of a footballing career. The word 'successful' introduces the idea of individual variation or even deviation from the template. So, career can be understood as meaning on the one hand the typical course of a particular calling (defined role) including its good and bad aspects, but on the other hand can be followed at an individual level. The role of drinker or drug taker can be conceptualized in the same way, although Edwards (1984) cautions that the concept of career applied to substance misuse may be no more than an 'analytically useful artefact'.

At the level of an individual user, career is synonymous with a detailed substance misuse history. The clinician or researcher seeks to understand that career by mapping and integrating all events, from the personal (e.g. bereavement), to the national (e.g. economic recession), and from the molecular (e.g. genetic make-up) to the sociological (e.g. legal system). This exercise of describing and formulating a substance misuse career demands an assiduous interview method combined with restrained judgement in the attribution of cause and effect.

A rather different but complementary concept is that of *natural history* which is rooted in the study of disease processes. Simply put, the idea suggests that a particular disease will, if untreated, follow a somewhat predictable course. As a consequence of exposure to toxic or foreign substances, which include psychoactive drugs, equally predictable biological changes occur, e.g. alcoholic gastritis, barbiturate enzyme induction, muscle cramps of opiate withdrawal or cocaine paranoia. In order to distinguish this process from a disease process, Edwards (1984) has proposed the term *natural history of reactivity*, which forms a useful bridge between career (the behaviour) and natural history (the disease). With the possible exception of alcohol, there has been little research on the relationship between pattern of substance use and biological consequences. At what point does tissue reactivity become a bona fide disease? Is it the case, for example, that neuronal tolerance to opiates becomes at least partially irreversible and is this then a disease? Is it the case that biochemical evidence of alcohol-related liver damage is reversible and not a disease? These grey areas are unresolved.

Nevertheless, such an integrative approach to career and natural history will enrich the clinician's understanding, and inform the choice of intervention by bringing realism and, often, optimism to a particular case. Analysis of career alone leaves the clinician without a tangible measure of outcome. Measuring outcome (Sobell *et al.*, 1987) has progressed to a point of being clinically unhelpful: there is no consensus on when follow up should be undertaken, or which of the multiple outcome variables are most critical. In a search for *core process* Duckitt *et al.* (1985) investigated the relationship between five categories of outcome (drinking behaviour, alcohol-related harm, social adjustment, mental health adjustment and socio-medical assessment) in 68 male drinkers followed up for ten to twelve years: a tentative conclusion placed dependence as a bridge linking drinking itself with the other variables.

The authors argue that while empirical, static measures have utility as outcome measures, it is equally important to consider whether an indication of the direction or path which the individual is taking can be gleaned from that snapshot of their career.

REPERTOIRE OF BEHAVIOURS: PATTERNS OF SUBSTANCE USE

Addictive behaviour in the broadest sense is best explained by social learning theory (Heather and Robertson, 1985). Understanding the phenomenon of dependence in psychological terms mediated through a learning process implies the possibility of unlearning dependence. It follows that the study of substance using careers might be expected to reveal a repertoire of behaviours as different sets of learning condi- tions operate.

Wille (1983) used a number of data sources (including interview and case notes) to follow up 40 abstinent heroin users at ten years: for half the group social stabilization preceded cessation of opiate use, while for the other half in-patient withdrawal of opiates led to lifestyle changes and a move away from drug use. For 90 per cent of the group the transition to abstinence involved a period of less than two years during which time there was intermittent use of opiates or other drugs as the decision to stop using them became consolidated.

In a similar exercise Saunders and Kershaw (1979) re-interviewed 99 subjects who were identified from a general population survey as excessive drinkers: they separately analysed self-report reasons for changing drinking behaviour among 41 'ex-problem drinkers', 37 'episodic over-consumers' and 19 'alcoholics'. In all three groups remission involved fairly major life circumstance change.

These and other studies suggest that favourable influences on drinking or drug-taking behaviour include marriage or the establishment of an important relationship, employment especially involving promotion or a work ethos intolerant of alcohol or drug use, financial restrictions, geographical relocation, religious or other group activity intolerant of alcohol or drug use, and adequate housing provision. The value of treatment has been questioned, and even dismissed as lacking potency in comparison to these naturally occurring life changes. Although major life events most dramatically illustrate that even markedly dependent drinkers and drug takers have the capacity for a repertoire of behaviours, the effectiveness of treatment should not be marginalized (Kleber, 1989; Saunders, 1989).

FACTORS INFLUENCING THE EARLY DEVELOPMENT OF CAREERS

Substance-using careers almost invariably start with an experimentation phase. Children have an awareness of alcohol and other drugs at an early age (Casswell *et al.*, 1988). The naive user starting out on their career will quickly accumulate knowledge and skills in the use of psychoactive substances. The first drug of use is likely to be low tariff, one that is legal, and approved socially, or at least in the sub-culture. In the UK cigarettes and alcohol will commonly be the first and second drug tried (Swadi, 1988).

In a study of 2159 school children aged 11 to 13 McNeill *et al.* (1988) found prior experimentation with cigarettes and being a girl most strongly predicted taking up smoking at the 30-month follow up: it was suggested that a general factor 'anticipation of adulthood' was also operating and that boys therefore would take up smoking later. The attitudes of teachers and friends, but not parents, was predictive.

In a cross cultural study of 774 18–21-year-olds, 613 fathers and 747 mothers from Dublin and London, O'Connor (1978) found that parental, particularly paternal, attitudes rather than actual behaviour most influenced the drinking habits of young people; peer group pressure was the most important determinant of how drinking was incorporated into their lifestyle.

Whether or not low tariff substances are successfully incorporated into a person's lifestyle or alternatively herald the start of a misuse career will depend on both social and personal factors (Plant *et al.*, 1985). These have much in common with factors predisposing to use of higher tariff substances. Early use of illegal or socially disapproved substances may retain an experimental component but may also be, to a lesser or greater degree, divergent from societal norms. Kandel *et al.* (1978) found that peer group use and non-conforming attitudes best predicted cannabis smoking for young people in New York. Dembo and Shern (1982), again in New York, report an orderly progression from drinking to cannabis smoking, and from cannabis smoking to hard drugs. The movement up to cannabis was accounted for by street socialization, that is to say a subcultural norm, while the movement to heroin required both peer use of heroin and impaired personal development. In similar studies of solvent use, Evans and Raistrick (1987) found that regular use was associated with a high incidence of family trauma, separation from biological parents, single-parent homes and periods of care from an early age. Cannabis and alcohol were seen as preferred but unaffordable drugs while amphetamine and LSD were used occasionally for specific effects. Davies *et al.* (1985) report (1985) on four chronic solvent users who shared histories of parental rejection or abuse and progressed to inhaling thence to snorting and injecting heroin.

ESTABLISHED CAREERS

Polydrug use

More established careers stand to be complicated by the use of pharmaceutical preparations which are obtained wholly or intermittently on prescription. Busto *et al.* (1983) report that out of 216 referrals for alcohol misuse, toxicology screening found 33 per cent of patients to be using benzodiazepines, of which 54 per cent were prescribed and 46 per cent illicit; 2 per cent also used codeine and 1.5 per cent barbiturates. Perera *et al.* (1987) found that 90 per cent of (mainly heroin) addicts also used benzodiazepines as hypnotics, anxiolytics, or main drug substitutes to intensify a 'high'. Of patient referrals for primary problems of benzodiazepine misuse Busto *et al.* (1986) report 56 per cent to be exclusively benzodiazepine users (median dose 15mg diazepam or equivalent) and 44 per cent to be multiple users (median dose 40mg diazepam or equivalent); other drugs most frequently used were alcohol 47 per cent, barbiturates 27 per cent, opiates 27 per cent, other analgesics 27 per cent and cannabis 4 per cent. In short, to study a single-drug career is to be blind to reality, and in particular the possibilities of substitution and supplementation.

The concern of clinicians and therefore the focus of much research is with individuals who have experienced troubles from their substance use. It must be stressed that whatever risk factors might operate for an individual, there is no inevitability that use of a particular substance will become misuse or that there will be a move to higher tariff drugs; hedonistic use of high tariff drugs such as cocaine, 'ecstasy' or heroin does not necessarily imply problem use. Murphy *et al.* (1989) report on continuous controlled use of cocaine in one third of 21 subjects followed for eleven years: only one of their subjects had a cocaine career leading to major social dysfunction. None the less 'soft' drugs (cannabis, solvents) are often a bridge to 'hard' drugs: the connections are speculative but probably include internalizing illegal or disapproved substance use as normal, attraction to an 'alternative' sub-culture, and experience and desire for more varied and powerful drug effects.

Typically the *experienced user* will have experimented with one or more sub-stances and opted for using one main substance: this choice will have been made taking account of pharmacological effects, legal status, availability and no doubt other idiosyncratic considerations. From a pharmacological standpoint alcohol and cannabis are likely to be favoured as recreational drugs; highly plastic, potent or addictive drugs are less attractive for most people (Edwards, 1974). Cannabis is extensively used as a main drug in its own right but perhaps more usually both cannabis and nicotine (cigarettes) are used alongside alcohol or opiates. Attitudes to nicotine as a drug are interesting: the Narcotics Anonymous programme advocates total abstinence from all chemicals with the exception of nicotine.

Alcohol

Vaillant and Milofsky (1982) in a 20-year follow up of 110 male problem drinkers identified from within the general population, found movement in and out of different drinking styles: 18 men had achieved asymptomatic drinking for two years or more but paradoxically 21 'securely abstinent' men (mean of ten years' abstinence) were those with highest dependence ratings and the highest problem scores. Child- hood variables had no predictive value on outcome. In a 4-year follow up of 758 men recruited through treatment agencies, Polich *et al.* (1981) reported markedly different outcomes depending on the orientation of the agency towards abstinence versus harm-free drinking: after taking out an overall 14 per cent mortality rate, abstinence orientated agencies achieved 14 per cent returning to normal drinking, 29 per cent totally abstinent and 57 per cent problem drinking compared to 46 per cent, 22 per cent and 32 per cent respectively from the harm-free orientated agencies. Taylor *et al.* (1985) in a 10-year follow up of male problem drinkers presenting for treatment have attempted to quantify the amount of movement between the categories 'abstinence', 'social drinking' and 'troubled drinking': 25 per cent were constantly within the troubled drinking category, 12 per cent continuously abstinent and the remainder moving between the two and occasionally into social drinking.

Heroin

Vaillant (1973) reports on a 20-year follow up of 100 heroin addicts in New York: 23 per cent were dead, 35 per cent stable and abstinent, 25 per cent continued using opiates and 17 per cent uncertain. Previous employment, staying in a constant social environment and marriage or important relationship prior to seeking treatment predicted a good outcome. Stimson and Oppenheimer (1982), in a detailed account of 101 heroin addicts followed for ten years, report 15 per cent dead, 38 per cent abstinent from all drugs and leading ordinary lives, 30 per cent receiving prescribed opiates but otherwise leading ordinary lives and 17 per cent either off drugs or still attending clinics but having no major problems.

One conclusion from these studies is that opiate addicts are more likely to grow out of their habit than drinkers. Addressing this very point Winick (1962) estimated that, of addicts known to the Federal Bureau of Narcotics, 73 per cent had stopped using by the age of thirty-seven and 95 per cent by the age of fifty-seven; the estimates were controlled for the proportion of addicts in each age band. In a similarly controlled study Temple and Leino (1989) showed that while heavier drinkers tended to die prematurely, older (fifty years or over) survivors were likely to drink within the same or higher consumption bands as reported at a first interview twenty years before. These differences between alcohol and heroin careers are reflected in mortality rates (standardized to per 1000 person years) reported on 8-year follow up (Barr *et al.*, 1984): from illness the death rate per cent for heroin addicts was zero (expected 1.4) and for drinkers was 21.7 (expected 8.9), while from accidents for addicts was 12.3 (expected 1.6) and drinkers 13.0 (expected 1.5).

CONCLUSIONS

In many ways these figures frustrate as much as they inform. There are the usual problems of comparing data across studies, there is an over-representation of male subjects and generalization into contemporary culture is uncertain. All that said, Edwards's assertion (1984) that the study of substance-use careers is a stimulus to understanding the impact of social and medical policy on both individual and groups of substance users is impressively supported. Longitudinal studies insist that there are ways out of damaging addiction careers: the challenge for the clinician is to persist with minimizing the harm until that way out is found.

ACKNOWLEDGEMENTS

Thanks are due to Gillian Tober (Tutor, Leeds Addiction Unit) for commenting on earlier drafts and to Angela Pearson for careful secretarial work.

REFERENCES

Barr, H. L., Antes, D., Ottenberg, D.J. and Rosen, A. (1984) 'Mortality of treated alcoholics and drug addicts: the benefits of abstinence', *Journal of Studies on Alcohol* 45: 440–52.

Busto, U., Simpkins, J., Sellers, E.M., Sisson, B. and Segal, R. (1983) 'Objective determination of benzodiazepine use and abuse in alcoholics', *British Journal of Addiction* 78: 429–35.

Busto, U., Sellers, E.M., Naranjo, C.A., Cappell, H.D., Sanchez-Craig, M. and Simpkins, J. (1986) 'Patterns of benzodiazepine abuse and dependence', *British Journal of Addiction* 81: 87–94.

Casswell, S., Gilmore, L.L., Silva, P. and Brasch, P. (1988) 'What children know about alcohol and how they know it', *British Journal of Addiction* 83: 223–7.

Davies, B., Thorley, A. and O'Connor, D. (1985) 'Progression of addiction careers in young adult solvent misusers', *British Medical Journal* 200: 109–10.

Dembo, R. and Shern, D. (1982) 'Relative deviance and the process(es) of drug involvement among inner city youths', *International Journal of the Addictions* 17: 1373–99.

Duckitt, A., Taylor, C., Brown, D., Edwards, G., Oppenheimer, E. and Sheehan, M. (1985) 'Alcoholism and the nature of outcome', *British Journal of Addiction* 80: 153–62.

Edwards, G. (1974) 'Drug dependence and plasticity', *Quarterly Journal of Studies on Alcohol* 35: 176–95.

— (1984) 'Drinking in longitudinal perspective: career and natural history', *British Journal of Addiction* 79: 175-83.

Evans, A. C. and Raistrick, D.S. (1987) 'Patterns of use and related harm with toluene-based adhesives and butane gas', *British Journal of Psychiatry* 150: 773–6.

Heather, N. and Robertson, I. (1985) *Problem Drinking: the New Approach*, Harmondsworth: Penguin.

Kandel, D.B., Kessler, R.C. and Arguiles, R.Z. (1978) 'Antecedents of adolescent initiation into stages of drug use: a developmental analysis', in D.B. Kandel (ed.) *Longitudinal Research on Drug Use*, Washington DC: Halstead.

Kleber, H.D. (1989) 'Treatment of drug dependence: what works', *International Review of Psychiatry* 1: 81–100.

McNeill, A.D., Jarvis, M.J., Stapleton, J.A., Russell, M.A.H., Eiser, J.R., Gammage, P. and Gray, E.M. (1988) 'Prospective study of factors predicting uptake of smoking in adolescents', *Journal of Epidemiology and Community Health* 43: 72–8.

Murphy, S.B., Reinarman, C. and Waldorf, D. (1989) 'An 11 year follow up of a network of cocaine users', *British Journal of Addiction* 84: 427–36.

O'Connor, J. (1978) *The Young Drinkers: a Cross National Study of Social and Cultural Influences*, London: Tavistock.

Perera, K.M.H., Tulley, M. and Jenner, F.A. (1987) 'The use of benzodiazepines among drug addicts', *British Journal of Addiction* 82: 511–15.

Plant, M.A., Peck, D.F. and Samuel, E. (1985) 'The predictors of alcohol, tobacco, and illicit drug use and misuse', in M.A. Plant, D.F. Peck and E. Samuel (eds) *Alcohol, Drugs and School Leavers*, London and New York: Tavistock, pp. 95–122.

Polich, J.M., Armor, D.J. and Braiker, H.B. (1981) *The Course of Alcoholism: Four Years After Treatment*, New York: Wiley-Interscience.

Saunders, J.B. (1989) 'The efficacy of treatment for drinking problems', *International Review of Psychiatry* 1: 121–38.

Saunders, W.M. and Kershaw, P.W. (1979) 'Spontaneous remission from alcoholism – a community study', *British Journal of Addiction* 74: 251–65.

Sobell, M.B., Brochu, S., Sobell, L.C., Roy, J. and Stevens, J.A. (1987) 'Alcohol treatment outcome evaluation methodology: state of the art 1980–1984', *Addictive Behaviours* 12: 113–28.

Stimson, G.V. and Oppenheimer, E. (1982) *Heroin Addiction: Treatment and Control in Britain*, London and New York: Tavistock.

Swadi, H. (1988) 'Drug and substance use among 3,333 London adolescents', *British Journal of Addiction* 83: 935–42.

Taylor, C., Brown, D., Duckitt, A., Edwards, G., Oppenheimer, E. and Sheehan, M. (1985) 'Patterns of outcome: drinking histories over ten years among a group of alcoholics', *British Journal of Addiction* 80: 45–50.

Temple, M.T. and Leino, E.V. (1989) 'Long-term outcomes of drinking: a 20 year longitudinal study of men', *British Journal of Addiction* 84: 889–99.

Vaillant, G.E. (1973) 'A 20 year follow up of New York narcotic addicts', *Archives of General Psychiatry* 29: 237–41.

Vaillant, G.E. and Milofsky, E.S. (1982) 'Natural history of male alcoholism', *Archives of General Psychiatry* 39: 127–33.

Wille, R. (1983) 'Processes of recovery from heroin dependence: relationship to treatment, social changes and drug use', *Journal of Drug Issues* 13: 333–42.

Winick, C. (1962) 'Maturing out of narcotic addiction', *Bulletin on Narcotics* 14: 1–7.

CROSS REFERENCES

Chapter 7

The role of genetic predisposition in alcoholism

Adityanjee and Robin M. Murray

Alcoholism shows a tendency to run in families though it does not generally follow simple Mendelian rules of transmission. In 1979, Cotton reviewed studies involving the families of 6,251 alcoholics and 4,083 non-alcoholics. Relatives of alcoholics consistently had higher rates of alcoholism than relatives of controls, and almost one-third of the alcoholics had at least one parent who was also alcoholic. This does not necessarily imply genetic transmission, since speaking French also runs in families but is not, of course, genetic. Systematic attempts to tease out the relative importance of heredity and intra-familial environmental influences started only in the 1940s, and in the main have consisted of twin and adoption studies.

TWIN STUDIES

One way of ascertaining whether there is a genetic contribution to alcoholism has been to compare concordance rates among monozygotic (MZ) versus dizygotic (DZ) twins. The former, of course, have identical genes while the latter share on average 50 per cent of their genes. Classical twin methodology implies that the finding of higher concordance rates for a characteristic in MZ than DZ twins indicates a genetic effect on that characteristic.

Table 7.1 summarizes the available studies. In the first of these which was carried out in Sweden, Kaij (1960) found that MZ twins were concordant for alcoholism more often than were DZ twins; there was a greater difference between MZ and DZ concordance rates for alcoholism than for alcohol abuse. A study of American Veterans found a higher concordance among MZ than DZ twins not only for alcoholism, but also for alcohol-related organ damage. However, the Maudsley study of Gurling and Murray (1987) showed no differences at all between MZ and DZ twins.

Researchers have also examined genetic effects on the drinking behaviour of normal twins (Table 7.2). For example, a Finnish study on normal drinking by Partanen *et al.* (1966) found that MZ twins were more similar than DZ twins in the quantity and frequency of the alcohol they drank but not in the adverse consequences of drinking that they experienced. More recently, Clifford *et al.* (1984) examined the drinking habits of 494 pairs of twins from the Institute of Psychiatry normal twin register. The results were rather similar to those of Partanen with approximately one-third of the variance in alcohol consumption appearing to be genetic in origin.

On the whole, the twin studies suggest the existence of a modest genetic contribution to both heavy drinking and alcoholism. However, twin studies have their

Table 7.1 Twin studies in alcoholism

Authors	Country	Sample source	Sex	Total no. of twin pairs	Concordance (%) MZ	DZ	MZ/DZ ratio	Remarks
Kaij, 1960	Sweden	Temperance Board	Males only	45[a]	71	32	2.2	Chronic alcoholism
Hrubec and Omenn, 1981	USA	Veterans Records	Males only	715	26.3	11.9	2.2	ICD8-9. Twins not interviewed
Gurling & Murray, 1987	UK	Maudsley Twin Register	Males and females	69	21	25	0.84	Alcohol Dependence Syndrome

Note: [a] Other pairs alcohol abusers

Table 7.2 Twin studies of normal drinking

Authors	Country	Sex	Total no. of	Heritability	
Partanen et al., 1966	Finland	M	902	0.39 for density 0.36 for amount	
Pederson, 1981	Sweden	M & F	137	0.28 (spirits drinking) 0.71 (heavy drinking)	No genetic contribution to beer or wine consumption
Kaprio et al., 1978	Finland	M & F	5044	0.37 (males) 0.25 (females)	
Clifford et al., 1984	UK	M & F	572	37% due to additive genetic 42% due to shared environment 21% due to unique environment	Variance in alcohol consumption

Table 7.3 Adoption studies in alcoholism

Authors	Source	No. studied Probands	Controls	Alcoholism in adoptees
Roe and Burke, 1945	Children placed by New York Charity	21 M 15 F	25	No cases of alcoholism detected in either group
Goodwin et al., 1973	Adoptees in Copenhagen area	55 M	78 M	Risk of alcoholism increased by > 3 times in those with a biological parent hospitalized for alcoholism
Cadoret and Garth, 1978	Adoptees placed by Iowa Children's Agency	4 M 2 F	78	Definite alcoholism in 2/6 of experimental group and 1/78 of control group
Bohman, 1978	Adoptees born illegitimmately in Stockholm	627 M & F	1148	23% of sons of alcoholic biological fathers were alcoholic, compared to 15% of controls

own weaknesses. For example, MZ twins are likely to have shared a more similar rearing environment than the DZ twins. Cohabiting is also an important confounding factor; living with a heavy drinking twin may induce the co-twin also to drink heavily or alternatively to be so revolted by alcohol as to become teetotal. These issues and publications referred to in the tables are reviewed in detail by Marshall and Murray (1989).

STUDIES OF HALF-SIBLINGS AND ADOPTEES

Because of the problems with twin studies, researchers turned to other approaches. Half-siblings provide a way of comparing related individuals, some of whom do, and some of whom do not share an alcoholic parent. Schuckit's group found that 20 per cent of the half-siblings of hospitalized alcoholics were also alcoholic (Schuckit, 1987). Furthermore, nearly two-thirds of the alcoholic half-siblings had a biological parent who was alcoholic compared with only 20 per cent of the non-alcoholic half-siblings. Those half-siblings who were alcoholic had not spent any more time in an alcoholic environment than the non-alcoholic half-siblings. Thus, what was important was receiving genes from an alcoholic parent rather than being raised by him or her.

Adoption studies provide another way of teasing apart genetic and family environment effects, since adoptees receive their genes but not their upbringing from their biological parents (Table 7.3). The first adoption study carried out by Roe in 1944 found no difference in drinking behaviour between children of alcohol abusers and children of controls. However, the results of this study have generally been disregarded on grounds of the small sample size and lack of proper diagnostic criteria.

Subsequent adoption studies in the USA and Scandinavia have produced data that support the hypothesis of genetic transmission of alcoholism (Goodwin et al., 1973; Cadoret and Gath, 1978; Bohman, 1978). The main findings of these studies are:

1 Sons of alcoholics are three to four times more likely to become alcoholic than sons of non-alcoholics. It makes little difference whether they are raised by their alcoholic parents or by non-alcoholic adoptive parents.
2 Sons of alcoholics are no more susceptible to other adult psychiatric disturbances than are sons of non-alcoholics where both groups have been raised by non-alcoholic adoptive parents.

ALCOHOLIC SUBTYPES AND GENE ENVIRONMENT INTERACTION

Thus, recent adoption studies have consistently shown a genetic effect on alcoholism. Research has, therefore, proceeded to trying to determine exactly what is transmitted, and how genes and environment interact in causing alcoholism. In this light, Cloninger sought to determine what were the characteristics of biological and adoptive parents which influenced the risk of alcohol abuse in the Swedish adoptees originally studied by Bohman.

The results of this re-analysis led Cloninger (1987) to postulate the existence of two types of alcoholism. He suggests that the more common type, which he calls milieu-limited (Type I) alcoholism, occurs in men and women, is usually not severe, and is associated with mild adult-onset alcohol abuse but not criminality in either biological parent. He suggests that both genetic predisposition and postnatal provocation are necessary for a person to develop this kind of alcoholism. In the Swedish adoptees, if there was either a genetic susceptibility or a provocative environmental milieu, but not both, then the risk of alcohol abuse was no greater than in the general population. However, if both occurred in the same person, the risk was doubled.

Cloninger claims that the other type (Type 2) is found only in men, and accounts for about 25 per cent of all male alcoholics in the general population. In the Swedish adoption study, the biological fathers of such individuals often had teenage onset of alcoholism and both extensive treatment for alcohol abuse and serious criminality; however, the biological mothers had no excess of alcohol abuse or criminality. In these families, the risk of alcoholism increased nine-fold in adopted-out sons regardless of the postnatal environment.

This simple theory is at first sight very attractive, but no one has yet been able to replicate Cloninger's findings of two types. More support has however accumulated for the idea that early onset alcoholism is especially likely to be familial.

NEUROPHYSIOLOGICAL MARKERS

Cloninger believes that vulnerability to alcoholism is a reflection of underlying differences in personality traits and temperament. However, others suggest that alcoholism is transmitted, not through the inheritance of a susceptible personality, but rather by some neurophysiological predisposition.

A number of studies have found that the EEG of sober and awake alcoholics tends to contain an excess of fast activity and to be deficient in alpha, theta and delta activity. The excess fast frequencies were at first thought simply to be a consequence of the degree of neuropsychiatric impairment in alcoholic patients. However, some studies have suggested that the pattern of fast EEG activity may be genetically transmitted. For example, one found that the sons of alcoholics (but not the daughters) showed a significant excess of fast EEG activity in comparison with controls. This implies that fast EEG activity could be a potential marker of genetic predisposition to alcoholism.

Evoked responses have also attracted attention. In a controlled study of the young sons of alcoholics, Begleiter found significantly reduced P3 voltage similar to that seen in abstinent chronic alcoholics. Thus, it may be that under certain circumstances, the P3 response reflects a genetically influenced susceptibility to alcoholism. Another potential marker, static ataxia (body sway), has now been found to be abnormal in four studies. It has to be said, however, that none of these 'so called' neurophysiological markers has yet been widely accepted as representing a reliable and specific marker for alcoholism.

Decreased intensity of reaction to alcohol may be a better marker of vulnerability to alcoholism. Schuckit and his colleagues showed that the sons of alcoholics rated themselves as significantly less intoxicated after drinking ethanol than did carefully matched control subjects. They also showed less neuropsychological impairment (Schuckit, 1987). These findings are consistent with the idea that some individuals may be prone to alcoholism because they are poor at estimating their own degree of intoxication, and perhaps, therefore, are more likely to exceed normal levels of consumption.

BIOCHEMICAL MARKERS

It could, of course, be that individuals susceptible to alcoholism could be so, not because of any abnormality of personality or CNS response to alcohol, but because they metabolize alcohol differently. Genetic and biochemical diversity both within and between different population groups appears to be the basis for differences in response to alcohol, and could also explain greater or lesser susceptibility to alcoholism.

For example, the low prevalence of alcoholism among the Oriental population has been attributed to an intolerance to alcohol. More than half of Oriental individuals show an unpleasant flushing reaction in response to alcohol, which appears to be genetically determined. Only a small minority of Caucasians have this flushing response. It has been suggested that the flushing reaction causes a low tolerance to alcohol which protects Orientals against the development of alcoholism.

Alcohol ingestion in individuals taking disulfiram (Antabuse) produces a reaction similar to the Oriental flush. Disulfiram inhibits the enzyme aldehyde dehydrogenase thus causing the accumulation of acetaldehyde; high levels of acetaldehyde have therefore been proposed as the mediator of the Oriental flush. Intravenous injection of acetaldehyde in humans will reproduce the flushing reaction, and Orientals who flush develop higher breath acetaldehyde concentrations than do non-flushing Caucasians. Researchers have therefore sought to find differences between alcoholics and controls in the genes that control alcohol metabolism.

MOLECULAR GENETICS

High acetaldehyde levels following alcohol consumption could result either from the possession of a particular active form of alcohol dehydrogenase (ADH) or a deficient form of aldehyde dehydrogenase (ALDH). There are five Class I genes for alcohol dehydrogenase in man. The important three, which code for isoenzymes involved in alcohol metabolism in the liver, have been mapped to the long arm of chromosome 4. Perhaps the consequent differences in enzyme activity could account for phenotypic variation in ethanol metabolism.

However, recently, more interest has been aroused by genetic variation in aldehyde dehydrogenase. Four separate genes have been identified but only two of the isoenzymes are likely to be involved in metabolizing acetaldehyde in the liver. About 50 per cent of Japanese and Chinese lack the active, high affinity ALDH2 isoenzyme whereas none of the Caucasian or negroid populations so far screened have shown this isoenzyme pattern. This lack of the active ALDH2 isoenzyme appears to be responsible for the flushing reaction. Furthermore, the frequency of alcoholism in Japanese people with the inactive ALDH2-2 allele is very significantly lower than in Japanese individuals with the more usual Caucasian type. Thus, there seems to be a relationship between a genetic variant of an enzyme involved in alcohol metabolism and drinking behaviour, or rather lack of drinking behaviour; possession of the ALDH2-2 allele appears to make alcohol consumption unpleasant, and therefore protects against the development of alcoholism.

ANIMAL STUDIES

Indirect evidence for the existence of genetic susceptibility to alcoholism comes from the production of strains of inbred rats that voluntarily consume large quantities of alcohol and rapidly become tolerant of its metabolic effects. Researchers have found neurochemical abnormalities in the alcohol-preferring strains of rats. Abnormal levels of serotonin, norepinephrine and dopamine have been reported in various parts of the brain and the relationship between neurotransmitters and alcohol consumption and tolerance is under investigation. This work is compatible with the evidence that inhibitors of norepinephrine and serotonin uptake are effective in reducing the voluntary consumption of alcohol by naive alcohol-preferring animals.

CONCLUSION

Alcoholism tends to run in families. Two out of three twin studies, and three out of four adoption studies have shown a genetic effect. Investigations of large non-patient samples of twins have shown that approximately one-third of the variance in normal patterns of alcohol consumption is under genetic control; the remaining two-thirds is divided between intrafamilial cultural effects (e.g. parental attitudes to drinking) and extrafamilial environmental factors (e.g. occupational pressure to drink or not to drink).

Suggestions that there are two distinct genetic types of alcoholism have not yet been replicated but alcoholics with a positive family history do seem to present earlier than those without such a history. Research continues into what exactly is transmitted – predisposing personality traits, a difference in neurophysiological response to alcohol, a metabolic difference, or some combination of these? At present, there is a great deal of interest in the possibility of genetic variation in the enzymes which control alcohol metabolism; the possession of an inactive variant of aldehyde dehydrogenase appears to protect a substantial proportion of Japanese against alcoholism but as yet no such differences have been found among Caucasians.

REFERENCES

Begleiter, H., Porjesz, B., Bihari, B. and Kissin, B. (1984) 'Event-related brain potentials in boys at risk for alcoholism', *Science* 225: 1493–6.

Bohman, M. (1978) 'Some genetic aspects of alcoholism and criminality: a population of adoptees', *Archives of General Psychiatry* 35: 269–76.

Cadoret, R.J. and Gath, A. (1978) 'Inheritance of alcoholism in adoptees', *British Journal of Psychiatry* 132: 252–8.

Clifford, C.A., Fulker, D.W. and Murray, R.M. (1984) 'Genetic and environmental influences on drinking patterns in normal twins', in N. Krasner, J.S. Madden and R.J. Walker (eds) *Alcohol Related Problems*, Chichester: John Wiley and Sons, pp. 115–26.

Cloninger, C.R. (1987) 'Neurogenetic adaptive mechanisms in alcoholism', *Science* 236: 410–16.

Cotton, N.S. (1979) 'The familial incidence of alcoholism', *Journal of Studies on Alcohol* 40: 89–116.

Goedde, H.W. and Agarwal, D.P. (1989) Alcoholism: Biochemical and Genetic Aspects, New York: Pergamon Press.

Goodwin, D.W., Schulsinger, F., Hermansen, L., Guze, S.B. and Winokur, G. (1973) 'Alcohol problems in adoptees raised apart from alcoholic biological parents', *Archives of General Psychiatry* 28: 238–43.

Gurling, H.M.D. and Murray, R.M. (1987) 'Genetic influence, brain morphology and cognitive deficits in alcoholic twins', in H.W. Goedde and D.P. Agarwal (eds) *Genetics and Alcoholism*, New York: Alan R. Liss, Inc., pp. 71–82.

Gurling, H.M.D., Murray, R.M. and Clifford, C.A. (1981) 'Investigations into the genetics of alcohol dependence and into its effects on brain function', in L. Gedda, P. Parisi and W.E. Nance (eds) *Twin Research 3, Part C, Epidemiological and Clinical Studies*, New York: Alan R. Liss, Inc., pp. 77–87.

Hrubec, Z. and Omenn, G.S. (1981) 'Evidence of genetic predisposition to alcoholic cirrhosis and psychosis', *Alcoholism: Clinical and Experimental Research* 5: 207–15.

Kaij, L. (1960) *Alcoholism in Twins*, Stockholm, Sweden: Almqvist and Wiksell. (Studies on the etiology and sequels of abuse of alcohol. Lund, Sweden, University of Lund, Department of Psychiatry.)

Kaprio, J., Sarna, S., Koskenvuo, M. and Rantasallio, I. (1978) *Baseline characteristics of the Finnish Twin Registry Section II History of symptoms and illness, use of drugs physical characteristics, smoking, alcohol and physical activity.* Helsinki, Finland: Department of Public Health Science, M37.

Marshall, J.E. and Murray, R.M. (1989) 'The contribution of twin studies to alcoholism research', in H.W. Goedde and D.P. Agarwal (eds) *Alcoholism: Biochemical and Genetic Aspects*, New York: Pergamon Press.

Partanen, J., Bruun, K. and Markkanen, T. (1966) *Inheritance of Drinking Behaviour.* Helsinki, Finland: Finnish Foundation for Alcohol Studies, pp. 14–159.

Pederson, N. (1981) 'Twin similarity for usage of common drugs', in L. Gedda, P. Parisi and W.E. Nance (eds) Twin Research 3, Part C, *Epidemiological and Clinical Studies*, New York: Alan R. Liss, Inc., pp. 53–9.

Roe, A., Burks, B.S. and Helman, B. (1945) 'Adult adjustment of foster children of alcoholic and psychiatric parentage. Memoirs of the Section on Alcohol Studies, No. 3', *Quarterly Journal of Studies on Alcohol*, New Haven: Yale University, p. 378.

Schuckit, M.A. (1987) 'Studies of populations at high risk for the future development of alcoholism', in H.W. Goedde and D.P. Agarwal (eds) *Genetics of Alcoholism*, New York: Alan Liss.

CROSS REFERENCES

Chapter 8

Economic aspects of the markets for alcohol, tobacco and illicit drugs

Alan Maynard

The economic approach to the analysis of the markets for alcohol, tobacco and illicit drugs deploys the conventional tool kit of the mainstream economist. A market is a network of buyers (demanders) and sellers (suppliers) and an important mechanism by which the demand for addictive substances is equated with its supply is price. If the price of these commodities is increased, other things being equal, the demand of buyers will fall. If prices fall, demand will increase. If the prices of alcohol, tobacco and illicit drugs rise then, other things being equal, this will induce suppliers to provide more of these commodities. If the prices fall, suppliers will be less willing to provide these addictive substances for their users.

These simple prepositions are hypotheses which can be tested by quantification and the deployment of sophisticated econometric techniques. However, before an example of these techniques is outlined in the second section of this chapter, the size of the markets is described in the first section. Both this description and the examination of the power of econometric techniques to elicit the determinants of demand for, as an example, tobacco, are, of necessity, only one of many possible examples of how the economic 'toolkit' can be deployed.

In the third section the techniques used by economists to evaluate intervention strategies are outlined. Such interventions may be preventive – for instance GP advice to stop smoking – or they may be treatments – for instance detoxification units. Because of the ubiquitous problem of limited budgets, choices have to be made as to what prevention and treatment regimes are to be funded. The economic approach to evaluation facilitates the prioritization of competing programmes in terms of their costs (which need to be minimized) and their benefits (improvements in health) which need to be maximized.

THE NATURE OF THE MARKET

What are the trends in the markets for addictive substances? The data on consumer expenditure for tobacco and alcoholic drinks are shown in Table 8.1 for the period 1979–88. It can be seen that over the period total expenditure on alcohol grew very little, by just over 1 per cent. The real values of the markets for beer and spirits declined marginally whilst that for wine, cider and perry grew considerably. It can be seen that over the period expenditures fluctuated considerably in the alcohol market. The real value of the tobacco market fell by 25 per cent almost continuously except for the last year in the time series.

Different but similar trends can be observed if consumption is measured by volume rather than price. In Table 8.2 it can be seen that alcohol consumption in terms

Table 8.1 Consumer expenditure in alcohol drinks and tobacco[1]

Year	Beer	Spirits	Wine, Cider and Perry	Total alcohol	Cigarettes
1979	9,568	4,168	2,500	16,236	7,883
1980	9,109	3,923	2,515	15,547	7,768
1981	8,561	3,693	2,692	14,946	7,109
1982	8,261	3,503	2,780	14,544	6,525
1983	8,412	3,597	3,050	15,059	6,480
1984	8,447	3,641	3,275	15,363	6,259
1985	8,416	3,831	3,404	15,651	6,112
1986	8,407	3,814	3,478	15,699	5,940
1987	8,485	3,881	3,661	16,027	5,902
1988	8,568	4,097	3,763	16,428	5,935

Source: Central Statistical Office

Note: [1]All data are adjusted for inflation and are given in terms of 1985 constant prices, £ million

Table 8.2 Consumption of alcoholic drinks and tobacco – quantities released for home consumption[1]

Year	Beer (million litres)	Spirits (million litres of pure alcohol)	Wine (million litres)	Cider and Perry (million litres)	Litres of pure alcohol per head of population aged 15 and over[1]	Cigarettes (thousand millions)
1979	6,824.4	105.5	454.3	231.5	9.74	124.6
1980	6,549.6	99.6	453.7	224.8	9.25	121.8
1981	6,231.6	94.6	486.7	240.8	8.90	109.9
1982	6,140.4	89.2	490.8	289.9	8.67	102.5
1983	6,223.2	91.7	535.9	325.8	8.94	102.6
1984	6,207.6	91.3	589.0	325.9	8.94	100.0
1985	6,151.2	97.3	618.1	317.4	9.02	99.7
1986	6,121.2	96.7	643.0	323.3	9.00	95.0
1987	6,198.0	98.2	684.0	322.7	9.16	101.6
1988	6,358.8	103.3	707.6	310.2	9.48	97.3

Sources: Monthly Digest of Statistics; HM Customs and Excise

Note: [1]Average alcohol strengths were taken as follows:

Beer: annual averages from HM Customs and Excise
Wine: less than 15% taken as 10% 15% or more taken as 17% sparkling wine taken as 12% made wine taken as 17%

Spirits: taken as 40%
Cider and Perry: taken as 4%

Different but similar trends can be observed if consumption is measured by volume rather than price. In Table 8.2 it can be seen that alcohol consumption in terms of litres of pure alcohol per head of population aged fifteen years and over fell from 1979 to 1982 and has gradually but steadily recovered to levels similar to those in

1979. The number of cigarettes used (in thousand millions) fell steadily and substantially (by 24 per cent) from 1979 to 1986 but since then has risen.

The size and growth trends in the markets for illicit drugs are difficult to determine. There are no good data about prevalence and values for the cocaine and marijuana markets. The heroin market can be 'guestimated' to be about 6 per cent of tobacco sales in 1984 (Wagstaff and Maynard, 1988), and it is possible that the size of the market has declined since then.

The data in Tables 8.1 and 8.2 demonstrate some interesting conclusions:

1. The quantity of alcohol consumed varies considerably over short periods, such as a decade, with the market shares of particular forms of alcohol moving quite differently from the total market trends.
2. The quantity of tobacco consumed varies considerably over short periods and that movement, as with alcohol, can be both upwards and downwards.

How can these trends be explained? What factors influence the demand for these products?

THE DETERMINANTS OF DEMAND

Economists are interested in exploring the determinants of both the demand and supply of alcohol and tobacco (e.g. see Godfrey and Hartley in Maynard and Tether, 1990). To illustrate their techniques an analysis of the determinants of tobacco use is presented here.

From the data in Table 8.1 and going further back in time to 1960 (see Hardman and Maynard, 1990) it can be seen that tobacco use (in terms of millions of cigarettes) peaked in 1973–4 and has declined steadily since then. During the period 1963–80 the real (inflation adjusted) price of tobacco declined substantially but unevenly: the tobacco index in 1963 = 100 and by 1980 = 56.7 (see Hardman and Maynard, 1990, table 1.9, page 21). Thus during this period the principal factor affecting demand was not price but the effectiveness of health warnings. Indeed this experience can be seen as a triumph for non-price manipulation of consumer demand.

Despite the perverse price (i.e. lower real taxation) policies of the government the influence of prices on demand is significant. The estimates of its value are affected by what consumption measure is used (volume or value) and what time period is covered. The technique used is to estimate the value of b_1, b_2, b_3, etc. in the following logarithmic equation using time series data, e.g.:

$$D = b_1 + b_2 P + b_2 Y + b_3 A + b_4 C, \text{etc.}$$

where
D = demand (measured in value or volume)
P = a price series
Y = an income (purchasing power) series
A = an advertising expenditure series
C = a dummy variable to represent health campaigns being 'on' or 'off'
b = the beta values give the elasticity of D to changes in P, Y, A, C, and other variables which can be incorporated into the analysis.

The values of the estimates of P and Y in the above equation by various authors for various periods using different time series data (sometimes quarterly, sometimes annual) are set out in Table 8.3. The most recent estimates (Godfrey and Maynard, 1988) estimated the price elasticity of tobacco to be −0.56, i.e. a 10 per cent increase in tobacco prices would produce a reduction in consumption of 5.6 per cent. The

Table 8.3 Examples of UK tobacco price and income elasticities

Study	Data	Own price elasticities	Income elasticities
Atkinson and Skegg (1973)	1951–1970 (annual)	0.0 (men) −0.35 (women)	0.36
McGuinness and Cowling (1975)	1957–1968 (quarterly)	−0.99 (SR) −1.05 (LR)	0.31 (SR) 0.33 (LR)
Redfar (1985)	1965–1980 (quarterly)	−0.23 (SR) −0.39 (LR)	0.12 (SR) 0.19 (LR)
Godfrey and Maynard (1988)	1956–1984 (annual)	−0.56	0.68

Source: Godfrey and Maynard (1988)
Note: SR = Short Run; LR = Long Run

estimated value of the income elasticity was 0.68, i.e. a 10 per cent increase in income (or purchasing power) would increase tobacco consumption by 6.8 per cent.

Estimates derived from the use of similar econometric techniques can be used to estimate the elasticity (i.e. regressiveness of demand to small changes in variables such as price and income) of demand for alcoholic beverages. As yet there are no estimates of elasticities in the market for illicit drugs because both price and quantity information are not available in the quantity or quality needed (see Wagstaff and Maynard, 1988).

These estimates facilitate the explanation of past trends and the prediction of future movements in the consumption of alcohol and tobacco. Additionally they can be used as the basis to predict future tax revenues and employment in these industries (see Godfrey and Maynard, 1988).

THE EVALUATION OF POLICY INTERVENTIONS

If policy-makers wish to reduce the ill effects of alcohol and tobacco use on the health of individuals they can deploy scarce resources either to educate people so that they avoid addiction to substances (health education) or to treat those who become addicted or users and, in doing so, have damaged their health (treatment). Both education and treatment practices use scarce resources. The problem facing policy makers is how to prioritize competing demands on these scarce resources. Is it more efficient to spend scarce resources on education or on treatment? What forms of education have what effects on the health of individuals at what cost? What is the 'best buy' (least cost, greater health improvement) in treatment? Is it cost effective to screen for alcohol and tobacco users?

Questions such as these tend to be answered inadequately if they are posed at all. Many policies, both in education and treatment, are adopted on the basis of rhetoric, emotion and assertion rather than on the basis of knowledge derived from carefully controlled trials which seek to measure both the clinical aspects of the intervention relative to some control, but also the economic aspects: the opportunity costs (alternatives foregone) to society of funding alternative actions. Ideally decision makers should be informed by the results of trials so that they know the effects of the intervention relative to the control in terms of their costs and the enhancements in the length and quality of life.

Unfortunately many interventions, both educational and treatment, have been evaluated imperfectly if at all. A good quality economic evaluation should address the following issues:

1. What is the question? The intervention to be evaluated has to be clearly identified and questions such as 'Do detoxification centres work?' are inappropriate. The question has to be precise, e.g. 'Do detoxification units of given characteristics affect subsequent drinking behaviour of client group X more than doing nothing or offering some other treatment to the same group?'
2. What are the alternatives? The alternatives (experimental and control) need to be identified clearly and specified fully.
3. Each alternative has to be defined clearly, i.e. it should be clear who does what to whom for each treatment package.
4. The costs of the alternatives should be identified, quantified and valued. These steps need to be taken separately. Some costs can be identified and quantified but are difficult to value, e.g. the time provided by carers (e.g. spouses) to look after high alcohol users may be identified but its quantification and valuation may be difficult. By distinguishing between identification, quantification and valuation it is possible to report results with more explicit degrees of incompleteness. Often studies imply they have covered all the relevant costs when in fact they are incomplete. By distinguishing the three stages in this way it is possible to check the difference between those costs that are identified and those that are valued and reach a judgement about the completeness of the costing.
5. The benefits of the alternatives should be identified, quantified and valued. The best outcome measure is one which values improvements in terms of enhancements in the length and quality of life of those being treated or given access to education. However, such outcomes raise difficulties about follow-up (longitudinal cohorts are costly) and the validity of competing improvements used to measure the quality of life (see Kind, 1988).

Often, because of the difficulty of measuring such benefits, intermediate outcomes are quantified, e.g. the number of high users or addicts identified by competing screening interventions. Such measures do not indicate whether cost-effective treatments are available for those identified by, for instance, screening programmes. Also intermediate measures may be non-comparable, e.g. is an alcohol screening programme of cost £10,000 which identifies 70 high users to be preferred to a drug screening programme costing £10,000 which identifies 70 'addicts'? How are 70 high alcohol users to be compared with 70 'addicts' when policy makers decide where to invest the scarce and limited £10,000? To answer this question it is necessary either to use value judgements (e.g. 'addicts are more valuable than heavy drinkers') or devise some measures of outcome (e.g. quality-adjusted life years (QALYs)) which indicate the health value of screening and treating competing groups of people who use these addictive substances.

6. The data, both costs, intermediate outcomes, and final outcomes, need to be analysed in marginal terms. Thus it is necessary to identify the cost of doing one more or one less screening procedure or treatment, and it is necessary to identify the effects of doing one more or one less on benefits too. By concentrating on the margin, policy-makers' choices are informed and focused on the benefits and costs of expanding or contracting activity by small amounts. If the marginal cost exceeds the marginal benefit the activity level should be reduced, if the marginal benefit exceeds the marginal cost the activity level should be increased until costs and benefits at the margin are equated (an illustrative example of the use of marginal analysis can be found in Maynard (1989), and this issue is discussed further by Drummond *et al.*, 1987).

7. Time preference has to be incorporated into the estimates of costs and benefits. Most people prefer to pay bills next year rather than now. Most people prefer to receive income now rather than next year. Thus individuals value streams of costs and benefits differently and depending when they impinge on choice. This time preference has to be incorporated into the evaluative framework (how this is done can be seen in, for example, Drummond *et al.*, 1987).

8. Because all evaluations – those in education and treatment of 'addicts' are no exception – use data and methods which are imprecise, it is necessary to carry out sensitivity analysis on all estimates of costs and benefits. This involves working out the effects of small changes in assumptions on results to determine how sensitive they are to such manipulations. If the results vary significantly with small variations in assumptions, their validity is that much more questionable.

If these eight processes are carried out the economic evaluations create an explicit framework where the details of the manipulations can be identified easily and reviewed. These criteria are a gold standard: if studies do not meet them their results may be incomplete and of ambiguous validity for policy-makers having to prioritize investments in a world of scarce resources.

CONCLUSION

The usefulness of economic techniques for analysing the networks of buyers and sellers of alcohol, tobacco and illicit drugs can be determined only by careful evaluation of what they have achieved. This approach offers a logic and explicit framework for investigating the choices of consumers, providers and regulators. It can never provide all the answers to the many questions that can be asked about the markets for addictive substances but alone and in conjunction with researchers from other disciplines it can illuminate some of their 'mysteries'.

REFERENCES

Booth, M., Hartley, K. and Powell, M. (1990) 'Industry: structure, performance and policy', in A. Maynard and P. Tether (eds) *Preventing Alcohol and Tobacco Problems*, vol. 1, Aldershot: Avebury.

Drummond, M.D., Stoddart, G.L. and Torrance, G.W. (1987) *Methods for the Economic Evaluation of Health Care Programmes*, Oxford: Oxford University Press.

Godfrey, C. (1990) 'Modelling demand', in A. Maynard and P. Tether (eds) *Preventing Alcohol and Tobacco Problems*, vol.1, Aldershot: Avebury.

Godfrey, C. and Maynard, A. (1988) 'Economic aspects of tobacco use and taxation policy', *British Medical Journal* 297:339–43.

Hardman, G. and Maynard, A. (1990) 'Consumption and taxation trends', in A. Maynard and P. Tether (eds) *Preventing Alcohol and Tobacco Problems*, vol. 1, Aldershot: Avebury.

Kind, P. (1988) *The Design and Construction of Quality of Life Measures*, Discussion Paper 43, Centre for Health Economics, University of York.

Maynard, A. (1989) 'The costs of addiction and the costs of control', in D. Robinson, A. Maynard and R. Chester (eds) *Controlling Legal Addictions*, London: Macmillan.

Maynard, A. and Tether, P. (eds) (1990) *Preventing Alcohol and Tobacco Problems*, vol. 1, Aldershot: Avebury.

Wagstaff, A. and Maynard, A. (1988) *Economic Aspects of the Illicit Drug Market and Drug Enforcement Policies in the United Kingdom*, London: HMSO.

CROSS REFERENCES

Section VII Prevention and policy

Section II

Clinical syndromes

Chapter 9

Alcohol and cerebral depressants

Robert M. Anthenelli and Marc A. Schuckit

This chapter presents a brief overview of the clinical syndromes associated with the abuse of cerebral depressant drugs, including alcohol. These substances are named for their shared ability to dampen central nervous system (CNS) activity while producing relatively little analgesic effect when taken in low to moderate doses. This class of drugs consists of *alcohol, barbiturates* and similar compounds, *benzodiazepines* and *carbamates* (see Table 9.1). An alternative classification scheme for these agents focuses on their major clinical target symptoms. Thus, the CNS depressants are often subdivided into *sedative-hypnotic, antianxiety* and *anticonvulsant* categories. However, it must be remembered that these specific clinical indications usually result from each drug's characteristic pharmacologic profile based on its route of administration, speed with which it enters the CNS, and rate of metabolism and excretion, rather than any major difference in CNS dampening effect.

Table 9.1 Cerebral depressants

	Drug type	Generic name	Trade name
I	Alcohol		
II	Barbiturates[a]		
	Ultrashort-acting	Methohexital	Brevital
		Thiopental	Pentothal
	Intermediate-acting	Amobarbital	Amytal
		Butabarbital	Butisol
		Pentobarbital	Nembutal
		Secobarbital	Seconal
	Long-acting	Phenobarbital	Luminal
III	Barbiturate-like	Ethchlorvynol	Placidyl
		Glutethimide	Doriden
		Methaqualone	Quaalude
		Methyprylon	Noludar
IV	Benzodiazepines	(see Chapter 14)	
V	Carbamates	Meprobamate	Miltown, Equanil
		Tybamate	Salacen, Tybatran
VI	Others	Chloral hydrate	Noctec
		Paraldehyde	–

Note: [a]Generic names of the barbiturates end in -al in the US, and in -one in Great Britain

All of the cerebral depressants have an abuse potential and can lead to psychological dependence. In addition, these agents are physically addicting and their repeated administration can produce withdrawal states marked by a similar pattern of signs and symptoms. Individuals abusing one type of drug from this category will develop cross tolerance to other agents in this group, and as a result, withdrawal states from one depressant may be treated by substituting another drug from this category (e.g. benzodiazepines to treat acute alcohol withdrawal). Finally, when taken in repeated high doses, all of these substances can produce intense sadness, impaired cognitive and psychomotor performance, an exacerbation of pre-existing confusional states, and withdrawal syndromes marked by prominent anxiety symptoms.

Many of the key issues surrounding alcohol and other cerebral depressants are covered elsewhere in this text (e.g. genetics, physical consequences, detoxification, rehabilitation) including Chapter 14 by Malcolm Lader devoted entirely to benzodiazepines. Here, we will focus on the usual course of clinical syndromes related to the psychological and physical addictive properties of CNS depressants. Alcohol will be the focus because most data are available from studies on this drug. The following sections will discuss the epidemiology and natural history of cerebral depressant abuse, and highlight clinically relevant topics.

EPIDEMIOLOGY

When considering alcohol, it is important to distinguish between drinking practices, problem drinking, and the clinical syndrome of alcoholism (Schuckit, 1985). Although ethanol use is frequently viewed along a continuum, it appears that only subsets of drinkers develop problems from their alcohol intake and that still fewer manifest the persistent pattern of serious life problems associated with alcoholism.

Drinking patterns and problem drinkers

Most men and women in Western countries imbibe alcoholic beverages, with several national surveys finding more than occasional drinking in approximately two-thirds of the population (Schuckit, 1985; 1989). Although the gender gap for the prevalence of alcohol use may be decreasing, particularly among younger drinkers, in general men are more likely to drink than women and imbibe more frequently and in greater quantities (Schuckit, 1985; 1989). Age plays a part, with the heaviest drinking occurring in men below the age of thirty. Correspondingly, as people grow older, they may be more likely to limit their use of alcohol as reflected by the higher proportion of abstainers in adults over the age of fifty years (Schuckit, 1985). (See Chapters 6 and 26.)

In keeping with the increased prevalence of alcohol use among young men, it is not surprising that between one-quarter and one-half of this group experiences transient alcohol-related problems (Schuckit, 1989). Difficulties such as a drunk driving arrest, arguments with friends and absenteeism from work are common among this cohort of drinkers, and there is some evidence that early advanced drinking may be related to a greater risk of developing alcohol problems or abuse.

However, the preponderance of data from follow-up studies shows that relatively isolated alcohol-related problems alone do not predict future alcoholism (Schuckit, 1989).

Alcoholism

No universal definition of alcoholism exists. As a result, estimates of the prevalence of the disorder vary depending on the restrictiveness of the criteria applied and the population surveyed. Using our preferred definition for alcoholism which requires multiple, serious life problems related to ethanol (e.g. marital difficulties, legal problems, job loss, alcohol-related illnesses), it is estimated that between 5 per cent to 10 per cent of American men and 3 per cent to 5 per cent of American women will suffer from alcoholism at some point in their lifetime (Schuckit, 1985; 1989). Using less rigorous criteria, a recent US survey found prevalence rates as high as 20 per cent for men and 10 per cent for women within some populations of the country (Schuckit, 1989). In Western Europe and Scandinavia, lifetime expectancy rates for alcoholism of about 3 per cent to 5 per cent for men and 0.1 per cent to 1 per cent for women have been reported (Goodwin, 1989). It must be noted that these are all rough estimates and that socioeconomic, demographic, ethnic and methodologic factors play an important role. For example, surveys of hospitalized general medical and surgical patients reveal rates of alcoholism as high as 20 per cent to 35 per cent for men because of the higher level of physical ailments associated with heavy drinking (Schuckit, 1985; 1989). These factors underscore the importance of considering survey techniques when interpreting epidemiologic data.

Another group in whom enhanced rates of depressant drug problems are likely to be seen consists of general psychiatric patients. For some of these men and women, the substance-related problems might be a consequence of the symptoms or impaired judgement inherent in their schizophrenia or mania. Others, however, may be presenting to psychiatric clinics because of *temporary* syndromes that are the result of their intoxication or withdrawal from brain depressants (Schuckit, 1989).

One way to begin to disentangle cause and effect, and to begin to establish the probable clinical course, is to assign *primary* and *secondary* labels based on the chronology of development of symptoms. For instance, in primary alcoholism the onset of multiple, serious alcohol-related life problems occurs without evidence of any major pre-existing psychiatric disorder or concomitant extensive drug use. These individuals, representing about 70 per cent of all 'alcoholic' patients seen for treatment, seem to have a different course, prognosis and response to treatment than the remaining 30 per cent of patients in whom alcoholism develops in the midst of another major psychiatric disturbance (usually the antisocial personality or major depressive disorder) (Schuckit, 1989). When alcoholism develops secondary to another psychiatric syndrome, the patient's course will most likely follow that of the primary disorder and require specialized treatments (e.g. lithium for manic-depressive illness) in addition to treatment for alcoholism.

Similarly, the primary versus secondary distinction appears to be clinically relevant among polydrug abusers. In this scheme the clinician again attempts to determine the chronology of development of symptoms with primary drug abuse indicating that the pattern of major life problems associated with substances other than alcohol developed *before* the onset of any serious ethanol-related difficulties. Although there are relatively few longitudinal studies available using this distinction, data from our laboratory show that primary drug abusers seem to have a different course and poorer outcome than do primary alcoholics when followed for up to one year after treatment in a substance abuse programme (Schuckit, 1989). Future epidemiologic studies of alcoholism need to address the apparent heterogeneity of the disorder more closely.

Other cerebral depressants

The epidemiology of sedative-hypnotic use, abuse, and dependence is somewhat more complicated because most studies combine benzodiazepines, barbiturates and barbiturate-like compounds under one rubric. Similarly, most sedative-hypnotic abusers show high rates of alcohol-related problems as well, further clouding the picture. Of the few clinical surveys employing the primary vs. secondary distinction described previously, it is estimated that about 3 to 7 per cent of psychiatric in-patients meet criteria for primary sedative-hypnotic dependence (Allgulander *et al.*, 1984). Among CNS depressants, benzodiazepines rank second to alcohol in use, having gradually replaced other drugs in this category because of their relative safety.

Focusing on barbiturates and similar compounds (e.g. methaqualone), it is convenient to divide abusers into two categories. The first group consists largely of teenagers and young adults who misuse illegally obtained depressant drugs often in combination with other substances (Schuckit, 1989). Among this cohort, the popularity of barbiturates seems to be declining in both the US and Canada, having reached its peak prevalence in the US in the mid-1970s (about 18 per cent) and decreasing in a fairly linear trend throughout the 1980s (Schuckit, 1989).

In contrast, a second group of depressant abusers has little in common with the traditional 'street-drug' culture and instead receives their supply of medication from physicians prescribing sleeping pills and anti-anxiety agents (Schuckit, 1989). These individuals, generally between the ages of thirty to fifty years, frequently increase their dose without their physician's advice and may seek prescriptions from several practitioners at once. Although fewer studies describing this population are available, using data encompassing sedative-hypnotic use overall (e.g. including benzodiazepine use), this group appears to consist predominantly of women who suffer symptoms of psychological and physical ill-health (Ashton and Golding, 1989).

CLINICAL MILESTONES

As with any clinical syndrome, the natural history of alcoholism is marked by some variability. However, once the diagnosis of *primary alcoholism* has been established, it is possible to predict the course of the disorder to some extent. Primary alcoholics typically experience their first major alcohol-related life problem (e.g. loss of a job, marital problems, accidents, arrests) in the mid-twenties to early thirties, with approximately half of those who will ever be diagnosed as alcoholic already having fulfilled the criteria by the age of 31 (Schuckit, 1989). Despite the occurrence of these serious alcohol-related difficulties, if an alcoholic presents for treatment, it is often not until his early forties. By this time, manifestations of the physical consequences of ethanol are likely to be present (alcoholic liver disease, gastritis, hypertension, pancreatitis) and laboratory tests frequently reveal state markers of heavy drinking (e.g. abnormal liver function tests and blood panels) (Schuckit, 1989). If excessive consumption persists, the alcoholic is likely to die 15 years earlier than expected among the general population (usually age fifty-five to sixty) with the leading causes, in approximate decreasing order of importance, being heart disease, cancer, accidents and suicide (Schuckit, 1989).

The drinking pattern of alcoholics is likely to fluctuate over time with very few people remaining persistently intoxicated until their demise. In any year, the alcoholic is likely to alternate between periods of abstinence, moderate drinking and episodes of severe alcohol misuse. It is estimated that in any given month roughly one-half of alcoholics will be abstinent, with a median of four months of being dry in any one- to two-year period (Schuckit, 1989). This fluctuating course of alcoholism belies the misconception of alcoholics as 'skid-row' drunks, when in fact the vast majority are blue- or white-collar men and women who may present to the clinic for reasons ostensibly unrelated to their drinking.

The possibility that alcoholics may be able to return to 'controlled' or permanent moderate drinking has been controversial. The problem centres around several factors including the definition of 'controlled drinking' and what is considered to be the overlap between ethanol misuse, abuse and dependence. Most follow-up studies and anecdotal reports indicate that only a very small proportion of severe alcoholics can maintain a pattern of stable moderate drinking over long periods of time (Schuckit, 1989). It is important to note, however, that higher rates of social drinking may be seen among those former ethanol abusers who had only relatively minor and fewer alcohol-related problems (Schuckit, 1989). Thus, we advocate that alcoholics be advised that abstinence is the most relevant goal of treatment for the following reasons: first, few alcoholics are likely to achieve any prolonged period of moderate drinking; secondly, the difficulty predicting who these people are; and thirdly, the natural course of alcoholism is marked by short periods of moderate drinking which usually give way to more excessive consumption and serious problems (Schuckit, 1989).

Finally, the prognosis for alcoholism is far from hopeless. Not only can one expect improvement with the variety of treatment interventions described elsewhere in this text, but there is also evidence that approximately 10 per cent to 30 per cent of alcoholics learn to abstain or to seriously diminish their drinking without any formal exposure to prescribed treatment (Schuckit, 1989). The chance of spontaneously remitting from alcoholism probably increases with the same factors that indicate a better prognosis for those entering treatment (e.g. family support, occupational stability, and absence of a police record). There is anecdotal evidence that men and women with spontaneous remissions tend to cite alcohol-related physical ailments, lifestyle changes, spiritual involvement or new relationships as having contributed to their decision to seek abstinence (Schuckit, 1989).

Much less is known about the course of problems associated with the other cerebral depressants. Polydrug abusers may use these agents illicitly in combination with other drugs (e.g. stimulants, opiates or alcohol) either to enhance their effect or to counteract the adverse effects of withdrawal (Schuckit, 1989). Of the few available longitudinal studies that have followed primary sedative-hypnotic abusers who initially had no concomitant abuse of alcohol or other drugs, Allgulander *et al.* (1984) found high rates of relapse with about half of the patients resuming their cerebral depressant abuse (including alcohol) and a chronic clinical course associated with high levels of psychological and physical morbidity. Suicide is an all too frequent occurrence among CNS depressant abusers. This unfortunate outcome is likely to be seen in about 10 per cent to 15 per cent of such individuals and might reflect the severe temporary mood swings that occur as a frequent consequence of high doses of depressant drugs (Schuckit and Monteiro, 1988). (See the chapter by Drs Glass and Marshall for a more thorough discussion of alcohol and mental illness.)

SOME CONCLUSIONS

This chapter has provided a brief sketch of the clinical syndromes associated with the abuse of alcohol and other cerebral depressants. Due to the constraints and the design of this handbook, we have limited our discussion to the epidemiology and natural history of CNS depressant addiction and refer the reader to the other pertinent sections of this text which, when taken together, form a more comprehensive overview. This includes Duncan Raistrick's contribution on career and natural history (Chapter 6).

It is our hope that the information presented above not only offers an update, but will also stimulate the reader to continue to keep abreast of the clinically relevant, exciting developments in this field. These include increasing knowledge about genetic influences (as discussed by Adityanjee and Robin Murray in Chapter 7), information about the relationship between psychiatric syndromes and the abuse of brain depressants (Schuckit and Monteiro, 1988), and efforts to better match individual patients to specific treatment approaches.

REFERENCES

Allgulander, C., Borg, S. and Vikander, B. (1984) 'A 4 to 6-year follow-up of 50 patients with primary dependence on sedative and hypnotic drugs', *American Journal of Psychiatry* 141: 1580–2.

Ashton, H. and Golding, J.F. (1989) 'Tranquillisers: prevalence, predictors and possible consequences. Data from a large United Kingdom survey', *British Journal of Addiction* 84: 541–6.

Goodwin, D.W. (1989) 'Alcoholism', in H.I. Kaplan and B.J. Sadock (eds) *Comprehensive Textbook of Psychiatry/V*, Baltimore: Williams and Wilkins.

Schuckit, M.A. (ed.) (1985) *Alcohol Patterns and Problems*, New Jersey: Rutgers University Press.

Schuckit, M.A. (1989) *Drug and Alcohol Abuse: a Clinical Guide to Diagnosis and Treatment* (3rd edn), New York: Plenum Medical Book Company.

Schuckit, M.A. and Monteiro, M.G. (1988) 'Alcoholism, anxiety and depression', *British Journal of Addiction* 83: 1373–80.

CROSS REFERENCES

Chapter 10

Opiates

Jerome H. Jaffe

DEFINITIONS AND TERMINOLOGY

Opium, the juice of the opium poppy, *Papaver somniferum*, consists of a mixture of chemicals. The major pure drug in opium is morphine; codeine also occurs naturally. Chemists have modified the morphine and codeine molecules to make other 'opiates' with generally similar actions, such as heroin (diacetylmorphine) and hydromorphone. In the late 1930s, German chemists synthesized several drugs (methadone, pethidine) which while not in any way derived from opium had almost all of the pharmacological actions of morphine and other opiates. The term *opioid* was then proposed to include both the opiates and their synthetic surrogates.

In the 1970s, several groups of researchers showed that the opioids acted on a family of receptors located on the membranes of neurons and other cells in the body, such as white blood cells. A *receptor* is a specialized structure in the membrane with a very specific shape. Each type of receptor is activated only by chemicals conforming to its special shape. Drugs which fit and activate a receptor are *agonists* for that receptor. Receptors control the permeability of the cell membrane or influence some biochemical system located within the cell. Some drugs fit the opioid receptors but do not activate them. These drugs, called *antagonists*, are capable of preventing other opioids from occupying the receptors or of displacing opioid agonists already at the receptors.

Shortly after the discovery of opioid receptors, it was found that organisms synthesize natural substances, *endogenous opioids*, which act on these opioid receptors. Most of these endogenous opioids are peptides, chains of amino acids, produced by the breakdown of larger precursor protein molecules. Three families of these larger precursor molecules are known, each under the control of distinct genes. These families of endogenous opioid substances have been named *enkephalins*, *dynorphins*, and *endorphins*. The body produces many specific peptides from each of the large precursor molecules. Researchers have reported that mammals actually produce their own morphine, although the significance of this finding is not yet clear.

The opioid receptors also can be generally grouped into several related families, now designated (on the basis of the way in which they were discovered) *mu*, *kappa*, and *delta* receptors, and there appear to be several subtypes of each of these groups. The significance of these various subtypes of opioid receptors is that when activated they produce different effects on a variety of bodily activities. For example, morphine and drugs similar to it appear to activate mu receptors preferentially; the pattern of effects seen when morphine is given is due to mu receptor activation. Tolerance and physical dependence associated with chronic use of morphine results from the cellular changes produced by chronic mu receptor occupation. Over the past decade, new drugs have been synthesized that act more selectively than any of the older opioids used in medicine, and even more selectively than any of the natural endogenous opioids. Most of these have not yet been approved for clinical use. However, some of the newly available mu opioid agonists are more than 1000 times as potent as morphine; that is, only 1/1000th the dose is required to produce the same effect. Some drugs can act as agonists at one receptor and as antagonists at another. These drugs are often termed agonist/antagonists and some appear to have a lower potential for abuse.

EFFECTS ON BODY AND BRAIN

Opioids that act on mu receptors produce a wide range of effects on the brain, spinal cord and nervous elements innervating other organs in the body, such as the gastrointestinal tract. Opioids suppress pain systems at the level of the spinal cord and within the brain. At high doses, this effect is sufficient to produce anaesthesia for surgical procedures. Opioids alter mood, typically producing a sense of euphoria in former opioid addicts, as well as a feeling of increased well-being and indifference to anxiety-provoking situations. Non-addict patients, however, often report only a sense of tranquillity with pain relief, and some complain of dysphoria and inability to think clearly. When addicts inject opioids intravenously, they report a brief but intense experience – a 'rush' or 'thrill' within a few seconds after injection, an effect not experienced when these same drugs are taken by mouth or injected under the skin.

In addition to effects on mood and pain perception, opioids affect the respiratory centre. With ordinary analgesic doses, these effects are not readily measured, but as the dose is increased, the effect becomes more pronounced until respiration no longer occurs spontaneously. The use of most mu opioids typically results in noticeable constriction of pupils and suppression of the cough reflex. Opioids have profound effects on the endocrine systems reducing release from the brain of the hormone ACTH (which causes release of stress hormones such as cortisol from the adrenal) and of the gonadotrophic hormones that stimulate release of testosterone and oestrogens from the gonads. These effects alter sex drive in men and women and reproductive function in women; considerable tolerance to these effects can develop with repeated use. Opioids can have important effects on the gastrointestinal tract and slow down the passage of food through the intestine. This makes opioids useful for the treatment of diarrhoea, but causes marked and often persistent constipation in addicts or in patients who need to take the drugs for treatment of pain.

OVERDOSE

The major toxic effect of opioid drugs is respiratory depression. Overdose is more commonly seen after intravenous use, but does occur with all routes of administration. The classic picture of opioid overdose includes stupor or coma, pinpoint pupils, severe respiratory depression and pale skin. There may also be pulmonary oedema, an accumulation of protein-rich fluid in the lungs that may lead to white froth coming from the mouth and nose. Blood pressure is not usually severely depressed. However, if respiratory depression is severe enough to cause anoxia (too little oxygen in the blood), there is damage to the brain and cardio-vascular system, and there may be dilated rather than constricted pupils and circulatory collapse. Overdose can be treated by means of artificial ventilation until the drug is metabolized, but it is preferable to administer an opioid antagonist such as naloxone.

HOW THE BODY METABOLIZES OPIOIDS

Although different opioids may have similar pharmacological properties in terms of actions at receptors, there are often important chemical differences that influence the way they are absorbed, metabolized, and excreted by the body. These differences in the metabolic pathways are sometimes the basis for very distinct profiles of action. For example, neither codeine nor heroin are active at opioid receptors, but they are both converted by the body into morphine which is inactive. Codeine is also distinct in that when it is absorbed from the intestines much of it is able to escape inactivation by the liver, whereas a very large proportion of morphine itself is inactivated. Heroin, like morphine, is largely inactivated by the liver when taken by mouth, but when it is injected its much greater solubility in lipids allows it to pass very rapidly and almost completely across the blood-brain barrier into the brain where, when converted to morphine and 6-monoacetylmorphine, it produces the expected opioid actions. The peak or most intense actions of intravenous heroin are experienced within two to fifteen minutes of its injection. The body's capacity to inactivate opioids like morphine, heroin, codeine, meperidine and hydromorphone is such that about half of the drug that enters the blood stream is inactivated in two to five hours; but some drugs such as methadone are inactivated and excreted much more slowly. Methadone has a half-life of 24 to 36 hours. Because of this, the level in the body will build up when it is given every day. Then, when the methadone is stopped, the drug in the body is inactivated and excreted over several days. The slow decrease in the body level results in a more prolonged but less intense withdrawal syndrome (see p.67). Unlike morphine, much of methadone escapes inactivation by the liver when it is absorbed from the intestine and it is therefore one of the opioids that is very effective when given by mouth. Because of their relatively rapid excretion from the body, drugs such as heroin, morphine, codeine, and meperidine can be detected in urine for only 2 to 3 days (except with the most sensitive assays, when they may be detected for a few days longer). Because almost all of it is converted to morphine in the body, very little, if any, heroin is found in urine. Methadone can often be detected for much longer.

EFFECTS OF REPEATED ADMINISTRATION: TOLERANCE AND PHYSICAL DEPENDENCE

Tolerance means that the same dose of a drug will produce a reduced effect, or that more drug is needed to produce the same effect achieved initially. With repeated use, tolerance develops to many of the effects of mu agonist opioids such as morphine and heroin. Tolerance does not develop at the same rate for every effect. For example, constipation and pupillary effects may persist when tolerance has already developed to effects on respiratory depression, mood, and pain perception. Considerable tolerance to the euphoric effects of heroin may develop after a few weeks, but there may still be a brief euphoric effect after an intravenous dose. Despite considerable tolerance, there is always a dose high enough to be lethal as a result of respiratory depression.

Tolerance to one mu agonist such as morphine results in a considerable degree of cross-tolerance to other mu agonists such as methadone or hydromophone. However, tolerance to mu agonists does not result in cross-tolerance to kappa agonists. Opioid tolerance is largely lost within a few days to weeks after withdrawal. Withdrawn addicts who attempt to use the high doses of drug to which they had become accustomed may experience a severe overdose.

Some aspects of tolerance may involve learning factors so that a drug user may experience more tolerance to a given drug under circumstances where it has been used previously than under novel circumstances.

When opioids occupy receptors they start a process of cellular adaptation (neuro-adaptation) that eventually forms the biological basis of the opioid withdrawal syndrome. Usually it takes several weeks of regular use of a short-acting drug such as morphine before abrupt discontinuation produces a measurable withdrawal syndrome. However, if the opioids are rapidly removed from their receptors by antagonists such as naloxone, some withdrawal symptoms are measurable in human volunteers within 24 hours after a single large dose of morphine. The morphine withdrawal syndrome consists of a wide range of signs and symptoms that tend to be opposite in direction to the effects produced by the drug itself (rebound effects). Thus, instead of tranquillity, euphoria, constricted pupils, and decreases in pain perception, respiration, spinal reflexes, and gastrointestinal motility, there is anxiety, dysphoria, muscle aches, increased respiration and sensitivity to pain, dilated pupils, hyperactive spinal reflexes (kicking movements, as in 'kicking the habit'), and abdominal cramps and diarrhoea. With short-acting opioids such as morphine, heroin, and meperidine (pethidine) the earliest components of the syndrome appear within 6 to 12 hours after the last dose, with the peak syndrome intensity at 24 to 48 hours, after which the intensity gradually declines over the next five to seven days. With drugs that are metabolized or excreted more slowly, such as methadone, withdrawal symptoms begin at about 24 to 36 hours, may not reach their peak until the third to fifth day and may be readily measurable for ten to fifteen days. However, with both long- and short-acting opioids, a more subtle protracted disturbance of mood and body physiology may persist for several months after the acute symptoms are no longer measurable.

MANAGING THE WITHDRAWAL SYNDROME

Although opioid withdrawal is painful and stressful, it is usually not fatal for healthy adults. In some countries, it is the policy not to provide treatment for incarcerated addicts in the belief that the discomfort of withdrawal will be a deterrent against relapse. In other countries, efforts are made to control symptoms and minimize discomfort. This can be accomplished in several ways, including gradual dose reduction and the substitution of longer acting drugs such as methadone. Once the patient is stabilized on enough methadone to prevent withdrawal for a day or two, the methadone dosage can be gradually reduced over five to ten days. The ensuing withdrawal under these circumstances is usually no worse than a case of severe influenza. Nevertheless, for ambulatory patients, such brief periods of withdrawal are rarely rewarded with prolonged periods of abstinence. For patients who were maintained on methadone, some clinicians in the United States advocate very slow withdrawal over a period of twenty-four weeks. Still others advocate more rapid withdrawal using the drug clonidine, originally developed for treating hypertension, to suppress some of the autonomic signs of withdrawal. In general, withdrawal or detoxification is relatively easy to manage. The more important and more difficult aspect of treatment is preventing relapse during the weeks and months after the acute withdrawal syndrome has subsided.

RECOMMENDED READING

Akil, H., Watson, H.J., Young, E., Lewis, M.E. *et al.* (1984) 'Endogenous opioids: biology and function', *Annual Review of Neuroscience* 7: 223–55.
Jaffe, J.H. (1990) 'Drug addiction and drug abuse', in A.G. Gilman, T.W. Rall, A.S. Nies and P.Taylor (eds) *Goodman and Gilman's The Pharmacological Basis of Therapeutics*, New York: Pergamon Press, pp. 522–73.
Jaffe, J.H. (1989) 'Drug dependence: opioids, nonnarcotics, nicotine (tobacco), and caffeine', in H.I. Kaplan and B.J. Sadock (eds) *Comprehensive Textbook of Psychiatry/V*, Baltimore: Williams and Wilkins, pp. 642–86.
Jaffe, J.H. and Martin, W.R. (1990) 'Opioid analgesics and antagonists', in A.G. Gilman, T.W. Rall, A.S. Nies and P. Taylor (eds) *Goodman and Gilman's The Pharmacological Basis of Therapeutics*, New York: Pergamon Press, pp. 485–521.

CROSS REFERENCES

Chapter 11

Cannabis

Bankole A. Johnson

Cannabis is a derivative of the Indian hemp plant, *Cannabis sativa*, which is a native of Central Asia. It is the most commonly used illicit drug with an estimated 200–300 million regular users worldwide. The non-medical introduction of the drug in Western Europe was by Napoleon's soldiers returning from Egypt at the beginning of the nineteenth century and its hedonic properties were subsequently promulgated by the infamous Club des Hashishins in Paris in the period 1840–60.

The earliest medicinal application was probably in the third century BC when Shen Nung, the Emperor of China, used it as a herbal remedy and psychic liberator. Therapeutic usage in the twentieth century has included the treatment of hysteria (abreaction), anorexia nervosa, epilepsy, rheumatism, bronchial asthma, pain, glaucoma and, most effectively, nausea induced by chemotherapy.

ABSORPTION, DISTRIBUTION AND ELIMINATION

There are several preparations of cannabis. The more familiar are ganja, marijuana, hashish oil and the Indian forms (charas and bang). These contain varying proportions of the leaves, stalk, shoots, flowers and resin from the plant. The potency of the preparation is influenced by the soil, climate, cultivation technique and the constituents of the mixture. The resin, which contains the tetrahydro-cannabinols (THCs) and related chemical compounds, is the most pharmacologically active part of the plant. Of these chemical compounds, Δ^9-trans-tetrahydrocannabinol, Δ^8-tetrahydrocannabinol and cannabidiol, respectively, are considered to be the principal active ingredients.

Cannabis preparations can be smoked, eaten mixed with foodstuffs, drunk as an extract, or rarely, injected intravenously. Smoking is the most efficient method of ingestion as up to 50 per cent of the preparation is absorbed and its full effects are manifest within a few minutes. The potency of a preparation of cannabis delivered by smoking is up to three times that of an equivalent amount ingested orally, as a result of more rapid absorption from the lungs, avoidance of first pass metabolism in the liver and the enhanced release of Δ^9THC from the pyrolysis of THC acids. Oral ingestion leads to slow absorption (about three hours) but results in a longer duration of effect than does smoking. The rate of absorption from intravenous injection is comparable to that from smoking but the intravenous route can be dangerous because of the increased risk of anaphylactic shock from undissolved particulate matter. Cannabis is lipophilic and is therefore rapidly distributed via the bloodstream to the adipose tissue of the lungs, liver, brain, adrenals, ovaries and testes. THCs can cross the placenta, enter breast milk and induce liver enzymes. The tight plasma binding of

THCs leads to important interactions with other drugs competing for such sites, for example, warfarin. It also accounts for poor penetration of the blood-brain barrier by THCs, with less than 1 per cent of the absorbed drug entering the brain. As serum levels fall, THCs leak back into the bloodstream; consequently after a single smoke of cannabis THCs can often be detected in the blood for up to 20 hours. Cannabis is metabolized by hydroxylation to more active constituents with half-lives exceeding 50 hours such as 11-hydroxy-tetrahydrocannabinol, followed by oxidation to less active constituents. The net effect of this is that, following a single smoke of cannabis, THCs can persist in the body for up to 30 days. Conjugation in the liver leads to the production of more water-soluble metabolites which are excreted slowly in the bile, urine, hair and faeces.

PHYSICAL EFFECTS

There is a clear but non-linear correlation between dose and effect. As a rough guide, the absorption of <50 mcg/Kg of Δ^9THC delivered by smoking usually results in the effects ascribed to 'low dosage' use, whilst the absorption of >250 mcg/Kg of Δ^9THC, also delivered by smoking, often culminates in the effects attributed to 'high dosage' use. Between these dosages there is a gallimaufry of effects; idiosyncratic reactions may occur, however, at any dosage.

Acute

The physical consequences commonly reported on acute 'low dosage' administration of cannabis are irritation of the bronchial mucosa, tachycardia, increased blood pressure, dry mouth, thirst, increased appetite, constipation, decreased intraocular pressure, ataxia and, rarely, photophobia and nystagmus.

Acute 'high dosage' administration is associated with drowsiness, bradycardia, bronchodilation, decreased blood pressure, hypothermia, cold extremities due to peripheral vasoconstriction, conjunctival infection, ptosis and a decrease in pupillary diameter.

Chronic

The chronic effects of cannabis are more controversial. They include a decrease in testosterone level and sperm count, libidinal drive, release of LH and FSH, fertility in women, foetal birth weight, gestational time and T cell function. Gynaecomastia has been reported. Enhanced in vitro antibacterial and antifungal activity have also been demonstrated. Chronic respiratory diseases, such as emphysema, may result from prolonged cannabis smoking. In addition, cannabis smoke may be more carcinogenic to lung tissue than cigarette smoke due to the higher content of polyaromatic hydrocarbons. An early report of cerebral atrophy following chronic heavy cannabis use has not been substantiated by further studies.

Tolerance

Tolerance to some of the effects of cannabis, especially to the subjective 'high', tachycardia, and decreased intra-ocular pressure has been described in chronic heavy cannabis users. However, this is somewhat contradicted by accounts of the phenomenon of reverse tolerance, which is the report of more subjective experiences by regular users in comparison to novices. When tolerance occurs, it develops with a few days of regular drug use and decays rapidly when the drug is withdrawn. In addition, there appears to be an upper limit to tolerance to cannabis which varies from one person to another. Cross-tolerance to the analgesic effects of THC and morphine has been demonstrated.

Dependence

The cessation of cannabis use in chronic users is often followed by withdrawal symptoms characterized by irritability, restlessness, appetite loss, nausea and insomnia. Nevertheless, other features of a dependence syndrome such as narrowing of repertoire, reinstatement or salience are not seen. There is no convincing evidence that craving or psychological dependence occurs.

PSYCHOLOGICAL EFFECTS

The psychological sequelae are not as closely related to dosage as the physical and there is a considerable range of clinical presentations. A single smoke of cannabis usually leads to euphoria, impaired co-ordination, disturbance of the passage of time (time appears to be slowed down), anxiety and sometimes depression. There is considerable interpersonal variation in the vulnerability of individuals to develop an acute toxic psychosis following cannabis use. However, with increasing dosage, usually the absorption of >250 mcg/Kg of Δ^9THC delivered by smoking, the appearance of psychotic phenomena becomes more likely. When this happens, apprehension, suspiciousness and morbid preoccupation often herald the emergence of confusion, memory impairment, depersonalization, derealization, delusions, auditory and visual hallucinations. 'Flashbacks', prolonged depersonalization and derealization can occur following chronic cannabis use.

Memory, cognitive and psychomotor performance

There are many pitfalls in the evaluation of psychological deficits attributed to cannabis. The potency of the substance supplied as cannabis can vary by a factor of up to 2,000. Also, there is a wide variation psychologically in interpersonal response to the administration of cannabis and the most widely available test for the detection of cannabis in the body, the urine cannabinoid level, gives no reliable clue as to the total amount of pharmacologically active cannabis in the body at that time.

The recognition and acquisition processes involved in the storage of short-term memory are the most affected by cannabis use, with the relative sparing of long-term memory. Despite the findings of a recent study to the contrary, more rigorously designed studies have cast doubt as to whether these harmful effects on cognitive function are progressive with chronic cannabis use. Interestingly, the reports on cognitive and psychomotor impairment following the use of cannabis have gained respectability by the demonstration of the preferential concentration and action of THCs in the hippocampal region of the limbic system.

The impairment of psychomotor and cognitive performance is of particular medico-social importance. The ingestion of even relatively modest amounts of cannabis can result in such a deterioration in co-ordination and reaction time as to make the operation of heavy machinery, driving or flying hazardous. The concomitant use of alcohol magnifies these deleterious effects. Some regular cannabis users insist that these dangerous effects on psychomotor performance are compensated for by an increase in the level of awareness in the sensations of hearing, sight and touch, but experiments under controlled conditions have not supported this claim.

Previous exposure may modulate the results of cognitive and psychomotor testing. For example, casual smokers often experience more impairment of cognitive and psychomotor performance than habitual users. Furthermore, placebo-controlled trials have suggested that habitual users are less able than casual users to distinguish the active drug, cannabis, from placebo. The psychological effects in habitual users may therefore, in part, be a re-enactment of an earlier response to exposure, or the result of personal experience.

PSYCHOSIS

Moreau de Tours in 1845 was the first to posit an association between the use of cannabis and psychosis, an issue which is still controversial. To elucidate this matter four important questions need to be answered: Can the drug provoke an acute organic reaction? Does it result in a characteristic pattern of symptoms, i.e. cannabis psychosis? Is it simply coincidental to the development of a psychosis? Can it precipitate or exacerbate a functional psychosis?

There is firm evidence that the absorption of a 'high dosage' >250 mcg/Kg of Δ^9THC delivered by smoking can provoke an acute organic state, the phenomenology of which has already been described. Lower dosages may produce a similar response as part of an idiosyncratic reaction. This acute organic reaction is virtually indistinguishable phenomenologically from delirious states produced by other psychomimetics, hallucinogens or toxins. One explanation of the psychomimetic effects of cannabis concerns its ability to alter brain amine levels and inhibit cholinergic neurotransmission. Indeed, the psychopharmacological basis for this effect has been strengthened by the recent discovery of a specific cannabinoid receptor – a G protein coupled receptor which inhibits adenylate cyclase activity in a dose dependent (to cannabinoids) and stereoselective fashion.

Functional psychosis has not been consistently demonstrated to occur more frequently among cannabis users than non-cannabis users and no unique set of psychotic symptoms following use can be reliably classified as constituting a 'cannabis psychosis'. Notably, the symptom pattern of psychosis following cannabis use, when it occurs, mimics hypomania more closely than schizophrenia and, characteristically, schizophrenic thought disorder is usually absent.

As evidence for the development of a functional psychosis as a result of cannabis use, most authors have cited a close temporal relationship between the intake of the drug and the development of a psychotic reaction. Unfortunately, this is no proof of causality, and there can be other explanations for this association. For instance, this sequence can be purely coincidental in regular cannabis users who, in addition, suffer from frequent relapses of an independent functional psychotic illness. It is possible that it is the development of a functional psychosis which provides the stimulus to take cannabis in an attempt to self-medicate. In addition, there may be a common, but at present unknown, aetiological factor which is the link between cannabis use and functional psychosis. Disappointingly, even recent studies, which have looked for a link between cannabis use and psychosis, continue to be of poor design. For example, a study which attempted to grade the exposure to cannabis over a fifteen-year period against the likelihood of developing schizophrenia in 45,570 Swedish conscripts did not even control for the use of other psychoactive substances such as amphetamines.

Although recent studies are providing stronger evidence that a functional psychosis can be provoked, aggravated or prolonged by the use of cannabis, there remains equally good attestation to the contrary. Therefore, no clear answer to this question can emerge until the methodological and ethical difficulties – which at present prevent proper placebo-controlled drug (cannabis) trials from taking place – are resolved, and the direct effects of cannabis studied in patients with a pre-disposition to psychosis.

PERSONALITY

It has often been argued that the chronic use of cannabis leads to an amotivational syndrome characterized by apathy, child-like thinking, loss of interest in achievement, disorganization of lifestyle and a propensity to a fantasy life. This conclusion has largely been based on studies of middle-class, highly motivated American college students who have often had little more than 'experimental' exposure to the drug. Nevertheless, the use of cannabis is not exclusive to the middle classes, and surveys which have included individuals from a more representative sample of the population have been unable to replicate the findings of these earlier studies.

AGGRESSION, VIOLENCE AND CRIME

A possible relationship between cannabis and violence was first reported by Marco Polo in the thirteenth century. During the twelfth century members of a Muslim Sect in Persia known as the Ashihin (Assassins) were said to have been enticed by their leader to commit murderous acts in defence of the sect by the promise of entry into 'Paradise', or induced into a suitably murderous state by the ingestion of a Secret Potion. The contents of this potion were never identified and the assertion that it was hashish was based on the notion that the term ashihin originated from hashishin, meaning one who uses hashish; though another possible derivation was from Hasan Ibn al-Sabbah, the leader's name.

Between 25 per cent to 50 per cent of unselected criminal populations abuse drugs, of which cannabis is perhaps the commonest. Attempts at exploring a possible mechanism by which cannabis may modulate aggressive or criminal behaviour has led to the examination of the following questions. Can the use of cannabis reduce, precipitate or exacerbate aggression, in either normal or pre-disposed individuals and, if so, in what circumstances?

Numerous commissions have been set up to answer these questions, but no consensus view has emerged, a fact highlighted by the President's Commission on Law Enforcement in 1967 which stated that 'the differences of opinion are absolute and the claims beyond reconciliation'. In the majority of cases the use of cannabis does not lead to an increase in aggressive behaviour. Moreover, in the minority of cases where a strong positive association was found between the frequency of cannabis use and an increase in aggression or criminal behaviour, there were often plausible non-causal explanations for the association. For example, social theorists have long pointed out that the use of cannabis is almost endemic in urban slums where high levels of criminal activity would also be expected, and the link might therefore be no more than coincidence or some other common denominator such as psychosocial deprivation.

Nothing has been established from case studies of crimes alleged to have been committed under the influence of cannabis. This is because 'street' cannabis is notoriously variable in its constituents and potency, and is often adulterated with other psychoactive substances such as phenylcyclidine, benzodiazepines, amphetamines or barbiturates. Thus, the evidence is often anecdotal and equivocal as to whether or not the individual was under the influence of cannabis or some other drug at the time.

It has been argued by those in favour of legalizing cannabis use that the cost of criminalization, in monetary and human terms, far exceeds the harmful consequences of the use of the drug. This view is supported by the American experience where the abolition of sanctions on the possession of small amounts of cannabis in eleven American States in 1973 has not led to any increase in incidence, prevalence or level of use. In addition, although cannabis users are statistically more likely to experiment with other illicit drugs when compared to non-drug users, the majority of cannabis users do not progress to more dependence-forming drugs such as opiates or cocaine. Opponents of the cannabis legalization lobby in Britain point to the fact that opinion polls conducted between 1969 and 1975 have consistently confirmed that only 8–12 per cent of the population is in favour of reducing cannabis-related penalties or legalizing the drug. Further, even if public opinion were to change, Britain is a signatory to the United Nations Single Convention (1961), a treaty binding signatory nations to prohibit the spread of 'addictive drugs'. Perhaps, more importantly there is still so much controversy surrounding the health hazards of cannabis use that, until this information is available, it may be prudent not to relax controls on its availability.

In rodents the direct administration of Δ⁹THC leads to aggression only under stressful conditions such as starvation or isolation. In man, the results of similar experimentation has been inconclusive due to the paucity of placebo controlled trials and the inappropriate measurement of psychosocial variables such as personality and hostility under sterile laboratory type conditions. It appears that in man, the social setting in which the drug is taken is crucial. Thus the disinhibiting effects of the drug with the release of aggression may only occur in situations where the atmosphere is already highly charged. These complex interactions between the personality of the drug user, previous experience with the drug and the impact of the social environment are poorly understood and in need of further systematic enquiry.

Up to 10 per cent of cannabis users may be at risk from developing an acute toxic psychosis. This toxic psychosis may result in aggressive outbursts and consequently enforced admission to psychiatric hospital. Interestingly, a recent report from a psychiatric hospital in a deprived urban city area has shown a significant increase in the number of such cases. It remains unclear whether all individuals who smoke cannabis are potentially at risk or only those who are in some way predisposed, for instance, by virtue of a family history and/or previous or current major mental illness. For this reason clinicians are universally unable to give any other advice to their patients, even in places where the use of the drug is legal, but to advocate total abstinence.

There is no direct correlation between the use of cannabis and violence and in the majority of cases, the crimes attributed to the use of cannabis concern the theft of property and the infringement of road traffic regulations.

Far too little attention has been paid to the finding that between 3.7 per cent to 37.0 per cent of drivers killed in road traffic accidents have significant levels of cannabinoids in their blood. Also, the disorientating effects of alcohol are additive to that of cannabis. At a time of great concern about the harmful effects of alcohol on driving, it is surprising that there has been no call for concomitantly drug testing drivers who fail the breathalyser test.

CONCLUSIONS

Cannabis has been therapeutically used for the treatment of hysteria, anorexia nervosa, epilepsy, rheumatism, bronchial asthma, pain, glaucoma and nausea induced by chemotherapy. Among the harmful physical sequelae of cannabis use, perhaps of greatest significance are the potential to suppress the immune system, impair reproduction, produce chronic respiratory disease and increase the risk of lung cancer.

Tolerance may develop to some of the effects of cannabis and withdrawal symptoms are often reported by regular users on cessation of drug use. However, craving or psychological dependence is not seen.

Chronic cannabis use is unlikely to lead to either a deterioration in personality or an increase in aggressive potential although 'flash backs', prolonged depersonalization and derealization may occur.

An acute toxic psychosis may follow cannabis intake with confusion, agitation, apprehension, paranoid ideation and perceptual disturbance. It remains unproven whether cannabis use can provoke, aggravate or prolong a functional psychosis, even in individuals at 'high risk' of psychosis. Therefore, future research effort needs to be directed at placebo controlled drug (cannabis) trials, using individuals from such 'high risk' groups to clarify the issue.

Finally, the marked cognitive and psychomotor impairment which may follow a single smoke of cannabis, an effect magnified by the concomitant use of alcohol, is an underrated hazard to the performance of skilled tasks such as driving. In future, appropriate legislation may need to be introduced to allow for motorists to be simultaneously tested for alcohol and drug (including cannabis) use, in order to improve road safety.

FURTHER READING

Abel, E.L. (1977) 'The relationship between cannabis and violence: a review', *Psychological Bulletin II* 84: 193–211.

Andreasson, S., Allebeck, P., Engstrom, A. and Rydberg, U. (1987) 'Cannabis and schizophrenia, a longitudinal study', *Lancet*, 1483–5.

Ashton, C.H. (1987) 'Cannabis: dangers and possible uses', *British Medical Journal* 294: 141–2.

Beaubrun, M.H. and Knight, F. (1973) 'Psychiatric assessment of 30 chronic users of cannabis and 30 matched controls', *American Journal of Psychiatry* 130: 309–11.

Campbell, A.M.G., Evans, M., Thompson, J.L. and Williams, M.J. (1971) 'Cerebral atrophy in young cannabis smokers', *Lancet* ii: 1219–24.

Dornbush, R.L., Fink, M. and Freedman, A.M. (1971) 'Marijuana, memory and perception', *American Journal of Psychiatry* 128: 194–7.

Edwards, J.G. (1982) 'Cannabis and the question of dependence', in *Report of the Expert Group on the Effects of Cannabis Use*, London: Home Office.

Fink, M. (1976) 'Effects of acute and chronic inhalation of hashish, marijuana, and tetrahydrocannabinol on brain electrical activity in man: evidence for tissue tolerance', *Annals of New York Academy of Sciences* 282: 387–98.

Fujiwara, M. and Ueki, S. (1979) 'The course of aggressive behaviour induced by a single injection of delta-9-tetrahydrocannabinol and its characteristics', *Physiology and Behaviour* 22: 535–9.

Ghodse, H.A. (1986) 'Cannabis psychosis', *British Journal of Addiction* 81: 473–8.

Hunt, C.A. and Jones, R.T. (1980) 'Tolerance and disposition of tetrahydrocannabinol in man', *Journal of Pharmacology and Experimental Therapy* 215: 33–4.

Ishbell, H., Gorodetzskky, C.W., Jasubski, D., Claussen, V., Spulak, F.K. and Korte, F. (1967) 'Effects of Δ^9-transtetra-hydrocannabinol in man', *Psychopharmacologica* (Berlin) 11: 184–8.

Janowsky, D.S., Meacham, M.P., Blaine, J.D., Schoor, M. and Bozzetti, L.P. (1976) 'Marijuana effects on simulated flying ability', *American Journal of Psychiatry* 133: 384–8.

Johnson, B.A., Smith, B.L. and Taylor, P.J. (1988) 'Cannabis and schizophrenia', *Lancet* i: 592–3.

Mason, A.P. and McBay, A.J. (1984) 'Ethanol, marihuana and other drug use in 600 drivers killed in single-vehicle crashes in North Carolina 1978–81', *Journal of Forensic Sciences* 29: 788–92.

Matsuda, L., Lolait, S., Brownstein, M., Young, A. and Bonner, T. (1990) 'Structure of a cannabinoid receptor and functional expression of cloned CDNA', *Nature* 346: 561–4.

Maugh, T. (1982) 'Marijuana "justifies serious concern"', *Science* 215: 1488–9.

Maykut, M.D. (1985) 'Health consequences of acute and chronic marihuana use', *Progress in Neuro-Psychopharmacology and Biological Psychiatry* 9: 203–38.

Moreau de Tours, J.J. (1845) *Hashish et de l'Alientation Mentale*, Paris: Masson.

Negrete, J.C. (1989) 'Cannabis and schizophrenia', *British Journal of Addiction* 84: 49–51.

Rottanburg, D., Robbins, A.H., Ben-Arie, O., Teggin, A. and Elk, R. (1982) 'Cannabis-associated psychosis with hypomania features', *Lancet* ii: 1364–6.

Soderstrom, C.A. and Carson, S.L. (1988) 'Update: alcohol and other drug use among vehicular crash victims', *Maryland Medical Journal* 37: 7, 541–5.

Thalore, V.R. and Skukla, S.R. (1976) 'Cannabis psychosis and paranoid schizophrenia', *Archives of General Psychiatry* 33: 383–6.

CROSS REFERENCES

Chapter 12

Tripping the light fantastic:
the phenomenon of the hallucinogens

John Strang and Harry Shapiro

The hallucinogens are the most extraordinary of all drugs. Whilst other drugs may amplify or dampen the normal experiences, it is the reported power to take the user on a journey beyond these experiences which accounts for the enduring fascination of the hallucinogens. This quality is conveyed in the writings of many authors including the following four key figures in the LSD story.

First there is Aldous Huxley who saw himself as a latter day prophet of hallucinogens which he viewed as a short cut to the transcendental experience. In his book *The Doors of Perception* Huxley (1954) describes how mescaline opens up the 'cerebral reducing valve' which normally tones down all our experiences, so that 'Mind at large seeps past the no longer watertight valve'. The 'other world' to which mescaline gave access was '... not the world of visions; it existed out there, in what I could see with my eyes open. The great change was in the realm of objective fact' (Huxley, 1954: 24).

The credit for the discovery of the hallucinogenic effects of LSD goes to Albert Hofmann, a chemist working for the Sandoz Pharmaceutical Company in Geneva. In 1943 he inadvertently absorbed small quantities of LSD in the laboratory and soon became restless and returned home where he 'perceived an uninterrupted stream of fantastic pictures, extraordinary shapes with intense kaleidoscopic play of colours: after some two hours the condition faded away' (Hofmann, 1980: 15). In his account he described many of the characteristics of the LSD experience:

> I lost all account of time. I noticed with dismay that my environment was undergoing progressive changes. My visual field wavered and everything appeared deformed as if in a faulty mirror. I was overcome with fear that I was going out of my mind. Occasionally I felt as if I were out of my body. I thought I had died. My ego seemed suspended somewhere in space from where I saw my dead body lying on the sofa.
>
> (Hofmann, 1980: 17)

He particularly noted one of the characteristic features of the LSD experience in which one sensation is experienced in another modality (termed synaesthesia) when he noted how '... acoustic perceptions such as the noise of water gushing from a tap or the spoken word were transformed into optical illusions' (Hofmann, 1980: 19).

Humphrey Osmond (1957) was one of the leading medical advocates of the therapeutic potential of LSD during the 1950s and first coined the term 'psychedelic' to describe compounds such as LSD or mescaline which 'enriched the mind and enlarged the vision'. He goes on to say 'It is this kind of experience which provides the greatest possibility for examining those areas most interesting to psychiatry which have provided men down the ages with experience they have considered valuable above all others' (Osmond, 1957).

The final quote is from Timothy Leary (1964), the psychologist turned guru who, during the 1960s, first exhorted youth to 'turn on, tune in and drop out'. He and other members of the League of Spiritual Discovery (LSD) described how 'a psychedelic journey is a journey to new realms of consciousness. The scope and content of the experience is limitless, but its characteristic features are the transcendence of verbal concepts, of space-time dimensions, and of the ego or identity' (Leary et al., 1964: 11).

WHAT ARE THE HALLUCINOGENS?

LSD is the most famous hallucinogen. Its chemical name is D-lysergic acid diethyl-amide which is chemically related to 5-hydroxytriptamine (5-HT), a neurotransmitter in the brain. Both psilocybin and dimethyltriptamine (DMT) are also closely related. It is not available naturally but has been widely synthesized in pharmaceutical laboratories until the 1960s and subsequently in highly productive illicit laboratories. Although originally sold on sugar cubes or microdots it has more recently been sold in stamp-like squares of paper impregnated with the LSD. The stamps typically carry a cartoon picture by which they are known (e.g. 'Supermans'). Production is cheap and purity is typically very high. Interestingly, sheets of stamps of virtually identical purity will sometimes include individual stamps with purities several times higher – this may contribute to 'the occurrence of unanticipated adverse reactions. Although LSD was originally available in an injectable pharmaceutical form, it is interesting that there has been no significant interest by drug users in the intravenous use of LSD or other hallucinogens – perhaps the reason is partly explained by Tyler (1986) who reports how intravenous use is 'a method wholly unsuitable since it slams the user straight into the intense hallucinogenic phase without even the shortish run-up that is provided when swallowing the drug' (Tyler, 1986: 138).

Hallucinogenic fungi ('magic mushrooms') are best considered in two categories. In the UK the most widely used magic mushrooms are the insignificant-looking 'Liberty Caps' (*psilocybe semilanceata*) which contain both psilocybin and psilocin. They grow in groups with a fine fragile flesh and a beige to brown pointed cap on top of a tall slim stem which may be two or three inches tall. Typically a couple of dozen Liberty Caps may be taken at one time. A richer variety of psilocybe mushrooms grow in Central and South America and were revered by the Aztecs who reserved use of the mushrooms for their priests and elders in religious ceremonies.

The other hallucinogenic mushroom which grows naturally in the UK is the classic 'Fly Agaric' (*amanita muscaria*). This is the mushroom or toadstool of fairy-tale fame with a bright red cap with white spots typically found growing in the mulch beneath birch trees. The mushroom is usually heated and dried and two or three mushrooms may be taken at once.

MDMA *(Ecstasy)* is classed as a hallucinogenic amphetamine – 3,4 methylene-dioxymethamphetamine or MDMA for short. Hallucinogenic amphetamines are a group of drugs with effects that combine those of amphetamine and LSD, although Ecstasy is not strictly hallucinogenic at normal dose levels. Within this group of drugs, there are over a thousand compounds. MDMA is part of the MDA (methyl-dioxy-amphetamine) family which are mainly derived from the oils of natural products such as sassafras, dill and parsley. The structure of each compound determines whether the effects are more like amphetamine or LSD. Ecstasy is at the milder end of the spectrum of potency, while others (usually wholly synthetic) such as PMA (para-methoxyamphetamine) and DOM (2,5-dimethoxy-4-methoxy-amphetamine) are very much stronger.

Phencyclidine (PCP) (1-[1-phenylcyclohexyl] piperdine) is also known as PCP or 'Angel Dust'. It was originally developed in the 1950s as a dissociative anaesthetic – so called because it dissociated the patient from bodily sensations and no pain was felt during surgery. Its use was soon discontinued when patients recovering from surgery became irrational, agitated and deluded as a side-effect of PCP. However, veterinary medicine continued using the drug until the late 1970s. PCP is generally accepted as a hallucinogenic, but it is actually difficult to classify because different doses produce different effects – stimulant, anaesthetic and analgesic as well as hallucinogenic.

Mescaline (3,4,5-trimethoxy-phenylethylamine) is the main psychoactive ingredient of the Peyote cactus. The plant is mainly found in Mexico and was used ceremonially by the Aztecs – indeed the word peyote means 'flesh of the gods'. It now forms part of the religious rituals of over forty American Indian tribes in the USA and western Canada. Peyote was the first hallucinogenic plant to be chemically analysed and a crystallized alkaloid had already been identified by the turn of the century. Because the dried cacti from which the alkaloid was extracted was called 'Mescal Buttons', the alkaloid was named mescaline. The chemistry of mescaline is similar to the neurotransmitter noradrenaline and the drug is active at oral doses of 0.2–0.4 grams. Aldous Huxley's main experience of hallucinogens (see elsewhere in this chapter) was with mescaline.

Other hallucinogens. It has been estimated that there are at least half a million species of hallucinogenic plant in the world, of which only about 150 species have been employed for their hallucinogenic properties. But hallucinogens are not confined to plant material and the endless number of chemical derivatives created in the laboratory. The Pacific Islands boast an hallucinogenic fish and the dried skin of one South American frog is revered for the hallucinogen in the salivary glands! However, among the more common hallucinogenic plants found around the world are the following: Belladonna (Deadly Nightshade) and Datura (these and others in the group contain atropine and scopolamine); nutmeg and mace; Morning Glory seeds; Iboga (a root found in Equatorial Africa) and Yage (a psychedelic drink made from the bark of the South American Ayahuasca vine).

THE USERS – WHO ARE THEY?

Even when LSD had a much higher profile, little was done to establish the extent and nature of its use. Two national surveys of drug use, conducted by OPCS in 1969 and the BBC 'Midweek' programme in 1973, reported 'ever used' figures for LSD at around 650,000 people or 1 per cent of the population. In 1982 National Opinion Polls (in a survey for the *Daily Mail*) interviewed 1326 people aged between 15 and 21 where a 3 per cent 'ever used' figure for LSD was recorded, while in 1985 the

News of the World commissioned Audience Research to conduct a further national survey of a representative sample of those aged between 16 and 34. In this survey 8 per cent said they had been to parties where LSD had been taken while 4 per cent said they had tried the drug themselves. Extrapolated nationally, this would again reveal an 'ever used' figure for LSD of around 650,000 people.

LSD maintains a persistent presence in the UK drug scene. Two examples demon- strate the broad church of LSD users. The first shows that LSD remains a favoured drug among those attending events previously associated with the 'alternative' society. The Sheffield branch of the 'Legalize Cannabis' campaign conducted an 'intended use' survey at the Stonehenge and Glastonbury Festivals in 1984. This revealed that 41 per cent and 30 per cent of respective festival-goers would be using LSD. Only cannabis was a more favoured drug. By contrast, LSD is also prevalent among groups for whom hippy ideology is anathema. The teenage magazine *The Hit* (26 October 1985) conducted a survey of drug use among its readers. A surprising 36 per cent of the 400 replies reported trying LSD. Again only cannabis was more favoured, but the results must be regarded with caution as alcohol and tobacco only registered 5 per cent between them, less than drugs like cocaine, barbiturates and amyl nitrite. By the late 1980s to early 1990s, LSD had apparently become part of the 'acid house party' scene, either taken on its own or allegedly mixed with MDMA as 'fantasy'.

PHARMACOLOGY

Only minute doses of LSD are required to produce the hallucinogenic effect. LSD is 100 times more potent for a given dose than psilocybin, and 400 times more potent than mescaline. Doses of well under 100 micrograms of LSD are sufficient to produce a major effect lasting many hours. These drugs have actions at multiple sites in the central nervous system. After oral consumption the effects may come on within a quarter of an hour and may last up to 12 hours. Although most attention has been paid to the psychic effects, there are also physical effects which are predominantly sympathomimetic (e.g. dilated pupils, raised blood pressure and pulse rate). Their exact mode of action on the brain remains uncertain but appears to be related to its structural similarity to 5-HT. In the 'normal' dose range the intensity of the psychological and physical effects of LSD are proportional to the dose. Tolerance develops rapidly so that users rarely take more than a few doses in quick succession; but conversely sensitivity to the drug returns rapidly. There is cross-tolerance between each of the hallucinogenic drugs described here. Physical withdrawal phenomena do not occur after abrupt cessation of intake of LSD and the other hallucinogens.

THE EXPERIENCE OF THE HALLUCINOGENS

The hallucinations described by the user of hallucinogenic drugs are usually not hallucinations in the strict sense of the word as used in psychiatry. First, they are recognized by users as being not real and as being ego-alien; second, they are usually enhancements or distortions of real perceptions rather than sensory phenomena whose origins are entirely from within the brain.

A trip begins about half an hour to one hour after taking LSD, peaks after two to six hours and fades out after about twelve hours, depending on the dose and having progressed through several phases. Exactly what happens when a drug is taken is often determined by what the user expects will happen and the situation in which the drug is used (e.g. alone or with a group or trusted friends).

Users often report visual effects such as intensified colours, distorted shapes and sizes, and movement in stationary objects. Distortions of hearing occur, as do changes in sense of time and place. Generally the user knows these effects to be unreal. True hallucinations are relatively rare.

A distinctive characteristic is the way in which the meaning of an experience may be altered. The experience of time or location in space may still be judged accurately, but the qualitative aspects of the experience and the importance attached to it may be fundamentally altered. Huxley describes it thus:

> Position and the three dimensions were beside the point. Not, of course, that the category of space had been abolished. When I got up and walked about, I could do so normally, without misjudging the whereabouts of objects. Space was still there; but it had lost its predominance. The mind was primarily concerned, not with measures and locations, but with being and meaning.
>
> (Huxley, 1954: 19)

Emotional reactions vary, but include heightened self-awareness and mystical or ecstatic experiences. Feelings of dissociation from the body are commonly reported. Unpleasant reactions are more likely if the user is unstable, anxious or depressed, and may include anxiety, depression, dizziness, disorientation and sometimes a shortlived psychotic episode including hallucinations and paranoia, commonly known as a 'bad trip'.

The same person may have good and bad 'trips' on different occasions, and even within the same trip. But whilst the LSD experience is variable compared with most other drugs, it is also relatively more open to the user's intentions and to the suggestions of others. Hence friendly reassurance may reduce the impact of a bad trip. Experienced users steer the trip towards the area they wish to experience or explore. It is difficult to combine a trip with a task requiring concentration, and driving will almost certainly be impaired. Suicides or deaths due to LSD-induced beliefs or perceptions, though much publicized, are rare. Fatal overdose was unreported in the literature until as recently as 1985.

In his chapter on 'The Acid Scene', Ken Leech (1973) describes three key elements to the LSD experience. The first is the effect of a kaleidoscope of intense light and colour with a broad heightening of all the senses, including cross-over between sensory modalities known as synaesthesia. The second is the element of depersonalization or ego-loss in which the drug taker experiences a separation of mind from body and a symbolic disintegration of the real world (it is this transcendence of the ego which Leech singles out as the fundamental characteristic of the psychedelic experience). The third element is the sense of illumination of reality and of the universe which accounts for the quasi-spiritual quality of the LSD experience.

COMPLICATIONS AND HAZARDS

The bad trip

It is perhaps inevitable that given the nature of the LSD experience, journeys to the outer reaches of the mind would include those to less beatific outposts. For each episode of taking hallucinogens, there is the risk that the experiences will be predominantly terrifying rather than exciting. According to regular users, this is said to be more common in the novice, and also in the individual who is already agitated or depressed prior to use of the drug. Although attention usually focuses on the 'hallucinations' or perceptual distortions, it should be noted that many of the features of the bad trip resemble those of a panic attack.

Treatment usually involves reassurance and general care until the effect of the drug passes (typically within a 12-hour period). Often this reassurance and care is provided by friends. When hospital admissions have been necessary for treatment of psychoses induced by hallucinogens, phenothiazines such as chlorpromazine are sometimes given during the acute stage. However, it should be borne in mind that there have been reports that the psychosis may have been aggravated by phenothiazines when it results from use of some of the rarer hallucinogens such as STP (4-methyl-2, 5-dimethoxy-a-methylamphetamine – called serenity, tranquillity and peace!) (see anecdotal reports by Leech, 1973; Hollister, 1982).

Adverse responses to use of LSD are also much more likely when the individual is unaware that they have been given the drug.

The flashback

For reasons that are not clear, the individual who has taken LSD may re-experience the original trip – usually in a muted and more abbreviated form. It is most unlikely that this is triggered by remaining amounts of the drug itself given that its half life is of the order of a few hours; these flashbacks may occur many months or even years later. As with the original trip, the flashback is often characterized by high levels of autonomic arousal with many of the features being similar to a panic attack, and it may well be that there are links here which have not been adequately explored (especially as both bad trips and panic attacks may be triggered by use of other drugs, such as cannabis). As with bad trips, the management usually involves general reassurance while awaiting the passage of time. If the problems become persistent then management should perhaps follow the lines of treatment for panic attacks.

Long-term psychosis (considering both drug-induced and drug-precipitated psychoses)

There is no doubt that a certain number of LSD users develop long-term psychotic illnesses. However, the real question which must be addressed is the extent to which this occurs more frequently (if at all) than already occurs in the general population. Certainly some of the reported cases of long-term psychoses as a result of use of LSD represent attempts on the part of the patient, the physician or the family to make sense of the onset of mental illness: thus, whilst understandable, they represent no more than retrospective rationalization and should not be seen as evidence for a true association. On the other hand even the drug-using fraternity themselves recognize that there are those who are permanently altered as a result of the LSD experience, and altered in such a way that they are subsequently damaged – the 'acid casualty'.

In this area it may be helpful to consider two different forms of drug psychosis. On the one hand, there is the true drug-induced psychosis in which the use of the drug (such as amphetamine, cocaine and LSD) directly causes the psychotic illness: in such cases the psychosis usually passes with the passage of the drug. On the other hand one might consider entirely separately the drug-precipitated psychosis in which the event of drug use (and perhaps especially an adverse reaction to drug use) acts as the trigger for an otherwise independent psychotic illness, whose time course and characteristics are then dictated by the illness itself and not by the characteristics of the drug.

THE LAW

LSD was first subject to special controls in the UK when in 1966 it was added to the list of drugs covered by the 1964 Drugs (Prevention of Misuse) Act. Currently it is controlled as a class A drug under the 1971 Misuse of Drugs Act, making its unauthorized possession, supply, manufacture and import criminal offences attracting the same maximum penalties as those relating to heroin, cocaine and the cannabinoids. Maximum custodial sentence for possession of a class A drug is seven years; those convicted of the more serious trafficking offences involving these drugs face up to life imprisonment. Lysergamide (lysergic acid amide) used in the manufacture of LSD, and a constituent of psychoactive varieties of Morning Glory seeds, is also a class A drug.

In 1979 there were 216 seizures of LSD with 208 persons being found guilty or cautioned for LSD-related offences. This represented the lowest point in a downward trend starting in 1971. However, by 1984 the figures had risen to a temporary high of 629 and 558 respectively; following which they dropped back down. The latest figures at the time of writing relate to 1989, during which the figures were 970 and 435 respectively.

The law in the UK regarding possession of hallucinogenic mushrooms has always been somewhat confused. As the law stands at present, it is not illegal to pick hallucinogenic mushrooms and eat them raw. However, any attempt to 'prepare' the mushrooms in any way (e.g. by boiling, drying or crushing) could be construed as an attempt to extract the psychoactive ingredient of the mushroom, rendering the user liable to prosecution for possession of a class A drug. Recently the definition of 'prepare' was extended to freezing where the defendant had 44 packages of 100 mushrooms in his freezer.

In the late 1960s concern in this country about the proliferation of hallucinogenic amphetamines in America prompted a precautionary controlling of specific drugs such as MDA and TMA (tri-methoxyamphetamine). However, in the mid-1970s after an illicit drug laboratory was raided in the Midlands, it was discovered that the chemist had prepared a hallucinogenic amphetamine not controlled at that time and was in possession of the formulae for other drugs of this type. Therefore in 1977, in order to stay 'one jump ahead' of the underground chemists, the government introduced an amendment to the Misuse of Drugs Act 1971 which placed these drugs in class A, and was designed to control all amphetamine-like compounds including MDMA.

MDMA is also in Schedule 1 of the regulations which prohibits doctors from prescribing it and is a Designated Drug meaning that a licence from the Home Office is required to use the drug for research purposes.

CONCLUSION

Aldous Huxley was wrong in his descriptions of the mode of action of hallucinogens, but perhaps his descriptions are as good as any other when describing the effects of this group of drugs. The reducing valve is open so that more of the wholeness of potential experience comes flooding through to the drug user. The user is swept headlong on a journey into poorly charted waters which contain both delights and dangers.

The present state of our relationship with the hallucinogens is perhaps best summed up in the concluding section of the chapter in *Drug Scenes* – the report on drugs and drug dependence from the Royal College of Psychiatrists (1987):

> It has to be conceded that experience with hallucinogens has been meaningful to many people; to those who have used these drugs as part of their religion over many centuries, to the creative writer, to the casual individual who has tasted exciting fantasies, and indeed to the patients who appear to benefit from them in psychotherapy. It is astonishing that a few micrograms of a chemical should open such windows, and society has not yet come fully to terms with this fact. At the same time it is extremely hard to judge the validity of the claims which people taking LSD have made for their intensely subjective experiences.
>
> The debate on hallucinogens should not seek to deny their strange magic. However, the case against them would seem to be overwhelming. Whatever the pleasure or even the arguable creative and therapeutic potential of drug-induced dreams, the resulting nightmares (the bad trips, flashbacks, psychotic illnesses and dangerous behaviour) are indeed too common, too unpredictable and too devastating to justify this form of experimentation with the human mind.
>
> (Royal College of Psychiatrists, 1987: 121)

REFERENCES

Hofmann, A. (1980) *LSD: My Problem Child*, London: McGraw-Hill.
Hollister, L.E. (1982) 'Psychotropic drug interactions', in S. Cohen, C. Buchwald, J. Solomon, J. Callahan and D. Katz (eds) *Frequently Prescribed and Abused Drugs: Their Indications, Efficacy and Rational Prescribing*, New York: Haworth Press, pp. 7–20.
Huxley, A. (1954) *The Doors of Perception*, London: Chatto and Windus.
Leary, T., Metzner, R. and Alpert, R. (1964) *The Psychedelic Experience: a Manual Based on the Tibetan Book of the Dead*, New York: University Books.
Leech, K. (1973) *A Practical Guide to the Drug Scene*, London: SPCK.
Osmond, H. (1957) 'A review of the clinical effects of the psychotomimetic agents', *Annals of the New York Academy of Sciences*, 66: 418–34.
Royal College of Psychiatrists (1987) *Drug Scenes*, London: Royal College of Psychiatrists.
Tyler, A. (1986) *Street Drugs*, London: New English Library.

CROSS REFERENCES
Chapter 13 Cocaine and the amphetamines
    Marian W. Fischman and Richard W. Foltin

Chapter 13

Cocaine and the amphetamines

Marian W. Fischman and Richard W. Foltin

The twentieth century has been marked by a series of stimulant abuse epidemics, with cocaine and amphetamine generally alternating in popularity. Beginning in the 1880s, these two drugs have shared repeated cycles of praise followed by universal condemnation as delight in their positive, mood-altering effects has been replaced by evidence of their substantial toxicity. This review briefly summarizes their effects in humans. More comprehensive discussions of this literature can be found in a number of recent reviews (e.g. Johanson and Fischman, 1989; Fischman, 1987; Kozel and Adams, 1985; Grabowski, 1984).

Amphetamine and cocaine, although pharmacologically different, share central nervous system stimulant activity and substantial abuse liability. Cocaine, the principal alkaloid of *Erythroxylon coca*, is the only naturally occurring local anaesthetic. Cultivated by the Indians of the Andean Highlands and portions of the South American Amazon valley for well over a millennium, coca leaves were not used in Europe until their active ingredient was isolated in 1855. Availability of coca extracts and cocaine in Europe and the United States was followed by a period of experimentation, resulting in euphoric public statements and widespread prescription by physicians for a variety of ills, from dyspepsia and neuralgia to alcoholism and melancholy. Enthusiasm was followed by general condemnation, as reports of its adverse consequences became well known. The first cycle of cocaine abuse thus began in the late 1800s, continuing through the early portion of the twentieth century. Amphetamine, on the other hand, synthesized in 1887, was not used as a bronchial dilator until the early 1930s. The CNS stimulant properties of the amphetamines were described in 1933, and reports of abuse soon followed. Amphetamines rapidly replaced cocaine in 'street' use since they were cheaper, more readily available, and had a longer duration of action. The optimism with which the amphetamines were greeted was, however, also followed by condemnation, paralleling the cyclic pattern of acceptance seen with cocaine.

These two drugs share a range of effects, most of which are related to their sympathomimetic properties. Amphetamine and cocaine increase concentrations of both dopaminergic and noradrenergic transmitters at the neuronal synapse, cocaine by blocking reuptake and amphetamine by both augmenting release and blocking reuptake.

MEDICAL USES

Cocaine has limited medical usefulness because of its substantial potential for abuse and toxicity. It is the only drug capable of causing both intense vasoconstriction and local anaesthesia. Because cocaine blocks nerve conduction, it was initially used extensively in ophthalmology. However, because it causes sloughing of the corneal epithelium when applied to the eye, its use is now limited to topical application in the upper respiratory tract.

Stimulant drugs are frequently used for the treatment of narcolepsy, obesity and childhood hyperactivity. Although patients with narcolepsy require large doses of amphetamine for prolonged periods of time, tolerance does not seem to develop to the therapeutic effects of the drug. The use of amphetamines in the treatment of hyperkinetic behavioural disorders in children, however, remains controversial, with care taken to limit treatment dose and duration. The major therapeutic utility of amphetamine is in short-term treatment of obesity. Because tolerance develops within 4-6 weeks, longer-term treatment should be intermittent, with drug-free periods interspersed. Amphetamine therapy has been unsuccessfully attempted in the treatment of Parkinson's disease, and, although suggested, neither amphetamine nor cocaine are efficacious in the treatment of depression. The therapeutic utility of these drugs is therefore, at best, limited.

BEHAVIOURAL PHARMACOLOGY IN HUMANS

Human volunteer subjects given single moderate doses of cocaine and amphetamine generally show a decrease in food intake and fatigue and an increase in activity, talkativeness, and reports of euphoria and general well-being. In addition, experienced stimulant users do not discriminate them when administered intravenously. At higher doses, repetitive motor activity (stereotyped behaviour) is often seen, and with further increases in dose, convulsions, hyperthermia, coma and death can ensue.

These drugs cause dose-related increases in heart rate and blood pressure. Intravenous cocaine (4–32 mg, single doses) has not been shown to have any effect on the electrocardiogram, respiratory rate and body temperature. Oral cocaine (30–200 mg/day, divided doses) does not affect pulse, temperature, blood pressure, or respiration. As with amphetamine, these oral doses do have a suppressive effect on both rapid eye movement sleep and total sleep.

TOXICITY

Toxicity associated with cocaine use has been related to virtually every physiological system evaluated. Although most of these reports are single case studies or clinical reports, with no independent verification of cocaine use (i.e. blood level), the abundance of reports gives credence to the claims of cocaine-related toxicity. Cardiovascular morbidity associated with cocaine use includes reports of cardiac ischemia, myocardial infarctions, cerebrovascular accidents, subarachnoid haemorrhage, and other abnormalities related to increased blood pressure. Cocaine has been shown to produce hyperpyrexia which can contribute to the development of seizures. In addition, there are data suggesting hepatotoxicity, and damage to the gastrointestinal tract, renal and pulmonary systems.

Cocaine HCl (hydrochloride) is inhaled into the nose, injected intravenously, or smoked, after conversion to the base. Amphetamines, most often taken in pill form, may also be injected intravenously and, most recently, smoking methamphetamine has been reported. Many medical complications of drug use are related to the route of administration. Perforation of the nasal septum, chronic rhinitis and loss of sense of smell can occur in those who inhale drugs, while parenteral use is associated with diseases (e.g. viral endocarditis, hepatitis and acquired immunodeficiency disease) introduced by dirty needles contaminated with the blood of previous users as well as extra substances in the drug. Thrombophlebitis and abnormalities in pulmonary function are more common in those who smoke their drug.

Cocaine toxicity may also result from an interaction with other drugs. Cocaine abusers, particularly those who smoke it or inject it intravenously, also frequently take heroin to counteract the overstimulation accompanying their high dose stimulant use. This kind of self-medication can also involve alcohol or other sedative-hypnotics.

One of the most significant consequences of chronic stimulant abuse is the development of behavioural pathology. A stimulant psychosis is characterized by paranoia, impaired reality testing, anxiety, a stereotyped compulsive repetitive pattern of behaviour, and vivid visual, auditory and tactile hallucinations. An experimental amphetamine psychosis, with symptoms resembling schizophrenia, has been produced in normal volunteers who received 120–700 mg/day for 1–5 days. More subtle changes related to repeated stimulant use include irritability, hypervigilance, extreme psychomotor activation, paranoid thinking, impaired inter-personal relations and disturbances of eating and sleeping. In view of these dramatic behavioural changes, the neurotoxicity of these drugs has been studied in non-humans. Repeated doses of methamphetamine result in long-lasting alterations in levels of dopamine in the striatum. The existence of such changes after repeated cocaine use has not been replicated, and this differential effect may be due to the different mechanisms of action of these two drugs related to their relative ability to release dopamine, as well as the pool from which that release occurs.

TREATMENT

A combination of behavioural and pharmacological approaches is most useful for the treatment of cocaine abuse (Kleber, 1988). A relapse prevention module, incorporated into many of the successful programmes, includes techniques such as breaking contacts with friends who use drugs, getting rid of cocaine-using para-phernalia, and avoiding situations that are associated with cocaine use and signal its availability. Classical conditioning techniques, still in the experimental phase, have included extinction procedures to eliminate conditioned responses that might be important in drug-use relapse. In addition, urinalysis (random, 1–3 times/week) to verify compliance with the treatment programme has been incorporated into the overall design of most programmes. Both in-patient and out-patient settings have been usefully employed, but factors such as severe depression or psychotic symptoms lasting more than 1–3 days, repeated out-patient failure, heavy intravenous or freebase use, concurrent dependence on other drugs and severe psychiatric or medical problems, suggest in-patient treatment. Although it is clearly easier to control drug taking on an in-patient unit, out-patient treatment has the advantage of allowing the patient to learn to cope with the stimuli which signal drug taking and promote relapse.

A number of pharmacological adjuncts have recently been tested in the treatment of cocaine abuse. These have either focused on treating a disorder for which cocaine users might be self-medicating (e.g. attention deficit disorder), or in looking for agents that might block cocaine-related changes, such as euphoria or withdrawal. Open trials have suggested that drugs such as lithium and methylphenidate might be useful in the former situation, while drugs such as amantadine, carbamazepine, bromocriptine, desipramine, and imipramine show promise for treating the cocaine abuser with or without any underlying psychopathology. A double blind placebo-controlled clinical trial found that desipramine maintenance resulted in significant decreases in cocaine 'craving', significantly increased cocaine abstinence, and significantly more patients retained in treatment.

Cocaine is generally taken in a 'binge-crash' cycle, with periods of repeated use alternating with drug-free periods. No clear evidence for physical dependence on cocaine exists, although it has been suggested that cessation of cocaine use is associated with a predictable series of symptoms, the 'crash', 'withdrawal' and 'extinction' phases. The crash phase (9 hours to 4 days) shows symptoms similar to those of major depression, but the withdrawal phase (1–10 weeks) is the period of maximal relapse potential to cocaine use. It is during this phase that pharmacological adjuncts to treatment might have their major bene- fit. During the final phase (of unlimited duration), stimuli which can trigger craving must be extinguished. Type of treatment may be related to stage of abstinence, with pharmacological adjuncts most appropriate during the withdrawal phase.

CONCLUSION

The ability of cocaine and the amphetamines to elevate mood and give the user a sense of behavioural enhancement most likely contributes to their appeal. The general facilitation of energy and alertness, and the restoration of performance which has deteriorated due to boredom or fatigue, all provide important data for understanding their use. The seductiveness of the psychomotor stimulants may be related to the notion that intermittent use is relatively safe, with dramatic subjective effects at doses that have small physiological effects. This, however, is not the way these drugs are used by the uncontrolled user. It is quite clear, for example, that many cocaine users take repeated doses frequently, often for several days, in cycles which resemble the patterns reported for the 'speed freaks' (amphetamine abusers) of the 1960s, and which resemble patterns obtained in the animal laboratory when availability is unlimited. Under such conditions, animals will self-administer cocaine or amphetamine until they are severely debilitated or until the experimenter stops the session. Severe toxicity has been frequently reported in users, but the extent of their excessive behaviour may be limited by drug availability.

Treatment is still in its early stages, and although no single approach has proven to be widely efficacious, it is likely that a combination of behavioural and pharmacological interventions will be most useful in treating those who abuse psychomotor stimulants. There are, as yet, a paucity of controlled clinical trials in this area, but it would appear that a relapse prevention module is invaluable in any treatment programme. Stimulant abuse epidemics have cycled repeatedly throughout the world, at least during the past hundred years, and understanding their etiology and treatment is of great importance in preventing their continuing toxicity.

REFERENCES

Fischman, M.W. (1987) 'Cocaine and the amphetamines', in H.Y. Meltzer (ed.) *Psychopharmacology: The Third Generation of Progress*, New York: Raven Press, pp. 1543–53.

Gawin, F.H. and Kleber, H.D. (1986) 'Abstinence symptomology and psychiatric diagnosis in cocaine abusers', *Archives of General Psychiatry* 43: 107–113.

Grabowski, J. (ed.) (1984) *Cocaine: Pharmacology, Effects, and Treatment of Abuse*, National Institute on Drug Abuse Research Monograph #50, Washington, DC: US Government Printing Office.

Johanson, C.E. and Fischman, M.W. (1989) 'The pharmacology of cocaine related to its abuse', *Pharmacological Reviews* 41: 3–52.

Kleber, H.D. (1988) 'Epidemic cocaine abuse: America's present, Britain's future?', *British Journal of Addiction* 83: 1359–71.

Kozel, N.J. and Adams, E.H. (eds) (1985) *Cocaine Use in America: Epidemiologic and Clinical Perspectives*, National Institute on Drug Abuse Research Monograph #61, Washington, DC: US Government Printing Office.

CROSS REFERENCES

Chapter 14

Benzodiazepine withdrawal

Malcolm Lader

Anxiety, tension and insomnia are experienced acutely, repeatedly or chronically by many people. Such symptoms are generally treated by a variety of pharmacological and non-drug methods. Of the medicaments used, the benzodiazepines have been regarded by medical practitioners and patients alike as safe and effective symptomatic remedies. Consequently, prescription of benzodiazepine anxiolytics and hypnotics has soared, almost completely ousting the barbiturates and other older compounds. Over the past ten years or so, it has become increasingly evident that long-term prescription of benzodiazepines is associated with a definite risk of dependence and that even short-term use may result in rebound on discontinuation.

WITHDRAWAL SYNDROMES

Rebound

Rebound insomnia is a specific type of withdrawal sleep disturbance, characterized by a worsening of sleep beyond pretreatment levels, following abrupt discontinuation of benzodiazepine hypnotics with medium to rapid elimination rates. It may occur even when the drug has been administered short-term in modest dosage. An analogous syndrome may be seen after the withdrawal of anxiolytics given for a few weeks only. In abruptly discontinued patients, anxiety may increase to an intensity above that in the pre-drug period. This rebound is particularly marked in patients stopping medium-acting compounds such as lorazepam. Tapering the dose should be regarded as good clinical practice even when the benzodiazepine has been administered for a short course of treatment.

Another form of rebound anxiety is 'interdose' anxiety in which levels of apprehension and tension rise just before the next dose is due. The ensuing dose is thus eagerly anticipated ('clock-watching').

Normal-dose withdrawal

This is the characteristic syndrome seen when patients are withdrawn from long-term treatment (say 3 months or so) with a benzodiazepine maintained within the recommended dosage limits (e.g. 30 mg/day or less of diazepam).

The withdrawal syndrome is characterized by shakiness, tremor, dizziness, insomnia, impaired concentration, nausea, dysphoria, headaches, incoordination, heightened sensory perception, lethargy, depersonalization, tiredness, blurred vision, facial burning sensation, hot and cold feelings, and muscle aching. The perceptual symptoms vary greatly from patient to patient, can be quite bizarre and often perplex the patient. The withdrawal syndrome supervenes despite tapering the dose. Many but by no means all of these symptoms are reported in patients with anxiety disorders and it might seem difficult if not impossible to distinguish between them. However, the withdrawal syndrome becomes evident 2–10 days after stopping the benzodiazepine (depending on its elimination half-life) and usually subsides over a few weeks; recrudescence of anxiety is much less predictable and it usually persists. Some patients commenced long-term benzodiazepine use for non-psychiatric reasons, e.g. muscle spasm, and first suffer psychological symptoms such as anxiety and insomnia on withdrawal. All these observations suggest that a distinction can usually be made.

The natural history of benzodiazepine withdrawal is not clearly understood. Although most patients experience a short-lived syndrome, some have protracted illnesses with severe and incapacitating symptoms. Nor is the eventual outcome well documented. In many studies total success, i.e. complete and sustained abstinence, was only attained in 30–70 per cent of patients. The factors governing outcome are unclear but patients with previous minimal or no psychiatric disturbance do best. In the comparisons between various benzodiazepines, distinctions should be made between:

1 Ease of identifying a withdrawal syndrome.
2 Severity and duration of the withdrawal.
3 Propensity to induce dependence.

Shorter-acting compounds are more likely than longer-acting ones to be associated with an identifiable syndrome because it is manifest within 48 hours or so rather than a week. Also, the syndrome is generally more severe, leading to a higher failure rate. Differences with respect to number 3 have not been established.

Neonatal withdrawal syndromes

A few reports have described apparent withdrawal symptoms in neonates following maternal exposure to benzodiazepines. The symptoms include tremor, irritability, hypertonia, high-pitched cry, gastrointestinal upsets and poor feeding. The benzo-diazepines readily cross the placental barrier and may accumulate in the foetus. Neonates have reduced metabolic capabilities which may explain why the withdrawal reactions have appeared at any time between a few hours and as long as nine days after delivery.

High-dose dependence and abuse

Benzodiazepine non-medical use comprises three main categories:

1 Sustained high-dose (supratherapeutic) use, almost always with physical dependence.
2 Sporadic high-dose abuse often in the context of polydrug abuse but increasingly on its own.
3 Overdose with self-harm intent.

It is uncommon for patients started on benzodiazepines for therapeutic purposes to escalate their doses. It is unclear why so few patients do steadily increase their doses while the vast majority remain at therapeutic levels indefinitely. A Drug Abuse Warning Network (DAWN) project in the USA found a positive relationship between the extent of non-medical use of tranquillizers and their availability through physicians' prescriptions.

Concern has been expressed about increasing benzodiazepine use among drug abusers. Amongst attenders at a London Drug Dependence Unit, nearly 60 per cent had benzodiazepines detected in their urine on one or more occasions. Benzodiazepines were easily the second most common drugs used, after methadone. Benzodiazepines were detected in a third of urine specimens obtained from over a 100 consecutive male admissions to an alcohol detoxification centre in Toronto. Temazepam has been available in liquid-filled capsules in the UK, and was being increasingly abused by intravenous injection.

MANAGEMENT OF BENZODIAZEPINE WITHDRAWAL

The most appropriate way to manage benzodiazepine withdrawal is universally accepted to be gradual tapering of the dose. The most severe symptoms of withdrawal such as epileptic fits and confusional episodes are more likely to follow sudden withdrawal, particularly with shorter-acting compounds. Views differ, however, as to the optimum rate of withdrawal. After even a short course of treatment, say 3-4 weeks, a week of half dosage is advisable.

After longer periods of time, especially when a shorter-acting compound has been used, 4 weeks is the minimum period and programmes as long as 16 weeks have been advocated. Indeed, some self-help agencies suggest a month of tapering for every year of benzodiazepine use. There is no evidence to support such a timetable. The regimen may become a morbid focus, the patient becoming obsessed with his or her symptoms. One strategy is to try a fairly brisk withdrawal, say over 6-8 weeks, and only to resort to more gradual tapering if the symptoms become intolerable.

Many physicians routinely substitute a long-acting for a short-acting benzo-diazepine, say 10 mg of diazepam for 1 mg of lorazepam. After stabilization, the diazepam is then gradually tapered off. Whatever the strategy, flexibility in the regimen and constant support are essential. The patient must be carefully followed up as a depressive illness is not uncommon and may need vigorous treatment. Such an illness may be reactive to the stress of withdrawal or represent recurrence of an earlier affective episode. In some patients, the illness has many biological features such as insomnia and loss of weight.

Adjunctive therapies have been tried. A beta-adrenoceptor antagonist may lessen some symptoms but clonidine is ineffective. Non-benzodiazepine anxiolytics such as buspirone are non-cross-tolerant with the benzodiazepines and do not help withdrawal. Some anecdotal reports have suggested that carbamazepine might be effective and phenobarbitone has been advocated.

Psychological support is most important. The treating physician should maintain close contact with the patient during withdrawal, and in the initial stages the patient should be seen at least weekly. With an in-patient daily contact has been found to be useful. At these meetings the physician should show that he understands the problems of withdrawal and be ready to offer guidance on non-medical as well as medical issues. The patient frequently displays numerous misconceptions and negative expectations about tranquillizers and withdrawal; these need to be elicited, identified, and corrected within a broadly educational framework.

The patient needs most advice concerning the management of the withdrawal syndrome itself. Most symptoms can be dealt with by reassurance and simple practical advice. With more persistent difficulties, the patient should be asked to keep a diary so that he may monitor particular symptoms that may provide important clues to the source of the difficulty. During the withdrawal period the patient is likely to attribute almost all physical and psychological changes s/he experiences to the withdrawal. This simplistic view must be corrected, for the patient may otherwise come to have unrealistic expectations about the likely outcome.

Formal psychological help has not yet been shown to be particularly effective. Relaxation treatment and training in anxiety management skills in the framework of group therapy is only moderately useful.

An important determinant of success in withdrawal seems to be the social support received by the patient. The process of withdrawal needs to be explained to the spouse, and in some cases children, and their support elicited whenever possible. In the absence of (or in addition to) family support the patient may find local self-help groups a useful adjunct.

However, the best way of avoiding dependence is by thoughtful prescribing. The duration of prescription of benzodiazepines should be decided in advance and set at a short period at the lowest possible dose. Intermittent flexible dosage should be encouraged, as it should result in lower total intake and a reduced dependence risk, and possible non-pharmacological interventions should be seriously considered. These considerations are particularly important in patients requiring hypnotics. Benzodiazepines should not be prescribed for normal people at times of acute stress such as bereavement or divorce, and a recent study found brief counselling by general practitioners to be as effective as benzodiazepines in cases of minor affective disorder.

CONCLUSIONS

Our perception of benzodiazepine withdrawal has moved from dismissing it as a minor abstinence syndrome to issuing official warnings about the dangers of withdrawal. It is now clear that a substantial proportion of chronic use is not justifiable in terms of the chronic or recurrent nature of anxiety disorders but reflects a dependence syndrome. Primary care practitioners are becoming increasingly adept at exploiting techniques to cope with anxiety disorders without resorting to tranquillizers. Anxiolytic benzodiazepines should be reserved for the short-term relief of anxiety which is disabling, severe or subjecting the individual to unacceptable distress.

FURTHER READING

Ashton, H. (1984) 'Benzodiazepine withdrawal: an unfinished story', *British Medical Journal* 288: 1135–40.

Busto, U., Sellers, E.M., Naranjo, C.A., Cappell, H., Sanchez-Craig, M. and Sykora, K. (1986) 'Withdrawal reaction after long-term therapeutic use of benzodiazepines', *The New England Journal of Medicine* 315: 854–9.

Higgitt, A.C., Lader, M.H. and Fonagy, P. (1985) 'Clinical management of benzodiazepine dependence', *British Medical Journal* 291: 688–90.

Petursson, H. and Lader, M.H. (1981) *Dependence on Tranquillizers*, Maudsley Monograph No. 28, Oxford: Oxford University Press.

Royal College of Psychiatrists (1988) 'Benzodiazepines and dependence: a College statement', *Bulletin of the Royal College of Psychiatrists* 12: 107–8.

Woods, J.H., Katz, J.L. and Winger, G. (1987) 'Abuse liability of benzodiazepines', *Pharmacological Reviews* 39: 251–419.

CROSS REFERENCES

Chapter 15

Tobacco smoking: an everyday drug addiction

Martin J. Jarvis

Tobacco use presents formidable problems throughout the world. Although consumption is now declining slowly in advanced industrial nations, it is increasing in developing countries. Cigarette smoking causes 350,000 deaths each year in the USA and 100,000 in the UK. Because the health effects, particularly lung cancer, are strongly related to duration of the habit, countries where smoking is on the increase will experience their tobacco epidemic in years to come. On present trends there will be more than 3,500,000 cases of lung cancer worldwide each year by the year 2025, of which more than 80 per cent will be in developing countries.

Within individuals, smoking is notorious for its tenacity. Most smokers want to give up, and try, often many times, to do so. Still the proportion who succeed is disappointingly low. In the UK, only one in three of those who have ever smoked cigarettes regularly give up before the age of sixty. Even those with direct personal experience of serious health consequences continue to smoke. As many as 38 per cent of smokers who have suffered a heart attack relapse to smoking while still in hospital, on average within 48 hours of coming out of intensive care.

Whilst smoking is a multifaceted issue, with important economic, social, psychological and political aspects, there is now an emerging consensus that at the heart of the problem lies the drug nicotine. This view received official endorsement with the publication of the 1988 Report of the US Surgeon General, entitled *Nicotine Addiction* (US Department of Health and Human Services, 1988).

NICOTINE AS AN ADDICTIVE DRUG

The Surgeon General concluded that nicotine is addictive in the same sense as heroin and cocaine, drugs that have generally been regarded as possessing a more significant dependence potential. The evidence leading to this conclusion can be summarized as follows:

1 Under appropriate reward schedules, nicotine functions as a robust primary reinforcer in animal self-administration paradigms.
2 Nicotine is a powerful psychoactive drug, acting at many sites in the brain and elsewhere. Chronic exposure to nicotine induces an increase in the number of brain nicotinic cholinergic receptors.
3 Nicotine has features which could provide the basis for both positively and negatively rewarding effects in humans. It is subjectively pleasurable and can enhance mood and performance. A well-defined withdrawal syndrome has an onset within 12 hours of the last cigarette and persists for several weeks. It is

alleviated by nicotine replacement but not placebo. Relief of incipient withdrawal effects could provide a powerful motive for continued use of tobacco.

4 Tolerance to nicotine's actions has been well established. Much of this is of the acute form, but chronic tolerance to the aversive effects experienced by novice smokers is also evident.

5 Compulsive use of tobacco is the norm. Although a small minority (5 per cent or so) of smokers smoke less than five cigarettes per day or on an intermittent basis, the typical smoker smokes about a pack of cigarettes each day, spaces those cigarettes at roughly equal intervals through the day, and rarely goes for as long as a day without smoking. In a recent study, patients seeking treatment for an alcohol or drug problem were asked to compare cigarettes with their main drug. Seventy-four per cent reported that cigarettes would be as hard to give up as their problem substance; 57 per cent said that cigarettes would be harder to give up; 45 per cent of cocaine users said that their urges to use cigarettes were as strong or stronger than their urges to use cocaine (Kozlowski *et al.*, 1989). Smokers frequently persist in their habit despite serious personal cost in the form of emphysema, limb amputation, laryngectomy, heart disease and lung cancer.

PATTERNS OF TOBACCO USE

Tobacco is burnt in cigarettes, pipes and cigars; taken nasally as finely ground 'dry' snuff, and orally as 'wet' snuff and chewing tobacco. The common feature is that all these different products and routes of administration permit the absorption of significant amounts of nicotine into the bloodstream. Absorption through the lungs is particularly efficient. Nicotine reaches the brain within seven seconds of puffing and inhaling the smoke from a cigarette, faster than uptake from intravenous injection. Once absorbed, nicotine is rapidly taken up by the brain and tissues throughout the body. It has an initial distributional half-life in blood of about ten minutes, and a terminal half-life of about two hours. This reflects metabolism to a pharmacologically inert form, cotinine, in the liver, and some excretion of nicotine unchanged in the urine (Benowitz, 1988).

The unfiltered cigarettes of the 1950s and earlier which yielded up to 30 mg of tar have now been superseded by filter-tipped brands of much lower delivery. Low-tar brands yielding less than 10 mg tar and 1 mg nicotine hold about 20 per cent of the UK market, with the great bulk of the remainder being accounted for by brands yielding between 10 and 15 mg tar and about 1.3 mg nicotine. The putative health benefits of smoking low-yielding brands is a subject of continuing controversy. It has become apparent that smokers regulate the amount they puff and inhale in response to changes in cigarette delivery (so-called 'nicotine titration'), with the result that measured smoke intakes from low-yielding cigarettes differ little if at all from those from higher-yielding brands.

EFFECTS OF NICOTINE ON MOOD AND PERFORMANCE

Nicotine's effects are subtle and do not draw attention to the fact that the user is taking a drug. This is perhaps one reason why it has taken so long to recognize cigarette smoking as a drug-taking behaviour. Unlike other drugs of abuse, nicotine rarely disrupts behaviour through intoxication. Overdosage tends to be self-limiting, in that the range of blood concentrations associated with desired effects is quite narrow, and higher levels quickly induce nausea and vomiting. Smokers maintain individually characteristic blood nicotine profiles over time, and regulate intake rather precisely to avoid exceeding preferred levels. At normal smoking levels, there is no impairment of the ability to socialize appropriately or of work performance.

Smokers' self-reports indicate that nicotine acts as a kind of mood regulator. While the pharmacological profile is that of a stimulant, smokers say, paradoxically, that it can both stimulate and sedate. They smoke to keep themselves going when working or to pep themselves up when bored. But they also report the strongest urges to smoke when emotionally upset or stressed. Even among teenaged novice smokers, the most common subjective effect of smoking reported is that of calming the nerves.

Laboratory studies have shown that nicotine enhances performance on simple tasks of psychomotor speed in non-smokers, and improves sustained vigilance in smokers. At present it is unclear whether these latter effects represent a real improvement in performance, or are merely a reversal of deprivation-induced deficits, since perforce the experiments are carried out after overnight abstinence from cigarettes. There is no evidence that smokers in general outperform non-smokers on any cognitive or performance tasks, although there is abundant evidence that smokers' abilities are impaired, at least in the short term, when they abstain from cigarettes.

THE SMOKING CAREER

Onset of cigarette smoking typically occurs in adolescence between the ages of 11 and 15. The profile of the young smoker is consistent with the idea that for many smoking represents 'anticipation of adulthood' among those who tend to be achieving less at school, have lower self-esteem, and are inclined to be generally rebellious. Children who take up smoking are also more likely to use other drugs, including alcohol. As many as 90 per cent of children who smoke more than two or three cigarettes go on to become regular smokers. Although children take up smoking for mainly psychosocial reasons, pharmacological motives soon achieve prominence. Nicotine intake per cigarette in teenage smokers is similar to that found in adults. Within a year or two of starting to smoke, many of these young people attempt to quit, but report withdrawal difficulties similar to those experienced by adults.

Levels of smoke intake characteristic of dependent adult smokers are reached by the late teens. This reflects higher cigarette consumption due to increased spending power. There is no evidence of any sex difference in smoke intake, although women tend to smoke fewer cigarettes per day than men.

With the widespread public awareness of the health effects, most smokers are now 'dissonant', in the sense that they would like to give up (at least if they could do so easily). But for most, motivation to quit remains fairly weak until the late thirties or forties, when effects on personal health begin to become apparent. Only one in three become permanent ex-smokers before the age of sixty, with no difference in cessation rates between male and female smokers.

SMOKING WITHDRAWAL

Within under a day of stopping cigarettes, smokers manifest a range of withdrawal symptoms (West, 1984). These are predominantly affective in nature, and comparison with placebo has shown that they are attributable to loss of nicotine rather than behavioural elements of the habit. Grossly observable behavioural changes are absent, but there is a decline of about 15 beats per minute in heart rate and reductions in levels of several hormones. Changes in mood include irritability, depression, restlessness, and difficulty in concentrating. Sleep is frequently disturbed, and there are strong cravings for cigarettes. The mood changes largely resolve within the first month, but increased hunger and appetite persists for at least three months, and may in the long term be one of the most difficult withdrawal effects with which to cope (Gross and Stitzer, 1989). Increased appetite appears not to apply to all food, but is manifested as a specific preference for sweet-tasting foods. Whether because of increased calorie intake, or because of removal of an effect of nicotine on metabolic rate, ex-smokers gain on average about 6 lb over the first year off cigarettes.

TREATMENT APPROACHES

Two broad classes of interventions designed to help smokers give up can be distinguished. Motivational approaches increase desire and intention to stop, while treatment methods offer specific strategies to overcome dependence (Jarvis and Russell, 1989). Mass media interventions and health education campaigns, which are primarily motivational in content, have been successful in making many smokers want to quit, but their effectiveness has been limited by the extent to which nicotine dependence constitutes a block for many smokers. Brief face-to-face advice by general practitioners given in the course of their everyday contact with patients induces a small (but clinically worthwhile) percentage of mainly light smokers to give up (Russell *et al.*, 1979), and the value of health professionals as smoking therapists might be increased by the availability of effective aids to overcome dependence. Despite much research, few treatment methods have been shown to be more effective than simple attention-placebo. One exception is nicotine replacement, as exemplified by nicotine chewing gum. Given in the context of group support, with adequate guidance and expectations, the gum alleviates withdrawal symptoms and has approximately doubled long-term clinic success rates from 15–20 per cent to 30–40 per cent. It has proved less successful in brief interventions in primary care, possibly because of inadequate attention to the critical issues of patient instructions and expectations. Promising new nicotine replacement methods currently being evaluated include transdermal delivery through skin patches and a nasal nicotine spray. Treatment methods are covered in detail in Chapter 40 by Petr Hajek.

REFERENCES

Benowitz, N.L. (1988) 'Pharmacologic aspects of cigarette smoking and nicotine addiction', *New England Journal of Medicine* 319: 1318–30.

Gross, J. and Stitzer, M.L. (1989) 'Nicotine replacement: ten-week effects on tobacco withdrawal symptoms', *Psychopharmacology* 98: 334–41.

Jarvis, M.J. and Russell, M.A.H. (1989) 'Treatment for the cigarette smoker', *International Review of Psychiatry* 1: 139–47.

Kozlowski, L.T., Wilkinson, A., Skinner, W., Kent, C., Franklin, T. and Pope, M. (1989) 'Comparing tobacco cigarette dependence with other drug dependencies', *Journal of the American Medical Association* 261: 898–901.

Russell, M.A.H., Wilson, C., Taylor, C. and Baker, C.D. (1979) 'Effect of general practitioners' advice against smoking', *British Medical Journal* 2: 231–5.

US Department of Health and Human Services (1988) *Nicotine Addiction: a Report of the Surgeon General*, Washington, DC: USDHHS.

West, R.J. (1984) 'Psychology and pharmacology in cigarette withdrawal', *Journal of Psychosomatic Research* 28: 379–86.

CROSS REFERENCES

Chapter 16

Volatile substance abuse

R.J. Flanagan, T.J. Meredith and J.D. Ramsey

The inhalation of volatile substances for recreational purposes ('glue sniffing', solvent abuse, volatile substance abuse (VSA)) is not a new phenomenon. Many early anaesthetics (diethyl ether, chloroform, nitrous oxide) were first inhaled deliberately to experience pleasurable sensations such as disinhibition and euphoria. Nowadays, solvents from adhesives (notably toluene), typewriter correcting fluids and thinners (usually 1,1,1-trichloroethane), 'butane' gas and pain relieving (PR) sprays and other aerosols are popular (Flanagan *et al.*, 1990) although a range of other products may also be encountered (Table 16.1).

MODES OF ABUSE OF VOLATILE SUBSTANCES

The physical form of particular products often determines the mode of abuse. Adhesives are usually poured into small plastic bags such as empty potato crisp packets. The top is gathered together and placed over the mouth and the vapour inhaled. Exhaled air is also re-breathed and carbon dioxide build-up (hypercapnia) and lack of oxygen (hypoxia) are added to the effects of the solvent. Skin contact with the adhesive may cause perioral eczema, a characteristic rash around the mouth (Meredith *et al.*, 1989). Typewriter correcting fluid and other liquids containing a volatile component may be poured onto fabric (a handkerchief or coat sleeve) and the vapour inhaled. Solvents may also be poured into containers such as empty washing-up liquid or bleach bottles prior to inhaling the vapour. White spirit and paraffin, although cheap and readily available, are not sufficiently volatile to be abused in this way. Petrol (gasoline), on the other hand, is commonly misused, especially in developing countries, and this can cause lead encephalopathy from absorption of tetra-ethyl lead used as 'anti-knock' (Meredith *et al.*, 1989).

Plastic bags may also be filled with gas from aerosol products, fire extinguishers or fuel gases. In addition, these two latter products may be inhaled directly from their containers. Aerosols are usually liquid or solid suspensions sprayed from containers containing a propellant gas; at room temperature 1 volume of liquefied propellant can give 200–300 volumes of vapour. The intended use of the product is immaterial, although those containing a high proportion of propellant, for example PR spray, deodorants and fly sprays, are preferred to those with relatively little propellant such as shaving foam. If some of the constituents are not respirable, as with aluminium chlorhydrate in antiperspirant sprays, then the product may be bubbled through water and the vapour collected. Alternatively, the product may be sprayed into a plastic bag and the aerosol allowed to settle.

Domestic natural gas is not abused, partly because it is not portable but primarily

Table 16.1 Some products which may be abused by inhalation

Product	Principal volatile components
Adhesives	
Balsa wood cement	Ethyl acetate
Contact adhesives	Toluene
Cycle tyre repair cement	Toluene and xylenes
PVC cement	Trichloroethylene
Aerosols	
Air freshener	Halons and butane
Deodorants, antiperspirants	Halons and butane
Fly spray	Halons and butane
Hair lacquer	Halons and butane
Local analgesic spray	Halons 11/12
Paint	Halons, butane and esters
Anaesthetic agents	
Gaseous	Nitrous oxide
Liquid	Halothane, enflurane, isoflurane
Local	Halons 11/12, ethyl chloride
Nail varnish remover	Acetone and esters
Domestic spot removers and dry cleaners	1,1,1-Trichloroethane
	Tetrachloroethylene
	Trichloroethylene
Commercial dry cleaning and degreasing agents	1,1,1-Trichloroethane
	Trichloroethylene
	Tetrachloroethylene
Fire extinguishers	BCF, Halons 11/12
Fuel gases	
Cigarette lighter refills	n-Butane and iso-butane
Butane	n-Butane and iso-butane
Propane	Propane and butanes
Paint stripper	Dichloromethane
	Toluene
Typewriter correcting fluid and thinners	1,1,1-Trichloroethane

because the principal component, methane, is not narcotic. However, the same is not true of the fuel gases (largely butane) used in cigarette lighters, small blow torches and camping gas stoves, and from larger containers (Calor Gas). These products are widely available generally in small, inexpensive packs, and are highly attractive to misusers. Cigarette lighter refills are sometimes abused by clenching the nozzle between the teeth but this carries the risk of a jet of fluid cooled to below −20°C causing cold burns to the throat and lungs. Consequent mucosal oedema may be marked and can cause respiratory difficulties. In addition, rapid chilling of the larynx may cause death because stimulation of the vagal nerve causes slowing of the heart and cardiac standstill.

PREVALENCE OF VSA IN THE UK

In secondary-school children selected at random from two London boroughs during 1984–6, Chadwick *et al.* (1989) reported a mean prevalence of previous or current VSA of 5.9 per cent. The rate ranged from 0.5 per cent to 9.6 per cent over the 16 schools surveyed with no marked sex difference. However, if subjects who had not been 'intoxicated' were excluded, the mean prevalence rate fell to 3.6 per cent. Similarly, in a survey of all but one of 28 secondary schools in an area of South Wales in 1985, of 4,766 pupils aged 11 to 19 years, 6.1 per cent had tried VSA and a further 0.7 per cent were current abusers; 3 pupils (0.1 per cent) reported 'sniffing' every day (Cooke *et al.*, 1988). Of those who had experimented, 58 per cent had already 'sniffed' by age 13 years. Two other recent studies have reported higher prevalence rates but the criteria used to select the schools surveyed are unclear. In any event, 3.5–10 per cent of young people in the UK have at least experimented with VSA and current users comprise some 0.5–1 per cent of the secondary school population.

Several factors contribute to the continuing popularity of VSA. The products misused are cheap and readily available. The packaging, for example that of typewriter correction fluid and thinner, is convenient and the packages are easily concealed or their possession is ostensibly legitimate. Unlike under-age drinking, VSA is not illegal and both the onset of effects and recovery can be rapid, a distinct advantage because a child can 'sniff' after school and still return home sober.

DETECTION OF VSA

The recognition of abusers can be difficult since many of the manifestations of VSA may appear similar to the normal problems of adolescence. However, a smell of solvent on the breath, adhesive marks on clothing and sores around the mouth should arouse suspicion, as should finding domestic products out of context (lighter refills under the bed) or in unusual quantities (Meredith *et al.*, 1989). Laboratory services may also help; many compounds can be detected in blood (using headspace gas chromatography) if the sample is obtained within two days or so of exposure. The exception is petrol which is a mixture of hydrocarbons; the blood concentrations of each component are usually too low to detect even after massive exposure.

If blood is sampled for laboratory analysis, certain simple precautions should be taken. The container should be made of glass and should preferably have a cap lined with metal foil. It should be well-filled and, ideally, should only be opened when required for analysis and then only when cold (4°C). However, samples submitted in far from ideal conditions may still give useful qualitative results (Meredith *et al.*, 1989). The measurement of urinary metabolites may extend the time during which exposure can be detected but, of the compounds commonly abused, only toluene, xylene, trichloroethylene and, to a lesser extent, tetrachloroethylene and 1,1,1-tri-chloroethane have suitable metabolites.

CLINICAL FEATURES

VSA can quickly give rise to pleasurable sensations such as feelings of well-being and euphoria. However, prolonged or intensive VSA often leads to less pleasant and more dangerous effects. Changes in perception may precede bizarre and frightening hallucinations, both visual and auditory. Ringing in the ears (tinnitus) is often reported while loss of balance (ataxia) and confusion may lead to accidents. Experienced abusers may deliberately use high doses to achieve a desired effect which is often hallucinations. Higher doses still may lead to unconsciousness with the attendant risk of death. Vomiting with the risk of suffocation from inhalation of stomach contents can occur at any stage.

There have been many isolated reports of chronic, sometimes permanent, damage from VSA affecting the central nervous system, heart, liver and kidneys, but most fail to prove a causal relationship. Nevertheless, some toxicity can be predicted because of that seen in individuals exposed to volatile substances during the manufacture and industrial use of these compounds. The evidence suggests that only a small minority of volatile substance abusers progress to heavy alcohol or illicit drug use but further data are needed (Edeh, 1989).

MORTALITY FROM VSA IN THE UK

Mortality in the UK has increased from 2 to 4 per annum in the early 1970s to 134 in 1988 and the underlying trend is still upward. Deaths occurred irrespective of social class and in all parts of the UK. The age at death ranged from 11 to 76 years but most (72 per cent) were aged less than 20 years (Flanagan et al., 1990). In contrast to the findings of prevalence studies, most (90 per cent) deaths occurred in males. In 19 per cent of deaths there was no history of previous VSA. The principal groups of compounds encountered were fuel gases, solvents in adhesives, other solvents and aerosol propellants. The first three groups each accounted for about 30 per cent of deaths (Flanagan et al., 1990). The exact mechanism of death is seldom clear although deaths from solvents in adhesives (mainly toluene) are much more likely to be from trauma (Figure 16.1) than from so-called 'direct' toxic effects. However, deaths from VSA, albeit some 100 per annum in the UK, are relatively few given the number of abusers indicated by prevalence studies.

LEGISLATION CONCERNING VSA

Actions have been taken against volatile substance abusers under the Public Order Act 1936, the Criminal Damage Act and Section 5 of the Road Traffic Act. Bye-laws such as those controlling litter and a British Rail bye-law which makes it an offence to be intoxicated on railway property have also been enforced. Offenders are safe from prosecution under the Licensing Act of 1872 and the Criminal Justice Act of 1967 because it has been ruled that VSA does not cause drunkenness.

The 1985 Supply of Intoxicating Substances Act made it an offence to sell, or offer for sale, substances to people under the age of 18 if the vendor knows or has reasonable grounds for believing that those substances are likely to be inhaled to achieve intoxication. A newsagent was sentenced to three months in prison for selling typewriter correcting fluid thinners to a 16-year-old who later died. On appeal, the sentence was increased to four months' imprisonment. The Solvent Abuse (Scotland) Act gives the Reporter powers to act in cases where children are involved. Scottish

Figure 16.1 Mortality from volatile substance abuse in the UK 1971–87 by mechanism of death

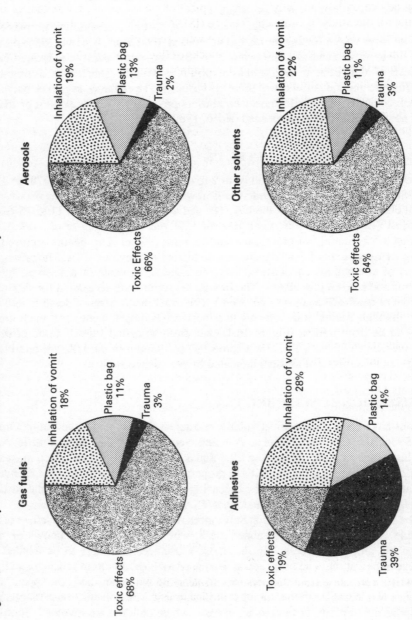

Gas fuels

Inhalation of vomit 18%
Plastic bag 11%
Trauma 3%
Toxic effects 68%

Aerosols

Inhalation of vomit 19%
Plastic bag 13%
Trauma 2%
Toxic Effects 66%

Adhesives

Inhalation of vomit 28%
Plastic bag 14%
Trauma 39%
Toxic effects 19%

Other solvents

Inhalation of vomit 22%
Plastic bag 11%
Trauma 3%
Toxic effects 64%

Source: Ramsey *et al.*, 1989

common law was employed against two shopkeepers who were sentenced (1983) to three years in prison, reduced on appeal, for supplying sniffing 'kits'.

PREVENTION OF VSA

The initial response to the problems posed by VSA was to try to reduce mortality by giving advice on how to 'sniff' safely. Typical of such a strategy was that of the Institute for the Study of Drug Dependence (ISDD) (1984): aerosol misuse was said to be particularly hazardous and warnings were given about 'sniffing' alone or in dangerous places such as on the roofs of blocks of flats. Although this approach was not evaluated systematically it was probably appropriate when dealing with habitual abusers. Voluntary restrictions were also placed on the sale of products such as contact adhesives and cigarette lighter refills. Since then, the main thrust has been in the field of education, not only of children and their parents and teachers, but also of retailers and health care professionals; excellent education packs have been produced (Lee, 1989), and the ISDD (1990a, 1990b) has produced booklets aimed at health care professionals and parents, respectively. In addition, some products have been reformulated to make them less amenable to abuse. Thus, the typewriter correction fluid Tippex appeared as a water-based product ('School and Study') but this formulation is slow to dry and thus less popular in normal use. To address this problem further 'solvent-free' products have been marketed.

CONCLUSIONS

We now have a reasonably clear picture of the volatile substances and products abused and the modes of abuse although the reason the practice is so widespread and enduring remains uncertain. School surveys have indicated the population at risk and mortality data are now collected and processed systematically. The annual VSA-related death rate is still increasing, although this could reflect increasing use of relatively dangerous products (cigarette lighter refills, aerosols) rather than an increased prevalence of VSA. Our knowledge of the chronic hazards of VSA is much less well developed, and the disruption caused to the families and friends of abusers and to the community at large must not be neglected and should be studied further.

NOTE

The views expressed in this article are those of the authors alone and in no way commit the Department of Health.

REFERENCES

Chadwick, O., Anderson, H.R., Bland, M. and Ramsey, J. (1989) 'Neuropsychological consequences of volatile substance abuse: a population based study of secondary school pupils', *British Medical Journal* 298: 1679–84.
Cooke, B.R., Evans, D.A. and Farrow, S.C. (1988) 'Solvent misuse in secondary school children: a prevalence study', *Community Medicine* 10: 8–13.
Edeh, J. (1989) 'Volatile substance abuse in relation to alcohol and illicit drugs: psychosocial perspectives', *Human Toxicology* 8: 313–17.

Flanagan, R.J., Ruprah, M., Meredith, T.J. and Ramsey, J.D. (1990) 'An introduction to the clinical toxicology of volatile substances', *Drug Safety* 5: 359–83.

Institute for the Study of Drug Dependence (1984) *Teaching about a volatile situation: suggested health education strategies for minimising casualties associated with solvent sniffing*, London: Institute for the Study of Drug Dependence.

—— (1990a) *Working with solvent sniffers*, London: Institute for the Study of Drug Dependence.

—— (1990b) *Parents: what you need to know about solvent sniffing*, London: Institute for the Study of Drug Dependence.

Lee, J.T. (1989) 'Volatile substance abuse within a health education context', *Human Toxicology* 8: 331–4.

Meredith, T.J., Ruprah, M., Liddle, A. and Flanagan, R.J. (1989) 'Diagnosis and treatment of acute poisoning with volatile substances', *Human Toxicology* 8: 277–86.

CROSS REFERENCES

Chapter 17

Pathological gambling: addiction without a drug

Sheila B. Blume

Games of chance have been popular since prehistoric times. Human beings invented gambling long before they learned to write, but throughout history societies have also been aware of the personal and social problems that accompany gambling and have seen fit to regulate, control or at times try to prohibit this behaviour. The lives of pathological gamblers have entered legend: kings who gambled away their kingdoms, wealthy families brought to ruin, and otherwise upstanding citizens turning to crime. Yet more often pathological gambling involves ordinary families struggling to maintain control while the gambling of one member emotionally and financially bankrupts their lives.

During the past decade there has been a slow but steady growth in clinical interest, professional education, treatment programmes, research and public policy measures aimed at prevention and treatment of pathological gambling. This is particularly true in the United States where gambling, both legal and illegal, has become a $240,000,000 a year industry, and where an estimated 1.5 per cent of the adult population are probable compulsive gamblers and another 2.8 per cent have gambling problems (Volberg and Steadman, 1988).

In 1980, the American Psychiatric Association included pathological gambling in its Diagnostic and Statistical Manual (DSM-III) for the first time. The diagnostic criteria were rewritten in the 1987 revision of the Manual (DSM-III-R), and are now almost exactly parallel to the criteria for psychoactive substance dependence. This revision reflects the growing acceptance and utility of the addictive disease model of pathological gambling (Blume, 1988), encouraged by the growth of Gamblers Anonymous since its establishment in 1957 (Gamblers Anonymous, 1984).

NATURE AND COURSE OF PATHOLOGICAL GAMBLING

This disorder is best conceptualized as dependence on the 'action' of gambling, an aroused, euphoric state compared by compulsive gamblers to the 'high' derived from cocaine or other drugs.

Gambling usually begins as a recreational activity during adolescence. The pathological gambler becomes interested in gambling and often begins as a winner. Males, offspring of problem gamblers and children of alcoholic parents are at increased risk. In about half of the cases, an upsurge in gambling activity begins with a big win, a sum equal to half a year's income or more (Custer, 1984).

With or without a big win, developing pathological gamblers derive an increasing proportion of their self-esteem from seeing themselves as smart or lucky gamblers. They become dependent upon gambling both as a solution to life problems and a remedy for dysphoric states. Bets must be gradually increased in size and frequency in order to produce the desired psychological effects. Much time and effort are devoted to handicapping, studying the sports page or following the market. As one gambler put it, 'When I'm not occupied with gambling I'm preoccupied with it.' Time away from friends, family and work and an unreasonable attitude of optimism characterize this early period. This attitude is sustained by concentrating on wins and making excuses for (or even denying) losses. The gambler often cannot account for money claimed to have been won.

The losing phase often begins with the kind of chance loss experienced by anyone who gambles. To compulsive gamblers, however, losses represent severe injuries to self-esteem and instead of cutting back they begin to 'chase losses', staking more in an effort to recoup money lost. This kind of betting accelerates losses. There are often ups and downs, compared by families to an 'emotional roller coaster'. However, the general trend is towards increasing debt and deterioration of social, vocational and interpersonal functioning. Family possessions, savings and legitimate sources of borrowing are exhausted.

Compulsive gamblers who have reached the desperation phase may engage in behaviours inconsistent with their previous moral standards, such as lying, embezzling and forgery. These are justified as temporary expedients until the next big win. Financial crises lead to the plea for a 'bailout', a large loan or gift meant to relieve immediate pressure, usually in return for a promise to give up gambling entirely. The bailout, however, like a detoxification for a heroin addict who wants to decrease his dosage, leads to more of the same. In both cases, there is an impairment of control and a craving stimulated either by dysphoric states or by exposure to others engaging in the behaviour. For both, abstinence is the appropriate treatment goal. Most compulsive gamblers who enter treatment or Gamblers Anonymous (GA) do so in the desperation phase. Depression and anxiety symptoms are common. Suicide attempts and other desperate acts, such as overt criminal behaviour, are also common.

There is also a special relationship between psychoactive substance dependence and compulsive gambling. In a recent study of our own, 9 per cent of 458 alcohol- and drug-dependent in-patients qualified for a lifetime diagnosis of pathological gambling and an additional 10 per cent had experienced gambling problems but did not meet full criteria. Most of these patients had not reached the desperation stage in their gambling. Although these patients tended to drink, take drugs and gamble at the same time, many reported patterns of increased gambling when they were separated from their drug for some reason. These patients are in danger of both relapse to alcohol/drug use if they gamble and to 'switching addictions' if their gambling problems are not addressed in treatment (Lesieur et al., 1986).

The causes of this disorder are unknown, although physiological, psychological and sociocultural factors have been thought to play a role.

CASEFINDING AND DIAGNOSIS

A convenient screening tool for the identification of pathological gamblers in clinical caseloads is the South Oaks Gambling Screen (SOGS) (Lesieur and Blume,

1988). It is a questionnaire based on DSM-III criteria and cross-validated to DSM-III-R. It can be given either as a paper-and-pencil test or in an interview format. A score of 5 or more out of 20 indicates probable pathological gambling, with 1 to 4 indicating some gambling problem. A copy of the SOGS and its score sheet are appended to this chapter. Subjects identified by the SOGS should undergo further investigation, including interviews with family members, to determine whether DSM-III-R criteria are met. This requires a minimum of four of nine symptoms which include frequent preoccupation, gambling larger amounts over a longer time than intended, increasing the size and frequency of bets to achieve the desired excitement, restlessness or irritability if unable to gamble, chasing losses, repeated efforts to cut down or stop, gambling interfering frequently with meeting obligations, gambling causing the sacrifice of important activity, and continuing to gamble in spite of mounting gambling-related problems.

TREATMENT

Treatment involves the following elements:

1   A thorough assessment of additional psychiatric and substance abuse diagnoses, as well as family, health, vocational and legal problems. These problems must be prioritized and addressed while the treatment of the pathological gambling proceeds.
2   Education about the addictive process, including cross-addiction and switching addictions.
3   Psychotherapy/counselling (group and/or individual) to help the patient attain abstinence and avoid relapse. This involves developing stable internal motivation for recovery, learning to handle dysphoric states and life problems without gambling, and rebuilding relationships and self-esteem. The pathological gambler is greatly helped by facing the entire amount of his/her indebtedness, working out a budget with his/her spouse, and repaying gradually. This process restores self-esteem, while declaring bankruptcy or arranging for family members to pay debts is a less helpful solution. The Fellowship of Gamblers Anonymous has experience in developing such repayment plans. GA offers group support, abstinent role models, opportunity to help others and a lifelong spiritually-based programme for living.
4   Family education and counselling are critical to recovery. Sometimes family members need referral for medical or psychiatric help. All should be referred to Gamanon for support and follow-up.

Few comprehensive follow-up studies have attempted to evaluate the effectiveness of treatment. Most of the patients presently seeking help do so late in the course of the illness. As research on this disorder advances – improved treatment, prevention, and earlier identification – a better chance of recovery will result. However, our current knowledge is sufficient to intervene successfully with many compulsive gamblers and their families.

REFERENCES

Blume, S.B. (1988) 'Compulsive gambling and the medical model', *Journal of Gambling Behavior* 3: 237–47.

Custer, R.L. (1984) 'Profile of the pathological gambler', *Journal of Clinical Psychiatry* 45: 35–8.

Gamblers Anonymous (1984) *Sharing Recovery Through Gamblers Anonymous*, Los Angeles, California: Gamblers Anonymous.

Lesieur, H.R. and Blume, S.B. (1988) 'The South Oaks Gambling Screen (SOGS): a new instrument for the identification of pathological gamblers', *American Journal of Psychiatry* 144: 1184–8.

Lesieur, H.L., Blume, S.B. and Zoppa, R.M. (1986) 'Alcoholism, drug abuse and gambling', *Alcoholism: Clinical and Experimental Research* 10: 33–8.

Volberg, R.A. and Steadman, H.J. (1988) 'Refining prevalence estimates of pathological gambling', *American Journal of Psychiatry* 145: 502–5.

CROSS REFERENCES

Chapter 4   Psychological theories of addiction
             Robert West
Chapter 38   Self-help groups
             Brian Wells

APPENDIX 1

SOUTH OAKS GAMBLING SCREEN

Name   Date

1. Please indicate which of the following types of gambling you have done in your lifetime. For each type, mark one answer: 'not at all,' 'less than once a week,' or 'once a week or more.'

	not at all	less than once a week	once a week or more	
a.	____	____	____	played cards for money
b.	____	____	____	bet on horses, dogs or other animals (at OTB, the track or with a bookie)
c.	____	____	____	bet on sports (parlay cards, with bookie, or at Jai Alai)
d.	____	____	____	played dice games (including craps, over and under or other dice games) for money
e.	____	____	____	went to casino (legal or otherwise)
f.	____	____	____	played the numbers or bet on lotteries
g.	____	____	____	played bingo
h.	____	____	____	played the stock and/or commodities market
i	____	____	____	played slot machines, poker machines or other gambling machines
j.	____	____	____	bowled, shot pool, played golf or some other game of skill for money

2. What is the largest amount of money you have ever gambled with on any one day?

___never have gambled   ___more than $100 up to $1000
___$1 or less   ___more than $1000 up to $10,000
___more than $1 up to $10   ___more than $10,000
___more than $10 up to $100

3. Do (did) your parents have a gambling problem?

____both my father and mother gamble(d) too much
____my father gambles (or gambled) too much
____my mother gambles (or gambled) too much
____neither one gambles too much

4. When you gamble, how often do you go back another day to win back money you lost?

____never
____some of the time (less than half the time I lose)
____most of the time I lose
____every time I lose

5. Have you ever claimed to be winning money gambling but weren't really? In fact, you lost?

____never (or never gamble)
____yes, less than half the time I lost
____yes, most of the time

6. Do you feel you have ever had a problem with gambling?

____no
____yes, in the past but not now
____yes

7. Did you ever gamble more than you intended to?

yes	no

8. Have people criticized your gambling?

yes	no

9. Have you ever felt guilty about the way you gamble or what happens when you gamble?

yes	no

10. Have you ever felt like you would like to stop gambling but didn't think you could?

yes	no

11. Have you ever hidden betting slips, lottery tickets, gambling money, or other signs of gambling from your spouse, children or other important people in your life?

yes	no

12. Have you ever argued with people you live with over how you handle money?

yes	no

13. (If you answered yes to question 12): Have money arguments ever centered on your gambling?

yes	no

14. Have you ever borrowed from someone and not paid them back as a result of your gambling?

yes	no

15. Have you ever lost time from work (or school) due to gambling?

yes	no

16. If you borrowed money to gamble or to pay gambling debts, who or where did you borrow from? (check 'yes' or 'no' for each)

	no	yes
a. from household money	( )	( )
b. from your spouse	( )	( )
c. from other relatives or in-laws	( )	( )

d.	from banks, loan companies or credit unions	( ) ( )
e.	from credit cards	( ) ( )
f.	from loan sharks ('Shylocks')	( ) ( )
g.	you cashed in stocks, bonds or other securities	( ) ( )
h.	you sold personal or family property	( ) ( )
i.	you borrowed on your checking account (passed bad checks)	( ) ( )
j.	you have (had) a credit line with a bookie	( ) ( )
k.	you have (had) a credit line with a casino	( ) ( )

© 1986 South Oaks Foundation

APPENDIX 2

SOUTH OAKS GAMBLING SCREEN SCORE SHEET

Scores on the SOGS are determined by adding up the number of questions which show an 'at risk' response:

Questions 1, 2 & 3 not counted:

_____ Question 4 — most of the time I lose
or
every time I lose

_____ Question 5 — yes, less than half the time I lose
or
yes, most of the time

_____ Question 6 — yes, in the past but not now
yes

_____ Question 7 — yes

_____   "   8 — yes

_____   "   9 — yes

_____   "   10 — yes

_____   "   11 — yes

         "   12 — not counted

_____   "   13 — yes

_____   "   14 — yes

_____   "   15 — yes

_____   "   16a — yes

_____   "   b — yes

_____   "   c — yes

_____   "   d — yes

_____   "   e — yes

_____   "   f — yes

_____   "   g — yes

_____   "   h — yes

_____   "   i — yes

Questions 16j & k not counted

Total = _____   (there are 20 questions which are counted)

0 = no problem
1–4 = some problem
5 or more = probable pathological gambler
©1986 South Oaks Foundation

Health risks and the addictions

Chapter 18

Disease and death caused by tobacco addiction

Keith Ball

Tobacco is one of the greatest causes of preventable disease and death in the world today, and is destined to produce a devastating pandemic unless urgent preventive action is taken. Martin Jarvis (Chapter 15) has clearly shown the strength of the addiction and David Simpson (Chapter 48) has described the essential steps needed to protect the health of future generations. In this chapter I will describe the size of the problem, some of the diseases caused by tobacco addiction and the effects it has had on some individuals whom I have personally observed.

WHO estimates that tobacco leads to at least two and a half million deaths in the world each year, and this number is likely to double within the next twenty years. In India alone it causes between 600,000 and a million deaths yearly (Sanghvi, 1989). It is an important cause of chronic disability and death from a wide range of neoplastic, vascular and respiratory diseases. If effective control measures are not taken tobacco addiction is likely to join AIDS as one of the two major lethal epidemics of the next century. In the UK and the USA, where cigarette use has been widespread for many years, both tobacco consumption and death rates from lung cancer and coronary heart disease are at last beginning to fall. In many countries including East Europe, the USSR, China and most developing nations the peak of the epidemic has not yet been reached. To make matters worse inhabitants of these countries tend to smoke much higher tar cigarettes than in the West, and in some are encouraged to do so by the aggressive promotion of the multinational tobacco companies. From the time tobacco use begins in a population, 30 or 40 years may elapse before the size of the problem becomes apparent, so long is the incubation period of tobacco-related diseases. Governments who encourage tobacco consumption as an easy source of revenue fail to recognize the appalling legacy they are leaving to later generations.

LUNG CANCER

In Western countries cancer of the lung is by far the most important of the cancers caused by tobacco. In the classic study of the smoking habits of British doctors it was shown that heavy smokers had over twenty times the death rate from lung cancer than non-smokers (Doll and Peto, 1976). The risk at the age of 50 is very much greater in those who start smoking before the age of 15 than for the minority who delay doing so until after the age of 20. Where teenage smoking is now increasing, as it is in many developing countries, an epidemic of lung and other cancers is almost inevitable in the years ahead. But the statistics alone tend to obscure some of the individual tragedies.

Prakash, a 62-year-old farmer, complained of cough and severe left chest pain for three months, and was admitted to a Bombay hospital. Radiograph showed a large cancer of his left lung eroding the chest wall which was inoperable. He had smoked 50 bidis a day for the last 45 years. (Bidis are the small cheap conical cigars made of high-tar tobacco smoked by many Indians and known as 'the poor man's smoke'.)

George Mwango, a 48-year-old farmer from Bulawayo, had six children and his wife was again pregnant. For many years he had smoked ten homemade cigarettes daily. He was in hospital because he was too short of breath to work. He had a complete collapse of his left lung due to a bronchial cancer. No treatment was possible and his days were numbered. The outlook for his wife and family was grim.

John, a 38-year-old lorry driver, started smoking at the age of 14 and since then had smoked up to 40 cigarettes a day. He came to a London hospital because he had coughed up blood, and a radiograph confirmed a lung cancer. Within three months the cancer had spread to the brain. He died and left a widow and five children between the ages of three and ten. She was admitted to a mental hospital with severe depression and his children were put into the care of foster parents.

Such patients illustrate not only the individual misery involved but also the social consequences for the family when the bread winner (or indeed the mother) dies.

ORAL CANCER

In the countries of South East Asia cancers of the mouth, tongue and pharynx are even more frequent than lung cancer. In India there are four times as many patients with cancers of the mouth and throat than of the lung. (By contrast in the UK cancer of the lung is far more common than oral cancer.) Oral cancers follow the use of pan (a mixture of tobacco, lime and areca nut), bidis and reverse smoking where some women place the lighted end of the cigar known as chutta inside the mouth.

Ahmed, a 30-year-old packer in a Bombay factory, was unable to swallow and had lost a lot of weight. He had smoked bidis for many years. He pointed to a large lump on the side of his neck. The light from the doctor's head mirror showed an extensive cancer at the back of his throat which was clearly inoperable. Radiotherapy was prescribed, but he was only likely to survive a few weeks.

OTHER CANCERS

Cigarette smoking can also cause cancers of the oesophagus, pancreas and bladder, and in recent years smoking in women has been shown to be an important risk factor for cervical cancer, one of the commonest malignancies in the Third World.

Even in Western countries only a small percentage of cancers caused by tobacco can be cured. In developing countries where the majority of these cancers now occur the chances of cure are remote. Prevention is their only hope.

CARDIOVASCULAR DISEASE

In Western countries cigarettes cause more deaths from coronary heart disease and stroke than from cancers. In men under the age of 45 at least 80 per cent of coronary deaths can be attributed to smoking. In a group of British soldiers under the age of 40 who survived a heart attack 93 per cent smoked an average of twenty-eight cigarettes daily (Lynch *et al.*, 1985). The risk of smoking is particularly great where other factors such as hypertension, raised cholesterol levels or a bad family history are present. Smokers who stop can greatly reduce their risk of a heart attack within a few years. Even after a heart attack stopping smoking can reduce by a half the chance of a fatal or non-fatal relapse. The American Heart Association considered smoking to be the most preventable cause of premature death in the USA.

> David, a 39-year-old HGV (heavy goods vehicle) driver from Liverpool, had just delivered a load of biscuits to a London factory when he collapsed with a sudden severe chest pain. On admission to hospital he was found to have an extensive myocardial infarction (heart attack). He had smoked fifty cigarettes daily and was about 40 pounds overweight. Although he recovered he needed to make major changes in his life style to improve his outlook.

> Mohammed, a wealthy Sudanese business man aged 42, smoked sixty Benson and Hedges cigarettes daily. For some years he had suffered from a duodenal ulcer and had developed angina of effort on walking a short distance. He was two stones overweight and took little exercise. He had severe coronary heart disease.

Coronary heart disease is rapidly increasing amongst the business and professional classes in developing countries and is a common cause of death both in Delhi and Khartoum. Cigarette smoking is an important factor.

PERIPHERAL VASCULAR DISEASE

At least 95 per cent of patients with obstruction to the arteries of their legs – the main reason for amputations – are cigarette smokers. Stopping smoking is by far the most effective treatment and if achieved early in the disease can prevent the need for operation.

> Natoo Patel, an Indian businessman aged 42, had arrived in London from Nairobi eight years earlier when he switched from smoking bidis to cigarettes. For three years he had had pain in his right leg when walking, and on admission to hospital incipient gangrene had developed which led to amputation. Despite this he was unable to stop smoking and when last seen was developing similar symptoms in his left leg.

CHRONIC BRONCHITIS (Chronic Obstructive Lung Disease)

Tobacco smoking is by far the most important cause of this disease, especially in those exposed to atmospheric pollution or a dusty environment. Tests of lung function show that many young smokers are already developing narrowing of their small airways. In a study of 405 schoolchildren cigarette smoking was associated with cough, sputum and shortness of breath on exertion. Stopping smoking can do much to reduce the progress of the disease but unfortunately many fail to do so until they are severely crippled.

> Elizabeth, a 57-year-old woman, had started smoking aged 18 which had resulted in severe chronic bronchitis. She was very short of breath and wrote: 'If people could only imagine the awful distress of trying to carry out everyday tasks such as washing or getting a meal, I am sure no one would ever smoke again.'

Chronic bronchitis is a major cause of prolonged disability caused by smoking especially in men working in polluted industries in developed countries and in women exposed to domestic smoky fires in the Third World, as in Nepal.

REPRODUCTIVE HEALTH

Women who smoke during pregnancy increase the risk of stillbirth and neonatal death, and their children are liable to a small but measurable delay in physical and intellectual development up till the age of eleven years. Indian women who chew tobacco increase their risk of stillbirth threefold especially if they are also malnourished or anaemic (Krishnamurthy, 1989).

Decreased fertility may occur in women who smoke, and the fact that the prevalence of impotence in men who smoke is increased has been attributed to arteriosclerotic changes in the penile arteries. Some studies have shown that smoking reduces the number and mobility of spermatozoa.

> Mary, aged 25, an Irish factory worker, smoked thirty cigarettes a day. She was 20 weeks pregnant when first seen and gave a history of one healthy baby aged four, one termination of pregnancy and one miscarriage. At 36 weeks she was admitted with back pains, ultrasound scan confirmed the absence of a foetal heart beat, intrauterine death was diagnosed and a stillborn infant was delivered. The placenta showed large clots with areas of fibrosis.

PASSIVE SMOKING

It is now known that non-smokers are at risk from inhaling other people's smoke. The smoke from the burning end of the cigarette contains considerably more toxic substances than the smoke breathed out by the smoker. Children whose parents smoke have more coughs and are more likely to have bronchitis and pneumonia than children of non-smokers particularly in the first year of life. It is now accepted that women who do not smoke have an increased risk of lung cancer if their husbands are smokers. It is likely that several hundreds of premature deaths in non-smokers each year in Britain are caused by other people's smoke.

Those who have had experience of the difficulty patients suffer in stopping smoking, even when they have had a heart attack or have the risk of losing a leg, fully accept that the use of tobacco is a true addiction. Doctors who daily see the tragic effects of this addiction on their patients become angry that governments do so little to control tobacco and allow the multinational companies to spend so much on promoting this lethal product.

REFERENCES

Doll, R. and Peto, R. (1976) 'Mortality in relation to smoking: 20 years' observations on British doctors', *British Medical Journal* 290: 1525–36.
Krishnamurthy, S. (1989) 'Tobacco use in pregnancy and reproductive outcome', in L.D. Sanghvi and P. Notani (eds) *Tobacco and Health. The Indian Scene*, Geneva: UICC and Bombay: The Tata Memorial Centre.
Lynch, P., Ineson, N., Jones, K.P., Scott, A.W. and Crawford, I.C. (1985) 'Risk profile of soldiers aged under 40 with coronary heart disease', *British Medical Journal* 290: 1868–9.
Sanghvi, L.D. (1989) 'Introduction', in L.D. Sanghvi and P. Notani (eds) *Tobacco and Health. The Indian Scene*, Geneva: UICC and Bombay: The Tata Memorial Centre.

CROSS REFERENCES

Chapter 19

Physical complications of drug abuse

Michael Farrell

One of the aims of drug treatment services is to foster a more health conscious drug-using population. Thorough physical and psychological assessment may be an important trigger to promoting a process of change. This could lead to less harmful drug use such as non-injecting drug use or preferably to a drug-free state. Increased attention is now focused on physical problems which may be due to human immunodeficiency virus (HIV) infection. As HIV-infected individuals become progressively more immunocompromised they will experience increased rates of infective complications such as pneumonia, septicaemia, endocarditis and tuberculosis. Health planners predict considerable increase in demands on both in-patient and out-patient medical treatment facilities with the spread of HIV in the drug-using population. Mortality rates in the drug-using population without HIV infection are estimated at 1–2 per cent per annum. Cumulative mortality of individuals infected with HIV is still uncertain but is estimated at 80–95 per cent.

TECHNIQUE SPECIFIC HAZARDS

Technique specific hazards are complications due to the mode of drug administration. HIV infection is undoubtedly the dominating complication of injecting drug use. However, there are a wide range of other physical complications. Some of these are directly related to poor sterile technique but others may arise despite careful aseptic precautions as normal skin flora are introduced into the blood stream during intravenous injection. Hepatitis and HIV may be transmitted by the sharing of injecting equipment but the true prevalence and incidence is confounded by the possibility of sexual transmission.

Infections

Skin

Normal skin flora such as *Staphylococcus aureus* and *Streptococcus pyogenes* frequently infect an injection site resulting in cellulitis. If this inflammation extends along the vein it may result in thrombophlebitis. A localized infection results in abscess formation which may require incision and drainage. If these abscesses are large they may leave behind indolent skin ulcers that require extensive cleaning and dressing. Skin infections are probably the commonest physical problem among injecting drug users.

Septicaemia

Despite laboratory studies demonstrating the immunosuppressive role of alcohol, opiates, cannabis and cocaine their actual role in compromising the immune status of drug users remains conjectural.

Most injecting episodes result in a minor bacteraemia which an efficient immune response will contain, but a septicaemia may develop if this is not contained. Septicaemia may also arise from a localized infection such as an abscess and may also result in endocarditis. Septicaemia should be suspected in any injecting drug user presenting with a raised temperature of undetermined origin. This condition should be vigorously treated in hospital with parenteral broad spectrum antibiotics after cultures have been taken to isolate and identify the organism. Systemic candidiasis (fungal infection) has recently been reported from Scotland. The fungus may originate either in the heroin or in lemon juice used to dissolve the drug. The infection then causes a systemic fever with joint pains and may cause a candidal ophthalmitis with resulting blindness. Anti-fungal agents, which are very toxic, may suppress the infection.

Endocarditis

Infection of the heart valves is estimated to occur in 2 per 1000 injecting drug users per year. A report from New York found bacterial endocarditis to be three times greater in HIV-infected drug users. The commonest organism is *Staphylococcus aureus* but other organisms such as *Streptococcus viridans, Enterococci* and *Candida albicans* may also be responsible. Endocarditis should be suspected in anyone with a fever and a changing heart murmur. Septic emboli may occur at distant sites. In non-injectors endocarditis usually occurs in the presence of existing valvular abnormalities but in drug injectors it occurs on normal valves. Acute infection results in erosive valve lesions and may result in acute heart failure. Early identification by two dimensional echocardiography and treatment targeted at the causative organism will result in a good recovery rate. If injecting continues studies suggest a high recurrence rate with high mortality.

Hepatitis

It is estimated that 50–80 per cent of injecting drug users have been infected with the hepatitis B virus. Infection may range from an asymptomatic attack to a fulminant hepatic necrosis. Progression to chronic hepatitis cannot be predicted on the basis of any of the clinical or epidemiologic variables of acute illness. Less than 10 per cent of infected individuals become carriers and 90–95 per cent develop antibodies to hepatitis B virus within 6 months but 5–10 per cent do not and become persistent carriers. Persistent carriers may go on to develop chronic active hepatitis, chronic persistent hepatitis or hepatoma (liver cancer).

The Delta virus is a defective hepatitis B-dependent virus that may be acquired as a co-infection or as a super-infection in an established hepatitis B carrier. Such infection significantly increases the severity of both acute and chronic hepatitis B infection. What has previously been termed non-A non-B hepatitis has now been termed hepatitis C. This appears to have a high prevalence among injecting drug users and a high rate of progression to chronic active hepatitis. The hepatitis core antibody test will identify the majority who have been exposed to hepatitis B virus. The hepatitis surface antigen and hepatitis E antigen will identify those who are more likely to infect others. Core antibody negative individuals should be offered hepatitis B immunization as should the sexual partners and intimate contacts of all drug injectors who are not already infected.

Pulmonary

Drug inhalation may be associated with asthma but the more common complications are that of pneumonia and tuberculosis. Recent American studies have shown an increased rate of pneumonia and tuberculosis in those that are HIV positive.

Pneumothorax may result from injecting into the neck if the needle penetrates the apex of the lung. Rare complications such as pulmonary hypertension may result from prolonged injection of inert material or particulate matter resulting in a gradual obliteration of the lung vascular bed.

Orthopaedic

Joint problems are less common but may result from direct infection, extension from an abscess or spread from septicaemia. Bone infection (osteomyelitis) is most often caused by septic embolism from a distant infected focus. The vertebrae are the most frequent bones involved with the thoracic, lumbar and cervical in that order of frequency.

Other injecting complications

Vascular

Venous access may frequently be a problem in individuals with a long history of injecting drug use. The femoral vein may be used as a route of access. Long-term groin injectors may have a sinus at their regular injection site. A deep venous thrombosis may occur at this site and may result in serious pulmonary thromboembolism (clot to the lungs). Anticoagulation is necessary. Continued injecting while anticoagualated may result in prolonged bleeding.

Repeated injection and superficial infections in the upper limbs may result in lymphangitis which can cause obstruction to the lymphatic drainage of the upper limb with resulting lymphoedema. It is this damage to the lymphatic drainage system that gives rise to the puffy hands seen in some long-standing injectors.

Arterial occlusion will result in an acutely painful swollen pale limb and may occur with injection of particulate matter inadvertently into an artery resulting in vasospasm, embolism or direct arterial injury. Immediate surgical management is essential to minimize tissue loss.

Renal

Renal problems appear to materialize in middle-aged long-term injectors as membranous glomerulonephritis or amyloid disease. In the earlier stages this can be detected by the presence of protein in the urine.

SUBSTANCE SPECIFIC COMPLICATIONS

A substantial proportion of the complications of drug use are infective in origin and arise mainly from injecting. However, each individual substance will cause problems in toxic doses or in lower doses may cause adverse reactions. Some of the main problems are briefly summarized here.

Drug overdose

Opiate overdose may occur in association with other drug use or after a period of abstinence or if the drug is of unexpectedly high purity. Opiate intoxication can be recognized when someone is comatose with pin-point pupils and slow, shallow respirations. Administration of the opiate antagonist naloxone 0.4-2.0 mg intravenously should reverse this situation. The dose required to displace the opiates from the receptor will depend on the magnitude of the original overdose. This reversal is one of the more dramatic sights of emergency medicine. If the person has taken a long-acting opiate such as methadone they should be observed in an intensive care setting for 24 hours to ensure that they do not become reintoxicated after the naloxone has worn off.

If there is no response to naloxone other central nervous system depressants are probably involved. Intensive care support to maintain respiration and blood pressure may be necessary until the effect of the drug has worn off.

Stimulants (amphetamine and cocaine)

The high level of use of cocaine in the general population in the US has resulted in a large catalogue of complications presenting to emergency rooms. These include myocardial infarction, cardiac arrhythmias, hypertension, cerebrovascular accident, seizures, hyperthermia. Inhalation of high temperature cocaine vapours may cause lung damage and pulmonary oedema.

Sedatives

Barbiturates and benzodiazepines may present with chaotic injecting behaviour but the commonest presenting problem is that of either intoxication or withdrawal. Both require appropriate medical supervision.

Solvents

Solvents may cause sudden death by asphyxia or inhalation of vomit or cardiac arrythmias on exercise. Long-term high-dose users may present with severe ataxia. The majority of the neurological deficits appear to be reversible on cessation of solvent inhalation.

Alcohol

Alcohol incurs the greatest range of physical health problems in the general population. Alcohol and polydrug abuse will substantially add to the range of physical complications in drug users. This is a particular problem in injecting drug users with underlying chronic liver disease. Full attention should be paid to drug users' alcohol intake and appropriate health promotion advice should be offered.

COMPLICATIONS IN WOMEN

Contraceptive, obstetric and gynaecological advice for drug-using women is an essential part of a comprehensive harm reduction strategy. Cervical erosions and genital ulceration may increase the risk of contracting HIV. Pregnancy in the drug-using population has increased rates of obstetrical and neonatal morbidity. Early antenatal clinic attendance and stabilization of drug use during pregnancy may substantially reduce this morbidity.

CONCLUSION

In the US the official Center for Disease Control (CDC) figures for AIDS in drug takers is considerably underestimated because HIV-infected drug takers are dying of drug-associated complications before they fulfil the CDC surveillance definitions of AIDS.

The advent of HIV has refocused attention on the physical problems of drug users. Basic clinical competence should include skills in the prevention, identification and initial management of drug-related physical complications.

Intensive attention has been paid to health education and counselling to reduce the incidence of risk-taking behaviour. This has led to a somewhat complacent view of non-sharing injecting behaviour. Safer injecting is still not safe and will continue to result in infective complications such as septicaemias, endocarditis and bacterial pneumonias. A substantial proportion of the physical problems described here may be ameliorated by appropriate attention to health education and harm reduction. Many of the most serious complications could be avoided by changing from injecting to non-injecting drug use.

FURTHER READING

Banks, A. and Waller, T.A. (1988) *Drug Misuse: a Practical Handbook for GPs,* Oxford: Blackwell Scientific Publications.
Barr, L.C. (1988) 'The surgical complications of drug abuse', *Surgery* 60: 1420–4.
Brettle, R., Farrell, M. and Strang, J. (1990) 'The clinical manifestations of HIV in drug users', in J. Strang and G. Stimson (eds) *AIDs and Drug Misuse,* London: Routledge.
Cregler, L. and Mark, H. (1986) 'Medical complications of cocaine abuse', *New England Journal of Medicine* 315: 1495–500.
Robin, H.S. and Michelson, J.B. (1988) *Illustrated Handbook of Drug Abuse Recognition and Diagnosis,* Chicago and London: Year Book Medical Publishers.
Sapira, J.D. and Cherubin, C.E. (1975) *Drug Abuse: a Guide for the Clinician,* Amsterdam: Excerpta Medica.
Sherlock, S. (1987) 'The natural history of hepatitis B', *Postgraduate Medical Journal* 63 (Suppl. 2): 7–11.

CROSS REFERENCES

Chapter 20

AIDS and drug use: 'To shun the heaven that leads man to this hell'

Alex Wodak

'All this the world well knows yet none knows well, to shun the heaven that leads man to this hell.'

(William Shakespeare)

The mortality rate reported for intravenous drug users (IVDUs) in Western countries in recent decades has been estimated at 2 per cent per annum (Thorley, 1981). This is approximately twenty times the mortality rate of their non-drug-using peers. In the 1980s a new disease of the immune system – AIDS – was recognized (Centers for Disease Control, 1981a, 1981b) and soon shown to be another potential complication of the injection of illicit drugs. By the mid-1980s, AIDS associated with intravenous drug use was recognized as a major public health problem in North America (Novick *et al.*, 1986; Marmor *et al.*, 1987) and Western Europe (World Health Organization, 1988). An increase in the mortality rate of IVDUs was reported in America and Western Europe in the late 1980s.

HISTORY

In 1981, a new immune deficiency disorder was reported in five homosexual/bisexual males one of whom was also an IVDU. Within a few years, this condition was termed the Acquired Immunodeficiency Syndrome (AIDS), and an aetiological agent was identified subsequently named the Human Immunodeficiency Virus (HIV). Intravenous drug use was soon recognized as a behaviour associated with the risk of developing HIV infection. HIV was identified in blood, semen and some other body fluids.

The sharing of needles and syringes and other injection paraphernalia, a common practice among IVDUs, is the major factor responsible for the spread of HIV in this population (Robertson *et al.*, 1986). Sexual transmission contributes to a lesser extent. A number of sexually transmitted diseases are known to facilitate sexual transmission of HIV infection and are also known to be prevalent among IVDUs.

In the early years of the AIDS epidemic in most Western countries, homosexual/bisexual males accounted for the majority of cases and appeared to be the largest reservoir of HIV infection in the community. Homosexual/bisexual male injecting drug users may often have acted as a bridge for HIV transmission by sharing injection equipment with other IVDUs. Rapid dissemination of HIV transmission has occurred frequently in populations of urban IVDUs. Subsequently, vertical transmission has resulted in the birth of a large number of infants infected with HIV. In most Western countries and now in some developing countries, sexual transmission from IVDUs to the non-drug-using heterosexual population represents the most likely means of dissemination of HIV infection to the general community.

The possible contribution of intoxication with alcohol and other drugs to risk behaviours associated with HIV transmission is still to be determined although it is known that the snorting or inhalation of cocaine by homosexuals/bisexual men is associated with an increased risk of infection (Stall *et al.*, 1986). This is presumed to be due to an increase in unsafe sexual practices. Cocaine use by IVDUs is also associated with an increased risk of contracting HIV (Chaisson *et al.*, 1989) and sexually transmitted diseases. In the mid-1980s the free base form of cocaine known as crack appeared in large quantities in the United States. By the late 1980s, a variety of forms of cocaine became increasingly available in a number of Western European countries.

EPIDEMIOLOGY OF AIDS AND HIV INFECTION IN IVDUs

In 1983, heterosexual IVDUs accounted for only 27.3 per cent of cumulative AIDS cases in New York City. By 1988, IVDUs constituted the largest risk group for newly diagnosed cases in New York City (Hospital Association of New York State, 1990). It is expected that by 1993, IVDUs will account for 50 per cent of new cases and homosexual/bisexual males will constitute 33 per cent of new cases.

HIV infection in New York City IVDUs began in the mid-1970s and reached a prevalence of 50 to 60 per cent by the early 1980s, subsequently remaining at that level (Des Jarlais *et al.*, 1989). HIV infection has now spread to IVDUs in areas surrounding New York City. The incidence of HIV infection in IVDUs appears to be declining in the west coast and the prevalence in west coast IVDUs is apparently stable at 10–15 per cent (Hahn *et al.*, 1989). Despite a decade and a half of HIV infection in IVDUs in the US, many cities still have a remarkably low prevalence of HIV infection in IVDUs.

In the second half of 1989, the number of newly diagnosed AIDS cases in IVDUs in Western Europe exceeded for the first time newly diagnosed cases in homosexual/bisexual males. The doubling time for AIDS cases in IVDUs is much shorter than for homosexual/bisexual males in Western Europe and the United States. IVDUs account for over 60 per cent of new AIDS cases in Spain and Italy; in most of the adjacent countries IVDUs and homosexual/bisexual males account for similar numbers of new diagnosed cases of AIDS. In Northern Europe, AIDS is less common and most cases are occurring in homosexual/bisexual males. The distribution in Western Europe of AIDS cases and prevalence of HIV infection in IVDUs is similar. The highest prevalence of HIV infection in Western Europe extends over the Northern Mediterranean coastline through Southern Spain, Southern France, Northern Italy, Switzerland and parts of Austria and Yugoslavia.

Although for many years it appeared that HIV infection in IVDUs was confined to countries with developed economies, in 1987/88 an epidemic of HIV infection occurred among IVDUs in Bangkok, Thailand. The increase in seroprevalence reached 4 per cent per month. Within a few years, seropositive IVDUs were reported from almost all of Thailand's seventy-five provinces. In the late 1980s, HIV infection was later reported in Polish IVDUs and scattered reports appeared regarding significant HIV infection of IVDUs in some South East Asian countries. AIDS cases involving IVDUs in Brazil increased from 3 per cent to 13 per cent of new cases between 1988 and 1989. The alarming possibility that HIV infection in IVDUs represented a new and major threat to public health in North America, Western Europe, South East Asia, Australia and South America was recognized.

CONSEQUENCES AND SPECIAL FEATURES

Although rapid spread of HIV infection among IVDUs has been documented in a number of cities (Robertson *et al.*, 1986), slower increases in HIV seroprevalence in IVDUs have been reported elsewhere. The proportion of seropositive individuals who go on to develop AIDS and other serious complications of HIV infection increases over time. Ultimately, most (if not all) people infected with HIV develop AIDS. The mean duration from HIV infection to the diagnosis of AIDS is 7–8 years but the range may be extremely wide (1–15 years). There is some evidence to suggest that IVDUs may progress to AIDS more quickly than other risk groups and that progression to AIDS is accelerated by continuing intravenous injection of street drugs. Both these observations remain tentative.

IVDUs represent the major conduit of HIV infection to non-drug-using heterosexuals, as sexual transmission from bisexual males to females occurs less frequently than from an IVDU to a non-drug-using sexual partner. Thus, the success or failure of efforts to control HIV infection in the general community in many Western countries depends to a large extent on containing the spread of HIV infection in IVDUs. Furthermore, IVDUs are sexually active, fertile and less compliant with birth-control techniques than average couples. Consequently, the spread of HIV infection to populations of IVDUs results within a few years in large numbers of HIV infected infants. The second wave of AIDS in IVDUs usually requires more resources than AIDS cases in homosexual/bisexual males because IVDUs frequently lack strong social networks, are often socially disadvantaged, and the social sequelae of HIV infection in families are immense, whether or not the children are also infected. In many countries, IVDUs from ethnic minorities appear to be disproportionately affected by HIV.

Following the epidemic of HIV infection in IVDUs in New York City, it was noted that the mortality rate of IVDUs increased substantially. Only part of this increase can be accounted for by AIDS. Seropositive IVDUs are at greater risk of developing life threatening infections even before developing AIDS. This increased mortality among seropositive IVDUs before the onset of AIDS has also been observed in Italy and Scotland.

Although widespread HIV infection had already occurred in IVDUs in some parts of the world several years before AIDS was first recognized, within a few years IVDUs were aware that this immune disorder was a devastating new complication of drug use. However, perception of personal risk remains low and high risk behaviours are still alarmingly common despite adequate knowledge and appropriate attitudes. Failure to personalize the risk of HIV infection has not however been unique to IVDUs.

The advent of HIV infection in IVDUs has had a dramatic effect on drug treatment services in many countries. The capacity of treatment services has been increased and treatment services liberalized to increase their attractiveness in many countries. The switch from an AIDS case load dominated by homosexual/bisexual males to a case load dominated by IVDUs has also required changes to centres providing treatment for complications of HIV infection with some difficulties encountered in mixing cases from different behaviour groups.

RESPONDING TO THE EPIDEMIC

The potential threat to public health, the financial cost and the immense human tragedy resulting from HIV infection in IVDUs began to be recognized in North America and Western Europe by the mid-1980s. Consequently, containing HIV infection in IVDUs became an urgent priority in many countries (Department of Health and Social Security, 1988, 1989; Presidential Commission on the Human Immunodeficiency Virus Epidemic, 1988). No single strategy can be considered a panacea, but the cumulative effect of multiple, partially effective strategies is now recognized. The earlier preoccupation with achieving behaviour change is now being supplemented by an equal concern to maintain behaviour change.

Education

Education of IVDUs was recognized as an important strategy in most countries early in the epidemic. Although IVDUs appear to have rapidly acquired an adequate understanding of the modes of HIV transmission, continuing education provides useful reinforcement to longer-term IVDUs as well as presenting important material to new recruits to drug use. IVDUs need to be provided not only with an adequate knowledge base and the means to achieve behaviour change (e.g. sterile needles and syringes), but also with techniques to achieve behaviour change.

Education has been carried out by a variety of techniques including mass media campaigns, pamphlets, posters, videos, directly from trained staff of alcohol and drug treatment centres and outreach workers. In some countries, IVDUs have contributed to the development and implementation of educational interventions by providing an authenticity and relevance often lacking in material prepared by health education professionals or the advertising industry. Education also needs to be considered as a comprehensive strategy. It is important that the community and policy makers, especially, are informed about AIDS and IVDUs in order to mobilize support for HIV prevention strategies. Health and welfare professionals, too, require education and training in order to ensure their assistance with implementation of prevention strategies and, ultimately, to improve the delivery of care for IVDUs with complications of HIV infection.

Preoccupation with provision of sterile needles and syringes has tended to result in far less attention being directed to unsafe sexual practices which are, in general, more resistant to change. The need for distribution of condoms and lubricants, together with exhortations for their use, have been well accepted in principle in many countries though utilization is often poor.

Harm reduction

The decision by most Western European countries to increase the availability of sterile needles and syringes was one of the first responses to the newly perceived threat of HIV infection in IVDUs. This increase in availability was achieved by establishing needle and syringe exchanges, distribution systems including vending machines and outreach programmes. Retail pharmacies have played an important new role as outlets for sterile injection equipment in many countries. In some countries, this strategy of providing sterile injection equipment provoked an acrimonious debate about whether this constituted 'condoning an illegal practice'. Reducing the spread of HIV infection in IVDUs is recognized by many as being more urgent and having a higher priority than reducing the incidence of intravenous drug use although this is seldom stated publicly. HIV infection now represents the most serious complication of intravenous drug use both for IVDUs and the general community. A hierarchy of outcome goals for HIV prevention and drug treatment has evolved:

1 intravenous drug use with shared injection equipment;
2 intravenous drug use with decontaminated, used injection equipment;
3 intravenous drug use with sterile injection equipment;
4 drug use without injection;
5 abstinence.

The focus on achieving a reduction in the risk of HIV infection and an improvement in other (mainly health) objectives despite continuing drug use is sometimes referred to as 'harm reduction'.

Decontamination of used injection equipment has been promoted as a means of reducing the spread of HIV infection in IVDUs. Bleach is regarded as the most suitable decontamination agent and is surprisingly safe even when inadvertently injected intravenously. Bleach decontamination has been considered acceptable in circumstances where increasing the provision of sterile needles and syringes has not been possible such as in some prisons or in the United States.

IVDUs in treatment appear to have a lower prevalence of HIV infection than IVDUs who are not in treatment. In addition, IVDUs in treatment for longer periods tend to have a lower prevalence of HIV infection than IVDUs in treatment for a shorter duration. IVDUs on higher doses of methadone tend to have a lower prevalence of infection than IVDUs on lower doses of methadone. These observations suggest that recruitment into treatment may reduce the risk of HIV infection (Ball *et al.*, 1988). Consequently, many countries have expanded the capacity and improved the attractiveness of the treatment system. In some cases, government guidelines regulating methadone maintenance programmes have been relaxed.

Research and evaluation

Research has played a critical role in developing strategies. Evaluation research has assessed the feasibility of certain strategies, determined their cost and unintended negative consequences. Evaluation of the effectiveness of strategies is complicated by the multiplicity of factors which influence HIV transmission. Changes in HIV risk behaviour have been measured although proof of causality is exceedingly difficult.

Research is required to improve the ability of IVDUs to gain greater control of their behaviour and thus resist unsafe injection practices and unsafe sexual practices. Pharmacotherapy for IVDUs (see chapter by Spencer Madden) could be enhanced by the development of a broader range of specific agents including treatment for compulsive psychostimulant users. A non-reusable needle and syringe has been suggested as a possible additional strategy but thus far the difficulties in development of a satisfactory design have prevented evaluation of this strategy.

Drug policy

In several countries, organizations of IVDUs have evolved or been encouraged to evolve (Friedman *et al.*, 1987). These organizations include past and present IVDUs. Through these organizations, IVDUs have been able to operate needle and syringe exchange, implement outreach programmes, develop peer-based education and contribute to policy development.

Drug policy may also influence the speed of HIV transmission among IVDUs. Supply reduction strategies are often evaluated by their success in achieving a high price and low purity of street drugs. However, high prices and low purity of street drugs increase the likelihood of drug injection (with the inherent risk of sharing of injection equipment) rather than consumption by alternative routes of administration such as smoking or swallowing. Drug policy may also have a major influence on the availability of sterile injection equipment or the effectiveness of needle and syringe exchange programmes. Furthermore, drug policy influences the guidelines for substitution treatment programmes and therefore affects their cost and attractiveness. The extent to which IVDUs can be diverted from prisons, where they may be at increased risk of HIV infection, to non-custodial forms of sentencing may also be influenced by drugs policy. In the presence of strictly implemented supply reduction policies, IVDUs are marginalized and ostracized which increases the difficulties of modifying their behaviour through educational interventions.

Considerable overlap exists between populations of IVDUs, prisoners and prostitutes. Therefore concern about prevention of HIV infection in IVDUs must include other important related groups. Education and provision of condoms are important strategies for prisoners and prostitutes. The provision of drug treatments in gaols and institution of urine testing for injectable substances may also contribute to a reduction of HIV transmission within prisons.

RESULTS OF IMPLEMENTATION OF STRATEGIES

A reduction in sharing of injection equipment has been documented in many countries although IVDUs often continue to share with regular sexual partners. Changes in sexual behaviour of IVDUs have been less impressive than changes in injection practices. Sexual behaviour of IVDUs with casual or commercial partners has changed most, and sexual practices of IVDUs with regular sexual partners have changed little if at all. Welcome as these changes are, it must be acknowledged that attempts to reduce HIV risk behaviours started from very high base-line levels.

CONCLUSION

The advent of HIV infection in IVDUs has resulted in the development of new perspectives on illicit drug use. New goals for prevention and treatment have been devised and gained reasonable acceptance in many countries. The advent of this epidemic increases the importance of efforts to reduce the demand for injectable drugs. Increasing use of cocaine in North America and Western Europe and its association with sexually transmitted diseases and HIV infection is an alarming development. HIV infection has had a devastating effect on some inner-city neighbourhoods with a high incidence of intravenous drug use. It is clear that the perspective on intravenous drug use has been irreversibly altered by HIV bringing with it the new challenge of reducing the spread of HIV infection and caring for IVDUs who are already infected. Efforts to improve our understanding of drug use must be increased, with the prevention of initiation of drug use acquiring an even increased urgency.

REFERENCES

Ball, J.C., Lange, W.R., Myers, C.P. and Friedman, S.R. (1988) 'Reducing the risk of AIDS through methadone maintenance treatment', *Journal of Health and Social Behaviour* 29: 214–26.
Centers for Disease Control (1981a) 'Kaposi's sarcoma and pneumocystis pneumonia among homosexual men – New York City and California', *Morbidity and Mortality Weekly Report* 30: 305–8.
— (1981b) 'Pneumocystis pneumonia – Los Angeles', *Morbidity and Mortality Weekly Report* 30: 250–2.
Chaisson, R.E., Bacchetti, P., Osmond, D., Brodie, B., Sande, M.A. and Moss, A.R. (1989) 'Cocaine use and HIV infection in intravenous drug users in San Francisco', *Journal of the American Medical Association* 261: 561–5.
Department of Health and Social Security (1988) *AIDS and Drugs Misuse. Part 1: Report of the Advisory Council on the Misuse of Drugs*, London: HMSO.
— (1989) *AIDS and Drugs Misuse. Part II: Report of the Advisory Council on the Misuse of Drugs*, London: HMSO.
Des Jarlais, D.C., Friedman, S.R., Novick, D.M., Sotheran, J.L., Thomas, P., Yancovitz, S.R., Mildvara, D., Webber, J., Kreek, M.L., Maslansky, R., Bartelme, S., Spira, T. and Marmor, M. (1989) 'HIV-1 infection among intravenous drug users in Manhattan, New York City, from 1977 through 1987', *Journal of the American Medical Association* 261: 1008–12.
Friedman, S.R., Des Jarlais, D.C., Sotheran, J.L., Garber, J., Cohen, H. and Smith, D. (1987) 'AIDS and self organisation among intravenous drug users', *International Journal of the Addictions* 22: 201–20.
Hahn, R.A., Onorato, I.M., Jones, T.S. and Dougherty, J. (1989) 'Prevalence of HIV infection among intravenous drug users in the United States', *Journal of the American Medical Association* 261: 2677–84.
Hospital Association of New York State (January 1990) *The Impact of AIDS in New York State*, New York: Albany.
Marmor, M., Des Jarlais, D.C., Cohen, H., Friedman, S.R., Beatrice, S.T., Dubin, N., el-Sadr, W., Mildvan, D., Yancovitz, S. and Mathur, U. (1987) 'Risk factors for infection with

human immunodeficiency virus among intravenous drug abusers in New York City', *AIDS* 1: 39–44.

Novick, D.M., Khan, I. and Kreek, M.J. (1986) 'Acquired Immunodeficiency Syndrome and infection with hepatitis viruses in individuals abusing drugs by injection', *Bulletin on Narcotics* 38: 15–25.

Presidential Commission on the Human Immunodeficiency Virus Epidemic (1988) Report of the Presidential Commission on the Human Immunodeficiency Virus Epidemic. Submitted to the President of the United States of America – Washington.

Robertson, J.R., Bucknall, A.B.V., Welsby, P.D., Roberts, J.J., Inglis, J.M., Pentherer, J.F. and Brettle, R.P. (1986) 'Epidemic of AIDS related virus (HTLV-III/LAV) infection among intravenous drug abusers', *British Medical Journal* 292: 527–9.

Stall, R., McKusick, L., Wiley, J., Coates, T.J. and Ostrow, D.G. (1986) 'Alcohol and drug use during sexual activity and compliance with safe sex guidelines for AIDS: The AIDS behavioural research project', *Health Education Quarterly* 13: 359–71.

Stimson, G.V., Alldritt, L., Dolan, K. and Donoghoe, M. (1988) 'Syringe exchange schemes for drug users in England and Scotland', *British Medical Journal* 296: 1717–19.

Thorley, A. (1981) 'Longitudinal studies of drug dependence', in G. Edwards and C. Busch (eds) *Drug Problems in Britain: a Review of Ten Years*, London and New York: Academic Press.

World Health Organization (1988) Report of the meeting on HIV infection and drug injecting intervention strategies. Geneva, 18–20 January.

CROSS REFERENCES

Chapter 21

Physical complications of alcoh

John B. Saunders

Alcohol is unique among psychoactive substances in having the capacity to cause widespread tissue damage. There is a vast array of physical complications which occur, sometimes singly, often multiply, in heavy drinkers. Physical sequelae may also be due to concomitant nutritional deficiency, to trauma sustained while intoxicated, or to infections as a result of reduced immune function. Alcohol is a risk factor for HIV infection and other sexually acquired disorders, because of its disinhibiting effects on behaviour.

The levels of alcohol intake associated with harm are better defined than for other psychoactive drugs. There is still, however, much controversy about whether there is a 'threshold' level of hazardous consumption. Some commentators conclude that there is a perceptible risk of harm with any level of regular drinking. What is clearer is that the great majority of persons who acquire chronic alcohol-related diseases, such as cirrhosis, pancreatitis and cardiomyopathy, do so on the basis of a mean daily alcohol intake of at least 60g[1] (men) or 40g[2] (women) sustained for at least five years. Women are more susceptible to physical sequelae than men, largely because of their lower lean body mass which results in proportionately higher blood alcohol concentrations after a standard drink than in men (Saunders *et al.*, 1981; Marshall *et al.*, 1983).

Certain complications, such as gastritis, acute pancreatitis, frontal lobe brain damage and trauma, appear to be related to heavy sessional drinking. The relationship between the pattern of drinking and physical sequelae is ill defined. The risk of trauma increases significantly when the blood alcohol concentration exceeds 50mg/100ml, and rises exponentially above this level.

ALCOHOLIC LIVER DISEASE

Alcoholic liver disease is one of the commonest causes of morbidity and mortality in the developed world. It exists in three main forms – fatty liver, alcoholic hepatitis and cirrhosis.

Fatty liver is a predictable metabolic response to alcohol and, in most individuals, is of little consequence. Frequently it is asymptomatic and is detected only by abnormal liver function tests, but it may cause pain in the right abdomen, dyspepsia, and nausea and vomiting. It resolves with abstinence over a period of two months and requires no specific therapy, other than abstinence and a nutritious diet.

Alcoholic hepatitis and cirrhosis are complications of longstanding heavy daily drinking. Alcoholic hepatitis is characterized by liver cell necrosis and inflammatory change, while cirrhosis implies permanent architectural distortion with surviving liver subdivided by strands of fibrous tissue. Alcoholic hepatitis typically presents with jaundice, fever and right abdominal pain, which may be accompanied by signs of hepatic decompensation such as ascites and encephalopathy. Cirrhosis can present with non-specific gastrointestinal symptoms, or with ascites, encephalopathy or haemorrhage from oesophageal varices. Both forms of disease can be asymptomatic, being detected on routine medical examination or abnormal liver function test results. Treatment involves abstinence, adequate nutrition, and measures to alleviate the signs of hepatic decompensation. Ascites is treated by sodium restriction and diuretics; encephalopathy by protein restriction and lactulose to reduce absorption of toxic nitrogenous compounds; and variceal haemorrhage, an acute medical emergency, by transfusion, vasoactive drugs (e.g. vasopressin, nitroprusside), oesophageal tamponade, and sclerosis of the varices. Propylthiouracil, an antithyroid drug, has been shown in a recent controlled trial to improve prognosis in patients with chronic alcoholic liver disease and may be the first drug to modify the disease process (see Saunders, 1989).

OTHER GASTROINTESTINAL DISEASES

Acute pancreatitis typically presents with mid-abdominal pain of variable degree, accompanied by nausea, vomiting and in severe cases hypotension and renal failure. Treatment includes rehydration, analgesia and correction of abnormal electrolyte status.

Chronic pancreatitis typically follows unremitting daily drinking for ten or more years (Worning, 1984). The usual presentation is with chronic upper abdominal pain and weight loss. In addition features of pancreatic exocrine insufficiency may be present (steatorrhoea and nutritional deficiencies indicating malabsorption) or endocrine (diabetes mellitus due to damage to the islets of Langerhans). Treatment of chronic pancreatitis involves abstinence from alcohol, correction of nutritional deficiencies and may require pancreatic enzyme supplements. Insulin is frequently required to control the diabetes. Management may be complicated by the development of dependence on opiate drugs presented for relief of pain.

Oropharyngeal and oesophageal cancers are strongly associated with heavy alcohol consumption, and **colo-rectal cancer** is a recently recognized association (Garro and Lieber, 1990).

Gastritis and peptic ulcer. Alcohol enhances back diffusion of hydrochloric acid through oesophageal and gastric mucosa. An alcoholic binge is commonly followed by mucosal erosions and bleeding. Bleeding is usually self-limiting and treatment usually entails only antacids or a short course of H_2 blockers such as cimetidine or ranitidine. Whether alcohol is an aetiological factor for peptic ulceration remains controversial, though complications such as perforation and haemorrhage are more common in alcohol-dependent persons.

CARDIOVASCULAR DISEASES

Alcoholic cardiomyopathy occurs typically in middle-aged men, mainly beer drinkers. The usual clinical presentation is a gradual onset of heart failure, with breathlessness on exertion and nocturnal dyspnoea. Peripheral oedema is a relatively early feature and may be followed by ascites. Atrial fibrillation is usual and this and other arrhythmias may be induced by a spell of unusually heavy drinking (the 'holiday heart syndrome'). Treatment involves usual anti-failure therapy, namely diuretics (e.g. frusemide, spironolactone), sodium and water restriction, digoxin for atrial fibrillation, correction of nutritional deficiencies and abstention from alcohol. The overall prognosis is poor: 80 per cent who continue to drink are dead within three years. There is a high incidence of thrombus formation in the dilated chambers and 40 per cent of patients will experience systemic embolism within three years.

Alcohol is now established as a risk factor for **systemic hypertension** (Saunders, 1987), and indeed 30 per cent of so-called 'essential hypertension' may be related to alcohol abuse. In most cases blood pressure falls (often to normal levels) upon abstinence, hence the importance of making the diagnosis. Treatment with antihypertensive drugs is poorly effective and alcohol abuse should be considered in all cases of ill-controlled hypertension.

Alcohol is also a risk factor for both **haemorrhagic and thrombotic stroke**. Heavy sessional drinking can result in haemorrhagic stroke, even when blood pressure is well controlled (Gorelick, 1989).

HAEMATOLOGICAL DISORDERS

Alcohol is a bone marrow toxin. The commonest manifestation of this is the appearance of enlarged red cells (macrocytes) in the peripheral blood. Approximately one-third of patients have evidence of co-existing folic acid deficiency. Thrombocytopenia is also a feature of marrow toxicity and in patients with chronic liver disease may be aggravated by hypersplenism.

NEUROLOGICAL DISORDERS

The neuropsychiatric complications of alcohol abuse, including the Wernicke-Korsakoff syndrome and cortical atrophy, are described by Kopelman in Chapter 22.

Alcohol-related fits occur principally during withdrawal, mostly within the first 48 hours. They are typical tonic-clonic fits, without focal features, and usually occur singly. Status epilepticus is rare. Conventional anti-convulsants such as phenytoin are not of proven benefit for either primary or secondary prophylaxis. The fits can be aborted by intravenous diazepam. Subsequent management is that of the withdrawal syndrome.

Cerebellar atrophy mainly affects the vermis and causes ataxia of stance and gait, with little if any evidence of incoordination of the limbs. The aetiology is poorly understood but is thought to reflect a combination of alcohol toxicity and thiamine deficiency.

Peripheral neuropathy results in sensorimotor disturbance, manifest by numbness, dysaesthesiae and paraesthesiae in a 'glove and stocking' distribution, and sometimes weakness of proximal or distal muscle groups (Walsh and McLeod, 1973). Recovery is slow, averaging one year, even with total abstinence. Thiamine should be prescribed.

MUSCULOSKELETAL DISORDERS

Acute myopathy presents with pain, tenderness and swelling of skeletal muscles. The distribution of muscles involved is symmetrical except where muscle groups have been traumatized due to prolonged recumbency. A severe form, acute rhabdomyolysis, is accompanied by myoglobinuria, which may lead to renal failure. Treatment involves rehydration and renal dialysis where appropriate.

Chronic myopathy is disputed by many as a discrete entity. Wasting and weakness of muscles in a proximal distribution is well recognized in chronic alcohol dependent individuals. Investigation reveals a neuropathic basis in most patients. Recovery is slow and often incomplete, even with total abstinence and adequate nutrition.

Osteoporosis affecting the spine results in back pain, wedge fractures and often a concomitant dependency on opioid drugs.

Avascular necrosis is a recently recognized association with heavy drinking (Bikle *et al.*, 1985).

Gout has entered popular folklore as a complication of alcohol abuse. It is caused by accumulation of uric acid, one of the many consequences of the metabolism of alcohol. Treatment involves colchicine or a non-steroidal anti-inflammatory drug for the acute attack, and, to prevent recurrences, allopurinol, aided by abstinence from alcohol.

ENDOCRINE DISORDERS

Alcoholic pseudo-Cushing's syndrome is caused by excessive glucocorticoid production and is manifest as a bloated facial appearance, obesity and hypertension. It is distinguished from true Cushing's syndrome by more ready suppression of cortisol levels by dexamethasone, and by resolution of the biochemical abnormalities with abstinence.

Gonadal atrophy affects both sexes, resulting in impotence and reduced spermatogenesis in men, and subfertility. The pathogenesis is multifactorial: direct effects on the testes and ovaries are compounded by suppression of hypothalamic and pituitary function (Morgan, 1982). Fertility in men usually recovers with abstinence, especially when detected at an early stage (Brzek, 1987). When chronic liver disease is present, subfertility may be permanent.

METABOLIC DISORDERS

As a result of the oxidation of alcohol, hydrogen equivalents are produced which fuel several subsidiary reactions, leading to the production of lactic acid, ketone bodies and neutral fats.

Alcohol-induced lactic acidosis occurs through failure of metabolism of pyruvate in the glycolytic pathway. It is seen mainly in elderly subjects with concurrent medical disorders. In addition to standard treatment of lactic acidosis, thiamine should be prescribed.

Alcoholic ketoacidosis is uncommonly diagnosed, in part because the ketone accumulation mainly involves beta-hydroxybutyrate, which is not detected by conventional diagnostic tests for ketone bodies. It presents with vomiting, dehydration, acidosis and frequently signs of malnutrition (Fulop *et al.*, 1986). Treatment entails rehydration, glucose, sometimes insulin and maintenance of plasma phosphate levels.

Hyperlipidaemia is found in over one-third of alcohol-dependent subjects. The proportions of cholesterol fractions and triglyceride change with time from the last drink, which means that employing the conventional classification of hyperlipidaemias is generally unhelpful. In most cases, abstinence results in resolution of the changes. Consumption of 20-40g alcohol per day increases HDL-cholesterol and is considered to lessen the risk of coronary heart disease.

Alcohol-induced hypoglycaemia occurs typically 6–12 hours after ingestion of large quantities of alcohol (100g) in a malnourished or fasting individual. In this situation glucose cannot be mobilized from depleted hepatic glycogen stores and the presence of alcohol inhibits gluconeogenesis. Hypoglycaemia commonly presents with grand mal fits (which are often assumed to be withdrawal fits), confusion, stupor or coma. Treatment involves the immediate adminstration of glucose intravenously. Thiamine should also be given.

Disturbances in electrolyte and acid-base status are common. Hypokalaemia, often accompanied by a metabolic alkalosis, is a predisposing factor for delirium tremens and requires prompt correction with potassium supplements (60–240 mmol/day). Hyponatraemia can complicate consumption of large quantities of dilute alcoholic drinks and may precipitate fits. Treatment is by water restriction; hypertonic saline is best avoided. Hypomagnesaemia is often found in withdrawal syndromes complicated by fitting and/or delirium tremens. It is corrected by 50–100 mmol magnesium per day.

FOETAL ALCOHOL SYNDROME

Foetal alcohol syndrome, first described twenty years ago, is now recognized as one of the two commonest causes of mental retardation in the developed world. The mean IQ of affected children is 70 and there is no improvement with time. The children have a characteristic facies, with a depressed bridge of the nose, thinning of the upper lip and absent philtrum, and low set ears (Jones *et al.*, 1973). Cardiac abnormalities are frequent.

MISCELLANEOUS CONDITIONS

Well-recognized **pulmonary complications** of alcohol abuse include lobar pneumonia, pulmonary tuberculosis and aspiration syndromes.

Common **traumatic sequelae** include rib fractures (often multiple and with no history of trauma), head injury, which may be complicated by subdural or extradural haematoma, and fractures of long bones.

Nutritional deficiency syndromes, virtually extinct in the non-alcoholic population in many developed countries, must always be considered in alcohol abusers. Thiamine deficiency is the commonest and presents with Wernicke's encephalopathy or beriberi heart failure. Pellagra, due to niacin (vitamin B3) deficiency, presents with a light-sensitive blistering rash, diarrhoea and confusion. Scurvy, due to vitamin C deficiency, is characterized by skin haemorrhages, gingivitis and deep haematomata. Treatment of these syndromes consists of the appropriate vitamin (best given by intramuscular or intravenous injection in the initial stages), together with a multivitamin preparation in case there is sub-clinical deficiency of other vitamins.

CONCLUDING REMARKS

Once the physical disorder is diagnosed and treatment is underway, attention can be focused on the management of the underlying drinking problem. Feedback about the presence of physical disease, especially when there is involvement of more than one organ system, is often a salutary experience for patients and helps develop a commitment to change the drinking behaviour. In general, patients with physical sequelae are best steered towards a goal of total abstinence. This certainly applies to those with chronic conditions such as cirrhosis and neurological complications. For those with reversible damage, a period of three months' abstinence is advised. Whether abstinence should remain the goal or whether moderated drinking can be attempted will depend on the previous pattern of drinking, the severity of dependence and the presence of a co-existing psychiatric disorder, issues which are discussed elsewhere in this volume.

NOTES

1   Equivalent to 4–5 'standard' drinks in North America and 6 in the UK and Australasia.
2   Equivalent to 3 'standard' drinks in North America and 4 in the UK and Australasia.

REFERENCES

Bikle, D.D., Genant, H.K., Cann, C., Recker, R.R., Halloran, B.P. and Strewler, G.J. (1985) 'Bone disease in alcohol abuse', *Annals of Internal Medicine* 103: 42–8.
Brzek, A. (1987) 'Alcohol and male fertility', *Andrologia* 19: 32–6.
Fulop, M., Ben-Ezra, J. and Bock, J. (1986) 'Alcoholic ketosis', *Alcoholism: Clinical and Experimental Research* 10: 610-15.
Garro, A.J. and Lieber, C.S. (1990) 'Alcohol and cancer', *Annual Review of Pharmacology and Toxicology* 30: 219–49.

Gorelick, P.B. (1989) 'The status of alcohol as a risk factor for stroke', *Stroke* 20: 1607–10.

Jones, K.L., Smith, D.W., Ulleland, C.W. and Streissguth, A.P. (1973) 'Pattern of malformation in offspring of chronic alcoholic women', *Lancet* 1: 1267–71.

Marshall, A.W., Kingstone, S., Boss, M. and Morgan, M.Y. (1983) 'Ethanol elimination in males and females: relationship to menstrual cycle and body composition', *Hepatology* 3: 701–6.

Morgan, M.Y. (1982) 'Sex and alcohol', *British Medical Bulletin* 38: 43–8.

Saunders, J.B. (1987) 'Alcohol: an important cause of hypertension', *British Medical Journal* 294: 1045–6.

—— (1989) 'Treatment of alcoholic liver disease', in M. Davis (ed.) *Therapy of Liver Disease*, London: Baillière Tindall, pp. 39–65.

Saunders, J.B., Davis, M. and Williams, R. (1981) 'Do women develop alcoholic liver disease more readily than men?', *British Medical Journal* 282: 1140–3.

Walsh, J. and McLeod, J. (1973) 'Alcoholic neuropathy: an electrophysiological and histological study', *Journal of Neurological Sciences* 10: 457–69.

Worning, H. (1984) 'Chronic pancreatitis: pathogenesis, natural history and conservative treatment', *Clinical Gastroenterology* 13: 871–94.

CROSS REFERENCES

Chapter 22

Alcoholic brain damage

Michael D. Kopelman

In discussing alcoholic brain damage, there are those syndromes which are more strictly neurological (in that they are predominantly characterized by physical signs and symptoms) and other syndromes which may be termed neuropsychiatric (in that they are predominantly characterized by cognitive, affective or personality change). The neuropsychiatric syndromes may, in turn, be subdivided into the acute/sub-acute and the chronic.

Within the compass of *neurological syndromes* can be included:

1 acute/chronic dysarthria and/or ataxia;
2 seizures resulting from alcohol withdrawal, hypoglycaemia, cerebral damage following, e.g. head injury, and the precipitation of epilepsy;
3 peripheral neuropathy;
4 various degenerative syndromes, e.g. of the corpus callosum (Marchiafava-Bignami disease), central pontine myelinosis, cerebellar atrophy and retrobulbar neuritis and/or optic atrophy.

These neurological syndromes will not be considered any further in this chapter (for further detail, see e.g. Lishman, 1987).

The *acute/sub-acute neuropsychiatric* syndromes include:

1 acute withdrawal syndromes and delirium tremens;
2 alcoholic hallucinosis;
3 alcoholic blackouts;
4 Wernicke's encephalopathy;
5 alcoholic pellagra encephalopathy.

Hepatic encephalopathy might also be included here but it is, of course, primarily the consequence of an extracranial physical disorder. It is discussed in the chapter on the physical complications of alcohol abuse (Chapter 21).

The *chronic neuropsychiatric* syndromes include:

1 a coarsening of personality, partly the consequence of frontal lobe dysfunction;
2 cognitive deterioration, which in an extreme form may be labelled 'alcoholic dementia' and is often associated with cortical atrophy;
3 the alcoholic Korsakoff syndrome.

The remainder of this chapter will discuss these acute/sub-acute and chronic neuropsychiatric syndromes in turn.

ACUTE/SUB-ACUTE SYNDROMES

Delirium tremens

In delirium tremens, there is commonly a *prodromal syndrome*, consisting of anxiety, sleeplessness, tremor, tachycardia and increased perspiration with sweaty palms. This is followed by the *delirium*, consisting of disorientation, a fluctuating level of awareness, hallucinosis, misperceptions, and a sense of intense fear, and by the '*tremens*' consisting of tremor, motor restlessness and autonomic overactivity. The hallucinations can be visual, in which case they often consist of small animals or insects; they can be tactile; and they can be auditory, in which case they are often threatening and persecutory. They are characterized by an intense reality and commonly produce a sense of terror in the subject. The autonomic overactivity involves increased psychomotor activity with tremulousness, agitation, intense perspiration and dehydration, and tachycardia with a weak pulse. The onset of the disorder usually occurs two to four days after alcohol withdrawal and is associated with the presence of infection or trauma in 50 per cent of cases and with liver damage in 90 per cent of cases (Lundquist, 1961). The episode usually terminates in a prolonged sleep after three days or less. Where mortality occurs, this usually results from cardiovascular collapse or concurrent infection. Treatment involves fluid and electrolyte replacement, sedation, and high potency vitamin replacement (Chick, 1989).

A retrospective survey of 121 cases between 1975 and 1984 found that the peak onset was during the second day in hospital, and the episodes lasted up to five days (Cushman, 1987). Visual hallucinations were present in 96 per cent of cases, auditory in 32 per cent, and tactile in 4 per cent. There was a past history of previous delirium tremens in 49 per cent of cases and withdrawal seizures in 37 per cent of cases. Moreover, the mortality was 4.9 per cent; this compares with a figure of 12 per cent reported in 1961 and 37 per cent reported in 1908 (Cushman, 1987). A further survey of 716 alcoholics seen between 1949 and 1969 found that the mortality rate of those who gave a history of delirium tremens was 29.5 per cent over a 15-year period (Nordström and Bergland, 1988). There is some evidence that the syndrome is precipitated by a 'resetting' of osmoreceptors, indicated by a change in the response to a water load in patients suffering withdrawal symptoms (Emsley *et al.*, 1987).

Alcoholic hallucinosis

This was first described by Wernicke in 1900. Kraepelin in 1913 differentiated alcoholic hallucinosis from delirium tremens in terms of

1 the absence of disorientation,
2 a predominance of auditory hallucinations,
3 a reduced amount of agitation and arousal,
4 a longer duration of the disorder.

In addition, it is appropriate to add:

5 that the disorder is not obviously related to alcohol withdrawal,
6 that the delusions are commonly said to be secondary to hallucinations.

It remains controversial how far a mild degree of 'clouding' of consciousness can be allowed within this diagnostic label. Cutting (1987a) found that auditory hallucinations were present in 98 per cent of a sample of 46 patients; these were derogatory or sexual in content in 76 per cent of cases and in the third person in 57 per cent. Delusions were present in 87 per cent of cases, but showed a pattern 'consistent' with the nature of the hallucinations in only 37 per cent. At follow up, a different diagnosis had commonly been given for subsequent episodes of psychiatric disorder; and the relationship of this disorder to schizophrenia is still debated (see Chapter 23 by Glass and Marshall).

Alcoholic blackouts

Acute, alcohol-related memory loss is said to occur in three forms, which probably reflect a continuum of severity (Goodwin *et al.*, 1969; Kopelman, 1987a). *State-dependent phenomena* have been reported in 60 per cent of subjects claiming blackouts. In such instances, the subject commonly hides money or drink when intoxicated, cannot find it when sober, but goes straight to it again after heavy drinking. In less dramatic form, such alcohol-related state-dependent phenomena can be demonstrated in healthy subjects in laboratory experiments. *'Fragmentary' blackouts* have been reported in 64 per cent of hospitalized alcoholics by Goodwin and colleagues. In this form of blackout, there is no clear demarcation of the onset or termination of the memory loss, and there are very commonly 'islets' of preserved memory within the amnesic gap. The amnesic gap tends to shrink through time, in a similar fashion to recovery from a head injury. *'En bloc' blackouts* have a very definite onset, and they end with the subject waking up and/or coming round with a sense of 'lost time'. There are usually no islets of preserved memory, and the memories do not recover through time. The memory loss can occur for a period of a few minutes or hours, and occasionally it lasts for a few days, giving rise to a fugue-like state, in which the subject may go wandering, sometimes travelling substantial distances and booking into hotels, before he or she 'comes round' unaware of what has been happening during the period of the 'blackout'.

A study of alcoholics who had had many blackouts, in comparison with those who had had very few, failed to find any significant difference on learning tests, suggesting that blackouts are not predictive of long-term cognitive impairment (Tartar and Schneider, 1976). Similarly, Ron (1983) failed to find any relationship between a history of blackouts and the presence of cortical atrophy on CT scan. Blackouts appear to be most closely related to

1 an early onset of the drinking history,
2 high peak levels of alcohol,
3 a past history of frequent head traumata.

Offenders, claiming amnesia for their offence, show a raised prevalence of alcohol abuse, and clinical assessments suggest that some of these cases may be instances of 'alcoholic blackout' (Kopelman, 1987b).

Wernicke's encephalopathy

This syndrome, first described by Wernicke in 1885, consists of ophthalmoplegia, nystagmus, ataxia and confusion. It is often, but not necessarily, accompanied by peripheral neuropathy. The full syndrome is seen relatively rarely, in part because the ophthalmoplegia responds well to treatment and recovers relatively rapidly, as does the confusion. Although they have closely overlapping neuropathology, Wernicke's encephalopathy does not necessarily terminate in Korsakoff's syndrome, and Korsakoff's syndrome does not necessarily follow Wernicke's encephalopathy (see p.147). The syndrome is a medical emergency, and patients can die from accompanying features of beriberi, including high-output cardiac failure. They should be treated with intravenous thiamine, and the other B vitamins should also be given (see below). Wernicke's encephalopathy can result from a variety of disorders other than alcohol abuse, all of which result in poor intake or absorption of thiamine, e.g. gastric carcinoma, other gastro-intestinal carcinoma, hyperemesis of pregnancy, haemodialysis, anorexia nervosa and other malignancy (see Kopelman, 1990a).

Alcoholic pellagra encephalopathy

In France, a combination of thiamine and pyridoxine is often given to alcoholics rather than multi-vitamins. It has recently been reported that French alcoholics are vulnerable to an alcohol-induced pellagra encephalopathy, resulting from nicotinic acid depletion (Serdaru et al., 1988; Hauw et al., 1988). Clinical features are a fluctuating confusional state involving global memory loss, visual hallucinations, restlessness alternating with apathy, and various physical signs (myoclonic jerks, hyper-reflexia, absent postural reflexes, a marked oppositional hypertonus and a rash on the back and chest). Clouding of consciousness can range from stupor to coma, and the confusional state is seen in all patients. The EEG is always abnormal with bilateral slow wave activity. Pathological features are neuronal chromatolysis (i.e. an enlargement of neurons with a reduction in size and eccentric placement of the nuclei), sometimes accompanied by degeneration of the corpus callosum and/or atrophy of the mammillary bodies and lesions in the thalamus. This finding confirms previous observations in Britain and Japan that nicotinic acid depletion can sometimes give rise to a confusional state, occasionally resembling the Wernicke–Korsakoff syndrome (Jolliffe et al., 1941; Lishman, 1981; Ishii and Nishihara, 1981).

CHRONIC SYNDROMES

Coarsening of personality

The coarsening of personality, seen in chronic alcoholics, is of course familiar. There is a loss of social, and sometimes sexual, inhibitions and a tendency to irritability, facile jocularity and abusiveness, not always directly related to acute intoxication. The consequences of this include family disruption (violence in the home and marital separation); an increased rate of accidents at home, work and on the road; and increased rates of absenteeism, redundancy, offending and vagrancy (Murray, 1986). Sexual impotence may also develop. Against this background of an insidious personality change, there may be acute episodes of so-called 'morbid jealousy' and/or 'pathological intoxication' (*mania à potu*), the latter involving senseless, violent behaviour, often of an extreme nature, followed by a prolonged sleep and amnesia for the events occurring during intoxication (Coid, 1979). The relative contributions of social, intrapsychic and pharmacological factors in producing these changes have been much debated. Whilst lay and clinical observation would appear to confirm the role of the direct 'disinhibiting' effect of alcohol, high rates of drunkenness are not associated with violence (for example) in all societies (Coid, 1986). There is some evidence that the presence of EEG abnormalities or other signs of organic brain disease are associated with a raised prevalence of 'pathological intoxication', but this remains controversial. More substantial is the increasing evidence that prolonged abuse of alcohol is associated with cortical atrophy particularly affecting the frontal lobes. Neuroradiological studies by Lishman *et al.* (1987) and Shimamura *et al.* (1988), an investigation of cerebral perfusion by Hunter *et al.* (1989), and neuropathological studies by Harper *et al.* (1987) all support this observation. It seems plausible that many of the more chronic personality changes seen in alcohol abusers (including the loss of inhibitions, irritability, facile jocularity and apathy) could be attributed to frontal lobe dysfunction.

Cognitive deterioration

A considerable number of studies (reviewed in Ron, 1983) have demonstrated mild to moderate degrees of cognitive impairment in subjects who have abused alcohol for many years. For example, Ryan and colleagues (1980) found that alcoholics were impaired at a short-term memory task, involving distraction of the subject's attention for a few seconds, paired-associate learning, and at a perceptuo-motor task ('digit symbol'). It appeared that these deficits persisted for several years, in that there was no significant difference between the performance of alcoholics who had been abstinent for between one and three months and those who had been abstinent for a period of one to five years on the memory tasks. On the other hand, a follow-up study, looking at these alcoholics after five years, did show a significant degree of further improvement on these tasks, suggesting that the recovery process may be very prolonged (Brandt *et al.* 1983). Ron *et al.* (1982) examined 100 alcoholic in-patients, finding that they were significantly impaired relative to controls on both verbal and performance IQ, immediate and delayed verbal memory, and at a card sorting ('frontal') task. Acker (1985; 1986), studying a similar series, found that females were more likely to become impaired earlier in their drinking history than were male alcoholics, consistent with findings for the physical complications of alcohol abuse. Hillbom and Holm (1986) compared alcoholics with a history of head injury with those who lacked a history of head injury, finding that, although the latter did significantly worse than controls at various cognitive tests, the head injury group were more severely impaired. Since the prevalence of head injury is two to four times higher in alcoholics than in the general population, Hillbom and Holm argued that head injury may contribute to the cognitive impairments commonly found in alcoholics.

Various studies have looked at the neuroradiological correlates of these cognitive abnormalities. For example, Carlen *et al.* (1981) found that alcoholics showed ventricular enlargement and sulcul widening on CT scan relative to age-matched controls. However, these neuroradiological changes were poorly correlated with performance on cognitive tests. Ron and her colleagues (Ron *et al.*, 1982; Ron, 1983) scanned 100 alcoholics between 12 and 120 days after alcohol withdrawal and, in a subgroup, a further scan was performed after 30 to 152 weeks. This study confirmed ventricular enlargement and sulcul widening, and also found enlargement of the Sylvian and inter-hemispheric fissures. However, as in Carlen *et al.* (1981), these changes were found to be poorly correlated with performance on cognitive tests, although in a more detailed analysis of an overlapping sample, Acker *et al.* (1987) found significant correlations between memory test performance and the size of the third ventricle, suggestive of thalamic or hypothalamic atrophy. In Ron's (1983) follow-up sample, there was some evidence that the ventricular enlargement diminished if subjects remained abstinent from alcohol. There have also been at least two studies of cerebral perfusion in alcoholics (Hata *et al.*, 1987; Hunter *et al.*, 1989), one of which found a generalized reduction of cerebral blood flow and the other found that frontal perfusion tended to be diminished in Korsakoff patients.

When these generalized cognitive impairments are severe, patients may be labelled as suffering 'alcoholic dementia'. Torvik *et al.* (1982) claimed that such dementia may result from the pathology commonly associated with Wernicke's encephalopathy, rather than from superimposed cortical atrophy. Others have argued that the dementia, when it occurs, may result from concomitant neurochemical depletion (Lishman, 1986), head injury (Hillbom and Holm, 1986), hepatic encephalopathy, vascular disease, or Alzheimer's disease (Victor and Adams, 1985). Whilst mild to moderate cognitive impairment following prolonged alcohol abuse undoubtedly occurs, the status of a severe, irreversible alcoholic dementia remains controversial.

Korsakoff's syndrome

Victor *et al.* (1971) defined this syndrome as 'an abnormal mental state in which memory and learning are affected out of all proportion to other cognitive functions in an otherwise alert and responsive patient'.

Three points should be made about this definition. First, no reference is made to 'short-term'/'long-term' memory or the extensiveness or pattern of the memory deficit. In fact, immediate recall of small quantities of information (so-called 'primary' or 'working' memory) is characteristically preserved, whereas the retrograde memory deficit may extend back many years or decades, as Korsakoff (1889) himself pointed out and as has been confirmed in modern experimental studies (e.g. Kopelman, 1989). Second, no reference is made to confabulation. 'Spontaneous confabulation', involving the fluent outpouring of erroneous material, is seen usually only as the subject emerges from the (Wernicke) confusional state; and confabulation is by no means pathognomic of the Korsakoff syndrome, occurring more commonly in Alzheimer and other dementias (Berlyne, 1972; Kopelman, 1987c). Third, the emphasis of the definition is on the memory deficit being 'out of all proportion' to other cognitive impairments. This does not exclude the possibility that there are other subtle or not-so-subtle cognitive impairments present. In fact, Butters and Cermak (1980), Bowden (1990) and Jacobson *et al.* (1990) have all emphasized that these impairments are similar to, but generally more severe than, the cognitive deficits seen in non-Korsakoff alcoholics. In particular, there is substantial evidence of frontal lobe dysfunction, which may contribute to some of the memory deficits (Janowsky *et al.*, 1989; Kopelman, 1991), and also of visuo-perceptual deficits (Jacobson *et al.*, 1990). Jacobson and Lishman (1987) have reported that patients given a clinical label of 'Korsakoff's syndrome' lie on a continuum with respect to the purity of their memory disorder, relative to the severity of these other cognitive abnormalities. However, it is still possible to isolate a group of patients with an 'acute' onset, who have a relatively 'pure' memory impairment (Cutting, 1978b; Kopelman, in press).

Not only has the purity of the memory disorder been called into question, but there is increasing recognition that its mode of onset can vary considerably (for review, see Kopelman, in press). Some patients first appear in coma, are usually seen by physicians, and if they recover are left with a residual Korsakoff syndrome. Others manifest the classical Wernicke syndrome and are the group most commonly seen by neurologists. A third group have an insidious onset, without initial medical or neurological signs, and may be first seen by psychiatrists. Finally there is a group, perhaps the largest of the lot, who are found to have the classical neuropathology at post-mortem but have not been diagnosed in life, presumably because they had only a mild degree of memory or other cognitive abnormality. In series in Australia and Scandinavia, this subgroup was found to account for 1–2 per cent of all autopsies, including about 12 per cent of alcoholics (Harper, 1979; 1983; Torvik *et al.*, 1982). It should also be noted that Korsakoff (1889) described his syndrome in a number of patients with disorders affecting nutrition/absorption in the *absence* of a history of alcohol abuse. Such cases have been reported less commonly in recent times (presumably because of improvements in medical care), but occasional instances have indeed been described (Beatty *et al.*, 1989; Becker *et al.*, 1990).

The classical neuropathology of what Victor *et al.* (1971) termed the Wernicke–Korsakoff syndrome involves micro-haemorrhages and endothelial proliferation (i.e. rupture and abnormal changes in the lining of blood vessels), together with focal areas of parenchymal necrosis, demyelination, gliosis and variable degrees of neuronal loss (i.e. degeneration of brain cells and tissue and nerve fibre linings with associated scarring). These abnormalities mainly occur in the so-called 'diencephalon', involving paraventricular and peri-aqueductal grey matter, the walls of the third ventricle, the floor of the fourth ventricle, and the cerebellum (i.e. deep midline and midbrain structures). Victor *et al.* (1971) argued that the critical lesion site for the production of memory deficit was the medial dorsal nucleus of the thalamus. However, two more recent studies have argued that atrophy of the mammillary bodies, together with concomitant lesions in the mammillary-thalamic tract and the anterior thalamus are the critical factors resulting in the memory disorder (Mair *et al.*, 1979; Mayes *et al.*, 1988). These lesions are induced by thiamine depletion and can be mimicked in experimental animals. Thiamine depletion also produces various neurotransmitter depletions, which may contribute to the *anterograde* memory impairment (McEntee and Mair, 1980; Butters, 1985; Kopelman and Corn, 1988). As mentioned above, concomitant frontal lobe pathology probably underlies some of the memory deficits (Mayes *et al.*, 1985; Janowsky *et al.*, 1989), and this may be true of the extensive *retrograde* loss characteristic of this disorder (Kopelman, 1991). Fuller details of the neuropsychology of the disorder have been reviewed elsewhere (Squire, 1987; Mayes, 1988; Butters and Stuss, 1989, Kopelman, in press).

CONCLUSION

In summary, the neuropsychiatric sequelae of prolonged alcohol abuse include both acute/sub-acute and more chronic syndromes. The acute phenomena include confusional states (delirium tremens, hepatic, Wernicke's, and alcoholic pellagra encephalopathy), hallucinosis and paranoid states (delirium tremens, alcoholic hallucinosis), and discrete episodes of memory loss (alcoholic blackouts). The chronic phenomena include a coarsening of personality, many features of which may well be attributable to the frontal lobe atrophy commonly described in alcoholics, cognitive deterioration which is associated with generalized cortical atrophy, and the more specific memory impairment (Korsakoff syndrome) resulting from diencephalic (and frontal) pathology. Although the clinical features of all these syndromes have now been well described and the aetiological basis of some is understood (thiamine depletion in the Wernicke and Korsakoff syndromes, nicotinic acid depletion in pellagra encephalopathy), we still lack knowledge about the underlying genetic, neurochemical, and pathophysiological mechanisms which bring them about. The cerebral changes which induce the clinical phenomena of delirium tremens or alcoholic hallucinosis, the pathophysiology of an alcoholic blackout, why thiamine depletion produces a particular pattern of neuropathological change but only in predisposed subjects, and the processes whereby alcohol causes cortical atrophy which is (at least) partially reversible after prolonged abstinence – all these issues remain to be further elucidated.

REFERENCES

Acker, C. (1985) 'Short report – performance of female alcoholics on neuropsychological testing', *Alcohol and Alcoholism* 20: 379–86.
— (1986) 'Neuropsychological deficits in alcoholics: the relative contributions of gender and drinking history', *British Journal of Addiction* 81: 395–403.
Acker, C., Jacobson, R.R. and Lishman, W.A. (1987) 'Memory and ventricular size in alcoholics', *Psychological Medicine* 17: 343–8.
Beatty, W.W., Bailly, R.C. and Fisher, L. (1989) 'Korsakoff-like amnesic syndrome in a patient with anorexia and vomiting', *International Journal of Clinical Neuropsychology* 11: 55–65.
Becker, J.T., Furman, J.M.R., Panisett, M. and Smith, C. (1990) 'Characteristics of the memory loss of a patient with Wernicke–Korsakoff's syndrome without alcoholism', *Neuropsychologia* 28: 171–9.

Berlyne, N. (1972) 'Confabulation', *British Journal of Psychiatry* 120: 31–9.

Bowden, S.C. (1990) The separation of cognitive impairment in neurologically asymptomatic alcoholism from Wernicke–Korsakoff syndrome: is the neuropsychological distinction justified?', *Psychological Bulletin* 107: 355–66.

Brandt, J., Butters, N., Ryan, C. and Bayog, R. (1983) 'Cognitive loss and recovery in long-term alcohol abusers', *Archives of General Psychiatry* 40: 435–42.

Butters, N. (1985) 'Alcoholic Korsakoff's syndrome: some unresolved issues concerning aetiology, neuropathology, and cognitive deficits', *Journal of Clinical and Experimental Neuropsychology* 7: 181–210.

Butters, N. and Cermak, L.S. (1980) *Alcoholic Korsakoff's Syndrome: an Information-Processing Approach to Amnesia*, New York: Academic Press.

Butters, N. and Stuss, D.T. (1989) 'Diencephalic amnesia', in F. Boller and J. Grafman (eds) *Handbook of Neuropsychology*, vol 3, Holland: Elsevier Science Publishers, BV.

Carlen, P.L., Wilkinson, D.A., Wortzman, G., Holgate, R., Cordingley, J., Lee, M.A., Huzzar, L., Moddell, G., Singh, R., Kiraly, L. and Rankin, J.G. (1981) 'Cerebral atrophy and functional deficits in alcoholics without apparent liver disease', *Neurology* 31: 377–85.

Chick, J. (1989) 'Delirium tremens', *British Medical Journal* 298: 3–4.

Coid, J. (1979) '"Mania à potu": a critical review of pathological intoxication', *Psychological Medicine* 9: 709–19.

—— (1986) 'Socio-cultural factors in alcohol-related aggression', in P.F. Brain (ed.) *Alcohol and Aggression*, London: Croom Helm, pp. 184–211.

Cushman, P. (1987) 'Delirium tremens: update on an old disorder', *Postgraduate Medicine* 82: 117–22.

Cutting, J. (1978a) 'A reappraisal of alcoholic psychoses', *Psychological Medicine* 8: 285–96.

—— (1978b) 'The relationship between Korsakoff's syndrome and "alcoholic dementia"', *British Journal of Psychiatry* 132: 240–51.

Emsley, R.A., Potgieter, A., Taljaard, J.J.F., Coetzee, D., Joubert, G. and Gledhill, R.F. (1987) 'Impaired water excretion and elevated plasma vasoprosin in patients with alcohol withdrawal symptoms', *Quarterly Journal of Medicine* 64: 671–8.

Goodwin, D.W., Crane, J.B. and Guze, S.B. (1969) 'Phenomenological aspects of the alcoholic black-out', *British Journal of Psychiatry* 115: 1033–7.

Harper, C. (1979) 'Wernicke's encephalopathy: a more common disease than realised: a neuropathological study of 51 cases', *Journal of Neurology, Neurosurgery and Psychiatry* 42: 226–31.

—— (1983) 'The incidence of Wernicke's encephalopathy in Australia: a neuropathological study of 131 cases', *Journal of Neurology, Neurosurgery and Psychiatry* 46: 593–8.

Harper, C., Kril, J. and Daly, J. (1987) 'Are we drinking our neurones away?', *British Medical Journal* 294: 534–6.

Hata, T., Meyer, J.S., Tanahashi, N., Ishikawa, Y., Imai, A., Shinohara, T., Velez, M., Fann, W.E., Kandula, P. and Sakai, F. (1987) 'Three-dimensional mapping of local cerebral perfusion in alcoholic encephalopathy with and without Wernicke–Korsakoff syndrome', *Journal of Cerebral Blood Flow and Metabolism* 7: 35–44.

Hauw, J.J., Baecque, C. de, Hausser-Hauw, C. and Serdaru, M. (1988) 'Chromatolysis in alcoholic encephalopathies. Pellagra-like changes in 22 cases', *Brain* 111: 843–57.

Hillbom, M. and Holm, L. (1986) 'Contribution of traumatic head injury to neuro-psychological deficits in alcoholics', *Journal of Neurology, Neurosurgery and Psychiatry* 49: 1348–53.

Hunter, R., McLuskie, R., Wyper, D., Patterson, J., Christie, J.E., Brooks, D.N., McCulloch, J., Fink, G. and Goodwin, G.M. (1989) 'The pattern of function-related regional cerebral blood flow investigated by single photon emission tomography with ^{99m}Tc-HMPAO in patients with presenile Alzheimer's disease and Korsakoff's psychosis', *Psychological Medicine* 19: 847–55.

Ishii, N. and Nishihara, Y. (1981) 'Pellagra among chronic alcoholics – clinical and pathological study of 20 necropsy cases', *Journal of Neurology, Neurosurgery and Psychiatry* 44: 209–15.

Jacobson, R.R. and Lishman, W.A. (1987) 'Selective memory loss and global intellectual deficits in alcoholic Korsakoff's syndrome', *Psychological Medicine* 17: 645–55.

Jacobson, R.R., Acker, C. and Lishman, W.A. (1990) 'Patterns of neuropsychological deficit in alcoholic Korsakoff's syndrome', *Psychological Medicine* 20: 321–34.

Janowksy, J.S., Shimamura, A.P., Kritchevsky, M. and Squire, L.R. (1989) 'Cognitive impairment following frontal lobe damage and its relevance to human amnesia', *Behavioural Neuroscience* 103: 548–60.

Jolliffe, N., Wortis, H. and Fein, H.D. (1941) 'The Wernicke syndrome', *Archives of Neurology and Psychiatry* 46: 569–97.

Kopelman, M.D. (1987a) 'Amnesia: organic and psychogenic', *British Journal of Psychiatry* 150: 428–42.

—— (1987b) 'Crime and amnesia – a review', *Behavioral Science and the Law* 5: 323–42.

—— (1987c) 'Two types of confabulation', *Journal of Neurology, Neurosurgery and Psychiatry* 50: 1482–7.

—— (1989) 'Remote and autobiographical memory, temporal lobe context memory, and frontal atrophy in Korsakoff and Alzheimer patients', *Neuropsychologia* 27: 437–60.

—— 1991 'Frontal dysfunction and memory deficits in the alcoholic Korsakoff syndrome and Alzheimer-type dementia', *Brain* 114: 117–37.

—— (in press) *The Alcoholic Korsakoff Syndrome and Alzheimer Type Dementia – a clinical, neuropsychological and neuropharmacological study*, London: Laurence Erlbaum Associates.

Kopelman, M.D. and Corn, T.H. (1988) 'Cholinergic "blockade" as a model for cholinergic depletion: a comparison of the memory deficits with those of Alzheimer-type dementia and the alcoholic Korsakoff syndrome', *Brain* 111: 1079–1110.

Korsakoff, S.S. (1889) 'Psychic disorder in conjunction with peripheral neuritis', translated and republished by M. Victor and P.I. Yakovlev (1955) *Neurology* 5: 394–406.

Lishman, W.A. (1981) 'Cerebral disorder in alcoholism: syndromes of impairment', *Brain* 104: 1–20.

—— (1986) 'Alcoholic dementia: a hypothesis', *Lancet* 1: 1184–6.

—— (1987) *Organic Psychiatry: The Psychological Consequences of Cerebral Disorder*, 2nd edn, Oxford: Blackwell Scientific Publications.

Lishman, W.A., Jacobson, R. and Acker, C. (1987) 'Brain damage in alcoholism: current concepts', *Acta Medica Scandinavica*, Suppl. 717: 5–17.

Lundquist, G. (1961) 'Delirium tremens: a comparative study of pathogenesis, course and prognosis with delirium tremens', *Acta Psychiatrica Scandinavica* 36: 443–66.

McEntee, W.J. and Mair, R.G. (1980) 'Memory enhancement in Korsakoff's psychosis by clonidine: further evidence for a noradrenergic deficit', *Annals of Neurology* 7: 466–70.

Mair, W.G.P., Warrington, E.K. and Weiskrantz, L. (1979) 'Memory disorder in Korsakoff's psychosis: a neuropathological and neuropsychological investigation of two cases', *Brain* 102: 783.

Mayes, A.R. (1988) *Human Organic Memory Disorders*, Cambridge: Cambridge University Press.

Mayes, A.R., Meudell, P.R. and Pickering, A. (1985) 'Is organic amnesia caused by a selective deficit in remembering contextual information?', *Cortex* 21: 167–202.

Mayes, A.R., Meudell, P.R., Mann, D. and Pickering, A. (1988) 'Location of lesions in Korsakoff's syndrome: neuropsychological and neuropathological data on two patients', *Cortex* 24: 367–88.

Murray, R. (1986) 'Alcoholism', in P. Hill, R. Murray and A. Thorley (eds) *Essentials of Postgraduate Psychiatry*, 2nd edn, London: Grune and Stratton.

Nordström, G. and Bergland, M. (1988) 'Delirium tremens: a prospective long-term follow-up study', *Journal of Studies of Alcohol* 49: 178–85.

Ron, M.A. (1983) *The alcoholic brain – CT scan and psychological findings. Psychological Medicine*, Monograph Supplement 3, Cambridge: Cambridge University Press.

Ron, M.A., Acker, W., Shaw, G.K. and Lishman, W.A. (1982) 'Computerised tomography of the brain in chronic alcoholism', *Brain* 105: 497–514.

Ryan, C., Didario, B., Butters, N. and Adinolfi, A. (1980) 'The relationship between abstinence and recovery of function in male alcoholics', *Journal of Clinical Neuropsychology* 2: 125–34.

Serdaru, M., Hausser-Hauw, C., Laplane, D., Buge, A., Castaigne, P., Goulon, M., Lhermitte, F. and Hauw, J.J. (1988) 'The clinical spectrum of alcoholic pellagra encephalopathy', *Brain* 111: 829–42.

Shimamura, A.P., Jernigan, T.L. and Squire, L.R. (1988) 'Korsakoff's syndrome: radiological findings and neuropsychological correlates', *Journal of Neuroscience* 8: 4400–10.

Squire, L.R. (1987) *Memory and the Brain*, Oxford: Oxford University Press.

Tartar, R.E. and Schneider, D.U. (1976) 'Blackouts – relationship with memory capacity and alcoholic history', *Archives of General Psychiatry* 33: 1492–6.

Torvik, A., Lindboe, C.F. and Rodge, S. (1982) 'Brain lesions in alcoholics', *Journal of Neurological Science* 56: 233–48.

Victor, M. and Adams, R.D. (1985) 'The alcoholic dementias', in J.A.M. Fredericks (ed.) *Handbook of Clinical Neurology*, vol 2 (46), Holland: Elsevier Science Publishers, BV, pp. 335–51.

Victor, M., Adams, R.D. and Collins, G.H. (1971) *Wernicke-Korsakoff Syndrome*, Philadelphia: F.A. Davis Company.

Wernicke, C. (1885) 'Acute haemorrhagic superior polioencephalitis', translated and republished by I.A. Brody and R.H. Wilkins (1968) *Archives of Neurology* 19: 228–32.

CROSS REFERENCES

Chapter 23

Alcohol and mental illness: cause or effect?

Ilana Belle Glass and Jane Marshall

The relationship between alcohol and mental illness is important both theoretically and practically. A knowledge of a consistency of the relationship has implications for aetiology, diagnosis, treatment and prognosis as well as service organization.

The association between alcoholism and psychiatric disorders has been the subject of many studies, reviews and even myths. Alcohol has been implicated as the agent responsible for a variety of psychiatric disturbances, and psychiatric problems have frequently been described as underlying all cases of alcoholism. Our understanding of this relationship has advanced slowly.

With the help of diagnostic criteria such as DSM (Diagnostic and Statistical Manual) III, IIIR and IV and the WHO (World Health Organization) ICD (International Classification of Diseases) 8, 9 and 10, insight is beginning to sharpen. As defined by these authorities alcohol abuse and dependence are now recognized as psychiatric disorders. Since psychiatric symptomatology may be present at many stages in the alcoholic career, symptoms must always be evaluated in the context of an entire process. There may be psychiatric factors which predispose some individuals to develop alcoholism and, conversely, alcoholism may play a part in the development of psychiatric disorders. Although psychiatric symptoms may arise as a result of acute or chronic effects of alcohol, any psychiatric disorder may co-exist independently with alcoholism.

As described in Chapter 29, a discussion on differential (and dual) diagnosis is imperative. Thus, a thorough history, including family history and mental state, may aid clarification. Psychopharmacological treatment options in relation to this assessment are described in Chapter 30. The value of psychotherapeutic techniques for disorders other than the addictions are not dealt with separately in this book but are, none the less, important.

Many studies have investigated the prevalence of drinking problems and psychiatric illness over the last twenty-five years. However, since diagnostic criteria for alcohol dependence and psychiatric illness varied, it has proved impossible to compare findings. Results indicate, however, that clinicians appreciate that patients who developed alcohol problems could also present with psychiatric disorders in addition. The Maudsley Hospital survey (Glass and Jackson, 1988) has drawn attention to the fact that 10 per cent of psychiatric patients have an alcohol problem, of which 40 per cent have an additional psychiatric diagnosis. As schizophrenia, affective psychosis, neurosis, personality disorder and drug addiction were found to be consistently associated, this chapter will deal with these disorders apart from the relationship between alcoholism and drug addiction.

ALCOHOLISM AND PSYCHOSIS

Schizophrenia

Prevalence

Analysis of this relationship is complex because there are a number of ways in which schizophrenia and alcohol can interact. Alcoholism may be chronic, and schizophrenia may arise coincidentally in the course of it. Schizophrenia might arise as a toxic effect of alcohol, or alcohol might exacerbate a chronic psychosis. Alcoholism might occur as a consequence of the psychosis.

As late as 1975, a review of studies on this issue reported prevalence rates for schizophrenia occurring in alcoholics of between 1 per cent and 33 per cent, and in schizophrenics abusing alcohol between 3 per cent and 63 per cent.

A recent study by Bernadt and Murray (1986) which assessed drinking behaviour in 371 psychiatric admissions showed that schizophrenics drank *less* than the mean amount drunk by patients admitted to hospital. Alcoholism has also been shown to be less common in relatives of schizophrenics than control subjects. These studies show no link between alcoholism and schizophrenia, and although they can occur together, it is uncommon.

Natural history studies

Apart from six studies attempting to clarify the issue of the relationship of schizophrenia to alcoholic hallucinosis, no long-term studies have been reported (Glass, 1989a; 1989b). The results of these studies, carried out between 1958 and 1978, some very comprehensive, were hampered by poor operational definitions and follow-up methodology. Taking into account these reservations, it appears that a very few cases of alcoholic hallucinosis develop schizophrenia.

Genetic studies

A number of studies which employ standard methods to ascertain a genetic contribution, i.e. adoption studies and twin studies (Kendler, 1985), have suggested that individuals suffering from schizophrenia and alcoholism have a predisposition to each illness separately.

Furthermore, there does appear to be a genetic component to the manifestation of alcohol-related problems like alcoholic psychosis and liver cirrhosis.

What is alcoholic hallucinosis?

This area is a controversial one, but many clinicians will be familiar with the following presentation: A heavy drinker complains of auditory hallucinations (noises, music or voices) often of a persecutory nature. The patient is not delirious, and no physical symptoms are present. Although this may follow relative or complete abstinence from alcohol, the problem may arise and recur while continuing to drink. Differentiation from schizophrenia is possible because thought disorder is not present, a family history of schizophrenia is negative, and there is no evidence of a complex delusional system. Of course, exclusion of a drug-induced psychosis by urine screening is necessary.

Nevertheless, the relationship of alcoholic hallucinosis to schizophrenia and delirium tremens is unclear. There appears to be a reasonable consensus that an acute illness, where auditory hallucinations predominate, associated with a history of heavy drinking, exists. Some authorities favour the view that it has much in common with delirium tremens (slight clouding of consciousness, presence of physical symptoms which may accompany an acute confusional state, other kinds of hallucinations). Others suggest a similarity to schizophrenia (clear consciousness, chronicity, predominantly auditory hallucinations). As mentioned above, review of follow-up studies to date reveals weaknesses in operational definitions and follow-up methodology. This array of fundamental definitions and assessment must render interpretations of these studies open to question, even where there appears to be agreement. At this stage, alcoholic hallucinosis might best be regarded as an organic psychosis. If it does resemble some type of schizophrenia, it is the non-familial, sporadic, paranoid form which is being linked to evidence of cerebral dysfunction.

In summary, it would appear that the more robust findings suggest that, although schizophrenia and alcoholism do occur together, this combination is uncommon. It is important, however, for the clinician to be aware of the possibility that the alcoholic patient who might have developed psychotic symptoms is not invariably suffering from a schizophrenic illness and long-term neuroleptics should not automatically be prescribed. The patient should be re-assessed after a month's abstinence, and this might give some indication as to the nature and the course of their illness, and treatment appropriately selected.

The following vignettes illustrate the way in which the variety of psychotic symptoms may present:

Alcoholic hallucinosis

Mr A came to the hospital saying that he wanted to stop drinking. He said that on several previous occasions when he had been drinking heavily he began to hear muffled noises as though people were muttering. At times he would actually hear voices which seemed real to him. Usually there were two voices and often they would comment on his actions. It could be very unpleasant, he said. When he was off drinking for a couple of weeks the noises would completely disappear. If he started to drink again, the noises sooner or later came back.

Visual illusions

Mr B and Mrs C were talking about their experiences when drinking. Mr B said that when he was drinking very heavily and sometimes went out for a walk he thought he saw an Alsatian dog running by his side, but when he tried to pat it, it seemed to disappear. This had happened on quite a few occasions recently.

He wondered whether Mrs C had ever had anything similar happen to her.

Mrs C said that sometimes when she had been sitting in her living-room she thought for a brief moment that her brother-in-law appeared, but when she started to talk to him he wasn't there.

Schizophrenic illness

Mr D was persuaded to go to his GP's surgery by his wife.

She told the GP that she was becoming more and more concerned about him. He was gradually becoming very emotionally withdrawn. He was also admitting to her, very reluctantly, strange feelings which he was having. She thought these feelings were, to say the least, very weird. He thought that there was a transistor in the flower pots.

This transistor was sending out signals which controlled what he thought and what he said. He felt like a robot, and this he put down to the influence of the signal. He believed that the television programmes were directing messages at him. He had taken to drink to try to dampen down these feelings, which had certainly begun to occur before he was drinking heavily.

Delirium tremens

A group of patients on an alcoholism treatment ward were exchanging experiences about the times they had tried to stop drinking.

Mrs E said that when she had decided to stop this time she had come to hospital because she was frightened of having the same experience as on the last occasion when she had decided to stop. She said that after three days off drink, she had become so confused that she didn't know where she was. She became so agitated on the third day off drink that she had to be taken to hospital as she needed a nurse to look after her all the time. She thought people were out to get her. She also reported seeing strange shapes and flashing lights. She later realized that these experiences were not real but at the time she was terrified out of her wits. The whole experience only lasted about a week.

ALCOHOLISM AND AFFECTIVE DISORDER

Prevalence

In summary, despite provoking much research interest in the past twenty-five years, the relationship between alcoholism and affective disorder is still poorly understood. Prevalence studies have focused mainly on the presence of depressive symptoms in alcoholics referred to specialized treatment centres with estimated rates of between 3 per cent and 98 per cent. Comparison of rates across studies is difficult because of the lack of rigorous and consistent diagnostic criteria for alcoholism *and* affective disorder. Often studies do not distinguish which is the primary problem (though this may be difficult in clinical practice), the syndrome–symptom dichotomy is not addressed and control groups are lacking. Assessment of depressive symptoms in alcoholics may be contaminated by variables such as personality, drug abuse, other psychiatric disorders (e.g. neurosis), as well as the alcohol-withdrawal state and possibly the phenomenon of craving. Chronic alcohol abuse is commonly complicated by depressive symptoms (during episodes of heavy drinking, in the withdrawal phase, secondary to alcohol-related adverse life events). These depressive episodes, although severe, are usually transient and improve with abstinence, thus may be a direct result of the pharmacological action of alcohol. One prevalence study which has attempted to overcome methodological problems is that of Bernadt and Murray (1986), which has already been mentioned. Using Research Diagnostic Criteria and the Present State Examination (PSE), they found a relationship between alcoholism and a high prevalence of affective syndromes. However, these affective syndromes were not severe enough to merit a secondary diagnosis. When the alcoholics were compared with a group of psychiatric patients similar prevalence rates for affective syndromes were found. This study underlines the need for control groups in prevalence studies.

Natural history studies

There is a paucity of natural history studies. Life time prevalence rates must be distinguished from current symptomatology and comparison made between alcoholics who continue to drink and those who maintain abstinence. Certainly some studies report that co-existing affective disorder may affect outcome in both male and female alcoholics (Hesselbrock *et al.*, 1986).

Genetic studies

Genetic factors are implicated in the aetiology of both alcoholism and affective disorder. This association is more clear-out for affective disorder. Twin and adoption studies of alcoholism have underscored the importance of environmental factors and the concept of familial alcoholism is being re-assessed. Research to date does not support a genetic association between alcoholism and affective disorder. In a recent study, Merikangas and colleagues (1985) examined the familial transmission of alcoholism and major depression amongst probands with alcoholism and depression. In all, 215 probands and 1331 relatives were studied. There was no control group. Their results indicated that at least for their group, alcoholism and depression were transmitted independently and were not manifestations of the same disorder.

Clinical features

Alcoholics commonly complain of feelings of depression, guilt and remorse, anxiety and irritability. Many report suicidal ideation. Sleep and appetite are disturbed. These symptoms are often set against a background of social disintegration – job loss, marital and family breakdown, financial and forensic difficulties, and physical illness.

Symptoms can be particularly intense following a period of binge drinking and may be severe enough to fulfil operational criteria for depression. However, many of the 'depressive symptoms' can also arise as a direct result of the toxic effects of alcohol, e.g. wakening early in the morning (a falling blood alcohol level), anorexia, weight loss and loss of libido.

In the majority of cases the symptoms recede over a period of three to four weeks with abstinence from alcohol. If symptoms of depression remain after this time they are likely to be due to a true depressive illness and antidepressants ought to be considered.

The issue of alcoholism and mania/hypomania has been poorly covered in the literature. A proportion of individuals with a bipolar affective disorder develop alcohol problems and vice versa but results in the limited studies carried out to date are conflicting and no inferences can be drawn. Many reports indicate that the manic phase is associated with heavy drinking; this association was *not* found in the Bernadt and Murray (1986) study. Further research on this question is needed.

The following case-histories illustrate some of the points raised in the preceding discussion:

Depressive illness

Mrs A, a married woman in her late thirties, had been drinking in a dependent fashion for some three years. For much of this time she had been depressed. Initially, she drank to relieve her depression but latterly she was finding that alcohol only served to lower her mood even further. She decided to stop drinking. Her low mood remained and did not improve.

When she was assessed she had been abstinent from alcohol for eight weeks. She described a feeling of black despair hovering over her and trying to get her in its grip. She would wake up at 5.00 a.m. unrefreshed and with her mind in a turmoil of confusion. The feeling of depression was very marked first thing in the morning. She described severe guilt feelings, had little hope for the future and her self-esteem was poor. Her appetite was negligible and she had no energy.

Objectively she was moderately depressed with psychomotor retardation. A tricyclic antidepressant was started and this led to a marked improvement in her mood over the next month. She remained on antidepressants for six months and maintained abstinence throughout this period.

At one year follow up she was still abstinent and euthymic.

Depressive illness

Mr D, a 49-year-old married unemployed man, had a twenty-year history of heavy drinking. For ten years he had demonstrated all the features of the alcohol dependence syndrome, but following in-patient treatment remained abstinent for one year. He began to drink heavily again following his father's death, in response to low mood, tearfulness, decreased appetite and weight loss, anergia and diminished libido. He experienced re-emergence of memory blackouts and severe withdrawal symptoms.

Following a failed out-patient detoxification his mood fell further and was accompanied by marked guilt feelings and poor self-esteem. Finally he thought that his wife and children would be better off without him, so he took an overdose of chlordiazepoxide together with a bottle of whisky and was admitted unconscious to a medical ward in his local hospital. He then had a severe haematemesis and at the time of transfer to an in-patient alcohol unit, he was thin, pale, undernourished with a tender abdomen and palpable liver. His haemoglobin was low, his liver function tests were elevated and a CT scan showed mild frontal atrophy.

He remained severely depressed over the next four weeks and there were prominent biological features. Although his depression was considered to be related to recent life events and alcohol, there were sufficient symptoms for an independent diagnosis, thus antidepressants were started. This led to a gradual improvement in his mood and he was finally discharged well on antidepressants.

Hypomania

Miss C, a 36-year-old single professional woman, had a five-year history of bipolar affective disorder and alcohol dependence.

She had been reasonably well for some two years, had been abstinent for the most part from alcohol and free from any major mood swings. Then, over a two-week period she developed a disrupted sleep pattern. She became very active and would talk in a loud animated voice. Slight pressure of speech was evident. She described considerable well being.

She began to think that a fellow member of her AA group was a reincarnation of Christ. She had a relapse of heavy drinking which lasted 24 hours. Over the next week she became increasingly restless and over-active, heard voices and saw visions of Jesus. She felt that she had been given special insight into God having created a world of extremes – black and white, love and hate.

Two days before admission she said that she had extra psychic powers and that all of the members of her family were going to die.

The symptoms subsided over a four week period in hospital during which time she was treated with neuroleptics.

In summary, alcoholics are prone to depressive symptoms particularly during and after periods of heavy drinking. These symptoms may last for several weeks after the last drink but in general should resolve with continuing abstinence. Antidepressants may have a place in cases of unresolved depression and are reported to be helpful in women alcoholics.

ALCOHOLISM AND SUICIDE

The rates of completed suicide in alcoholics are higher compared with rates in non-alcoholics of similar age. Kessel and Grossman's (1961) follow-up study of in-patient alcoholics indicated that 8 per cent killed themselves. Studies from other countries report equivalent figures. About 30 per cent of attempted suicides are alcoholic. Those at greatest risk include older men with a long history of alcoholism, a history of depression, previous attempts and significant physical and social sequelae of their alcohol abuse.

The alcoholic presenting with suicidal ideation should be admitted and detoxified under careful medical and psychiatric supervision. Assessment and re-assessment of the mental state will be necessary so that informed decisions concerning treatment and continued risk can be made.

There is increasing evidence that other forms of self-destructive behaviour, e.g. fatal accidents, overdoses, are also more common amongst alcoholics, and there is debate as to whether these are, in fact, covert suicides.

The following case-history describes the complexity of dealing with such a clinical problem:

Mr B, a 42-year-old married self-employed man with a long history of binge drinking, was admitted to hospital because of suicidal ideation.

His wife had left him one month previously because of his alcohol consumption and his intolerable behaviour. He'd lost his business as a result of his alcohol problem and friends had been deserting him because of his drinking.

On the day of admission he had been feeling particularly depressed and overwhelmed by his circumstances and had consumed about three bottles of vodka. He visited his GP, got a letter for the hospital but on his way home impulsively decided to kill himself and walked in front of a car. He was not injured, collapsed on the pavement and was taken home. Later that day, when he had sobered up somewhat, he was still feeling depressed and suicidal, therefore brought himself to hospital. He described a low mood, sleep disruption with early morning wakening and initial insomnia, poor appetite and nutrition, weight loss and decreased libido. The future looked bleak. He expressed suicidal ideation but had no formed intent or plans.

After a rather stormy detoxification his mood improved. His sleep returned to normal as did his appetite. Two weeks after admission there was no evidence of a depressive disorder.

ALCOHOLISM AND NEUROTIC DISORDERS

Despite numerous reports indicating the co-occurrence of neurotic symptoms and disorders with alcohol use, abuse, intoxication and withdrawal, the figures quoted vary greatly. This is related to the array of diagnostic criteria, research methodologies (life-time prevalence or current symptomatology), rating scales applied to in-patient and out-patient alcoholic or neurotic samples.

There is a dearth of basic data on prevalence, natural history studies, the role of genetic predisposition and treatment efficacy studies comparing behavioural, pharmacological and psychotherapeutic strategies.

Most work has centred on anxiety states: generalized anxiety, panic attacks and phobic states (Stockwell and Bolderston, 1987).

These indicate that in some instances anxiety states do precede the development of alcoholism. Thus it is imperative to assess patients once they are abstinent. If, thereafter, anxiety is thought to be a problem in its own right, appropriate treatment interventions should be considered. Counselling, behavioural psychotherapy and pharmacotherapy, if successful, mitigate the anxiety and as a consequence, alcohol abuse, as demonstrated in the following case report:

A 23-year-old man was admitted to a surgical ward because of recurrent attacks of pancreatitis. This was just one of a number of alcohol-related physical problems: hepatitis, gastritis, convulsions and delirium tremens, he had experienced. From the age of 16, when he began drinking, his consumption escalated to one and a half bottles of spirits a day.

He said that part of the reason he drank was due to anxiety. On further questioning it became clear that he often experienced sweating, tremulousness, a feeling of being unable to cope and agitation. Furthermore, he admitted to spending most of his time indoors and avoided going out, using public transport and doing shopping. This seemed to precipitate his drinking bouts because of the anxiety it generated.

After in-patient detoxification he was discharged home. He was given a self-help manual for coping with his phobic symptoms. His mother agreed to help with the self-exposure homework. He continues to attend the alcohol unit out-patient department and a day centre specializing in alcohol problems.

ALCOHOLISM AND PERSONALITY PROBLEMS

The most complicated relationship to unravel remains that between alcohol abuse, alcoholism and personality problems, especially sociopathy. Many persons diagnosed as sociopaths or as suffering from psychopathic personality disorder engage in excessive drinking; many alcohol abusers exhibit antisocial behaviour such as criminal activity, violence and aggressive behaviour. The diagnosis of personality disorder itself is subject to criticism and controversy.

Schuckit (1973) has suggested three aetiological links:

1 Alcohol abuse as a symptom of antisocial behaviour.
2 Alcohol abuse leads to antisocial behaviour.
3 A common factor underlying both alcoholism and sociopathy.

Temporal sequencing, he suggests, can aid diagnosis. If antisocial behaviour precedes alcoholism by 7–10 years, the primary diagnosis is that of sociopathy.

Cloninger and Bohman's studies (Bohman *et al.*, 1981; Cloninger *et al.*, 1981; Clonginer, 1987) have concluded that there are two forms of alcoholism which have distinct genetic and environmental causes, and which differ in their association with criminality, severity of alcohol abuse and expression in biological parents. This is covered more extensively in Chapter 7 and the association of criminal activity with alcohol consumption is discussed in Chapter 44.

A clinical illustration follows:

A 25-year-old woman was admitted to an alcohol treatment unit because her drinking had escalated over the five years since the birth of her child. She drank to relieve anxiety, and was drinking two bottles of vodka a day. Her boyfriend had left recently because of her drinking, and she had begun to have fits. She reported that she had also been taking diazepam over this time.

Her mother died when she was 10, and there was a family history of depressive illness and alcoholism. She regularly missed school, and had not taken examinations, nor had she ever been employed. She had had many boyfriends, but no long-standing relationships. She had had numerous arrests for prostitution and shop-lifting since the age of 16.

ALCOHOLISM AND EATING DISORDERS

Interest in the relationship between eating disorders and alcoholism has burgeoned only recently. Once more, lack of operational criteria and rating scales reduced much information to anecdote and speculation.

However, studies are now beginning to suggest that it is well worth pursuing further the link between these two disorders, and the possibility of a common aetiological factor. Whether treatment should be directed at each condition separately, or whether there is a need for an approach for the two conditions combined, is as yet untested.

A clinical example illustrates:

Ms A G, a 23-year-old lady, was referred to an alcohol treatment unit for a drinking problem which she had had since the age of 16. At the time of referral she was drinking two bottles of wine a day. This began in the setting of increasing conflict at home. She experienced withdrawal symptoms when she abstained, and she has had periods of up to one year when she has managed to remain abstinent.

She also admitted to a long-standing eating problem. She had had periods of anorexia nervosa, when her weight dropped to six and a half stone, she was amenorrhoeic and she hardly ate for fear of putting on weight. At time of consultation she was having episodes of bingeing and vomiting (bulimia nervosa), and her weight had stabilized at eight stone.

She was thought to be an intelligent young woman, and had a steady relationship with a caring boyfriend. She was advised to begin an out-patient detoxification programme and counselling. In the longer term, individual psychotherapy was considered a possibility.

PATHOLOGICAL JEALOUSY

In this curious syndrome, feelings of jealousy become so extreme that they can impinge destructively on the lives of those involved. The association with alcoholism is well recognized, and it may be symptomatic of a number of other psychiatric illnesses including paranoid schizophrenia and depressive illness. There is still much to learn about the sequence and interaction of the jealousy and drinking behaviour.

A clinical example illustrates some of the features:

Mr F was admitted to hospital because he was threatening to assault his wife. He had a history of heavy alcohol consumption over many years and had always been a jealous person. He complained that she was unfaithful to him. He would check up on her arrangements and would rummage through her possessions for evidence of these liaisons. She denied his claims, but this just seemed to provoke more anger and abuse. He said that he found this experience unpleasant and, although he had repeatedly tried to stop drinking because of the increasingly violent nature of his threats, he was worried he might harm his wife. This time he wanted some help. After managing to abstain from alcohol for some time, there was a diminution of his jealousy and an improvement in his marital relationship.

CONCLUSION

While it is well documented that psychiatric disorder and alcoholism co-exist, very few reports examine the interaction of various conditions and the nature of the particular relationships that may exist between them. Psychiatric disorder may pre-date, predispose to, or arise as a result of the alcoholism. It may exist independently, though it could influence the outcome of the alcoholism. Research which elucidates the prevalence, genetic contribution and natural history of associated disorders might offer new leads for treatment interventions. This has implications for aetiology and service development.

Clinically, decisions about treatment will depend upon the symptomatology at the time of assessment, evaluation of family history, time course of the illness and the patient's condition after detoxification from alcohol and other drugs.

REFERENCES

Bernadt, M.W. and Murray, R.M. (1986) 'Psychiatric disorder, drinking and alcoholism: what are the links?', *British Journal of Psychiatry* 148: 393–400.

Bohman, M., Sigvardsson, S. and Cloninger, C.R. (1981) 'Maternal inheritance of alcohol abuse: cross-fostering analysis of adopted women', *Archives of General Psychiatry* 38: 965–9.

Cloninger, C.R. (1987) 'Neurogenetic adaptive mechanisms in alcoholism', *Science* 236: 410–16.

Cloninger, C.R., Bohman, M. and Sigvardsson, S. (1981) 'Inheritance of alcohol abuse', *Archives of General Psychiatry* 38: 861–8.

Glass, I. B. (1989a) 'Alcoholic hallucinosis: a psychiatric enigma. 1. The development of the idea', *British Journal of Addiction* 84: 29–41.

—— (1989b) 'Alcoholic hallucinosis: a psychiatric enigma. 2. Follow-up studies', *British Journal of Addiction* 84: 151–64.

Glass, I.B. and Jackson, P. (1988) 'Maudsley Hospital Survey: prevalence of alcohol problems and other psychiatric disorders in a hospital population', *British Journal of Addiction* 83: 1105–11.

Hesselbrock, V.P., Hesselbrock, M.N. and Workman-Daniels, K.L. (1986) 'Effect of major depression and antisocial personality on alcoholism: cause and motivation pattern', *Journal of Studies on Alcohol* 47: 207–12.

Kendler, K.S. (1985) 'A twin study of individuals with both schizophrenia and alcoholism', *British Journal of Psychiatry* 147: 48–53.

Kessel, N. and Grossman, G. (1961) 'Suicide in alcoholics', *British Medical Journal* 2: 1671–2.

Merikangas, K.R., Leckman, J.F. and Prussoff, B.A. (1985) 'Familial transmission of depression and alcoholism', *Archives of General Psychiatry* 42: 367–72.

Schuckit, M.A. (1973) 'Alcoholism and sociopathy: diagnostic confusion', *Quarterly Journal of Studies on Alcoholism* 34: 157–64.

Stockwell, T. and Bolderston, H. (1987) 'Alcohol and phobias', *British Journal of Addiction* 82: 971–9.

CROSS REFERENCES

Chapter 24

Adolescence: the genesis of addiction

Harry Zeitlin and Harith Swadi

It was only in the second half of this century that adolescent substance abuse became recognized as a serious problem. In the early fifties substance abuse in children and the notion of adolescent addicts was almost unthinkable. First reports of teenage solvent abuse in America appeared in 1959 in the *Denver Post*, and the use of marijuana and psychedelic substances gained momentum during the youth movement in the early sixties. Since then the stereotypical drug 'junkie' has been getting younger and adolescents and young adults have become the initial marketing target of any new substance.

Apart from the natural concern for adolescents, there are major reasons to justify the increasing interest in adolescent substance abuse. Rising prevalence, changes in pattern of use, continuity to adult addictive behaviour, different aetiological factors and management requirements all make this a special area for study.

AN EPIDEMIOLOGICAL PERSPECTIVE

Exposure of very young children to the non-medical use of substances by adults is common, but reports of substance abuse among primary school pupils are rare, most being for older secondary school age children (11+). The prevalence, patterns and frequency of use show considerable regional variations which appear to be linked to availability, socioeconomic status of the area, publicity, local cultural character-istics and drug use sub-cultures. In general, the prevalence is higher in urban areas and inner cities.

In Britain, unlike the USA, there are no nationwide statistics about adolescent drug abuse. However, prevalence of cigarette and alcohol use have been well surveyed and for British secondary school children, 10 per cent to 20 per cent are regular smokers and 60 per cent to 90 per cent regularly drink alcohol, 10 per cent drinking 'more than moderately'. That is not very different from American high school children among whom it is found that about one-fifth smoke daily, though up to 30 per cent drink heavily.

For drug abuse, reports from various parts of the UK indicate that 5 per cent to 20 per cent of school age children have ever tried at least one drug with 2 per cent to 5 per cent using weekly or more often. By comparison, more than half American high school students have tried at least one drug, marijuana being the commonest. In 1987 that drug alone was reported to be used daily by 3.3 per cent of teenagers. Overall about 5 per cent of adolescent drug users in the USA meet the criteria for 'dependency' and it may well be a matter of time before British rates reach the same levels.

PATTERNS OF USE

Introduction to drug use starts more often between the ages of 13 to 14 than in the later teens. In a large London-based study among 11- to 16-year-olds the proportion who had ever tried any drug (including solvents) doubled from 13 per cent in 11-year-olds to 26 per cent among 16-year-olds. For repeated use there was an eight-fold rise from 2 per cent to 16 per cent across the same age range (Swadi, 1988).

Perhaps the most worrying aspect is the apparent continuing trend to earlier initiation into substance use. The present age of induction of about 13 to 15 years has to be seen in the context of a steady fall over two decades from the age range of 18 to 20 years.

Almost all drug users have already used alcohol, and the age of induction into alcohol use is generally about two years earlier. For alcohol there is also a threefold increase in prevalence since 1970. This is made more significant by the evidence that the earlier initiation into alcohol and drug use, the higher the risk of progressing to more dangerous patterns of use and of subsequent behavioural and social problems (Robins et al., 1986).

Sex differences in patterns of substance abuse in the young are changing. Tobacco smoking has now become more common among teenage girls than boys and, whilst heavy drinking remains the province of boys, moderate alcohol use shows no significant sex differences. Girls tend to start psychoactive substance use later than boys, but once started their use is more committed.

There are important age-related differences in the type of drugs used. Compared with adults, adolescents have less involvement with opiates and cocaine and the main substances used are alcohol, cannabis and solvents. Use of several drugs is the rule rather than the exception and recent evidence suggests that there is a resurgence in the use of amphetamine-related substances. There are increasing reports of the so-called designer drugs like 'ecstasy' (MDMA) and cocaine in its 'crack' form among adolescents and young adults in the UK.

AETIOLOGICAL FACTORS

Whilst in any one case it may be possible to 'understand' why drug abuse has occurred, generally causation remains as much the subject of speculation as of fact. Possible biological, psychological and social factors have been considered and there is a consensus that aetiology of substance abuse is multifactorial. Age of introduction to substance abuse is a more general risk factor and use by or before mid-teens carries a high risk of continuing abuse (Robins et al., 1986). Robins and her colleagues found three particular risk factors: alcohol problems in parents, school failure and early smoking. Other commonly cited factors are curiosity, inappropriate media handling of drug issues, peer influence, family dynamics, general social pressure, social isolation, low self-esteem and genetic influences.

Substance abuse is associated with a variety of behavioural and emotional problems but particularly with delinquency and conduct disorder. The nature of the relationship is complex as some of the disturbance follows rather than precedes drug abuse and there is an unresolved debate as to whether some start to use drugs to cope with anxiety or misery.

There is consistent evidence that family influences are of paramount importance in a variety of ways. Substance abuse in a parent provides a powerful role model but even in non-abusing parents attitude to drug behaviour in others has a major influence. The latter is thought to have more influence on attitudes to alcohol rather than other drugs possibly because of more family openness about alcohol. Absence of a family attitude and loss of parental control are also important, leaving a young person much more influenced by peer group pressures. It appears that parental attitudes have more influence on whether an adolescent takes drugs or not, whereas peer pressures affect the patterns of use.

The role of peers is interesting as both poor peer relationships and adverse peer pressure are cited as causative factors. Having a drug-taking friend is more likely to initiate drug taking and also to reinforce that activity once started. It may be that the difficulty in peer relationships excludes vulnerable children from identification with more constructive groups.

Once initiated, adolescents discover the mood-altering effects of drugs and alcohol and subsequent use is largely determined by pharmacological factors and social and psychological reinforcing mechanisms. Volatility of mood, normal in adolescents, may make this group particularly susceptible.

COURSE

Untreated, some adolescent abusers stop after a few occasions of use, some continue to use on a less frequent basis or go in and out of use, others develop chemical dependency and some die, usually of an accident or an overdose.

There is some consistency in the sequence of stages of involvement followed by young abusers, though the progression from stage to stage is not inevitable (Kandel, 1975). Kandel described the stages as use of: (1) beer or wine, (2) spirits or tobacco, (3) marijuana, (4) other illicit drug. Almost all using other illicit drugs will have previously taken marijuana, so that whilst most do not progress in this way, marijuana has deservedly gained the reputation of being the 'gateway' to drug abuse. Progression to a 'higher ranked' drug is directly related to the intensity of use at the prior stage and this pattern holds regardless of such variables as gender, ethnicity, socioeconomic class and geographic location. Continued use also relates to the type of drug. Not surprisingly rates of conversion from occasional to regular use are higher for heroin and cocaine than for marijuana.

Outcome for abusers is gloomy not just for continuing drug abuse but also in terms of a high rate of psychiatric and social problems. Aggression, anti-social behaviour, occupational and marital problems are common. Drug abusers are more likely to be charged with crimes both in childhood and adult life. Some of the later problems are the independent continuity of childhood disturbance that predated the onset of drug abuse. It is probable though that co-existence of drug abuse makes that continuity more likely. However, at least one study (Robins *et al.*, 1986) indicates that very similar behavioural and social problems arise in previously non-delinquent abusers and must be considered to occur also as the consequence of drug abuse.

MANAGEMENT

Most Out-patient Drug Treatment Programmes are planned for adult addicts and have to adapt with difficulty to the special needs of adolescent clients. Apart from the different aetiological factors and drug-use patterns, adolescents respond to different therapeutic techniques.

Adolescent abusers are notoriously difficult to 'access' unless they are obliged by a statutory order, or by good parental control (which makes substance abuse less likely anyway). Rarely is there a need for detoxification programmes in adolescents. Drug abuse among adolescents is usually not an isolated phenomenon and work with abusers in this age range must take into account normal and pathological processes that occur in adolescence other than those solely due to drug abuse. There should be as full an assessment as possible of the adolescent's psychiatric, physical and social state. The results of the assessment determine the suitable therapeutic approach and counselling, group therapy, and individual psychotherapy are all recognized means of treatment. However, recently family therapy is being seen as an approach likely to succeed with adolescent abusers (Fishman *et al.*, 1982).

Whatever the therapeutic approach, there should always be the facility to have involvement with parents and to address the care and educational needs of the adolescent. This country needs a more active policy for the management of adolescent abusers, to develop a special service that is both multi-disciplinary and multi-agency. The problem is sufficiently large and unique to merit training 'super-specialists' in adolescent substance abuse.

PREVENTION

The morbidity during adolescence, the long term continuity to adult drug abuse, and the associated psychological, social and physical disability make prevention a high priority. Unfortunately, except for smoking, so far there is little evidence that current prevention programmes are effective in reducing prevalence. Few 'before' and 'after' assessments of prevalence have been carried out in the United Kingdom. Moreover, there is evidence from other countries that many of the techniques of preventative programmes currently used are at best only effective for selected groups and at worst counter-productive. 'Scare' tactics have been found to increase interest in drugs; Factual Information programmes, Social Skills Training, 'Just Say No' campaigns, Affective Education and the Alternatives Approach all tend to have limited effects in selected populations when used alone (Swadi and Zeitlin, 1987). The disappointing results of primary prevention has prompted the birth of the 'harm-minimization' approach, i.e. teaching safer and less damaging methods of use. Apart from ethical considerations, for an adolescent population, this would seem a hazardous approach as it neither delays initiation nor prevents identification with drugs.

Most prevention programmes are targeted at 14- to 15-year-olds (Swadi, 1989) although the steep rise in prevalence commences a year or two before this. It is also apparent that the earlier the age of initiation the more likely a progression to addictive behaviour and the higher the rate of psychosocial disturbance in adult life. The two important aims of prevention should be to influence children before they are exposed to attempts to initiate them to drugs and to prevent initiation if possible but to delay initiation 'at all costs'. This implies working with primary school and first-year secondary school children and developing programmes which are aimed at inducing individual and group drug resistant identities.

Apart from such whole population approaches, an equally fruitful task may be identifying and targeting those with known risk factors.

FROM ADOLESCENCE TO ADULTHOOD

Since only a minority of adult addicts start drug use in adulthood, the importance of adolescence for adult addictive behaviour cannot be stressed too strongly particularly with regard to service planning. At a London treatment centre, 92 per cent of the clients reported starting before the age of 19 years (mean starting age 15.5 years) (Sheehan *et al.*, 1988). However, only 5 per cent to 10 per cent of adolescent abusers go on to become adult problem users and the majority do not get more involved nor continue drug abuse into adult life. It may be that the continuity in addictive behaviour represents a continuity in the factors that led to or maintained it, and this requires further study. Until then the remaining 90 per cent of teenage experimenters must be considered vulnerable and a potential source of future social morbidity that could swamp existing resources for adults. Service planning should take this, as well as regional, local and cultural variations, into account.

REFERENCES

Fishman, H., Stanton, M. and Rosman, B. (1982) 'Treating families of adolescent drug abusers', in M. Stanton and T. Todd (eds) *The Family Therapy of Drug Abuse and Addiction*, New York: Guilford.

Kandel, D. (1975) 'Stages in adolescent involvement in drug use', *Science* 190: 912–14.

Robins, L., Helzer, J. and Przybeck, T. (1986) 'Substance abuse in the general population', in J. Barrett and R. Rose (eds) *Mental Disorders in the Community: Progress and Challenges,* New York: Guilford.

Sheehan, M., Oppenheimer, E. and Taylor, C. (1988) 'Who comes for treatment: drug misusers at three London agencies', *British Journal of Addiction* 83: 311–20.

Swadi, H. (1988) 'Drug and substance use among 3,333 London adolescents', *British Journal of Addiction* 83: 935–42.

— (1989) 'Adolescent drug education programmes: methods and age targeting', *Pastoral Care in Education*, June: 3–6.

Swadi, H. and Zeitlin, H. (1987) 'Drug education to school children: does it really work?', *British Journal of Addiction* 82: 741–6.

CROSS REFERENCES

Chapter 25

Why women need their own services

Jo Coupe

Long before research studies dealing specifically with women's substance abuse issues were set up, some of the most closely observed descriptions of addiction problems for women could be found in literature, mostly in fiction, but also often described in biographies and autobiographies. Cult heroine Marilyn Monroe is but one such example of a woman overtaken by addiction problems. Also, life stories continue to pepper the national dailies and are to be found in abundance in women's magazines. In recent years there has been an increasing awareness and acknowledgement that substance abuse issues for women are a serious topic in their own right. These have to be set within the context of the overall concept that society affects women's lives at every level, and more importantly that this differs from the impact it has on men.

Although women's issues have moved forward from the 'Cinderella' position they previously occupied, considerable resistance is still evident. Some of this has been created in part by the way research concentrated on single topics, relentlessly pursued, but remote from the context of women's lives. This has tended to result in important research findings, such as that physiological gender differences render women 'at risk' of earlier or more severe health problems than men, being interpreted pejoratively. It seemed that women were being told that they were intrinsically 'bad' if they dared to admit to a substance abuse problem, and that not only were they damaging themselves but creating irreversible damage to their progeny. A purely medical perspective has tended to create barriers for women who are faced with real life situations in which change does not always appear achievable. It is to be hoped that research will reveal that the now widely accepted focus on 'harm minimization' as a goal of treatment will attract more women towards services before their problems become too severe.

THE SOCIAL CONTEXT OF WOMEN'S SUBSTANCE PROBLEMS

Problems of addiction, more often than not, describe a condition as it relates to men. However, the process of socialization is gender-bound and, for women, is mainly geared to the maintenance of dependency roles. A feminist perspective conceptualizes the transmission of the particular 'female' psychological make-up, via the mother–daughter relationship, in an unbroken succession and involves a social requirement for women to adopt roles of deference, submission and passivity. This can generate many complicated feelings, and any substance used by an individual woman may tip over into addiction in an attempt to quell inner disturbances. Substance dependency in women, however, offends the sensibilities because of adherence to the concept of women as key carers, who are required to exercise high standards both as wives, mothers and workers. Women have been socialized out of access to pleasure, which might otherwise provide relief, because they are not only heaped with responsibility, but they also tend to feel guilty if they do manage to escape these duties. Thus, as a substitute for pleasure, and as a relief from guilt, women may seek alleviation through a variety of routes, such as drinking or taking tranquillizers. Adopting a contrary lifestyle, which becomes a reality for women using illegal drugs, is a further option. If women's pleasures were legitimized, they might be less at risk of being caught up in a vicious circle of using more and more drugs to counteract the inevitable social stigma which follows. The main character in Sheila MacLeod's *Axioms* illustrates these points in describing a fairly common social situation from which dependency problems can easily be triggered. In bemoaning her fate at the breakdown of her marriage, she says to herself 'They are all doing as they please. It is only Claudia who doesn't know how to please herself, having lost the habit. They have all conspired to cast her in the conventional role of wife and mother, whose services are no longer required. Oh, alcohol, friend of the useless and rejected, here I come ...' (MacLeod, 1985).

EFFECTS OF SUBSTANCE ABUSE FOR WOMEN

The danger and damage consequent upon a regular pattern of substance abuse is a cause for concern in various ways.

Alcohol

Women absorb alcohol, from the stomach and small intestine into the bloodstream, more quickly than men. Thus they become more intoxicated even if they drink smaller amounts. The differences are exaggerated during the pre-menstrual phase and during ovulation. In pregnant women, alcohol crosses the placenta into the circulation of the foetus, which is particularly vulnerable to damage in the first stage of pregnancy. Difficulties start to occur with heavy consumption of alcohol because only the liver can metabolize alcohol in order for it to be eliminated, and it performs this function at a slower rate than for men. For some time after ingestion, blood alcohol concentrations can impair many functions leading to accidents in the home or on the road, and releasing confusing emotional reactions due to the disinhibiting effects of alcohol on the central nervous system. Statistically the onset of drinking problems occurs at a later stage chronologically than in men, but it is alarming that serious cerebral and liver damage occurs much earlier in the drinking history, and develops at a much faster rate, than in male counter-parts. Evidence, from studies using CT scan techniques, revealed 'structural evidence of brain damage, after an average heavy drinking history of three to four years in women, as against seven to eight years in men' (Jacobson, 1986).

Foetal alcohol syndrome

Research concerning what is commonly known as 'foetal alcohol syndrome' encounters several problems and makes it difficult to be conclusive about the syndrome. In particular, as a group, alcohol-abusing mothers, tend to avoid attending antenatal services. Reliance upon self-report of alcohol consumption at key stages in pregnancy casts doubt upon results. It is also difficult to attribute specific birth abnormalities in the common situation of women abusing a variety of substances. However, babies born to alcohol-abusing mothers are noted to have the following characteristics:

1 growth deficiency (undersized and fails to show catch up growth in the first few months of life);
2 abnormalities of the head and face (small circumference of the cranium, shortened eyelids and under-developed upper lip and flattened wide nose);
3 mental handicap;
4 associated features (various joint abnormalities, heart defects and birth marks).

Social problems

Alcohol plays a major part, too, in exaggerating mood swings which accompany the menstrual cycle, and which have been causally related to the commission of crime, often of a violent nature. There is also considerable documentation of the part alcohol plays in terms of family breakdown and in non-accidental injury to children: reception into care arises when women are no longer able to sustain their role as carers. As in all instances of abuse, research now indicates that the experience of such abuse in childhood is a predisposing factor for the development of a similar alcohol problem in that child's later life.

Opiates

Many of the health risks of illegal heroin use are secondary, rather than specific to the drug itself, as the quality of opiates bought on the street is very variable. Injecting drug users, despite Health Promotion campaigns, are clearly prone to infection through use of 'dirty' equipment and because they may have less opportunity to practise 'safe sex'. Women who fund their drug habit by prostitution are 'at risk' of catching genito-urinary infections and are highly represented in figures relating to HIV infection.

Crime, a further secondary factor, becomes endemic once all legitimate forms of funding are exhausted. Whereas burglary used to be a male-dominated offence, in towns and cities where drug users are known to live, women now appear increasingly in the drug-related burglary statistics.

A damage-laden mythology has built up around heroin, yet its physiological effects are arguably less problematic than those of alcohol, although heroin acts similarly to alcohol in entering the blood stream to cause potential damage to a foetus. Women who are regular users of heroin often have secondary amenorrhoea because opiates prevent the secretion of gonadotrophin by blocking stimulation of the hypothalmus by the pituitary gland, thus preventing ovulation. Many heroin users believe that the drug acts as a natural contraceptive and so often become unintentionally pregnant.

Pregnancy

There are implications for women heavily into opiates in coping with pregnancy, arising mainly from the social pressures of their situation. 'Many drug-using women report a reluctance to attend antenatal clinics because of fears of staff attitudes to their problems and worries that their baby will be taken into care' (Gerada and Farrell, 1990).

There is no firm evidence that drug addicts, as an identified group, make poor parents, but society seems convinced that they do. Women alcohol and drug abusers are generally seen as 'rejecting their proper place, incapable of motherhood because of a lifestyle which is initially wilfully perverse, and then, inescapably pathetic' (Perry, 1979).

It is not surprising that many births occur with scant antenatal preparation, or that obstetric complications, such as premature delivery, arise because of poor nutrition and minimal health care. Low birth weight appears to be the most direct opiate effect and there is also a serious complication of injecting drug use because of the vertical transmission of HIV. Studies now suggest that between one quarter and one half of babies born to infected mothers are also infected. In addition, babies exposed to opiates during pregnancy may be born in a state of withdrawal and show signs of hyper-activity, irritability and respiratory distress.

Management of the pregnant opiate user

Because of the complexity of problems which can accompany a pregnant drug user, it is likely that a multidisciplinary approach will be most effective in reducing infant mortality and morbidity rates. It is helpful, in alleviating the fears of the women involved, to have one person in a team of 'carers' to co-ordinate the various departments involved.

The general aims of management will be to:

1 Identify and attract drug using women to the service.
2 Provide antenatal and health care.
3 Advise towards reducing all illicit opiates and replace with oral methadone (during the second trimester).
4 Co-ordinate management ante- and post-natal care, with the multidisciplinary team.

(Gerada and Farrell, 1990)

In this sense the medical input that may be required is but one link in a wider chain of support from drug treatment agencies.

Nicotine and tranquillizers

It is unfortunate that there has been a greater emphasis on health problems attached to alcohol and opiates, at the expense of drugs which attract less media attention. Benzodiazpepines and nicotine, seemingly 'innocents abroad', constitute enormous health risks for women. Both are killer drugs. Nicotine is linked particularly to cancer and has the effect of contributing to low birth weight in babies. The adverse effects of tranquillizers, taken in cocktails along with other drugs and alcohol, are highly represented in overdose and suicides. Tobacco advertising continues to target vulnerable groups of young people. Statistics reveal that while tobacco consumption overall shows a downward trend, women as a category have not significantly reduced their consumption, and indeed, amongst teenage girls, the figures continue to rise. As far as tranquillizers are concerned, although greater awareness about the hazards of prescribing are having their effect, nevertheless, it is estimated that 12 per cent of women in the United Kingdom consume these drugs on a daily basis for more than one month in any year (Royal College of Psychiatrists, 1987).

ARE SERVICES GEARED UP FOR WOMEN?

The medical profession has been mainly responsible for the setting up of services to deal with drug and alcohol problems. Their power has been legitimized through the setting up of Alcohol Treatment Units and Drug Dependency Units within psychiatric hospitals. Now it is recognized that a purely health-orientated response to substance abuse problems has failed. In 1985, all Health Authorities were authorized to provide locally based services and this resulted in the emergence of many Community Teams which are multidisciplinary in composition. Initially, owing to additional funding being available from central government, services were directed mainly towards drug abusers. Increasingly, local teams have amalgamated drug and alcohol services. Although theoretically this means that services have become more accessible to women, there are still drawbacks to provision. These are partly structurally engendered by the failure of workers to co-operate effectively across disciplines, and partly owing to the lack of adequate training facilities for staff members. Such training as is acquired may not have had any focus whatever on areas of concern to women, so that the need to tailor services to encourage take-up by women can be easily overlooked. The composition of any one area team is therefore a critical factor in whether or not services are 'user-friendly' to women.

Carers and women workers – a paradox?

Women have been socialized to accept a predominant role as carers. They are highly represented by choice or opportunity, at all levels, as workers, in drug and alcohol services. The mere fact of being female is not enough to ensure the kind of attitudinal change necessary to the delivery of services sensitive to women's needs. Ironically, many women workers at the so-called coal-face act as filters for the medical profession's 'cult of expertise'. It appears that some of these women adopt a defensive stance in order to maintain their traditional framework of values, but the underlying identification with women patients or clients creates role confusion, which then exhibits itself paradoxically in a back-lash of over-reaction and antagonistic attitudes. This is aptly illustrated by an article which appeared in the *Midwives Chronicle and Nursing Notes* in July 1986, which displays stereotypic and punitive attitudes to pregnant women drug users. 'These women, then enter pregnancy in a haphazard, passive manner and briefly develop a positive response. Unfortunately, often they cannot sustain this positive attitude, since they are unable to feel adequate concern for their own physical well-being, and view the foetus as an intruder' (Kroll, 1986).

Race, religion and culture – special areas of weakness

Drug and alcohol problems rarely present tidily, and they often arise against a backdrop of complex social problems which are not easy to resolve. The experiences of women are also necessarily a product of culture, resulting in differences in response to religion, race and social class. All recent research indicates that women are '20 times as likely as men, to receive opposition from family and friends, regarding treatment entry' (Jordan and Oei Tian, 1989). According to a report by DAWN (1989), the mere fact of their being in a Western culture, encouraged them to drink alcohol in larger quantities than they would in their countries of origin. These women feel doubly oppressed on account of gender and race. DAWN concludes that

> although many agencies and individuals are reluctant to consider providing services for black communities, this is a service that should not be under-estimated. For generations, the black communities have taken care of themselves, often without any financial support. Many of the black women who responded to the study, stated that they would not even consider approaching an all-white agency for advice and support, such is the stigma which attaches to the perceived reputation the black community has for being drug takers. This image appears to be perpetuated by a racist press, by many professionals and by the Police and legal system.

> (DAWN, 1989)

Regrettably, the most common solution has been for women to present to their local doctor when problems start to overwhelm them, and for a prescription for a tranquillizing drug to be supplied. Society's belief in slick solutions to deep-seated social and psychological problems needs to be radically restructured and not to be solved by means of a liquid cosh. Nowhere is this more vividly illustrated than within the prison system.

> Although many women entering prison are already taking large doses of tranquillizers, they are given little or no help in cutting down. In 1983, 247 women in Holloway Prison and 295 in Cookham Wood were being prescribed psycho-tropic drugs. In a far larger male prison in Pentonville, only 39 such prescriptions were used.

> (Padel and Stevenson, 1988)

CONCLUSION

Even this brief 'dip' into the complex area of women's dependency shows that there is no one way of alleviating problems. Comprehensive training, within all the relevant disciplines, needs to address the specific difficulties women face. The single most important contribution to developing services which address women's problems in a serious, yet not 'off-putting', manner must be for the people involved in creating and running these services to have their consciousness raised about the necessity to find realistic solutions for women. It is essential that co-operative ventures run by women themselves need to be actively encouraged within local communities, particularly by those groups who have traditionally held the power of the purse over resources and those who have responsibility for solving health and social problems.

REFERENCES

DAWN (Drugs Alcohol Women Nationally) (1989) *Black Women and Dependency: A Report on Drug and Alcohol Abuse*, London: DAWN.
Gerada, C. and Farrell, M. (1990) 'Management of the pregnant opiate user', *British Journal of Hospital Medicine* 43: 138–41.
Jacobson, R. (1986) 'Female alcoholics: a controlled CT brain scan and clinical study', *British Journal of Addiction* 81: 661–70.
Jordan, C. Majella and Oei Tian, P.S. (1989) 'Help-seeking behaviour in problem drinkers: a review', *British Journal of Addiction* 84: 979–88.
Kroll, D. (1986) 'Heroin addiction in pregnancy', *Midwives Chronicle and Nursing Notes* 99: 153–7.
MacLeod, S. (1985) *Axioms*, London: Methuen, pp. 100–1.
Padel, U. and Stevenson, P. (1988) *Insiders: Women's Experience of Prison*, London: Virago, p. 202.
Perry, P. (1979) *Women and Drug Use: An Unfeminine Dependency*, London: ISDD.
Royal College of Psychiatrists (1987) *Drug Scenes: A Report on Drugs and Drug Dependency*, London: Gaskell, p. 154.

FURTHER READING

Camberwell Council on Alcoholism (1980) *Women and Alcohol*, London and New York: Tavistock.
Eidenbaum, L. and Orbach, S. (1985) *Understanding Women*, London: Pelican.
Ernst, S. and Goodison, L. (1981) *In Our Own Hands: a Book of Self-help Therapy*, London: The Women's Press.
Ettore, B. (1989) 'Women, substance abuse and self-help', in S. Macgregor (ed.) *Drugs and British Society: Responses to a Social Problem in the Eighties*, London and New York: Routledge, pp. 101–115.
NIDA (1985) Research Monograph 59: Consequences of Maternal Drug Abuse, Rockville, USA.
NIDA (1986) Research Monograph 65: Women and Drugs: A new era for research, Rockville, USA.
Summers, A. (1986) *Goddess: The Secret Lives of Marilyn Monroe*, London: Sphere.

CROSS REFERENCES

Chapter 37 Family therapy for alcohol problems
            Ian Bennun
Chapter 45 Drug use and criminal behaviour
            Trevor Bennett
Section VI Services

Chapter 26

What about the elderly?

Peter Crome

The elderly (post-retirement) now comprise 20 per cent of the population in the UK and other developed countries. People are living longer and to reach the age of 85 or over must now be regarded as unexceptional. Medical and social care of the elderly with drug and alcohol problems has been and still is a relatively neglected area within the addictions field. Similarly, research into this problem has been largely ignored and where it has been carried out it has tended to be in 'older' people (55 to 75 years) rather than in the very old (70 years or more).

HOW THE ELDERLY DIFFER FROM THE YOUNG

The aetiological, diagnostic and therapeutic problems in the elderly are best understood if placed within the general concepts of how elderly people differ from those who are young.

Medically: The elderly have a higher prevalence of almost all serious diseases including the major killers – cardiovascular disease, respiratory disease and cancer, and the major disabling diseases including arthritis and Parkinson's disease. What is more, with advancing years they are more likely to have more than one serious physical problem. They are the major consumers of therapeutic drugs and are prescribed large quantities of classes of drugs which are potentially addictive. In one study 37 per cent of all women aged 75+ were given one or more prescriptions for psychoactive drugs in a single year.

Psychiatrically: The prevalence of depression is highest in the elderly. Rates of 10 per cent to 40 per cent are quoted depending on definition. Many more elderly people are unhappy. Dementia is essentially a disease of old age, 20 per cent of over 80s probably have this condition. Alcohol is a factor in a third of elderly suicides.

Physiologically: There is a wide range of changes in almost all organs of the body. Of particular relevance is a variable but significant alteration in their ability to clear exogenous substances including drugs from their bodies. Elderly people have higher blood alcohol level for a given mg/kg dose. As a rule both therapeutic and side-effects of drugs are enhanced. About 10 per cent of hospital admissions are due to drug side-effects.

Financially: Elderly people as a whole are one of the poorest groups in the UK. The present state retirement pension provides an income below the official poverty line.

Socially: Elderly people are much more likely to be bereaved, to be retired, to be separated from family and to be geographically isolated.

The consequences of these problems to an individual with drug or alcohol problems are variable. Some retired people might reduce the amount they drink because they have less money or because the stress of work has been alleviated. Others might drink more because they have more free time on their own or engage in social activities which have a high drink-related component (Busby *et al.*, 1988). As a rule, however, prevalence rates for all types of substance abuse are lower in the elderly than in younger subjects. There are two main factors producing this. First, younger people who abuse are less likely to reach old age than non-abusers (survival of the fittest). Second, fewer elderly people start abusing drugs or alcohol at an old age. A third possible factor is that the elderly are more likely to stop using addictive substances. There is a paucity of comparative information on the success rates of treatment in young and old but it is possible that target-organ damage by cigarette smoke or alcohol may increase motivation to stop. Severe bronchitics may not be able to inhale. Disabled, housebound elderly people may have difficulty in getting access to alcohol and cigarettes. Elderly alcoholics are more likely to be institutionalized and thus be denied access to alcohol.

It is also necessary to consider that people in their eighties today will have lived through a different set of life events at formative stages in their personal development (e.g. World Wars, the depression of the 1930s) than people who were 80 three decades ago. Differentiation between cohort effects and true ageing effects is, therefore, important.

ALCOHOL

In a recent UK community study in Newcastle it was found that 13 per cent of respondents drank enough to put them at risk from liver damage (Bridgewater *et al.*, 1987). Figures in the range from 2 per cent for women to 20 per cent for men have been found in the United States. Generally accepted screening procedures have not yet been established for the elderly and physical markers such as mean corpuscular volume and gamma glutamyl transpeptidase are less reliable indicators since they may be influenced by many other common physical disorders found in old age. In geriatric medical practice alcohol abuse may present in non-specific ways, such as falls, accidental hypothermia, malnutrition, generalized weakness due to myopathy, confusional states and decreased self-caring skills, although classical presentation with both physical (liver disease, bleeding varices) and psychiatric (depression, psychosis) does occur. Confusion presenting a few days after hospital admission suggests the possibility of delirium tremens. Dustbin inspection for empty bottles should form part of the medical home visit to an elderly person.

Elderly drinkers may be divided into two groups – drinkers who become old and those who start drinking in later years. The former are more likely to have physical complications, such as liver disease, neuropathy and cardiomyopathy. They are more likely to have underlying personality problems than those who start drinking later. This latter group often start drinking in relation to some of the stressors outlined above. They are less likely to have a family history of alcoholism and more likely to be psychologically stable. They are also more likely to present with problems associated with intoxication – e.g. falls and confusion – rather than chronic illnesses complicating alcohol abuse.

DRUGS

Official statistics from most Western countries indicate that there are very few elderly illicit drug users and that those that there are mainly became addicted many years ago. However, following their therapeutic use, elderly people may become addicted to narcotics and benzodiazepines. These latter drugs and milder narcotics such as dextropropoxyphene are prescribed on such a large scale that it must be the exceptional older person who has not been prescribed them at some time in his or her life or does not have easy access to them at home. Although therapeutic barbiturate prescribing is now uncommon there are still many elderly people who are addicted to barbiturates and other related drugs which were first prescribed for them many years previously and continue to be prescribed. These patients tend to be treated by their own general practitioners and are almost invariably never registered as addicts. Many of these patients appear to be 'stable' with the clinical consequences of their addiction only coming to light when they are admitted to hospital for other conditions and suffer withdrawal reactions when the drugs are suddenly discontinued.

Elderly husbands and wives often swap medication, and this sharing of drugs often extends to neighbours and relatives. There are isolated examples of abuse of almost all other classes of drugs, including laxatives which cause chronic diarrhoea and diuretics which may cause postural hypotension, falls and electrolyte imbalance. It should be remembered that the forcible administration of drugs to elderly people does occur within both families and institutions and this needs to be considered within the whole context of 'elder abuse' (physical, financial and social). Even within institutions for the elderly severely mentally infirm there are wide variations in the patterns of prescribing suggesting that there is much over-prescribing.

SMOKING

Approximately 15 per cent of the over-65s are smokers. This figure is lower than all other adult age groups. Amongst the elderly more men than women smoke. This is probably a generational effect and one would expect to find a more even sex distribution in years to come. There is some evidence to suggest that elderly smokers are more psychologically addicted than younger people but that their pharmacological addiction, in terms of amount of tar and nicotine inhaled, is less. It needs to be stressed that there is good evidence that even in later years giving up smoking improves morbidity and mortality from the common smoking-related illnesses such as ischaemic heart disease, chronic obstructive airways disease and lung cancer.

ATTITUDES TO THE ELDERLY

Ageism, Western society's attitude to the elderly, is complicated and varied. It is essentially negative and reflects the low status of the elderly in the community. Typical attitudes in response to the discovery of an elderly addict frequently include reluctance to refer for specialist help either because of a real or suspected belief that agencies are not interested in this problem or because they think that such intervention will prove ineffective. Health professionals working specifically with the elderly may share such beliefs. It is also not uncommon for people to collude with elderly alcoholics in the belief that 'it is all they have to live for' and that treatment would be cruel and not kind.

PREVENTION AND TREATMENT

Prevention strategies should be modified to the needs of the elderly. It is worthwhile to discuss drug and alcohol problems in pre-retirement education (where it exists), in elderly people's social groups and most important, by physicians when prescribing. Health professionals need to be made aware of the problem through their continuing education. In the UK the recently introduced general practitioner annual check-up of the over-75s gives an additional opportunity to review the possibility of drug or alcohol abuse. Treatment facilities, both in the community and in hospital, need to recognize that the elderly have specific problems. Access must be easy: there is no value in placing an elderly person with a hearing deficit in a group where he cannot hear what other people say. For the very old, treatment is best carried out by the local psychogeriatric service which is usually community rather than institutionally based. Hopefully such a unit enjoys close working contact with the local authority home care services. Treatment in its broadest sense needs to be directed to the underlying causes of the addiction and to its consequences – medical, financial and social.

CONCLUSION

Addiction of all types may occur in the elderly. Both diagnosis and treatment present special difficulties. Nevertheless, age alone should never be a barrier to therapy which can prove successful, and which can improve the quality of life even in those of advanced years.

REFERENCES

Bridgewater, R., Lee, S., James, O.F.W. and Potter, J.F. (1987) 'Alcohol consumption and dependence in elderly patients in an urban community', *British Medical Journal* 295: 884–5.
Busby, W.J., Campbell, A.J., Borrie, M.J. and Spears, G.F.S. (1988) 'Alcohol use in a community-based sample of subjects aged 70 years and older', *Journal of the American Geriatrics Society* 36: 301–5.

FURTHER READING

Crome, P. and Patterson, L.J. (1989) 'Drugs and the elderly: adverse reactions, abuse and overdosage', in P. Turner and G.N. Volans (eds) *Recent Advances in Clinical Pharmacology 4*, Edinburgh: Churchill Livingstone, pp. 159–72.
Lisansky Gomberg, E.S. (1982) *Alcohol Use and Alcohol Problems among the Elderly*, Rockville: National Institute on Alcohol Abuse and Alcoholism.
McKim, W.A. and Mishara, B.L. (1987) *Drugs and Aging*, Toronto and Vancouver: Butterworths.

CROSS REFERENCES

Section IV

Screening and detection

Chapter 27

The process of help-seeking in drug and alcohol misusers

Margaret Sheehan

It is well documented that only a small proportion of drug and alcohol misusers present for treatment and often at an advanced stage of the problem (DHSS, 1982; Thom, 1984). Earlier treatment involvement can enhance outcome (Zahn and Ball, 1972). Why then do people delay for so long before seeking help? What can we understand of the barriers to seeking help?

THEORETICAL PERSPECTIVES

A number of authors have considered the process of help-seeking from different perspectives and in relation to a variety of populations. Although the views expressed are wide ranging, there are also commonalities. There is agreement that people may have symptoms or other distressing difficulties for some considerable time before seeking professional help. Zola (1973) concluded that 'there is an accommodation physical, personal and social to the symptoms and it is when this accommodation breaks down that the person seeks, or is forced to seek, medical aid'. In his view there are five types of triggers to the decision to seek medical aid. These are:

1 The occurrence of an interpersonal crisis.
2 The perceived interference with social or personal relations.
3 Sanctions.
4 The perceived interference with vocational or physical activity.
5 A kind of temporalizing of symptomatology.

A different perspective is that of Kadushin (1958/9) in his work on how people decided to undertake psychotherapy. This included people whose problems were brought to their attention by others, and those who felt the problem lay elsewhere, in someone else. However, those who recognized and accepted that the source lay within themselves had the best chance of being accepted for and continuing treatment.

Help-seeking as a career with different stages was suggested by Brannen and Collard (1982) in their study of people seeking help for marital problems. These steps were: the recognition of something being wrong; the interpreting and labelling of a problem as being of a particular kind; disclosing the problem or turning to someone else who was significant; the decision to seek help from a particular agency; and finally the approach to the agency itself.

The idea of a process and the interplay of a number of factors both internal and external are central to these views on help-seeking. They need to be understood in terms of individual psychological characteristics as well as the wider social context in which they are located.

BARRIERS TO TREATMENT

Many studies of drug and alcohol misusers have reported that there is a considerable gap between the time people start using drugs or alcohol problematically and approaching for help (Thom, 1987; Sheehan *et al.*, 1988). Why is it that people wait for so long? Undoubtedly there is an inability or unwillingness to recognize that a problem exists or that it merits attention only when it is at a very advanced stage. As alcohol is a legal drug in our society many people are unclear as to what constitutes normal or problem drinking. Conversely, although opiate drugs are illegal many young people may not be aware of the possibility of addiction when they first start using. This underestimate and misunderstanding of the extent of the problem are amongst the reasons cited for not seeking help. Both men and women have experienced the fear of being stigmatized and labelled as a result of requiring help for alcohol problems. Feelings of shame, guilt, embarrassment, fears of failing treatment and not getting on with the treaters have been mentioned by drug and alcohol misusers alike as problems in approaching for help (Sheehan *et al.*, 1988; Thom, 1986). To define oneself as an alcohol or drug misuser may act as an incentive towards seeking help but is not a necessary prerequisite. A combination of some or all of the following have been known to be significant in the self-definition of alcohol as a problem: increased consumption, alcohol-related problems, a belief in the disease concept of alcoholism and disruption to a number of life areas (Skinner *et al.*, 1982; Hingson *et al.*, 1980). For drug misusers the subjective experience of dependence and chronicity of the problem were part of the self-definition (Oppenheimer *et al.*, 1988). These problems were seen in conjunction with other life stresses. The foregoing emphasizes the importance of education about the risks of alcohol and drug consumption and the value of early intervention by the primary-care system.

The accessibility of specialist services may also act as a barrier, both in terms of their structure and the perception of what is on offer. Help may initially be sought from informal social networks, as an approach to specialist service may be too daunting. Such a service may be seen, rightly or wrongly, to deal with certain sections of the population only and not take the needs of particular groups, such as women and ethnic groups, into account. Research on drug misusers who were new to treatment showed how little was known of the service which was being approached and what was on offer (Sheehan *et al.*, 1988). This illustrates the necessity of making known the diversity of services available and so demystifying the routes to treatment.

REASONS/TRIGGERS TO HELP-SEEKING

Life events, in addition to increased alcohol consumption and a subjective experience of dependence on drugs, have been shown to be important triggers to help-seeking. People may experience a wide variety of life events in the period prior to seeking help. Some or all of the following have been identified as important: serious health problems, marriage break-up or disruption, the loss or threat of losing a child, violence on the part of the respondent and job disruption. In a study of treatment-seeking addicts, the life events that threatened relationships with either partners or children, although mentioned by few people, were a powerful impetus to seeking help when they occurred. Other triggers identified were needing immediate medical attention and legal pressure (Thom, 1987; Oppenheimer *et al.*, 1988). There can be other influences on the decision to seek help apart from life events. Amongst these is a sense of impaired functioning, both in psychological terms (such as depression) or in physical terms (such as feeling ill much of the time). The positive or negative intervention of a partner was a more important factor for male alcoholics than for female alcoholics. The possibility of a major positive change in one's life – forming a new relationship, looking forward to the birth of a grandchild – could also lead people to seek help with their alcohol problem.

CONCLUSIONS

It is clear that there are a variety of reasons that bring alcohol and drug misusers into treatment. To ignore what brings them for help can have a negative effect on treatment retention (Zola, 1973). Finally a greater understanding of the issues discussed are required if educational activities are to enhance earlier detection and treatment take up. For many it is external events and circumstances that act as the trigger. The reasons given for coming for help therefore need to be identified by clinicians to enhance their therapeutic effect.

REFERENCES

Brannen, J.M. and Collard, J. (1982) *Marriages in Trouble: the Process of Seeking Help*, London: Tavistock.
DHSS (1982) *Treatment and Rehabilitation: Report of the Advisory Council on the Misuse of Drugs*, London: HMSO.
Hingson, R., Scotch, N., Day, N. and Culbert, A. (1980) 'Recognising and seeking help for drinking problems', *Journal of Studies on Alcohol* 11: 1102–17.
Kadushin, C. (1958/9) 'Individual decisions to undertake psychotherapy', *Administrative Science Quarterly* 3: 379–411.
Oppenheimer, E., Sheehan, M. and Taylor, C. (1988) 'Letting the client speak: drug misusers and the process of help seeking', *British Journal of Addiction* 83: 635–47.
Rounsaville, B.J. and Kleber, H.D. (1985) 'Untreated opiate addicts. How do they differ from those seeking treatment?', *Archives of General Psychiatry* 42: 1072–7.
Sheehan, M., Oppenheimer, E. and Taylor, C. (1988) 'Who comes for treatment: drug misusers at three London agencies', *British Journal of Addiction* 83: 311–20.
Skinner, H.A., Glaser, F.B. and Annis, H.M. (1982) 'Crossing the threshold: factors in self-identification as an alcoholic', *British Journal of Addiction* 77: 51–64.
Thom, B. (1984) 'A process approach to women's use of alcohol services', *British Journal of Addiction* 79: 377–82.
— (1986) 'Sex differences in help-seeking for alcohol problems – 1. The barriers to help-seeking', *British Journal of Addiction* 81: 777–88.
— (1987) 'Sex differences in help-seeking for alcohol problems – 2. Entry into treatment', *British Journal of Addiction* 82: 989–97.

Zahn, M.A. and Ball, J.C. (1972) 'Factors related to cure of opiate addiction among Puerto Rican addicts', *International Journal of the Addictions* 7: 237–45.
Zola, I.K. (1973) 'Pathways to the doctor – from person to patient', *Social Science and Medicine* 7: 677–89.

CROSS REFERENCES

Chapter 28

Screening and early detection of alcohol problems

Morris Bernadt

WHAT IS SCREENING?

The United States Commission on Chronic Illness defined screening as

> the presumptive identification of unrecognised disease or defect by the application of tests, examinations, and other procedures which can be applied rapidly. Screening tests sort out apparently well persons who probably have a disease from those who probably do not. A screening test is not intended to be diagnostic. Persons with positive or suspicious findings must be referred to their physicians for diagnosis and necessary treatment.

This definition is geared towards medical illness and one might wonder what application there is in the field of alcoholism.

WHY SCREEN FOR ALCOHOLISM?

Alcohol-related problems are common and often unrecognized. For example, a fifth or more of all acute male admissions to medical wards in Britain and the United States are associated with alcohol abuse; yet there is evidence of widespread default in detection both in hospital and general practice. Thus, at a London teaching hospital 64 per cent of the medical and surgical case records made no mention of, or only a vague comment about, alcohol intake, and in a Manchester general practice 80 per cent of alcoholics were not identified. Thus, it might seem desirable to screen all individuals in certain high-risk populations.

Research studies have evaluated screening for excessive alcohol consumption, alcohol abuse, hospital diagnosis of alcoholism and alcohol dependence. Some of these are dimensional rather than categorical, i.e. there is a continuum between those with the disorder and the rest of the population, but this need not be a serious problem. What is essential however are clear criteria to define a case.

SCREENING PERFORMANCE

The commonly used measures to assess screening performance are sensitivity, specificity, predictive value of a positive test result and predictive value of a negative test result. The two predictive values are sometimes abbreviated as positive predictive value (PPV) and negative predictive value (NPV). What these measures do is to separate out how well a screening instrument detects those with the condition and those without it (sensitivity and specificity respectively); with predictive values the measures examine separately positive and negative test results.

Table 28.1 Screening outcome

| | | Screening test result | |
		negative	positive
	absent	true negatives a	false positives b
Alcoholism			
	present	false negatives c	true positives d

Sensitivity is the proportion of alcoholics that have a positive test. In Table 28.1 the alcoholics are the sum of c and d; of these, d have a positive test result so sensitivity is d/c + d. *Specificity* is the proportion of non-alcoholics (the non-alcoholics are a + b) who have a negative test result (the group a), so specificity is a/a + b. *Predictive value of a positive test result* refers to the proportion of those with a positive test result who are alcoholic; in the table the positive test results are b + d, of which d are alcoholic, so PPV is d/b + d. *Predictive value of a negative test result* is the proportion of those with a negative result (the total of negative results is a + c) who are not alcoholic (a). Therefore NPV is a/a + c. The table also shows true and false positives and true and false negatives.

An effective screening instrument must pick up most cases with the condition, i.e. be of high sensitivity. Sensitivities of 90 per cent or more are regarded as satisfactory. To be administratively effective a substantial proportion of the positive test results must be cases of alcoholism, i.e. PPV must be reasonably high; values above 40 to 50 per cent are sought.

SCREENING INSTRUMENTS

During the early 1970s, American workers described *questionnaires* that had good screening performance for the populations studied. The best known of these is the Michigan Alcoholism Screening Test (MAST). This consists of twenty-five questions which are observer-rated, i.e. there is an interviewer. Some of the questions deal with attitudes towards drinking (either the individual's or relatives'), most deal with alcohol-related disabilities and a few deal with alcohol dependence. The Brief MAST, a ten-item observer-rated questionnaire, was found to perform as well as the longer MAST (Pokorny *et al.*, 1972: 342). Another variant is the self-administered Short Michigan Screening Test (SMAST) which has thirteen questions.

The process of shortening the interview reached its apotheosis with the CAGE questionnaire which has four items! CAGE is an acronym formed from the key features of each question:

'Have you ever felt you should *cut* down on your drinking?' 'Have people *annoyed* you by criticizing your drinking?' 'Have you ever felt bad or *guilty* about your drinking?', 'Have you ever had a drink first thing in the morning to steady your nerves or get rid of a hangover (*eye-opener*)?'

(Mayfield *et al.*, 1974: 1121)

With a cut-off point of two positive answers out of the four questions, the CAGE sensitivity is as good as longer screening interviews, but its specificity has usually been found to be somewhat worse – at approximately 75 per cent, it means that there is a false positive rate of about 25 per cent.

A Washington University group described a branching interview (an algorithm). Here, the question to be asked depended on the answer to the previous question. Half the alcoholics were identified by affirmative responses to two questions and 96 per cent of non-alcoholics were detected by their answering negatively to four questions – only question one was common to both groups. Overall, the mean number of questions asked was 5.5 (Reich *et al.*, 1975: 847).

In contrast, European researchers seemed more interested in *laboratory tests*. Alcoholic populations were found to have raised values of red blood cell mean corpuscular volume (MCV) and serum gamma glutamyl transferase (gamma GT), aspartate transferase (AST), alanine transferase (ALT), the ratio of AST to ALT, alkaline phosphatase, urate, cholesterol and high-density lipoproteins. Other tests include an abnormal serum transferrin (described as desialylated or 'carbohydrate deficient') and detection of alcohol in breath, saliva, sweat, blood and urine.

With some laboratory tests initial enthusiastic reports of sensitivities in excess of 90 per cent have been followed by other studies demonstrating sensitivities of 30 per cent or less. One reason for this is that initial studies often compare a group of severe alcoholics with normals whereas follow-up studies include individuals in an intermediate position.

When screening interviews were compared with laboratory tests in the same individuals, the screening interviews performed much better. These had, after all, been designed for the very purpose. Laboratory tests had often fortuitously been found to be abnormal. It is not surprising that a screening questionnaire made up largely of items enquiring about certain attitudes to alcohol and alcohol-related disabilities should be congruent with systems of diagnostic criteria (e.g. DSM-III) which specify for a diagnosis the same attitudes to alcohol and the same alcohol-related disabilities. Contrast this with gamma GT, the physiological function of which is unknown.

Several comparative studies showed that screening interviews had sensitivities above eighty per cent whereas the best laboratory test, usually gamma GT, had a sensitivity in the range thirty to forty per cent (Bernadt *et al.*, 1982: 327; Skinner *et al.*, 1986: 1706). The laboratory tests do have high specificities, meaning that if one is a non-alcoholic one will very likely have a negative test. The positive and negative predictive values in questionnaires have had higher values than the laboratory tests.

Combining interview and laboratory tests

If one uses a battery of tests, with the composite instrument registering positive if one of the single tests is positive, one gets very high sensitivity, but a sharp decline in specificity. That is, the alcoholics are bound to register positive on one of the tests, but so will a substantial proportion of non-alcoholics.

There are sophisticated statistical techniques, e.g. discriminant analysis which allows simultaneous assessment of a number of variables, due weighting of each in terms of its importance in differentiating alcoholic individuals from non-alcoholic, and the use of the whole range of each measure with avoidance of arbitrary cut-off points. With discrimination analysis each individual can be allocated a discriminant score indicating the likelihood of the condition being present. Results are encouraging if the variables include questionnaire or clinical history items, but if the variables are composed exclusively of laboratory tests screening performance plummets (Bernadt *et al.*, 1984: 85).

PRACTICAL PROBLEMS

Although screening questionnaires are highly cost-effective they are hardly ever used, even with high-risk populations. Why is this? The most important characteristic for the detection of alcoholism is a high index of suspicion. Might it be that where personnel are appropriately perceptive to diagnostic cues screening is not required, whereas where there is diagnostic blindness the need for detection is not appreciated? It could be that a more direct approach than screening is to heighten staff awareness rather than to attempt to institute screening in their departments.

Ironically, it is laboratory measures which are, in practice, occasionally used for screening. Certain professional groups, e.g. civil servants, undergo annual health screening. Automated analysis of a wide range of biochemical and haematological tests is done enabling a check to be made on those measures affected by alcohol, low sensitivity notwithstanding.

THE EFFECT OF PREVALENCE

Screening performance is affected by the prevalence of alcoholism. Conventional wisdom is that it is the predictive values that are altered but there are reasons why sensitivity and specificity are too.

With falling prevalence there is a marked reduction in PPV and a small rise in NPV. This is an arithmetical consequence of their definition. It can be seen if one compares two hypothetical populations where the prevalence in the first is 20 per cent and in the second, 2 per cent. Supposing there are a 1,000 individuals in each population. In the first population, of the 1,000, 200 will have the condition, leaving 800 without it. Assume the screening test has a false positive rate of 10 per cent and a false negative rate of 10 per cent. Then of the 200 affected individuals, 20 will be falsely negative leaving 180 true positives (see Table 28.2). Of the 800 unaffected individuals, 80 will be falsely positive leaving 720 true negatives.

Sensitivity = 180/180 + 20 = 90%
Specificity = 720/720 + 80 = 90%
PPV = 180/180 + 80 = 69.2%
NPV = 720/720 + 20 = 97.3%.

Table 28.2 The effect of prevalence on screening outcome

		Twenty per cent prevalence		Two per cent prevalence	
		Screening test result		Screening test result	
		negative	positive	negative	positive
Alcoholism	absent	720	80	882	98
	present	20	180	2	18

In the second population of a 1,000, 20 will have the condition leaving 980 without it. Of the 20 with it, 2 will be false negatives and 18 true positives (see Table 28.2). Of the 980 without the condition there will be 98 false positives and 882 true negatives. Note that now most of the positive test results are false positives.

Sensitivity = 18/18 + 2 = 90%

Specificity = 882/882 + 98 = 90%

PPV = 18/98 + 18 = 15.5%

NPV = 882/882 + 2 = 99.8%.

Sensitivity and specificity have remained the same, NPV has increased very slightly, but PPV has dropped from 69.2 per cent to 15.5 per cent. Thus, in the first population about two-thirds of positive results would have been those affected whereas, in the second population, only one in six or seven positive results identifies an affected individual.

What is often not appreciated is that prevalence also affects sensitivity and specificity. Because level of alcohol consumption and alcohol-related disabilities are continuously distributed in the population, a high prevalence will be associated with relatively more severe cases. Screening interviews and laboratory tests will more readily register positive with the severe cases than with those in the borderland between case and non-case and hence will be more accurate. In contrast with low prevalence there will be a far smaller proportion of severe cases and those cases that there are are more likely to be borderline where the screening instrument will have more difficulty in accurately identifying cases. Thus sensitivity declines with a lowering of prevalence. With specificity, accuracy in identifying non-cases will be easier in those individuals totally symptom-free, because even if some truly absent symptoms are incorrectly perceived as being present there are unlikely to be sufficient such errors to meet criteria for caseness. With low prevalence there will be relatively more of these individuals so specificity will be high. Thus lowering the prevalence raises the specificity.

The message is that prevalence affects all measures of screening performance. Therefore in applying research findings to clinical practice one must ensure that one's patient population has a reasonable prevalence – a prevalence of 10 per cent or greater is satisfactory.

PRESENT STATUS OF SCREENING AND EARLY DETECTION

Screening interviews are largely used for recruiting subjects for research trials. Although they are quick to administer and cheap they seem not to have 'caught on'.

Laboratory tests, though more expensive and having worse performance, are nevertheless included in annual health screening of certain professional groups.

For early detection what is crucially important is a high level of awareness of problems related to alcohol.

REFERENCES

Bernadt, M.W., Mumford, J., Taylor, C., Smith, B. and Murray, R.M. (1982) 'Comparison of questionnaire and laboratory tests in the detection of excessive drinking and alcoholism', *Lancet* 1: 325–8.

Bernadt, M.W., Mumford, J. and Murray, R.M. (1984) 'A discriminant-function analysis of screening tests for excessive drinking and alcoholism', *Journal of Studies on Alcohol* 45: 81–6.

Mayfield, D., MacLeod, G. and Hall, P. (1974) 'The CAGE questionnaire: validation of a new alcoholism screening instrument', *American Journal of Psychiatry* 131: 1121–3.

Pokorny, A.D., Miller, B.A. and Kaplan, H.B. (1972) 'The Brief MAST: a shortened version of the Michigan Alcoholism Screening Test', *American Journal of Psychiatry* 129: 342–5.

Reich, T., Robins, L.N., Woodruff, R.A., Taibleson, M., Rich, C. and Cunningham, L. (1975) 'Computer-assisted derivation of a screening interview for alcoholism', *Archives of General Psychiatry* 32: 847–52.

Skinner, H.A., Holt, S., Sheu, W.J. and Israel, Y. (1986) 'Clinical versus laboratory detection of alcohol abuse: the alcohol clinical index', *British Medical Journal* 292: 1703–8.

CROSS REFERENCES

Chapter 29

Tell me about the client: history-taking and formulating the case

Ilana Belle Glass, Michael Farrell and Petr Hajek

The following exchange will reverberate in the minds of students, clinicians and examiners.

'Tell me about the client.'

'Would you like to know the history, the diagnosis or the formulation?'

This chapter focuses first on taking a substance-abuse history and, subsequently, on formulating the case. Clearly, taking a competent substance abuse history must be embedded in a thorough psychiatric and medical history and readers are referred to the *Oxford Textbook of Psychiatry* (Gath *et al.*, 1989).

Furthermore, such an assessment should be seen as an important beginning for any programme. Investment of time at this early stage will be multiply rewarded, for this prepares the groundwork for later action in many ways. Generating a sense of reassurance, support, commitment and integrity during an assessment is a positive factor in catalysing change. Advice and education, too, is often indirectly provided during the initial consultation. An essential ingredient of the history-taking process is establishing what the client perceives his or her problems to be, and his or her views as how best to tackle these difficulties. Much of this emanates from a receptive and responsive ambience.

ASKING THE RIGHT QUESTIONS

The following outlines the basic information about the client's alcohol, drug, smoking and HIV status which should be gathered in the course of history-taking. The drug and alcohol history are presented in the form of a checklist, whereas for smoking and HIV brief descriptive accounts are presented (Edwards, 1987; Ghodse, 1989; Strang *et al.*, 1989).

Taking an alcohol history

1 Personal history

Birth and developmental milestones, family atmosphere, school performance and general conduct in school, educational achievement, occupational history, sexual and marital history. Attempt to correlate social problems with evolving drinking problem. Enquire about impact of alcohol problem on lifestyle.

2 Family history

Brief vignette of father and mother and other siblings should include: age, age at death, occupation, relationship with client. History of psychiatric problems or substance abuse in immediate family and also enquire about maternal and paternal family history.

3 Drinking history

i Alcohol consumption (units) in the past 24 hours
ii Alcohol consumption (units) in the past month
iii Alcohol consumption (units) in the past 6 months
   (1 unit =1 glass table wine = $^1/_2$ pint beer = 1 measure spirits = 1 measure sherry. 16 units = $^1/_2$ bottle spirits = 2 bottles wine = 8 pints beer = 4 cans extra strong lager)

4 Drinking career

i Age of:
   First drink ever
   Regular week-end drinking
   Regular evening drinking
   Regular lunch-time drinking
   Early morning drinking.
ii Withdrawal symptoms: tremor, night sweats or morning nausea, convulsions.
iii Delirium tremens.
iv Other features of dependence: tolerance, compulsion to drink, salience of drink-seeking behaviour, rapid reinstatement after abstinence.
v Periods of abstinence.

5 Alcohol-related problems (past and present history)

i Physical: e.g. gastritis, hepatitis, cirrhosis, neuropathy, pancreatitis.
ii Psychological: e.g. anxiety, depression, phobias, delusions, suicidal ideation or attempts, hallucinations.
iii Social: e.g. marital, occupational, financial problems.

6 Other drug use

Quantity, route of use, complications:
i Tobacco
ii Cannabis
iii Benzodiazepine or other sedatives
iv Cocaine/amphetamine
v Opiates

7 Abstinent periods

   Duration of abstinence.
   Perceived source of help or reason.
   Triggers for relapse.

8 Previous treatment history

General Practitioner, counselling, general or psychiatric hospital out-patient and in-patient, dry hostels, medication, self-help group (e.g. AA, Drinkwatchers), response to treatment.
   Explore goals of present treatment.

9 Forensic history

Charges, convictions, fines, imprisonments, e.g. drinking and driving, drunk and disorderly, violent incidents.

10 Occupational history

Relationship of job loss to drinking, promotions, demotions, present employment status.

11 Sexual history and HIV risk behaviour

See section on HIV counselling, p. 195.

12 Marital history

Relationship of sexual and marital difficulties to drinking.

13 Present life situation

Family and social supports, non-drinking friends, leisure activities and occupational prospects, financial status, accommodation.

Taking a drug history

1 Personal history

Birth and developmental milestones, family atmosphere, school performance and general conduct in school, educational achievement, occupational history, sexual and marital history. Attempt to correlate social problems with evolving drug problem. Enquire about impact of drug problem on lifestyle.

2 Family history

As for alcohol history, ask about other family members with problems resulting from alcohol, drugs or nicotine.

3 Drug history

This section should attempt to give a clear picture of initiation into drug use accounting for each specific drug and initiation into injecting if appropriate. The evolution of drug use with the development of personal and social problems as a consequence of drug use. It is advisable to chart the type, quantity and route of use of each individual drug. Alcohol consumption should also be checked as a routine part of a drug history.

i   Drug use in the past 24 hours
    Detailed and sensitive questioning around this will not only provide information about drug use and drug dependence but should give a vivid picture of the individual's lifestyle and daily stresses and strains.
ii Drug use in the past month
    Drug use is often atypical on presentation to services and it is advisable to attempt to draw a picture of drug use over the previous four weeks.

4 Drug-using career

It is worthwhile exploring the evolution of drug use with particular reference to when the person thought that drug use had become problematic and what was the nature of such problems. The problems the drug user identifies may be radically different from the problems you identify.

Age at first drug use for individual drugs.

Age for regular drug use for each drug.

Age for dependent drug use.

Routes of drug use oral/inhaled/intravenous.

Approximate quantities used.

Periods of abstinence.

5 Injecting history

This should cover first injecting experience. It is quite common for the first injecting episode to involve sharing of equipment and this should be sensitively explored. It is advisable to ask how often have you shared rather than asking have you ever shared.

i   Time course:

First time injected.

Duration of injecting.

Daily frequency of injecting.

Knowledge about HIV transmission.

ii Injecting site:

Site of injecting: arms, legs, groin, neck.

Any physical problems at site or systemically.

Knowledge about source of clean injecting equipment.

6 HIV risk

(See section on HIV counselling, p. 195)

The frequency of sharing, number of different people shared with and knowledge of methods to clean equipment help to assess HIV risk-taking behaviour. Sensitive exploration of sexual risk-taking behaviour is important and is frequently left unmentioned in the assessment of drug takers.

First time shared.

Last time shared.

Frequency of sharing.

Sharing with partner or dealer.

Knowledge about cleaning injecting equipment.

Does partner use drugs, inject or share.

Heterosexual or homosexual activity, high risk sexual behaviour.

Condom use.

7 Drug-free periods

Self, General Practitioner, Drug Dependence Unit, Community Drug Team, or other, e.g. prison.

Duration for which client has been drug-free.
Mode of relapse.
If time spent in prison, time from release to first drug use.

8 Treatment history

Periods of treatment by:
Out-patient/General Practitioner detoxification.
In-patient detoxification.
Rehabilitation community.
Describe treatment and response to treatment, including medical and psychiatric problems.
Explore goals of present treatment.

9 Forensic history

Previous court cases, duration in prison and nature of offence. Court cases pending. Past and present involvement with the criminal justice system should not be used to prognosticate.

10 Alcohol history and smoking history

See pages 191 and 196.

11 Occupational history

12 Marital history

13 Home environment

Drug-using contacts and cues.
Drug-free supports.
Occupational skills or interest in acquiring skills.
Non-drug-using leisure activities.

HIV counselling

This check list mentions the key points and should be complemented by a fuller text for acquisition of such skills for actual practice.

Pre-test counselling

1 Knowledge about HIV and HIV transmission.
2 Knowledge about means to reduce the risk of transmission.
3 Knowledge about HIV test.
   a Nature of antibody test.
   b Possibility that test could be negative for up to three months after acquiring the virus.
   c Differentiation between seropositive status and AIDS.
   d Implications of seropositive state for length of survival with clarification of present estimated length of survival of up to ten years.

e   Explore how patient would cope if seropositive.
f   Ask about suicidal thoughts or plans, or thoughts about relapse to chaotic drug use.
g   Concern about possibility of spreading virus to others.
h   Sources of support in the period awaiting test result and in immediate period after receiving result.
i   Explain about social difficulties that may arise as a result such as life insurance and health insurance cover.
4 Explore risk-taking behaviour with specific aim to use this very important session to consider significant modification in injecting and sexual behaviour.

Post-test counselling

1 For patients who are seronegative this is an important opportunity to explore changes in risk-taking behaviour. Research shows counselling and testing may have a significant impact in modifying risk-taking behaviour.
2 If the patient is positive then the counselling should be conducted over a number of sessions to provide appropriate support. This should include reiteration of the significance of HIV positive status and the differentiation from clinical AIDS, and the possibility of a long period of well-being.
3 The patient will need to decide who they can tell and to consider if there are any sexual or drug-related contacts that need to be told that they have been exposed to HIV.
4 Need to explore mood and suicidal thoughts. Information about support organizations for positive individuals which will provide additional support and counselling should also be given.
5 Ensure contact with ongoing medical support such as HIV clinic and advise on the way to cope with intercurrent illness. In general, advise quick referral to HIV clinic if the patients experience an illness that they feel to be different from past experience.

Taking a smoking history

Helping smokers quit rarely depends critically on taking a detailed substance-use history. Smoking careers are often depressingly similar and few guidelines can be offered to front-line clinicians for tailoring treatment on the basis of assessment. A standard treatment is often applied, especially where group methods are used. There exist a number of questionnaire and objective methods to assess various facets of smoking history, smoking behaviour and the intake of constituents of tobacco smoke (Jarvis, 1989). Some measures, such as the gas chromatography of salivary cotinine, are extremely sensitive and accurate. However, most of these methods have their main application in a research, rather than clinical, context. Nevertheless, a basic assessment can in principle provide some potentially useful data, and it gives an opportunity for preparing clients for treatment.

The variable which is most relevant for treatment is *motivation to give up smoking*. It is obvious that smokers who are not sure that they want to give up need a different approach from those who find they are unable to quit on their own, despite being well motivated to do so. The former could benefit from educational approaches focusing on the health risks of smoking and benefits of quitting, while the latter need help in overcoming their dependence, and there may be no need to spend precious time on further motivational input. A simple question such as 'How much do you want to stop smoking?' can lead to a useful discussion and assist decisions about the type of advice or treatment offered. The number, duration and circumstances of *previous attempts to quit* can serve as a useful indirect indicator of motivation and can inform treatment considerations as well.

Average daily *cigarette consumption* is usually recorded as the smokers' main relevant characteristic. It can be supplemented by measurement of *expired-air carbon monoxide*, which is the simplest and cheapest way to objectively assess actual smoke exposure. The correlation between these two measures in dependent smokers is relatively low (< 0.5). In the clinic setting, translating both cigarette consumption and CO (carbon monoxide) readings into treatment recommendations is rather difficult. However, portable CO monitors have other uses as well. The demonstration of elevated CO levels can have a motivational influence on clients; recent ex-smokers may find encouragement in seeing the immediate health benefits of quitting in the fast drop in CO levels; and measuring CO at each session encourages honest reporting of smoking and reinforces the goal of total abstinence.

Dependence on tobacco is a variable of potential importance for tailoring treatment. Several questionnaire measures of dependence have been proposed, based primarily on indications of smoke intake (cigarette consumption, extent of inhalation, cigarette yield) and/or difficulty doing without cigarettes (e.g. Fagerstrom Tolerance Questionnaire, Horn-Russell Smoking Motivation Questionnaire). *Latency to the first cigarette of the day* is often considered a good reflection of both of these hypothetical signs of dependence. Cigarette consumption alone has been found to predict outcome in samples of general practice and hospital patients. It seems that in the general population, lighter smokers tend to find quitting easier, and by inference need less support. In clinic clients, however, such correlations seldom approach clinical significance. So far no measure of dependence on tobacco has been developed which can reliably predict withdrawal discomfort and outcome in a clinic population, and on which treatment decisions could be confidently based.

Certain types of treatment for smokers may require specific data on other variables such as motives for smoking, tempting situations, psychosocial resources and coping repertoire. This is however beyond the scope of a brief section on general pre-treatment assessment.

MAKING SENSE OF THE INFORMATION: WHAT'S BEST FOR THE CLIENT

By synthesizing a history, you are in a position to communicate your view on or opinion of the client. It is the summation of the information accrued, both fact and impression. The essence of comprehensive history-taking is to be able to amalgamate those features into a meaningful picture of the person which relates to your strategy of treatment. Each practitioner develops a personal style, but most will find that at some stage or another, the following points will be discussed.

Introduction

You should briefly introduce the client by giving the name, age, sex, nationality, religion, marital status, occupation and employment status. Any outstanding feature which might have a bearing on the whole history should be made explicit at this stage.

For example:

Dr H W is a 45-year-old single-handed general practitioner who is not working at the present time. She has been divorced for some years and currently lives alone. She was born in Australia. The reliability of her history is questionable, partly because of her knowledge as a medical practitioner.

The presenting complaint in the context of the medical and psychiatric history including that of substance misuse

This section should enable you to form a mosaic about the pattern of health, discomfort and illness in the recent past: the reason for the present consultation.

Demarcation of drug and alcohol use, misuse and dependence is pivotal. Quantification, in units of alcohol, grams of heroin or cigarette equivalents, is useful information. The effect generated by these substances and the routes of administration should be described.

Clarification of the onset, frequency, duration and intensity of any psychological symptoms is helpful. It is important to identify the possible relationship of these symptoms to substance misuse, be it as a result of intoxication, withdrawal or specific psychological effects.

The impact of the presenting problems on the client's social, occupational, sexual and marital roles should be assessed.

The presenting complaint should be set in the context of the client's background. Previous episodes of substance misuse, as well as psychiatric and physical illnesses, require evaluation. This involves the assessment of severity, duration and response to treatment. The agencies, counselling services, hospitals, including doctors and therapists caring for the client, must be summarized. Prescribed medication and possible drug interactions must be noted.

A comparison between the present problem and previous difficulties should be made.

Salient features of the pre-morbid personality should be described, as should any forensic history.

Attention should be drawn to family illnesses bearing some similarity or significance to the client. Relevant details relating to the client's parents, siblings or children might be included. The quality of the home environment and supportive network are useful to gauge.

Possible past and recent aetiological factors should be identified. These include separation, adoption, divorce, birth injury, immigration, bereavement, head injury, unemployment, promotion, marriage and physical illness. Those which might have predisposed, precipitated or maintained the client's problems require emphasis.

For example:

Dr H W was admitted to a drug and alcohol unit in a psychiatric hospital after her general practitioner had been called to her and found her to be confused and agitated. There were rumours that she had attempted to prescribe amphetamines for herself.

Review of her life history revealed that for many years Dr H W had been prescribed a variety of psychoactive drugs ostensibly for headache. During this time she had been married and had a family. Her medical career had been chequered in that she worked in a number of hospitals and practices in an attempt to gain specialist qualifications. She finally began to work in a group practice, but found difficulty in getting along with the partners. A few years ago she decided to take over a practice single-handedly.

Over the previous two years she had become increasingly depressed and anxious, and had been an in-patient in a psychiatric hospital. There she was prescribed anxiolytics and antidepressants. Although she appeared to make a reasonably good recovery initially and was able to work adequately for a while, the situation deteriorated.

More recently her general practitioner had been called to see her because she had developed an ulcer on her thigh. He also noted that she was emaciated, and she admitted that she had not been functioning well. She was finding it difficult to look after herself and run the practice. She felt desperately isolated as she was not in touch with any of her three children, and she had few friends. She was unable to sleep, felt depressed again, and was lacking in energy. She was referred to the out-patient drug and alcohol unit. She would only admit to taking the occasional glass of wine or psychotropic drug. The psychiatrists assessing her again wondered whether she might be depressed, and it was while arranging a further assessment that she had to be admitted.

Aetiological factors in the past included a disrupted childhood and a family history of mental illness. Her premorbid personality, that of a 'worrier and perfectionist', pointed towards rigidity and obsessionality. More recently, she had been socially and professionally isolated, which had been stressful.

Mental state on admission

It is necessary to describe relevant features, positive and negative findings, of both the physical and mental condition of the client. If the therapist is not a physician, it is important to realize that a physical examination may be necessary for clients who have a history of drug and alcohol problems.

Comment on the physical condition of the client should therefore focus on the physical signs of withdrawal from drugs or alcohol, stigmata of liver disease, neurological dysfunction, sites of infection at points of injection, and associated infections.

Mental state examination involves assessment of level of consciousness, alertness, and orientation as well as degree of co-operativeness. Ease with which rapport has been established calls for comment. The client's ability to provide a coherent history will tell much about their intelligence, cognitive state and insight into their condition.

It is worth paying attention to the general state of dress and grooming. Similarly, evidence of agitation, calmness or detachment from the problem should be appraised. Pattern of sleep, appetite, energy level, mood state and suicidal ideation are useful indicators of specific and general psychological dysfunction.

Any suggestion of abnormal experiences, such as delusions and hallucinations, should be probed fastidiously. Clients are often embarrassed to elaborate on these. Cognitive function, likewise, requires meticulous evaluation, for otherwise important leads may be missed.

For example:

On admission Dr H W was examined. She was observed to be very thin, with an ulcer on her left thigh. She was noted to have a staring mask-like facies, to be sweaty and have a fine tremor.

She was agitated and smoked almost continuously. It was difficult to get a coherent history, as she was distractable. There was little eye contact and rapport was difficult to establish. She seemed oblivious to the enormity of her situation and kept denying that she was abusing drugs or alcohol.

She admitted to feeling frightened and anxious, to sleeping poorly and to eating irregularly and inadequately. She said she was feeling depressed, and was tearful, but she reported that she did not have any thoughts of suicide.

She denied any abnormal experiences. Difficulty in attending and concentrating jeopardized evaluation of her memory.

Diagnosis and differential diagnosis

At this stage the therapist has the opportunity of deciding on what basis he or she comes to a tentative conclusion regarding a diagnosis. There may only be one diagnosis, but more often than not, there is more than one. Each diagnosis must be clearly substantiated. Those features in favour of the proposed diagnosis must be enunciated and inconsistencies should be stated.

Clear criteria for dependence must be specified. A decision must be reached as to whether the patient is presently withdrawing, or is intoxicated, or simply 'using' or drinking regularly to excess.

The possibility of an associated depressive illness, dementia, anxiety or phobic state, or a schizophrenic illness preceding substance misuse must be considered.

If it is not possible to be certain about the diagnoses because there is insufficient information, this should be stated. The most intelligent approach is to point to the difficulty of disentangling the history because of lack of independent information, but to propose a plan as to how to remedy the deficit.

For example:

Dr H W has been party to ill health for the last 25 years.

She has suffered psychological (depression, anxiety) and physical (headache) symptoms and syndromes. In retrospect, some of her physical problems could reflect her psychological difficulties. In order to contain her distress she has been treated with a variety of psychotropic drugs. She seems to have coped with some of her problems by abusing drugs prescribed for both her physical and psychological distress. A number of the drugs prescribed had the potential to induce dependence. To what extent she may be dependent on one or more drugs and alcohol is presently unclear since not only is she denying the development of dependence syndrome (e.g. tolerance, withdrawal symptoms, relief drinking or drug taking, craving), but she is denying drug abuse. Observation on the ward may clarify this.

In addition, she has had life-long difficulties relating to people both personally and professionally. She seemed unable to adjust to her role as mother, as wife and as a practising doctor. This has added to her lack of support and vulnerability, and exacerbated the stresses involved in running a single-handed practice. Although a controversial diagnostic category, it is likely that she has a disturbed personality, and many would describe her as having a personality disorder.

The question as to whether she has a depressive illness must remain open because it is extremely difficult to be certain of a diagnosis made whilst the client is taking psychoactive drugs.

Once she has been withdrawn from all drugs for four to six weeks, her capacity to function without these agents may then be reviewed. Similarly, with regard to any possible cognitive deficit, astute observation on the ward may reveal the possibility of a confusional state, Wernicke's encephalopathy or a dementing condition.

Management: investigations and treatment

The programme of investigation and treatment will depend in large part on what the client perceives his or her problems and goals of treatment to be. Assessment of motivation, triggers to help-seeking, reasons for using substances, and stage of the drug-using career may point to suitability for treatment.

The investigations carried out should be summarized. It includes not only blood tests, X-rays and brain scans, but also information accrued from other sources. The reasons for requesting tests should be spelled out, and the results obtained from the tests or questionnaires disclosed.

Confirmatory or contradictory evidence may be from the client's general practitioner, other specialists, family members, friends, and employers. Consent, preferably written, should be sought from the client in order to obtain information from independent informants. If the client is admitted to a treatment unit, then observations by nurses, doctors, occupational therapists and other members of the treatment team is valuable material.

The range of treatment options and goals in the short and long term should be described. This is covered in the sections on treatment skills and service organization in this book. This includes treatment of concurrent physical or psychiatric illness. There is no simple formula which will answer a client's needs. A strategy for monitoring and feedback on the decisions made or contracts negotiated should be recorded. Contingency plans should be discussed in case the proposed programme fails.

For example:

Routine biochemistry and haematology indicated that she had most likely been drinking to excess since her gamma-glutamyl transferase and MCV were raised. Her urinary drug screen revealed barbiturates, benzodiazepines and opiates.

Further information was provided by her general practitioner, her practice staff, her family and several colleagues. This information confirmed the suspicion that she had been taking a wide variety of psychotropic drugs over many years. These were prescribed both for psychological and physical complaints. The quantity and frequency were difficult to determine precisely because she tended to deny her problems.

She was observed on the ward by the registrar (resident), the nurses (particularly one key-worker) and the occupational therapist. She seemed unable to become involved in the group therapy offered and found occupational therapy unrewarding. She chose not to participate in the activities on the ward.

Initially she resisted attempts to form a relationship with her key-worker, but this improved. In time, she admitted to having injected drugs occasionally.

Her headaches were assessed by a neurologist who thought that they did not have any neurological basis.

Since it was not possible to be certain as to which drugs she had been abusing, it was decided to observe her initially, without prescribing additional medication which might obscure the picture. Within three days of admission to the ward she developed a fit. At this point she was prescribed a decreasing regime of diazepam. After several weeks as an in-patient she was discharged home. It was suggested to her that she join the self-help group, Narcotics Anonymous.

She agreed that her general practitioner carry out random urinary drug screens and to be supervised in the out-patient department monthly. She agreed not to work until her case had been reviewed by the authorities.

Prognosis

Those factors which indicate a good prognosis and those which might undermine it should be specified.

Factors such as length of illness, previous episodes of illness, pre-morbid personality, response to treatment, supportive network, level of motivation to improve, degree of insight into illness are only some of the features which may be assessed to provide some idea of possible outcome.

For example:

At this stage it is difficult to be confident of a favourable outcome, although there are some grounds for cautious optimism.

Positive factors are that during her stay on the ward she began to admit to abusing drugs and alcohol in the context of the ward group and with her key-worker. In addition, she volunteered that she would not work until the relevant authorities had reviewed her case, and until she had attended meetings at Narcotics Anonymous, organized her practice so that she would have maximum support when she returned to work, and arranged domestic help to lessen the stress on her everyday life. She was willing to comply with suggestions for regular screening and assessment.

Negative features are her long history of instability and abuse of drugs to contain unpleasant feelings, as well as a poor response to past treatment, which it is fair to say, did not focus on her polydrug abuse.

CONCLUSION

A thorough history is the substrate for a considered opinion about the client: what's best for the client. The objective of this chapter, therefore, is not only to provide a system for history-taking, but also to suggest a scheme for synthesizing the information gathered. This is the cornerstone of the practitioner in the substance abuse field.

REFERENCES

Edwards, G. (1987) *The Treatment of Drinking Problems*, Oxford: Blackwell.

Gath, D., Gelder, M. and Mayou, R. (1989) *Oxford Textbook of Psychiatry*, Oxford: Oxford University Press.

Ghodse, H. (1989) *Drugs and Addiction Behaviour. A Guide to Treatment*, Oxford: Blackwell.

Jarvis, M. J. (1989) 'Helping smokers to give up', in S. Pearce and J. Wardle (eds) *The Practice of Behavioural Medicine*, Oxford: Oxford University Press.

Strang, J., Bradley, B. and Stockwell, T. (1989) 'Assessment of drug and alcohol use', in C. Thompson (ed.) *Instruments of Psychiatric Research*, Chichester: John Wiley & Sons.

CROSS REFERENCES

Section II   Clinical syndromes
Section III   Health risks and the addictions
Section IV   Screening and detection
Section V   Therapeutic skills

Section V

Therapeutic skills

Chapter 30

Detoxification and pharmacotherapy: alcohol

John Peachey

Drugs are used in alcoholism treatment to treat alcohol withdrawal symptoms, to assist maintenance of abstinence and to treat mental health disorders that either lead to or resulted from excessive drinking. Considerable care and clinical skill are required in prescribing drugs to alcohol-dependent patients. The treatment must be safe, economical and effective. Treatment is commenced only after the diagnosis is established and the short- and long-term treatment goals are agreed upon. The choice of drug, its dose and the dosage schedule are determined by the medical and psychiatric status of the patient, as well as the pharmacological properties of the drug including its toxicity. Monitoring patients' compliance and drinking behaviour during treatment is essential in view of the potential for alcohol-drug interactions, for developing cross-dependence with certain psychotherapeutic drugs, and the risk of impulsive behaviour and self-harm. Duration of treatment or any alterations depend upon drug toxicity and success in attaining treatment goals. In this chapter, guidelines are discussed for the safe and effective use of drugs in the treatment of alcohol-dependent patients.

DRUG TREATMENT OF ALCOHOL WITHDRAWAL

Detoxification is the first step in the treatment of alcoholics. The treatment goals are threefold: to provide symptomatic relief, to prevent withdrawal complications and to encourage the individual to enter alcoholism treatment following withdrawal (Sellers, 1988a).

Treatment rationale

The benzodiazepines (BZDs) (Table 30.1) possess cross-tolerance with alcohol and are preferred over other sedative-hypnotics such as the barbiturates because of their relatively low dependence liability and toxicity, and their anticonvulsant activity. Diazepam and chlordiazepoxide have a long duration of action due to hepatic metabolism to active metabolites which have half-lives of up to 100 hours. Since cumulative toxicity can occur with repeated use, lorazepam and oxazepam, which are not metabolized in the liver, are recommended for patients with impaired hepatic function. Chlormethiazole is used in Britain, but it is not available for use in Canada or the United States. Phenothiazines and butyrophenones are ineffective in alcohol withdrawal and should be avoided, except when indicated for treatment of psychotic symptoms. Following withdrawal, patients are offered counselling and referral for alcoholism treatment.

Table 30.1 Some drugs which are often used in alcoholism treatment

Generic name	Trade name	Major property	Therapeutic dose (mg) (daily maximum dose mg)
ANTIANXIETY DRUGS			
Benzodiazepines			
Diazepam	Valium[R]	Long acting	5 (20)
Chlordiazepoxide	Librium[R]	Long acting	25 (100)
Oxazepam	Serax[R]	Intermediate acting	15 (60)
Lorazepam	Ativan[R]	Intermediate acting	1 (6)
ANTIDEPRESSANT DRUGS			
Tricyclic agents			
Amitriptyline	Elavil[R]	Sedative effects	25 (200)
	Triptizol[R]	Anticholinergic effects	
Imipramine	Tofranil[R]	Sedative effects	25 (200)
		Anticholinergic effects	
Desipramine	Pertrofane[R]	Few side effects	25 (200)
	Pertrofan[R]		
ANTIPSYCHOTIC DRUGS			
Phenothiazines			
Chlorpromazine	Largactil[R]	Low potency	25 (800)
Trifluoperazine	Stelazine[R]	High potency	2 (20)
		Neurological side effects	
Thioridazine	Mellaril[R]	Low potency	25 (600)
	Melleril[R]		
Butyrophenones			
Haloperidol	Haldol[R]	High potency	2 (20)
	Serenace[R]	Neurological side effects	

Note: R = Registered

Adverse effects

Drug treatment should ensure optimal conditions for safe withdrawal without producing unwanted toxicity. The patients' medical condition is assessed prior to and during withdrawal treatment. BZDs are used only when necessary, in the smallest effective dose.

Clinical use

Mild withdrawal: patients with mild alcohol withdrawal symptoms (mild tremor and nausea, mild tachycardia of 100 to 110 bpm, slight sweating and insomnia) usually respond satisfactorily to reassurance and general support in a quiet and friendly environment without drug therapy.

Moderate to severe withdrawal: indications for the use of a BZD include moderate to severe alcohol withdrawal (noticeable tremor, nausea and vomiting, malaise, anxiety, depression and/or irritability, heart rate >110 bpm, profuse sweating, and hypertension) and a history of withdrawal seizures and/or delirium tremens. Patients are admitted to hospital if they have severe alcohol withdrawal symptoms, fail to respond to drug treatment in two or four hours, or have medical, psychiatric or surgical disorders including recent head injury, current withdrawal seizures and delirium tremens, and mood disorder. Withdrawing patients may have poor nutrition, poor hydration or an infection which require urgent medical treatment. Parenteral thiamine is administered on admission to prevent Wernicke's encephalopathy, and multivitamin oral preparations are prescribed to treat vitamin deficiency.

Two strategies for BZD treatment of withdrawal are used. In the first, equivalent doses of 10 mg of diazepam or 50 mg chlordiazepoxide are administered orally several times a day as needed, for 3 to 4 days until the patient is asymptomatic. A second treatment strategy is to administer a loading oral dose of BZD consisting of 20 mg diazepam hourly until the patient becomes mildly sedated and/or withdrawal symptoms improve. A complication of the former strategy is cumulative toxicity in the form of daytime drowsiness and hang-over for several days after withdrawal. With the second dosage regimen, most patients respond in the first 12 hours of treatment with 60 mg diazepam or less and further doses of diazepam are not necessary. Compared to the 'as needed' drug administration, diazepam loading usually results in the use of less drug, and less drug toxicity.

Chlormethiazole (CMZ) is used in the United Kingdom but is not available in Canada and the United States. The usual dose of CMZ is 500 mg three or four times daily for 3 to 7 days, with gradual dose reductions thereafter. In severe withdrawal, CMZ may be given orally in doses up to 2 grams four times daily. CMZ is also available for intravenous administration. Treatment with a BZD or CMZ is generally not indicated for longer than 2 weeks.

Withdrawal complications: Two complications of alcohol withdrawal are withdrawal seizures (usually by the third day) and delirium tremens (usually around days 4 to 7). Patients who have a history of withdrawal seizures should receive diazepam for seizure prophylaxis as three 20 mg doses hourly (for severe withdrawal symptoms) or every 6 hours if the withdrawal symptoms are less severe. An alternative regimen is phenytoin 100 t.i.d. for five days. Patients who have seizures for the first time require further investigations to rule out epilepsy after withdrawal is completed. The decision to continue phenytoin treatment will depend on the eventual diagnosis; however, continued administration of phenytoin is not recommended for patients with alcohol-withdrawal seizures alone.

Delirium tremens is described by Michael Kopelman in Chapter 22. Haloperidol in 2 to 5 mg doses is effective in the treatment of acute delirium tremens.

DRUG TREATMENTS FOR CESSATION OF DRINKING

The alcohol-sensitizing drugs disulfiram and calcium carbimide are used specifically with the aim to assist the alcoholic to stop drinking (Peachey and Annis, 1984) (see Table 30.2).

Table 30.2 Alcohol-sensitizing drugs: pharmacology and toxicity

	Disulfiram	Carbimide
Alcohol-sensitizing action		
Onset:	delayed 12 h.	about 1 h.
Duration:	several days	24–36 h.
Adverse clinical effects		
Minor:	drowsiness	–
	lethargy	–
	halitosis	–
Major:	liver damage[a]	–
	–	hypothyroidism[b]
	peripheral neuropathy[c]	–
	psychiatric[d]	–
	inhibition of drug metabolism[e]	–

Notes: a – idiosyncratic hepatic necrosis (potentially fatal) – very rare
   b – in patients with pretreatment reduced thyroid function
   c – axonal degeneration in susceptible patients
   d – depression and/or psychosis in susceptible patients
   e – inhibition of hepatic mixed function oxidases resulting in reduced body clearance of drugs (e.g. diazepam, amitriptyline, phenytoin, warfarin) which undergo hepatic metabolism, resulting in cumulative toxicity

Treatment rationale

These drugs inhibit aldehyde dehydrogenase, the enzyme responsible for the metabolism of acetaldehyde to acetic acid. In the presence of alcohol, disulfiram and carbimide produce an acetaldehyde-mediated reaction consisting of tachycardia, flushing, tachypnoea and shortness of breath, hypotension and dizziness, nausea and vomiting, and shock. The fear of experiencing the reaction is usually a sufficient deterrent to prevent drinking; experiencing the reaction strengthens patients' resolve not to drink.

Adverse effects

Although disulfiram and carbimide are safe when administered in therapeutic doses under optimal treatment conditions, adverse clinical effects can occur as a result of drinking during treatment, drug–drug interactions, or direct drug toxicity.

Common side effects with disulfiram include drowsiness, lethargy and a bothersome metallic-like taste which are controlled by reducing the dose and/or taking the drug at bedtime. Less common but potentially harmful adverse effects include hepatotoxicity, peripheral neuropathy, and exacerbation of pre-existing depression or psychosis. Carbimide produces few adverse clinical effects; one exception is a decrease in thyroid function in patients with reduced thyroid function. Disulfiram, but not carbimide, inhibits the hepatic metabolism of other drugs such as phenytoin and diazepam, resulting in increased blood and tissue concentrations and possible drug toxicity. For this reason, carbimide may be indicated in patients who require treatment with other drugs.

Clinical use

The alcohol-sensitizing drugs are used for patients when the treatment goal is abstinence and there are no major medical problems. Patients also receive counselling and other treatments which are necessary for recovery.

The choice of alcohol-sensitizing drug is determined by its availability (carbimide is not available in the USA and only on a named patient basis in the UK), and the pharmacological actions and toxicity. The therapeutic dose of disulfiram is 250 mg once daily, and for carbimide 50 mg twice a day to ensure continuous protection against drinking. Intermittent protection may be recommended for patients who have been abstinent but need protection during periods of increased risk of drinking. Disulfiram has a slow onset of action and therefore must be taken at least 12 hours before the patient enters a high-risk drinking situation. Carbimide can be used when needed just prior to or during potential drinking situations because of its rapid onset of action (within one hour).

DRUG TREATMENTS FOR CO-EXISTING MENTAL HEALTH DISORDERS

A major challenge for general practitioners is the patient who abuses alcohol and has a co-existing mental health disorder (Levy and Mann, 1988; Kofoed *et al.*, 1986; Kosten and Kleber, 1988). As is discussed by Ilana Glass and Jane Marshall in Chapter 23, diagnosis is often difficult since excessive drinking can result from, or contribute to, a wide range of psychiatric and medical disorders. Alcoholism often develops prior to the onset of psychiatric disorders and may result in anxiety, affective or psychotic organic brain disorders. These disorders generally resolve once the patient has recovered from the effects of the alcohol.

Patients with psychiatric disorders may also develop persistent alcohol-related problems that complicate the course of their psychiatric illness and its treatment. These patients are diagnosed as having alcoholism which is secondary to the primary psychiatric disorder. These patients require treatment for maintenance of abstinence as well as treatment of the primary mental health disorder.

A comprehensive medical and psychiatric history, physical examination and clinical laboratory tests (e.g. haematology, biochemical, metabolic and liver function tests) as well as toxicology tests (alcohol and drug screen) must be completed before drug treatment is started. The diagnosis of co-existing psychiatric disorders can only be confirmed after the person has been completely detoxified and has recovered from the effects of alcohol and other drugs in two to four weeks.

Drug treatment of anxiety disorders

Excessive use of alcohol can contribute to the development of anxiety neurosis and insomnia either directly or indirectly as a result of its disruptive effect on job performance, relationships, and financial and legal status. Persons with a primary anxiety disorder often use alcohol and other sedative-hypnotics symptomatically.

Benzodiazepines

Treatment rationale

Approximately a third of alcoholics also have an anxiety disorder. BZDs are often prescribed on the premise that, by reducing anxiety, they would eliminate the urge for alcohol. This attractive theory has not been borne out in practice and BZDs are not indicated as a primary treatment for alcohol dependence.

Adverse effects

Although the BZDs have a high therapeutic index (or safety margin), adverse effects can occur with their use in alcoholics. BZD treatment of anxiety in alcohol-dependent patients may result in BZD dependence; patients often find it as difficult to stop the BZD as to stop drinking. Routine use can interfere with alcoholism treatment by hindering development of insight and motivation in some patients; repeated BZD treatment can slow patients' cognition, interfere with memory and, in high doses, produce depression. BZDs increase the risk of injury from motor vehicle accidents in patients already at high risk. The lethality of BZDs is enhanced when they are taken in combination with other central nervous system depressants, including alcohol; BZDs should be used with great caution in impulsive and suicide-prone patients.

Clinical use

BZDs are adjuncts in alcoholism treatment, to be used in combination with counselling and other psychological treatments. BZDs are primarily used as anxiolytics and hypnotics. Since the symptoms of anxiety and insomnia generally resolve after several days of abstinence, BZD treatment is selective and time-limited (<14 days).

BZDs are prescribed in therapeutic doses (Table 30.1) only when the anxiety disorder is sufficiently severe to interfere with normal daily functioning. Longer-acting BZDs (e.g. diazepam, chlordiazepoxide, lorazepam) may be preferred since they seem to have less abuse/dependence liability than the short-acting derivatives (e.g. triazolam). However, long-acting drugs (e.g. diazepam) produce day-time drowsiness and cumulative toxicity, especially in patients with reduced drug meta-bolism. Other drug treatments include imipramine for patients with panic disorder.

Drug treatment of affective disorders

Depressive symptoms are recorded in over a half of alcoholics undergoing withdrawal. For most, the affective disturbance is secondary to alcohol abuse. Although organic mood disorders secondary to alcohol resolve after one to three weeks of abstinence without specific drug treatment, they may be sufficiently severe to require hospitalization (Nakamura *et al.*, 1983).

Antidepressants

The tricyclic (TCA) and related antidepressants are often used in the treatment of depression in alcoholics (Table 30.1). The monoamine oxidase inhibitors (MAOI) are not generally used to treat depression because of the risk of adverse effects and drug–drug interactions.

Treatment rationale

TCAs relieve depression by increasing the availability and activity of synaptic norepinephrine (NE), dopamine (DA) or serotonin (5-HT) in the central nervous system through inhibition of their inactivation by neuronal uptake.

Adverse effects

TCAs which possess significant anticholinergic, antiadrenergic and antihistaminic activity (e.g. amitriptyline) are likely to produce cardiotoxicity, autonomic side effects and sedation. Desipramine and some of the atypical antidepressants (e.g. fluoxetine) may be preferred to avoid cardiotoxicity and other side effects. Monitoring plasma TCA levels is recommended to determine an optimal dose of the drug for treatment efficacy and to avoid toxicity.

Clinical use

TCAs are indicated in the treatment of patients with a diagnosis of major depression. The starting dose of TCA is 50–75 mg/day of imipramine or its equivalent (Table 30.1). The dose is increased every other day by 25 to 50 mg to at least 150 mg/day of imipramine or its equivalent. To avoid drug toxicity dosages above 200 mg of impiramine or its equivalent are generally not used. Patients may receive a therapeutic trial of TCA for four or five weeks before the decision is made to change or stop the treatment. Some favourable responses to treatment include improvement in activity level, sleep, appetite, mood, or social interest.

Lithium

Lithium is only indicated for alcohol-dependent patients who, after thorough assessment, are considered to have a diagnosis of a bipolar mood disorder.

Treatment rationale

The mood-stabilizing effects of lithium in patients with recurrent affective disorders appear to reflect normalization of the functional activity of neurotransmitters due to changes in the electrolyte balance across neuronal cell membranes.

Adverse effects

Lithium has a low therapeutic index. Blood lithium concentrations rise and fall rapidly during treatment; an aim of treatment is to maintain levels above 0.9 mEq/l but less than 1.25 mEq/l since adverse clinical effects are associated with higher blood concentrations. Blood levels in terms of free lithium ion are measured 12 hours after the previous dose, and at monthly intervals during treatment. Patients need to be monitored carefully during treatment for side effects and toxicity.

Clinical use

Use of lithium is restricted to patients with a bipolar affective disorder who are able and willing to comply with treatment guidelines and who have no medical contraindications such as hypothyroidism.

Lithium is formulated as 300 mg of lithium carbonate (or 8.12 equivalents of lithium since each gram-molecular weight contains two equivalents of lithium). Lithium is administered in divided doses to maintain blood concentration at about 1.0 mEq/l. Since lithium is used to prevent recurrence of major affective disorders, treatment may be continued for many months or years.

Drug treatment of psychosis

Psychotic symptoms in the form of hallucinations and delusions are usually transient in alcohol-dependent patients (Schuckit, 1982). The diagnosis of an underlying psychotic illness, such as schizophrenia, must be considered when psychotic symptoms persist for longer than a few weeks.

Psychotic symptomatology in alcohol-dependent patients is mainly seen in two alcohol-related states: alcohol withdrawal delirium and alcoholic hallucinosis. Also, schizophrenic patients may drink excessively, resulting in exacerbation of their psychosis. Antipsychotic drugs are primarily indicated for these clinical states.

Treatment rationale

Most antipsychotic drugs (phenothiazines, thioxanthines and butyrophenones) interfere with the actions of dopamine as a synaptic neurotransmitter in the brain by blocking dopamine receptors, thereby exerting antagonism of dopamine-mediated synaptic neurotransmission. Some antipsychotic agents (e.g. thioridazine) possess minimal antidopamine actions but exert significant anticholinergic actions. Other antipsychotic drugs, e.g. molindone, act mainly through serotonin pathways.

Adverse effects

The antipsychotic drugs exert not only significant beneficial clinical effects but also undesirable autonomic, neuroendocrine and neurological effects. Some important neurological extrapyramidal side effects are dystonia, Parkinsonism, or akathesia, which occur within days or weeks of the start of treatment. An antiparkinsonism agent such as benztropine can be used to control these extrapyramidal side effects.

Clinical use

Since the psychotic symptoms are usually related to alcohol use and remit spontaneously in a few days, antipsychotic drugs are often necessary for a few days only. Acute alcohol withdrawal and other medical disorders should be treated concurrently. Unlike schizophrenic illnesses, alcohol-induced organic disorders respond to relatively small doses of drug. Haloperidol is used in doses of 2 to 5 mg orally or intramuscularly, up to 10 mg/day, until the control of symptoms has been achieved. Other antipsychotic agents for use in alcoholics are listed in Table 30.1. Their potential side-effects in patients with physical complications of alcohol abuse, especially liver damage, should be carefully considered before doing so and should probably be reserved for acutely disturbed patients.

CONCLUSION

Although drugs play a major role in the rehabilitation of the chronic alcoholic, they are adjuncts to other therapies directed at the amelioration of alcohol-related problems. Except in certain acute situations, drugs are used only after there is sufficient evidence to support a diagnosis.

Drugs are used in the context of an alcoholism treatment plan which includes all elements of therapy required by the patient (Sellers, 1988b). Short-term as well as long-term treatment goals are established which form the basis for later evaluation of the treatment outcome. The therapist must be aware of the nature, purpose and consequences of the drug treatment, and the dose, frequency and duration of administration. The patients' condition must be systematically monitored during treatment with respect to compliance, alcohol or drug use and adverse drug effects. Treatment outcome is evaluated at regular intervals, and the drug treatment is revised, as necessary, to accommodate changes in the patient's condition.

REFERENCES

Kofoed, L., Kania, J., Walsh, T. and Atkinson, R.M. (1986) 'Outpatient treatment of patients with substance abuse and coexisting psychiatric disorders', *American Journal of Psychiatry* 143: 867–72.

Kosten, T.R. and Kleber, H.D. (1988) 'Differential diagnosis of psychiatric comorbidity in substance abusers', *Journal of Substance Abuse Treatment* 5: 201–6.

Levy, M.S. and Mann, D.W. (1988) 'The special treatment team: an inpatient approach to the mentally ill alcoholic patient', *Journal of Substance Abuse Treatment* 5: 219–27.

Nakamura, M.M., Overall, J.E., Hollister, L.E. and Radcliffe, E. (1983) 'Factors affecting outcome of depression symptoms in alcoholics', *Alcoholism: Clinical and Experimental Research* 7: 188–93.

Peachey, J.E. and Annis, H. (1984) 'Pharmacological treatment of chronic alcoholism', *Psychiatric Clinics of North America* 7: 745–56.

Schuckit, M.A. (1982) 'The history of psychotic symptoms in alcoholics', *Journal of Clinical Psychiatry* 43: 53–7.

Sellers, E.M. (1988a) 'Alcohol, barbiturate and benzodiazepine withdrawal syndromes: clinical management', *Canadian Medical Association Journal* 139: 113–20.

—— (1988b) 'Defining rational prescribing of psychoactive drugs', *British Journal of Addiction* 83: 31–4.

CROSS REFERENCES

Chapter 31

Detoxification, pharmacotherapy and maintenance: drugs

J.S. Madden

The term 'detoxification' is generally used in substance misuse practice to signify the withdrawal process from alcohol or a drug, together with treatment that may be advantageous during withdrawal. The management of overdose is excluded. Pharmacotherapy here denotes drug treatment of dependence apart from organic complications such as superadded infections. Maintenance treatment is a particular form of therapy for opioid dependence that involves administration for a prolonged period of a less harmful form of substitute drug.

DETOXIFICATION

The withdrawal symptoms and signs that follow cessation of a drug which induces physical dependence can be eased by chemical treatment. The therapeutic regime may take the form of phased removal of the original preparation; this strategy is applicable to benzodiazepines and to the proprietary liquid compounds which contain opioids. For heroin and most opioids it is more usual to employ oral methadone in decreasing dosage. There is a growing and desirable impetus towards drugs which suppress withdrawal features although of a different pharmacological class to the original substance and which are not themselves liable to lead to dependence.

Opioids

As already noted proprietary mixtures containing opioids and that are taken orally can be withdrawn gradually. The compounds can be phased out over a period of two to three weeks on an in-patient basis. A longer time interval of months is appropriate outside hospital.

Oral methadone in a liquid form (e.g. a linctus or fruit juice preparation) that cannot be injected is the usual basis for withdrawal from heroin and other illicit opioids. Methadone suppresses withdrawal features from the opioid class of drug (i.e. the drug is cross-dependent). Non-injectable forms of methadone (not tablets nor ampoules) avoid the rapid euphoria and conditioned attractiveness of injecting or smoking techniques as well as the infective risks of injections. Methadone induces dependence with an abstinence syndrome which is slower in onset, less severe at its height but more lengthy than that from heroin. Although the withdrawal features that follow the termination of a methadone regime are more prolonged and troublesome than those provoked by heroin cessation, the substitution and then the phased removal of methadone is an acceptable method of detoxification for patients and therapists.

Methadone has a long plasma half-life of 1 to 1.5 days. There is therefore no need to administer the drug more than once daily; this is advantageous for patients or clients outside a hospital, who can be asked to collect their supply each day. The stratagem of daily issue avoids the provision of large quantities that are intended to last several days but which can be consumed prematurely or sold, with the resultant deficit met by renewed recourse to illicit drugs. Daily attendance furthermore favours development of a therapeutic relationship with staff and allows urine testing to determine concurrent use of other drugs. Repeated consumption of other substances militates against the objectives of treatment, directly by continued illicit intake and indirectly by maintenance of a lifestyle that preserves contact with the drug subculture.

An initial dose level of 30 to 40 mg once a day of methadone generally suffices to keep an out-patient comfortable. Higher amounts up to 60 or 80 mg a day are infrequently required and lengthen the withdrawal period unduly. The length of the regime is flexible, depending on patient progress. Since clinical judgement rests mainly on self-reports of withdrawal symptoms, a blend of sympathetic concern and firmness is needed by the therapist. For out-patients a regime of less than a month rarely succeeds in promoting more than a brief break from heroin. Longer courses allow time for the subject to benefit from counselling and adopt a different lifestyle. Some clients require especially prolonged regimes that may include a period of stabilization at a particular dose level before further drug reduction. The latter process approximates in all but name to a period of 'maintenance treatment'.

Dose reductions for an out-patient can take place at first by amounts of 5 mg each week. Below 20–25 mg as a daily dose withdrawal is more gradual, perhaps with weekly decrements of 2 mg. It may be desirable to hold the patient for a time at the 20–25 mg level.

Urine testing for illicit drugs accompanies the regime. Testing is preferably conducted on days not anticipated by the patient though practical exigencies of staff time may thwart this requirement. A urine that is positive for heroin metabolite, particularly in the early part of treatment, may not warrant termination of methadone but rather offers an opportunity to discuss difficulties with the subject. Repeatedly positive urinanalyses point to a failure of treatment at the particular time and to an assessment of alternative strategies such as in-patient detoxification. Urines that are positive for nonopioid drugs, as for example stimulants or sedatives, allow the therapist to give prompt guidance regarding avoidance of contact with drug-taking acquaintances.

In-patients are generally content with a lower starting amount of methadone in the order of 30 mg daily. For patients in hospital it is common, despite the lengthy half-life of methadone, to divide its intake into two daily doses during the early stage of withdrawal. A short withdrawal regime of ten days is humane but with a patient who has fragile motivation may lead to premature self-discharge to resume heroin. An in-patient regime of three weeks is more likely to ensure compliance and allow development of a therapeutic relationship with staff.

Benzodiazepines have been employed to counteract opioid withdrawal symptoms. Their use is not recommended outside hospital. Benzodiazepines, as discussed by Malcolm Lader in Chapter 14, produce a type of physical dependence whose abstinence features, unlike those of opioids, carry severe medical risks even in subjects who are otherwise healthy. Drug misusers are able to inject crushed tablets or the contents of capsules when given psychoactive drugs in these forms. Repeated intake of benzodiazepines can produce a range of psychological symptoms and so compound problems for drug misusers and their therapists.

There are nonopioid alternatives that are preferable to benzodiazepines. Clonidine is an alpha$_2$–andrenergic agonist that activates presynaptic receptors of noradrenaline (norepinephrine) and so reduces by negative feedback noradrenergic activity. Neurones in the locus coeruleus of the brain stem which release noradrenaline are normally subject to inhibition through their own presynaptic noradrenaline receptors and through their opioid receptors. Repeated intake of an opioid drug mimics and thereby reduces inhibition from the endogenous opioids of the brain; drug withdrawal then provokes a hyperactivity of the noradrenaline-releasing neurones which endures until the endogenous opioid inhibition returns to normal. It is hypothesized that clonidine suppresses the withdrawal overactivity of central noradrenergic neurones (of which half are located in the locus coeruleus) by its effect on their noradrenaline receptors.

One 50 microgram tablet of clonidine can be taken on four occasions throughout the first opioid-free day. On the second day the doses are doubled and retained at the higher level during three days. From the fifth day when the underlying opioid-abstinence syndrome is abating, the drug is reduced by one tablet daily so that by the twelfth day administration has ceased. This schedule usually avoids the side effect of hypotension with resulting dizziness which the drug can produce. The patient is warned of possible dizziness and advised to remain quietly at home; the recom- mendation, if followed, has of course the advantage of controlling drug-seeking behaviour. Alternatively the patient is asked to attend each day for an issue of clonidine and determination of dose level after assessment of clinical response, including blood pressure. Attendance has the advantage of allowing counselling on the psychosocial measures needed for continued abstinence. In hospital daily amounts up to 800 micrograms (16 tablets) in divided doses can be employed. These are withdrawn gradually from the fifth day of admission.

Abrupt cessation of clonidine when given to treat hypertension has led to dangerous rises of blood pressure. Although the risk is largely theoretical when the compound is administered over a short period to a drug misuser, clonidine should be withdrawn in stages. This advice is enjoined on the patient. Lofexidine is a similar compound that is reputed to possess less hypotensive and sedative effects than clonidine. There are no reports of dependence on either drug.

Clonidine is absorbed transdermally. In the United States the drug is available in a patch that adheres to the skin and delivers the drug during the course of a week. The method avoids the hazard that is sometimes encountered with clonidine tablets of deliberate overdose in an attempt to boost the beneficial effects of the compound.

Diphenoxylate and loperamide are drugs employed in oral form by some practitioners to alleviate withdrawal diarrhoea and abdominal pain. Although both are opioids their dependence potential is small, especially from loperamide. They can be prescribed to complement clonidine.

Benzodiazepines

The abrupt cessation of an opioid is usually distressing to patients but is not medically hazardous. The possible exceptions are elderly or physically ill subjects. In contrast, sudden stoppage of benzodiazepines is liable to provoke convulsions, agitation, delirium or more prolonged though less dramatic symptoms. Their medical administration should never cease abruptly.

A phased reduction over a period of weeks is appropriate for a person whose regular intake is of recent onset. Benzodiazepines should not be issued outside hospital to a person who had been taking them illicitly because of the risk of their misuse, perhaps intravenously, by the recipient or others.

Many subjects dependent on benzodiazepines have been receiving drugs of this category on prescription for some months or years. In their case drug reduction should occupy a period of several months, occasionally longer than a year, in order to minimize the risk of a variety of prolonged withdrawal symptoms. The features can arise during and persist for a lengthy period after overhasty benzodiazepine withdrawal. They include anxiety, phobias, panic attacks, depression, depersonalization and disturbances of perception (Ashton, 1984).

The following regime is suitable for a patient who has been taking benzodiazepines chronically on prescription. Dose reductions should take place at intervals of one to four weeks, though two weeks is often preferred. The pace of removal is negotiated with the patient and largely determined by the latter. Diazepam is a commonly prescribed benzodiazepine. Dose levels of diazepam above 30 mg daily can be reduced by 1–2 mg decrements. From a daily level of 30 mg downwards 1 mg decreases are suitable although in the final stages patients may prefer 0.5 mg reductions.

Withdrawal of lorazepam is particularly likely to induce prolonged symptoms. It is often helpful to transfer a patient from lorazepam to diazepam. One to 1.5 mg of the former is equivalent to 10 mg of the latter.

Patients who are reducing benzodiazepines require support and reassurance. Self-help groups are beneficial. Cognitive and behavioural techniques exist for the anxiety and phobias that may supervene. Depressive symptoms may warrant antidepressant medication.

Barbiturates and other general sedatives

Included in this category are barbiturates, chlormethiazole, methaqualone, glutethamide and meprobamate. Their abrupt cessation induces abstinence features of agitation, tremulousness, delirium and convulsions. The syndrome is similar to that which follows stoppage of alcohol or benzodiazepines except for two qualifications. Fits are more common than with alcohol cessation and the prolonged symptoms that may follow benzodiazepine removal are not encountered. Phased withdrawal of the compounds over a period of two to three weeks is appropriate. The process is more readily achieved in hospital.

Cocaine

The frequent heavy use of cocaine promotes feelings of depression and anxiety after its termination. Counselling with psychological and social support forms the basis of therapy. Non-addictive pharmacological aid is under development.

It is hypothesized that repeated intake of cocaine depletes neurone vesicles of dopamine and that the depletion mediates the dysphoria and drug craving which follows cocaine cessation. Dopamine agonists have therefore been employed in treatment. Bromocriptine acts as an agonist directly at postsynaptic receptor sites for dopamine. Amantadine releases dopamine and noradrenaline from presynaptic storage vesicles and delays the reuptake of these neurotransmitters. Both compounds have been used to reduce the anhedonia and craving of cocaine withdrawal.

Antidepressant drugs, particularly the tricyclic compound desipramine, are also employed. Tricyclics have the risk that their retarding effect on cardiac conduction might be synergistically prolonged by cocaine if the subject resumes the latter substance.

In considering the pharmacological approaches it should be noted that the clinical effects of dopamine agonists supervene quickly, while those of tricyclic antidepressants take two to three weeks to unfold but are possibly more enduring. The treatment of cocaine misuse, including pharmacological intervention, has been reviewed by Lee and Ellinwood (1989).

Amphetamine-like drugs

There are many compounds that resemble amphetamines in chemical structure and activity. Their discontinuance leads to a phase of lethargy and depression. The symptoms require respect from the therapist for the malaise of the patient or client, with reassurance that they will remit. Medication is not appropriate.

Phencyclidine

Phencyclidine (PCP) is considered to possess sedative, hallucinogenic and stimulant properties. Its removal has been reported to produce an amphetamine-like withdrawal syndrome. The features involve depression, need for sleep, increased appetite and PCP craving (Rawson et al., 1981). The condition is not severe enough to warrant medication.

Cannabis

The regular intake of large amounts of cannabis can lead to physical dependence. The withdrawal features include tension, anorexia, loss of weight and impaired sleep (Jones et al., 1976). The abstinence syndrome is not severe and does not require treatment by drugs.

Hallucinogens, atropine-like drugs, volatile inhalants, simple analgesics

Individual misuse of the above drugs is usually intermittent and therefore on a priori grounds unlikely to lead to physical dependence and to an abstinence syndrome.

Occasionally their intake is regularly repeated but even then physical dependence does not ensue. Their removal after a phase of regular consumption leads to an improvement and not to a deterioration of the subject's sense of well-being.

Methadone maintenance

The term applies to substitute medication for another opioid, usually for heroin. Methadone is given in a liquid non-injectable form to enable the subject to cease other forms of opioid usage and to change to a more stable lifestyle. If the previous drug intake involved injections then the attractiveness and physical risks of injection procedures are avoided. The strategy is not universally employed and has met diversity and fluctuations of attitude amongst therapists. The contradictory views can be reconciled if the process is regarded as a holding period while the patient or client is encouraged to make significant changes in thinking and behaviour that favour eventual abstinence. Viewed in this light there is not a clear or radical distinction between methadone maintenance and a lengthy period of methadone detoxification.

The dose which is employed is similar to that required at the start of a less prolonged withdrawal regime. Thirty to 40 mg of methadone given once daily usually suffice. Occasionally amounts as high as 60 mg in a day may be needed but the therapist should aim to keep the daily level below 50 mg. Large amounts over 60 mg daily have been given with the intention of blocking the euphoric effect of heroin and thereby rendering pointless further heroin intake. The high quantities of prescribed drug involved in methadone blockade promote prolonged dependence and are no longer favoured.

Methadone is issued daily to regulate its intake and minimize its illicit dissemination. Consumption within clinic premises is preferable. If this is not possible arrangements are made for daily issues by a pharmacist. Frequent counselling and urine testing for heroin and other illicit drugs are important. Otherwise the regime degenerates into mere drug provision and the client can simply utilize the prescribed substance to supplement illegal drug supplies.

It is possible with time to establish trust between patient and professional staff so that the former can be saved the inconvenience of daily attendance at a clinic or pharmacy. Sufficient methadone to last for a few days is then issued for the client to take home. An alternative drug for this stage that has been studied experimentally is levo-alpha-acetylmethadol (LAMM). The effects of LAMM endure for 72 hours so that the drug can be taken on just three occasions in a week.

It is usual in the United States to commence withdrawal from methadone after a year of maintenance treatment (Kleber, 1989). The reduction phase occupies three to six months. Since withdrawal symptoms and drug craving can be prominent at dose levels below 25 mg and may lead to relapse onto heroin some patients are retained on longer regimes.

Many other legal preparations, including stimulants, general sedatives and opioids in forms that can be injected, have from time to time been suggested or tried as substitutes for street drugs. Their use can provoke chaotic behaviour, including violence; this drawback applies both to stimulants and sedatives. Further caveats should be entered against preparations which can be injected (tablets and capsules as well as ampoules enter the injectable category). Injectable drugs attract high prices on the illicit market. They continue the practice of injecting with its attendant risks of overdose and of infection. Viral infections can of course ensue if injection equipment is shared, even occasionally. Therefore substitute drugs apart from oral methadone are not advised as a treatment for illicit drug users.

Management of opioid dependence in pregnancy

The therapist has two individuals to consider – the mother and the foetus. Sudden cessation of opioids by a pregnant female is associated with foetal distress and intrauterine death. A methadone schedule can prevent the fluctuations of foetal exposure to opioids that accompany irregular illicit usage. The regime promotes compliance with antenatal care and allows guidance of the mother towards a drug-free state. Slow detoxification employing methadone and monitoring of the foetus is often practical, with a satisfactory outcome for mother and foetus. In some instances it is not possible to achieve methadone removal before labour.

An infant born to a mother who has been taking methadone or another opioid will show withdrawal features. The neonatal abstinence syndrome can comprise irritability, convulsions, tremor, muscle rigidity, sneezing, yawning, lacrimination, rapid breathing, vomiting, diarrhoea and a shrill cry.

Fortunately the course of the condition is naturally towards recovery. Differences between centres in its reported severity may reflect varying patterns of drug usage, including polydrug intake (Alroomi *et al.*, 1988). Therapy takes the form of medication for neonatal irritability, as by phenobarbitone or chloral hydrate. An opioid may be given temporarily; fits require an anticonvulsant. Babies that are low in weight (perhaps because of maternal self-neglect combined with tobacco smoking), require maintenance of fluid, electrolyte and calorie balance together with correction of associated metabolic anomalies.

Naltrexone blockade

Naltrexone inertly occupies the mu receptor sites for opioids and so competitively prevents drug euphoria. Naltrexone, which is taken by mouth, is employed for this reason to block the agreeable effects of heroin and thus render heroin usage unrewarding. The side-effects of the drug take the form of yawning, stretching and a stimulant effect on thought and speech. They are infrequent. There is no withdrawal syndrome from cessation of naltrexone.

Like other opioid antagonists naltrexone can provoke abstinence features in a patient who has recently been taking an opioid agonist, so it is necessary to ensure that the recipient is over the withdrawal phase from the original drug. This requires five to seven days of abstinence from heroin or ten to fourteen days abstention from methadone. It may be desirable to administer a test dose of 400–800 micrograms of naloxone subcutaneously to assess if this powerful antagonist precipitates the opioid abstinence syndrome during the following 45 minutes. Alternatively 200 micrograms of naloxone may be given intravenously; if no adverse reaction occurs after

30 seconds a further test dose of 600 micrograms can be injected. If naloxone does not provoke withdrawal features then neither will naltrexone.

The initial dose of naltrexone is 25 mg (half a tablet), followed if there are no withdrawal features either by a further 25 mg an hour later or by 50 mg the following day. Mild abstinence symptoms can be treated by clonidine for a few days in daily amounts of 100–300 micrograms. Naltrexone can be taken in daily doses of 50 mg, but it is more usual to space administration through the week. For example, 50 mg can be ingested on Mondays and Wednesdays and 150 mg on Fridays.

An alternative starting procedure involves rapid detoxification with clonidine and naltrexone (Vining et al., 1988). Clonidine is given in decreasing dosage over five days, while naltrexone is raised in single daily increments from 12.5 mg to 100 mg on the fifth day.

Naltrexone given experimentally in high levels of 300 mg a day has increased liver enzymes. It is therefore recommended that the drug is avoided if liver dysfunction is initially present and that hepatic enzymes are monitored for at least two months. It is possible that the lower doses employed in treatment make the advice overcautious.

The main difficulty rests with patient compliance. To obviate this drawback it is advantageous for the drug to be administered by a relative or another person after the patient has agreed to the supervision.

CONCLUSION

Pharmacotherapy often forms an integral part of treatment but does not occupy the cardinal role. Counselling is the central process; its techniques are described in other chapters.

A promising area for progress lies in the development of drugs that relieve withdrawal symptoms but are not themselves addictive. Antidepressants are not vulnerable to misuse, except for the amphetamine-like tranylcypromine, but in practice are not usually required. Lack of compliance is a major hurdle to widespread employment of drugs which could block the euphoric results of misused substances.

There are some modest gains in the techniques of matching pharmacological treatments to the needs of subjects. The briefer methods for detoxification, and naltrexone blockade, are best suited to the more determined patients. Detoxification with oral methadone is a useful means of attracting clients into therapy. The consideration draws magnified importance since the advent of HIV disease amongst misusers who inject drugs. Detoxification on a recurrent basis may be required; this approach is popular with out-patients and is associated with psychological and social benefits (Tennant, 1986).

Heroin injectors who are infected with HIV virus deteriorate more rapidly towards disease manifestations if they incur further inoculations with the virus. Methadone can lead some drug misusers with HIV infection towards general improvement in health and to treatment of their infected status or disease.

Subjects whose opioid dependence appears firmly entrenched often enter the stage of disenchantment and turn to treatment (Stimson and Oppenheimer, 1982;

Madden, 1984). They can benefit from an intermediate step of psychological and social stabilization on methadone. Passive prolongation of methadone regimes is undesirable, with the exception, in the interests of the subjects, of certain patients who have HIV infection. The practice inhibits spontaneous progress towards remission, saps staff morale and obstructs the flow of subjects through clinics. The latter process inhibits rapid acceptance of new clientele. Therapist disillusion has also arisen from realization that the simple provision of methadone without careful monitoring of patients often fails to check their use of illicit drugs.

Personnel who treat drug misusers acquire certain assets. Shrewdness is needed to assess the severity of withdrawal symptoms and to determine whether subjects continue to obtain drugs from other sources, whether on prescription or illicitly. Despite care, therapists are sometimes deceived, so equanimity and good humour are indispensable when deception is encountered.

Drug-dependent persons are understandably hesitant or fearful of treatment, although they appreciate that therapy entails some discomfort. They are more likely to enter and remain in treatment if they sense the concern and experience of therapists. Such professional attributes are evinced in part by readiness to minimize physical or mental distress, but more fully by keenness to guide clients towards constructive goals by means of a blend of clarity, flexibility and tenacity.

REFERENCES

Alroomi, L.G., Davidson, J., Evans, T.H., Galea, P. and Howat, R. (1988) 'Maternal narcotic abuse and the newborn', *Archives of Disease in Childhood* 63: 81–3.
Ashton, H. (1984) 'Benzodiazepine withdrawal: an unfinished story', *British Medical Journal* 288: 1135–40.
Jones, R.T., Benowitz, N. and Rackman, J. (1976) 'Clinical studies of cannabis tolerance and dependence', *Annals of the New York Academy of Sciences* 282: 221–34.
Kleber, H.D. (1989) 'Treatment of drug dependence: what works', *International Review of Psychiatry* 1: 81–9.
Lee, T.H. and Ellinwood, E.H. (1989) 'Progression, complications and treatment of cocaine misuse', *Current Opinion in Psychiatry* 2: 408–13.
Madden, J.S. (1984) *A Guide to Alcohol and Drug Dependence* (2nd edn), Bristol: Wright, pp. 253–4.
Rawson, R.A., Tennant, F.S. and McCann, M. (1981) 'Characteristics of 68 chronic phencyclidine abusers who sought treatment', *Drug and Alcohol Dependence* 8: 223–7.
Stimson, G.V. and Oppenheimer, E. (1982) *Heroin Addiction: Treatment and Control in Britain*, Edinburgh: Churchill Livingstone.
Tennant, F.S. (1986) 'Benefits of recurrent, outpatient heroin detoxification', *International Journal of the Addictions* 20: 1685–91.
Vining, E., Kosten, T.R. and Kleber, H.D. (1988) 'Clinical utility of rapid clonidine–naltrexone detoxification for opioid abusers', *British Journal of Addiction* 83: 567–75.

CROSS REFERENCES

Chapter 32

Behavioural treatments for alcohol problems

D. Adrian Wilkinson and Martha Sanchez-Craig

Behavioural treatments for alcohol dependence, like other behavioural approaches, embody an attitude towards treatment more than a defined set of techniques. The attitude stems from the assumptions that: alcohol dependence is largely the product of normal learning processes; alcohol consumption is functional for the drinker; as a learned behaviour, excessive drinking can be 'unlearned' if its functions are understood. These assumptions impel the therapist to investigate *antecedents* (environmental, emotional and cognitive) of episodes of excessive drinking, and *consequences* that maintain the behaviour. The behavioural approach involves testing *individualized treatment strategies* and abandoning those that fail to work.

People often think of behavioural approaches as involving punishment with electric shock or nausea-inducing drugs. In fact, behaviour therapists have shown that electrical aversion therapy is ineffective for alcohol problems, but aversion therapy using nausea is sometimes effective (Miller and Hester, 1986). However, most behavioural techniques do not involve aversive procedures. The therapy typically involves therapist and client talking together to solve the client's problems. What is unique in the behavioural approach is the nature of the discussions and the techniques used to help the client.

Behavioural treatments are conceptually rooted in the work of the Russian reflexologists, which culminated in Pavlov's description of the processes of conditioning at the turn of the century. Their enterprise shaped an enduring attitude to psychological research and treatment. The central feature of this attitude was a determined operationalism, rejecting subjectively defined psychological entities, and demanding objective description of all scientifically valid phenomena. This position was adopted by the North American behaviourists, of whom B.F. Skinner has been most influential. The principal objective of all these scientists was to describe the processes of learning in humans and other species.

In the 1950s and early 1960s it became acceptable among many clinicians and researchers to view some phenomena of abnormal psychology (including 'alcoholism') as the manifestation of maladaptive conditioning or learning, rather than as a symptom of psychopathology, characterological deficiency, or physiological abnormality. This general view was applied to excessive drinking, and resulted in some radical innovations to research on the subject. Specifically, clinical and research interest focused upon the problem behaviour itself (rather than psychological characteristics of the drinkers), giving priority to the objective description of drinking in alcoholics. This was accomplished by housing alcoholics in laboratories and giving them access to alcohol under various conditions. The results of these studies seriously undermined the credibility of the currently influential disease construct of alcoholism (see Sobell *et al.*, 1981, for review).

The laboratory studies revealed that drinking alcohol by alcoholics did not occur for relief of withdrawal, and did not inevitably occur in the presence of alcohol, which was often 'hoarded' until a large quantity had been saved. In addition, alcoholics would drink moderate quantities to retain access to social and recreational activities, if excessive drinking caused the removal of these amenities. The results of this body of research (and parallel studies with animals) were inconsistent with a number of predictions from the disease model of alcoholism, wherein 'loss of control' in the presence of alcohol, and 'craving' due to withdrawal are central constructs. Behavioural researchers concluded from these studies that alcohol consumption in alcoholics should be viewed more as functional behaviour gone awry rather than as symptoms of an underlying disease process.

EVOLUTION OF BEHAVIOURAL TREATMENTS

The earliest treatments deriving explicitly from theories of learning were aimed at the elimination of alcohol consumption by making the act of drinking unpleasant (aversive conditioning). This could be achieved, for example, by means of pairing drinking with chemically induced nausea, or by structuring undesirable consequences for drinking (e.g. loss of social contacts or money).

A clinically influential finding of the laboratory studies was the demonstration that management of contingencies for drinking could induce moderate levels of consumption in alcoholics. This suggested that moderation of consumption might be an achievable goal of treatment outside the laboratory, as some clinical outcome studies of conventionally treated alcoholics had purported to show, thereby causing a storm of controversy (Heather and Robertson, 1983). As a result of this convergence, behavioural approaches to treatment have been particularly prominent in attempting to facilitate moderation of consumption in alcohol-dependent clients. More recently clinical research has focused on identifying the characteristics of clients for whom such a goal is most feasible. A further development of the behavioural approach was the inclusion in treatment programmes of training in skills that were presumed to be deficient among problem drinkers, such as relaxation skills and improvement of social competence. This elaboration arose from the general principle that drinking is functional behaviour. Hence, being able to achieve the perceived benefits of drinking by alternate means should protect against a return to excessive use of alcohol.

The most profound change in the behavioural approach occurred after the work of Bandura and others legitimized the study of 'cognitive' variables by behaviourists. The idea that thoughts control behaviour is ancient and incontrovertible. The oddity of behaviourism was its avoidance of this 'mentalist' hypothesis, because it meant abandoning operationalism. The 'cognitive revolution' in psychology involved the development of methods for experimentally demonstrating the role of cognitive events in the production of behaviour. The new behaviourists claimed to be able to measure the effects of cognitive variables and called their approach 'cognitive-behavioural'. It was believed to retain the scientific purity of the behavioural approach, while admitting the reality and importance of thoughts in relation to actions.

In the field of alcohol studies, an outgrowth of the development of cognitive-behavioural psychology was the demonstration that expectations about alcohol played an important role in the development of drinking and its consequences. The principal method of studying alcohol expectancy effects involved giving subjects alcohol or placebo, and instructing them that they were receiving or not receiving alcohol. In numerous studies the belief that they had consumed alcohol had as much effect on subjects' behaviour (social, aggressive, sexual) as did the actual consumption of the drug (see Wilson, 1988, for review). The ideas of expectancies and the subject's interpretation of events were incorporated into cognitive-behavioural models of alcohol abuse, treatment (Sanchez-Craig *et al.*, 1987) and relapse (Marlatt and Gordon, 1980).

A second outgrowth of acceptance of the role of cognitions among the causes of drinking was an increased emphasis upon the drinker as an agent of change and a source of information. Client self-observation became an integral component of attempts to understand drinking, but still with the behaviourist emphasis on objective description and quantification. Like the behavioural scientists, clients were now urged to record the 'ABCs' (Antecedents, Behaviours, and Consequences) of their thoughts, emotions and actions in relation to drinking and the experience of temptations to drink.

TYPICAL ATTRIBUTES OF BEHAVIOURAL TREATMENTS

One can identify a number of crucial attributes of the behavioural approach to the treatment of excessive drinking. The individual attributes are not necessarily unique to behavioural treatments, but their combination is. These attributes may be succinctly described as follows:

Focus on drinking

The principal objective of treatment is to change the drinking of the client, so that it no longer causes problems. This contrasts with methods that aim at some other change in the client (e.g. in personality, psychodynamics, pharmacologic state or physiology) leading to changes in drinking.

Ongoing assessment of drinking

The behavioural approach is characterized by emphasis on recording the level, pattern, circumstances and consequences of drinking by the client at admission and throughout treatment and follow-up. These measures are taken because: (a) it is not assumed that a problem-free outcome must involve total abstention from alcohol; (b) it is assumed that significant improvements (short of successful outcome) should be noted and can occur without total abstention; and (c) it is assumed that deterioration can occur and a prompt response by a change of treatment strategy should be instituted.

Individualized treatment goals and plans

If alcohol dependence is learned, it can be learned in a variety of circumstances and physical or emotional states. This implies that goals and treatments should be individualized to reflect this variety in the conditions of learning. Because the functions attributed to alcohol use vary among individuals, the treatments should vary according to these presumed functions. Thus, among clients who use alcohol as an aid to sleeping, the treatment plan would differ from that for clients who use alcohol to facilitate social interaction or to ameliorate negative emotion. Also, in behavioural treatment flexibility is accepted concerning the goal of treatment; hence the nature of the goal should be precisely specified so that outcome can be assessed. Abstinence is abstinence (if one has any regard at all for the English language), but moderate drinking can involve variations in quantity, frequency and setting of consumption.

Flexibility of treatment goals and plans

The general approach to treatment is empirical. It is assumed that alcohol consumption serves some real or imagined function for the drinker, and that careful examination of the circumstances of drinking can reveal these functions. The topography of drinking, and its antecedents and consequences (cognitive, emotional, behavioural, and environmental), are described and reviewed extensively in assessing the client's problem. An hypothesis is formed concerning the events in the client's mind and environment that are maintaining the drinking, and then a plausible strategy for undermining these supports of the excessive drinking is formulated. This strategy may involve attempts to alter the environment of the client, his or her expectations about the effects of drinking, the consequences of drinking, or some combination of these. If the strategy fails, the hypothesis concerning the functions and supports for drinking are re-evaluated.

Brief treatment – long follow-up

The theoretical description of excessive drinking as a form of learned behaviour suggests two things about treatment duration. As humans are flexible behaviourally, it should be possible to produce changes in their behaviour very rapidly. However, since the habit of heavy drinking is typically longstanding and ingrained by the time people come into treatment, the tendency to revert to the habit is likely to persist for a long time after the behaviour is restrained and to extinguish slowly. Furthermore, as with most habits, re-acquisition is likely to be rapid. All of these features suggest that the most effective use of treatment resources is likely to involve fairly brief initial phases of treatment, with extensive follow-up and preparation of the client to anticipate urges or temptations to re-engage in the behaviour for a considerable time after it has been brought under control. (Marlatt has termed such preparation of the client 'Relapse Prevention').

PHILOSOPHIC BASES OF BEHAVIOURAL TREATMENTS

Paradoxically, the philosophic basis of behavioural approaches is not uniform, although their epistemology and scientific roots are common. Some approaches are rather deterministic and tend to involve collaborating with the client to restructure his or her physical and social environment so that the environmental change decreases the probability of drinking. The 'Community Reinforcement' model admirably represents this paradigm (Sisson and Azrin, 1989). Other approaches derive more from an existential philosophy, emphasizing the autonomy, responsibility and thoughts of the client (e.g. Sanchez-Craig, 1990) and using terms such as 'self-control' in describing the focus of the treatment strategy. Since clients vary in a similar manner amongst themselves, it is likely that matching the clients' concepts of themselves with the philosophic thrust of the treatment will increase the effectiveness of treatments.

IMPACT OF BEHAVIOUR THERAPY

Behavioural treatments of alcohol problems are much less common in most parts of the world than treatments based upon a conception of alcohol dependence as disease. Where the behavioural approach to alcohol problems has had its greatest impact is in the evaluation of treatment programmes. The methods for assessing the outcome of treatment, developed by behavioural scientists, have been almost universally adopted where such evaluations occur. It remains to be seen whether clinicians will prove as prepared to adopt the behavioural approach as the scientists have been.

REFERENCES

Heather, N. and Robertson, I. (1983) *Controlled Drinking* (rev. edn), London: Methuen.
Marlatt, A. and Gordon, J.R. (1980) 'Determinants of relapse: implications for the maintenance of behavior change', in P.O. Davidson and S.M. Davidson (eds) *Behavioral Medicine: Changing Health Lifestyles*, New York: Brunner/Mazel, pp. 410–52.
Miller, W.R. and Hester, R. (1986) 'The effectiveness of alcoholism treatment: what research reveals', in W.R. Miller and N. Heather (eds) *Treating Addictive Behaviors*, New York: Plenum, pp. 121–74.
Sanchez-Craig, M. (1990) 'Brief didactic treatment for alcohol and drug-related problems: an approach based on client choice', *British Journal of Addiction* 85: 169–77.
Sanchez-Craig, M., Wilkinson, D.A. and Walker, K. (1987). 'Theory and methods for secondary prevention of alcohol problems: a cognitively-based approach', in W.M. Cox (ed.) *Treatment and Prevention of Alcohol Problems: A Resource Manual*, New York: Academic Press.
Sisson, R.W. and Azrin, N.H. (1989) 'The community reinforcement approach', in R. Hester and W.R. Miller (eds) *Handbook of Alcoholism Treatment Approaches*, New York: Pergamon.
Sobell, M.B., Cappell, H. and Sobell, L. (eds) (1981) 'Contribution of basic research to the treatment of substance abuse', Special issue: *Addictive Behaviors* 6: 185–269.
Wilson, G.T. (1988) 'Alcohol use and abuse: a social learning analysis', in C.D. Chaudron and D.A. Wilkinson (eds) Theories on Alcoholism, Toronto: Addiction Research Foundation, pp. 239–87.

CROSS REFERENCES

Chapter 3   Behaviour pharmacology of addiction
             I. P. Stolerman
Chapter 4   Psychological theories of addiction
             Robert West
Chapter 33   Behaviour therapy of drug dependence
             Charles P. O'Brien and Anna Rose Childress

Chapter 33

Behaviour therapy of drug dependence

Charles P. O'Brien and Anna Rose Childress

Behaviour therapy is generally defined as a treatment characterized by deliberate attempts to modify specific behaviours for therapeutic purposes. Typically the therapist focuses on behaviours which lead to the obtaining and administration of drugs. This is in contrast to non-directive therapies which do not target specific behaviours, but rather they encourage self-expression and help the patient in general to understand feelings and relationships. In practice, there is no need for a sharp separation between directive and non-directive therapies. Patients may best be managed by a combination approach involving different techniques used at different times during the course of therapy. In this chapter, although we will focus on behaviour therapy per se, in a complicated condition such as addiction, a narrow focus on behaviour therapy alone would rarely be indicated except for research purposes.

ANALYSIS OF THE BEHAVIOUR OF DRUG ABUSE

The critical aspect of treatment is not detoxification or simple removal of the drug from the body. Depending on the drug, detoxification can be accomplished in many ways; but after a brief abstinent period, return to drug use is likely unless there is effective intervention. The therapist can analyse the patterns of behaviour which lead to relapse and develop strategies which can help the patient resist the pressure to resume drug-taking.

One aspect of the pressure to relapse involves spontaneous craving for the drug. Craving refers to strong internal urges to obtain and administer a specific substance. Craving is often reported by recovering addicts in treatment and thus can be used as a subjective measure of change. Although the concept of craving has been criticized as being poorly defined, it can be useful in monitoring the effects of treatment. Craving is usually increased prior to a 'slip' or relapse to drug use. There is no objective measure to validate craving in clinical situations and there is some difference of opinion as to its meaning. Operationally, however, patients seem to understand the concept and to be able to rate its strength as they perceive it.

Substances are abused because they are reinforcing: they produce some desired effect. Having tried the substance once, the user is motivated to repeat the process and take it again. This means that abused drugs and, by association, drug-related environments and people have reinforcing, discriminative and eliciting properties. The properties of these drug-related stimuli are not easy to dissociate: a single stimulus – for example, the sight of a drug dealer – can simultaneously: (1) attract the patient because of the close association between the dealer and the powerful primary reinforcing properties of the drug, (2) signal the patient that a response contingency is in effect, i.e. drug-seeking behaviour is now very likely to be reinforced (discriminative properties), and (3) trigger strong physiological arousal, drug craving and other drug-related responses in the patient (eliciting properties) because of the dealer's repeated association with drug administration and drug effects.

The actual drug-using environment is likely to be even more complex. The typical situation contains not just one stimulus (e.g. the dealer) with multiple properties, but many stimuli (e.g. the location itself, the presence of regular drug users, the sight of drug paraphernalia), each with multiple properties, all potentially interacting and contributing to the final end-point behaviour of drug-seeking and drug-taking. Therapeutic techniques have been developed in an attempt to modify the properties of these stimuli and reduce the likelihood of relapse.

TREATMENTS ADDRESSING REINFORCING PROPERTIES OF DRUGS

Drug-seeking behaviour is powerfully reinforced thousands of times over the natural course of the patient's addiction. Current behavioural treatments addressing these reinforcing properties include operant extinction and contingency management. Operant extinction requires devising a situation in which the patient is exposed to drug-related stimuli and may go through the motions of seeking drugs without the occurrence of the usual reinforcement. Drug-seeking behaviour would no longer be reinforced and should eventually extinguish. In animal research, operant extinction of 'drug-seeking' is quite straightforward: omitting the reinforcing consequence (either the drug itself or a drug-related stimulus secondarily reinforcing because of its association with the drug) when the animal emits the behaviour causes the behaviour eventually to cease (extinguish). In clinical situations it is difficult to extinguish drug-seeking in a way strictly analogous to the experimental case because drugs are difficult to remove completely from the environment.

One tool for operant extinction is a pharmacologic treatment that specifically blocks the reinforcing actions of a drug even if the drug is administered. Naltrexone, a specific opiate antagonist, provides this opportunity for opiate abusers. Though not popular among most opiate abusers (who often want to retain the option of feeling opiate effects), naltrexone may be a useful tool among subgroups of opiate abusers with a high incentive for abstinence, e.g. medical professionals who will lose their licence to practise if they relapse and ex-prisoners on probation who risk re-incarceration if they relapse or return to drug-related crimes. Though naltrexone permits rapid operant extinction of drug-seeking behaviour, the effects are usually confined to the period when the patient is on the naltrexone and aware that reinforcement is unavailable. When the patient discontinues the naltrexone, however, drug-seeking behaviour will again be reinforced, and it often resumes. Methadone reduces the reinforcement of street opiates through a different mechanism. Persons maintained on methadone, a long-acting opioid, become cross-tolerant to all opioid (opiate-like) drugs. Tolerance refers to the fact that the taking of a substantial dose of an opioid alters the body such that the response to all other opioid drugs is reduced. Thus the perception of pleasure when usual doses of street opiates are taken is markedly decreased resulting in diminution or cessation of street opiate use. With the recent upsurge of cocaine abuse, research is underway to find pharmacologic agents which will specifically and effectively block the reinforcing effects of cocaine, but none is available at present.

CONTINGENCY MANAGEMENT

Another way of addressing the reinforcing properties of drugs and their associated stimuli is to find strong positive or negative reinforcers that will encourage competing non-drug behaviours and/or discourage drug-use behaviours. For example, Crowley (1984) found that cocaine abusers were more likely to maintain abstinence if they knew a signed 'confession' of their relapse would be sent to their medical licensing board or employer. Several variants on these contingency management and contracting techniques have been tried, including positive reinforcement for clean urines using money or increased methadone dosages. The most clinically useful of the contingency techniques incorporate reinforcers with a connection to the relevant community outside the treatment setting (e.g. letters of progress to employer or family). Use of these relevant reinforcers helps extend the influence of treatment beyond the immediate treatment setting, into the patient's family and the community.

TREATMENTS ADDRESSING DISCRIMINATIVE PROPERTIES

Stimuli associated with drug use can act as discriminative stimuli (SDs), signalling the patient that a response contingency is in effect. For example, the sight of a shooting gallery or 'crack' house cues the patient that drug seeking is likely to be reinforced. A basic behavioural approach to the discriminative properties of drug-related stimuli is to change an SD for drug seeking (the sight of a dealer, the onset of craving) into an SD for some alternative behaviour which will be reinforced, but not by drug use. The alternative behaviours may include avoidance (immediate withdrawal from the 'high risk' situation), assertive refusal of drug offers, engaging in a pleasurable physical activity or deep relaxation. The reinforcers for these behaviours may include an increased sense of mastery, self-control and self-efficacy (Marlatt, 1982).

TREATMENTS ADDRESSING ELICITING PROPERTIES

Drugs themselves are powerful eliciting stimuli. They trigger a wide range of subjective and pharmacologic effects. Stimuli repeatedly paired with drug administration (the sight of a dealer, a particular drug-related location) can acquire the ability through classical conditioning to elicit a wide range of conditioned responses, including drug-like, drug-opposite or drug compensatory effects, and drug craving. Many of these elicited responses could play a role in the high rate of relapse which characterizes substance-abuse disorders. Two basic approaches to the eliciting properties of drug-related stimuli include (1) counter-conditioning of other less problematic responses to the same drug-related conditioned stimulus (CS), and (2) attempts to weaken the eliciting power of the drug-related CS through classical extinction (repeated presentation of the CS not followed by drug administration). The latter procedure is also commonly referred to as 'cue exposure'.

Counter-conditioning

Counter-conditioning is most often encountered in the form of classical aversive conditioning, in which an aversive stimulus such as emetine-induced nausea or small electric shock is repeatedly paired with characteristic stimulus properties of the abused drug or with actual drug administration. The goal is a conditioned aversion, such that stimuli (sight, taste, smell) associated with the substance will trigger nausea or repulsion instead of craving/desire to use.

Though aversive emetine conditioning has been used in the treatment of more than 30,000 alcoholism in-patients over the past four decades, controlled studies of its presumed benefits lag far behind. Aversion therapy has been used very little in the treatment of patients dependent on drugs other than alcohol (Wolpe, 1965). When attempts have been made to conduct controlled studies in our centre, very few patients agreed to participate in a study which involved discomfort.

Classical extinction (cue exposure)

There is a recent and growing literature which clearly demonstrates that a variety of physiological and subjective responses can be elicited in abstinent former drug-dependent persons by initial exposure to both drug-related and alcohol-related cues. Though the nature and direction of the physiological responses vary across studies, the subjective reports often have one response in common: patients experience increased craving during initial exposure to cues associated with drug or alcohol administration.

With repeated, non-reinforced exposure to these cues (also called classical or Pavlovian extinction), both physiological and subjective responses to these conditioned cues tend to diminish. Several groups have used this principle to reduce the physiological and subjective responses to alcohol-related cues. Our own work focused initially on the use of extinction (cue exposure) procedures in treating opiate abuse patients. In general, this early work showed that repeated exposure to opiate-related stimuli (drug-related audio tapes, videotapes, paraphernalia and rituals) significantly reduced the conditioned craving and conditioned withdrawal symptoms which occurred upon initial presentation. Problems encountered in this early work included the persistence of conditioned physiological responses and incomplete generalization of extinction to actual cue situations outside the laboratory.

More recent work with patients recovering from cocaine dependence (Childress et al., 1988) demonstrates significant responses to cocaine-related cues after 28 days of therapeutic community treatment. Patients are typically surprised by the intensity of the craving for cocaine which occurs when they watch videos of typical situations which they will undoubtedly encounter when they leave the safety of the hospital or therapeutic community. These subjective feelings of craving are usually accompanied by marked autonomic changes consisting of increased heart rate, reductions in skin temperature and other signs of autonomic activation. The cues which are most effective are those which are specific to the patient's drug of choice and his preferred mode of administration (e.g. smoking or intravenous use).

We have studied groups of opiate-dependent and groups of cocaine-dependent patients over time and repeatedly exposed them to cues previously derived from similar patients. The responses produced by these cues can be very difficult to extinguish despite many repetitions over several months. This suggests that former addicts continue to be at risk when they return to environments laden with drug-related stimuli. Interestingly, the drug naltrexone, discussed earlier as a tool for operant extinction, could also potentially facilitate the classical extinction of conditioned craving and other responses. Being on naltrexone prevents the patients from experiencing drug effects, and the patient can have repeated, non-reinforced exposure to drug-related cues, experience urges, without clinical risk of relapse or re-addiction. It remains to be tested whether the effects of this classical extinction would generalize to a period when the patient has discontinued naltrexone.

Studies of clinical outcome suggest that patients who receive the treatment combination of extinction plus psychotherapy (another adjunctive treatment found useful in our substance-abuse populations) tend to have better retention in the out-patient treatment phase and fewer drug positive urines than patients in the other three comparison treatment packages. Though these relative differences are encouraging, we hope to increase the absolute magnitude of the benefits by teaching patients to actively combat the conditioned craving and arousal which they experience in response to cocaine-related stimuli. We have tested several 'coping with craving' techniques in the treatment of cocaine dependence (Childress *et al.*, 1990) and feel they will significantly enhance the effectiveness of passive cue exposure.

MULTI-MODAL BEHAVIOUR THERAPY

Our tentative conclusion based on our research, literature reviews and clinical experience is that combined treatment tailored to the individual patient is the preferred clinical approach at present. Cognitive-behavioural therapy in the Beck model has been demonstrated to be effective in opiate addicts (Woody *et al.*, 1983). Cognitive aspects include explanations to the patient about the causes of relapse and the presumed conditioning mechanism for the sudden appearance of craving in certain situations. Patients can be given specific homework assignments involving places and situations to avoid at first and then to approach under safer circumstances after practice in role-playing sessions during therapy. Specific techniques to cope with craving can be practised. These might involve relaxation techniques, thought-stopping and imagery. Cue exposure can be combined with these cognitive behavioural techniques. Thus the patient can have a bout of craving precipitated by imagery or drug-related stimuli during a session and then he can practise coping techniques with the aid of the therapist.

Of course, such combinations of treatment techniques make outcome research very difficult. It would be far simpler to give only one pure treatment to each patient so that we could determine which ingredient is producing the change in outcome. Unfortunately, addiction is such a complicated disorder involving so many different types of problems that a single treatment technique is unlikely to produce measurable effects.

CONCLUSION

In recent years there has been an encouraging increase in the amount and quality of research on behavioural treatments for substance abuse. Some of the most promising approaches combine behavioural treatments with each other (e.g. relapse prevention and cue exposure) or with other forms of treatment (e.g. psychotherapy), attempting to maximize impact on the multiple determinants of drug use. We are approaching the time when a patient may be systematically evaluated to develop a profile of vulnerabilities (e.g. cue responsivity, psychiatric symptoms, family problems, occupational problems) to determine rationally the treatment or combination of treatments of greatest potential benefit.

ACKNOWLEDGEMENTS

This work was supported by the V.A. Medical Research Service and NIDA Project DA 03008. Portions of this chapter appeared in a NIDA monograph of the 1988 Proceedings of the Committee on Problems of Drug Dependence.

REFERENCES

Childress, A.R., Ehrman, R., McLellan, A.T. and O'Brien, C.P. (1988) 'Conditioned craving and arousal in cocaine addiction', *Problems of Drug Dependence, NIDA Monograph Series*, DHHS pub no. (ADM) 88–1564, pp. 74–80.

Childress, A.R., Hole, A., DePhillipis, D., Urschel, H. and O'Brien, C.P. (1990) 'Active techniques for coping with conditioned drug craving and arousal', manual available from first author, Center for Studies in Addiction, University of Pennsylvania Department of Psychiatry, Philadelphia, PA. 19104.

Crowley, T. (1984). 'Contingency contracting treatment of drug-abusing physicians, nurses and dentists', *Behavioral Intervention Techniques in Drug Abuse Treatment, NIDA Research Monograph* 46: 68–83.

Marlatt, G.A. (1982) 'Relapse prevention: a self-control program for the treatment of addictive behaviors', in R.B. Stuart (ed.) *Adherence, Compliance and Generalization in Behavioral Medicine*, New York: Brunner/Mazel.

O'Brien, C.P., Ehrman, R. and Ternes, J. (1986) 'Classical conditioning in human opioid dependence', in S. Goldberg and I. Stolerman (eds) *Behavioral Analysis of Drug Dependence*, San Diego: Academic Press, pp. 329–56.

Wolpe, J. (1965) 'Conditioned inhibition of craving in drug addiction: a pilot experiment', *Behaviour Research and Therapy* 2: 285–7.

Woody, G.E., Luborsky, L., McLellan, A.T., O'Brien, C.P. and Beck, A.T. (1983) 'Psychotherapy for opiate addicts: does it help?', *Archives of General Psychiatry* 40: 639–48.

CROSS REFERENCES

Chapter 34

An alternative to psychotherapy

George Vaillant

My thesis is that the patient who tells us that he drinks because he is depressed and anxious may in fact be depressed or anxious because he drinks. He may draw attention from the fact that it is painful for him to give up alcohol. The alcoholic's denial may be simultaneously at a conscious, unconscious and cellular level. In no other mental illness is the deficit state so clearly a product of disordered chemistry and yet the secondary conflicts and associations so dynamically fascinating to psychiatrists. The greatest danger of this is wasteful, painful psychotherapy that bears analogy to someone trying to shoot a fish in a pool. No matter how carefully he aims, the refracted image always renders the shot wide of its mark.

Consider the scenario of *Who's Afraid of Virginia Woolf?* We see George and Martha locked in a sadomasochistic marital struggle. Drawing on his protagonists' childhoods, Edward Albee fills his audience in on the complex roots of their current conflict. The therapists in the audience may speculate that if George and Martha could come to terms with their parental introjects and learn openly to love each other through psychotherapy, their need for alcohol would vanish. But let us look at that scenario more closely. In fact, the sadism between George and Martha rises parallel to their rising blood alcohol. People mindlessly torture each other – and their therapists – because they have a disease called alcoholism far more often than people misuse alcohol to punish those they love.

Let me approach the problem from a different tack. Once compulsive drinking is established, any excuse justifies a drink. Consider well-analysed training analysts who chain-smoke. Despite their access to previously repressed parental introjects and despite deep understanding of their oral needs, analysts continue to smoke. Do they do it from an unconscious death wish or from intractable habit? There is reasonable evidence that premorbidly many alcoholics are no sicker than many heavy smokers. To formulate their habit in terms of their 'retrospective' accounts of parental deprivation or psychological conflict would be a grave error.

At this point, I shall describe the Cambridge Hospital programme for treating alcoholics. The administrative control of the programme is in the Department of Medicine and in its own non-psychiatric community board. A cornerstone of this programme is to avoid sustaining therapeutic alliances with alcoholics so as to avoid transference and, it is hoped, thereby to avoid the lion's share of the ensuing countertransference. The staff has been deliberately recruited from the psycho-dynamically naive. The reason for this philosophy is that even if alcoholics can learn to tolerate their transference, therapists of alcoholics seem to have extraordinary difficulty in tolerating theirs. For example, for years I was associated with two psychoanalytically oriented, sophisticated, humane community mental health centres. In both there was an unwritten sign over the entrance to in-patient and out-patient services. The sign said: 'Alcoholics need not apply'. This stemmed from senior staff's countertransference, not from the needs of the community.

In contrast, if the Cambridge Hospital alcohol programme shuns psychotherapy, if it phobically avoids transference, it also treats more alcoholics than any other programme in Massachusetts. It has a walk-in service sixteen hours a day, seven days a week; patients are seen without appointment. The staff has learned to accept, not reject, the twenty-time repeater; to offer hope and experience to the ten-time repeater; and to offer education and treatment to the one thousand alcoholics who are seen each year for the first time. Alcoholics' needs for welfare, shelter, detoxification and referral are met day and night. Getting alcoholics to return for subsequent visits is not a problem.

However, when an alcoholic comes for a return visit, he sees whatever counsellor is on duty. This could be any one of ten individuals. Even group leadership is on a rotating basis so that patients will come to groups to work on their problem of alcohol, not out of alliance to an individual. Again, on the detoxification unit, a patient is welcome to return as many times as he needs detoxification, but on every admission the patient is assigned a new counsellor. The focus of the programme is to produce alliance first to the institution Cambridge Hospital and from there through step-wise progression to encourage the patient to move on to an alliance with Alcoholics Anonymous. This organization, by its very emphasis on anonymity, strives to avoid sustaining individual alliances. A member is taught to ally himself with his peers' strengths – not with those of his therapist.

Let me explain this unusual approach: Why does it help treatment to regard alcoholism as a disease, not a psychiatric disorder? Why does it help to violate the usual principles of doctor–patient alliance?

First, alcoholism is a disorder with unexpected relapses and intense needs for help at unexpected times. The alcoholic, like the unconscious, has little sense of time. Unexpected relapses tend to be destructive to any ongoing relationship, and this includes the most selfless therapeutic alliance. The patient literally is not under his own control. One of the advantages of a walk-in clinic, a hot line and AA, is that they do not expect the patient to be in control. If we treat alcoholism by trying to sustain a therapeutic alliance, we expect the alcoholic's symptoms to be dynamically determined, controllable through insight and affected by the state of the transference. However, once we feel that there is a dynamic relationship between our response and the patient's drinking, we develop superstitious and magical ideas about our powers, and this leads to hyper-vigilance, then mistrust and finally rupture of the alliance. It is no accident that the first step of Al-anon, as well as AA, is 'We admitted we were powerless over alcohol'. Rather than engender therapeutic nihilism, the Cambridge Hospital programme paradoxically has this motto as its cornerstone. Our treatment staff are asked to attend Al-anon regularly. The whole treatment philosophy is designed to alleviate the enormous staff guilt generated by the seemingly inexplicable failure of some alcoholics to recover. Teaching staff to 'let go' of patients when they leave allows them to welcome those who may return.

Similarly, we try to involve the closest family member of every patient admitted. The task of family therapy is not just to view the patient's alcoholism in the context of his ongoing family relationships but also to view his ongoing familial battles from the perspective of the 'disease', alcoholism.

The second reason for avoiding psychotherapy is that if the onset of alcoholism is facilitated by object loss, it is even truer that alcoholism causes object loss. There is probably no group of people more exquisitely lonely than chronic alcoholics. They have replaced virtually every meaningful person in their lives with inanimate bottles. The temptation of the sensitive therapist to step in and try to fill that loneliness leads to overwhelming demands, e.g. crises on weekends, at Christmas or in the early hours of the morning. The therapist withdraws, and the alcoholic's misperception that his loneliness is too great to bear is confirmed. So, again, it is important to avoid therapeutic relationships leading to intense transference and countertransference.

The third reason for the Cambridge Hospital's philosophy is a paradox of alcoholism. Dynamic treatment can serve to increase, rather than lessen, the patient's denial that he has a problem with alcoholism. For if alcoholism is regarded as a symptom, then misunderstood relapse only increases the patient's guilt towards his therapist. If alcoholic sadism is regarded as dynamically, not chemically, engendered, shame is immense. But if the patient's rages and relapse to alcohol are a symptom not of his unacceptable ambivalence, but of his matter-of-fact illness, then the patient's guilt is reduced and he can keep his alcoholism in consciousness. Not only can he remember that his marriage and childhood were 'allegedly' intolerable, he can also see as intolerable the 'fact' that he now truly has difficulty controlling his drinking.

The fourth reason for avoiding psychotherapy is that alcoholism is sometimes preceded and is always followed by profoundly low self-esteem. By definition, a sustained therapeutic relationship and its accompanying transference present the therapist as a powerful and reliable figure enhancing the alcoholic patient's low self-esteem and exacerbating his contempt for his own incomprehensible unreliability. Alcoholics learn to displace this rage at self to contempt for the reliability, the tolerance and the sobriety of their long-suffering therapists. A therapist can only experience this as ingratitude. In response, the patient can only conclude that his ego strengths can never be allied with his therapist's.

In contrast, the anonymous peer groups in Alcoholics Anonymous ask only that the patient accept help from those who are as vulnerable as himself; and equally important, of course, AA allows him to help in return. An alliance is forged and self-esteem goes up. True, AA has a system of 'sponsors' and 'pigeons' but one definition of a pigeon is 'someone who keeps the sponsor sober'! Thus we have another paradox. Psychotherapy asks that the patient admit helplessness to his doctor, encourages him to say how little he has to be grateful for, but insists that he be independent enough to pay for the privilege. AA costs the patient nothing but shows him that he is independent enough to help others and encourages gratitude for the smallest blessings. That such an approach involves denial of emotional suffering is true; but research into serious medical illness is slowly teaching us that denial can be lifesaving.

Fifth, there is also evidence that a small group of alcoholics have been so profoundly deprived in childhood that the reliving of early rejections in psychotherapy may be unbearable. If most alcoholics are not premorbidly sociopathic, a very high percentage of sociopaths are alcoholic. Thus a significant fraction of alcoholics have had early childhoods similar to those of severe delinquents and poly-drug users. Some alcoholics have suffered early maternal neglect which may impair their capacity to care for themselves. However, the yearnings involved make their appearance in the transference, and that is where the danger lies. The fact that the subject never had an adequate mother becomes amplified by the transference rather than relieved. Psychoanalysis helps us love the parents that we have had but does not provide the parents that we never had. Doctors, wishes aside, are not mothers, and the analyst's couch is no bassinet. There are times in life when the affects associated with early abandonment may best be left alone. The period during which an alcoholic gives up alcohol may be one such time.

Indeed there are precious few ways that adults acquire sustaining parental introjects. There are few ways that an adult can truly find a mother substitute. One way is by loving group membership, for example, in AA or the church; another is becoming a mother substitute himself, for example, being a matron in an orphanage or a twelfth-stepper in AA.

The sixth and final justification for the Cambridge Hospital philosophy is the worthy psychodynamic goal that alcoholics must be taught 'the inviolable unity of their own selves'. I think that to achieve that goal, alcoholics must learn that their drinking behaviour is not a reflection of their dynamic unconscious, but just the reverse. Often what emerges in the therapy of an alcoholic is psychological confabulation in order that the patient can continue his chronic addiction. The chief complaint 'I drink because my wife left me' masks the fact that 'my wife left me because I drank', and the self-loathing that derives from the secret belief 'my wife left me because I am bad because I could not stop drinking'; hides the more bearable and admissible fact that 'my wife left me because I could not stop drinking because I was powerless over a disease'.

Psychotherapists encourage and focus upon the affects of anger and sadness, but in chronic alcoholism interest in the patient's 'poor me's' and 'resentments', instead of uncovering old wounds, merely brings forth reflex confabulation to explain unconsciously conditioned relapse to alcohol. Without prospective study appreciation of this fact is immensely difficult and the alcoholic's anger and depression become major foci of psychotherapy.

To conclude, once an alcoholic has achieved stable sobriety, he will have the same needs for and capacity to benefit from psychotherapy as would another member of the population. But bald facts from the lives of 268 men, prospectively followed from their sophomore year in college until age fifty, underscore the theoretical points of this chapter. Twenty-six of these men at some point lost control over their use of alcohol. One-half sought psychotherapy and on the average received about two hundred hours of psychotherapy. With time, one-half of these men have achieved stable remission from their alcoholism – usually through abstinence. In only one case did psychotherapy seem to be related to the remission; in many cases it seemed to deflect attention away from the problem.

NOTE

This chapter is an extract from 'Dangers of psychotherapy in the treatment of alcoholism', the author's chapter in M.H. Bean and N.E. Zinberg (eds) *Dynamic Approaches to the Understanding and Treatment of Alcoholism*, published in 1981 by the Free Press (A Division of Macmillan Publishing Co., Inc.), New York.

Chapter 35

Individual therapy with drug takers: getting started

D. Colin Drummond

Views about the nature of drug addiction have undergone considerable change. Addiction to drugs has been seen at various times as being due to social conditions, disease, internal conflict, personality disorder, economics, conditioned learning, faulty cognitions and genetic inheritance. Some theories continue to enjoy popularity, a few to the point of evangelism. Other less celebrated causal theories have not survived the passage of time. A bewildering array of prescriptive treatments for addiction, derived from these theoretical models, await the therapist's choice. These are discussed in this section of the book.

While each approach to the therapy of the drug taker may have its merits, it would be incorrect to assume that any particular method, even if practised to perfection, can offer the complete answer. Therapy should be tailored to individual needs. Since highly technical or jargonistic language accompanies many therapies, it is understandable that the training therapist or generalist feels unskilled and impotent. A general practitioner recently told a research worker, 'I don't do anything for addicts, I just talk with them.' Such a self-deprecating view underlines the lack of perceived importance which is often attached to basic interpersonal therapeutic skills. The importance of these basic skills cannot be overemphasized.

GETTING STARTED

Genuineness, non-possessive warmth, unconditional positive regard and accurate empathy were identified by Rogers (1957) as important personal attributes of the effective therapist. Without these qualities, which are now generally accepted as being important in all types of therapy, the development of an effective therapeutic relationship will be difficult. With drug takers, who often feel alienated from society and especially antagonistic to authority figures, the adoption of a non-judgemental attitude is all the more important in creating a trusting relationship.

In addition to a trusting relationship, the needs of the patient cannot be met without an adequate understanding of the nature of the patient's problem. This includes an understanding of the patient's perception of the problem as well as the 'bare facts'. This requires an effective interviewing technique. Irrespective of the therapist's particular theoretical orientations, an understanding of psychodynamic principles is important (Brown and Pedder, 1979).

At the outset of the interview, the therapist should orientate the patient by self-introduction and a brief outline of the nature and purpose of the meeting. If the patient has been referred by a colleague, it is important to make reference to this. The patient's view of the problem should then be explored with the use of open-ended questions. An example of this would be 'can you tell me how you came to be referred to see me?' The interview should proceed with further open-ended questions by the therapist, moving where appropriate to more closed questions. An example of a closed question would be 'how long have you injected heroin?' Clearly, these two types of question attract a different kind of response. The use of closed questions early in the interview tends to dissuade the patient from expanding on personally important themes.

At certain times during the interview it may be appropriate to make interpretations in order to clarify the patient's feelings. Sometimes patients find it hard to say what they feel about events which have had a strong emotional impact on them. The extent to which one feels able to make interpretations will depend on both one's experience and the strength of the therapeutic relationship. Often one has a sense of what the patient is not saying but displaying in other ways either verbally or behaviourally. An example would be 'you seem very angry about that, can you tell me more about it?' In a sense one is giving the patient 'permission' to talk about feelings of which they may be ashamed or afraid.

The therapist must also ensure that what the patient is telling them is accurately understood. Apart from conducting interviews in an unhurried manner, careful listening should be supplemented by the therapist periodically summarizing and reflecting information back to the patient for confirmation. Not only does this reduce the possibility of misinterpretation, but it can also help the drug taker to reflect upon and make sense of their experiences.

There are different views on the taking of notes during therapeutic interviews. It is important for the therapist to keep a record of the interview. The patient should be asked, however, if they have any objection to this. They may be concerned about disclosing sensitive information such as their criminal or sexual behaviour if they believe, perhaps correctly, that people other than the therapist may have access to the information. During subsequent interviews it is less desirable to write, as this can be very distracting for the patient, but a record should be made after the interview. As a general point, it is preferable not to record sensitive information in case records.

It is usually unproductive to conduct therapeutic interviews when the patient is intoxicated with drugs or alcohol. Clearly this can sometimes be difficult to ascertain. If the patient arrives for a therapy session in a clearly intoxicated state, however, it is important to discuss this with them in a non-judgemental manner and ask them to return on another specified occasion, if necessary later the same day, when they are no longer intoxicated. Setting limits without rejection can be testing for both the therapist and the patient, but can lead to a more effective therapeutic relationship.

SETTING GOALS

When therapist and patient come together they may harbour very different ideas about what constitute appropriate goals of therapy. The therapist coming from a background in the caring professions aims to eliminate pain and suffering. Complete abstinence from drugs might be seen as the necessary goal to achieve this. The patient on the other hand may be highly ambivalent, seeing many advantages as well as disadvantages about continuing to take drugs. Thus, it is the therapist's task to help the patient to set and work towards a goal which is realistically attainable and congruent with their expectations.

Before the advent of HIV infection in drug injectors, some therapists tended to be rather more directive in encouraging an abstinence goal from the outset. Now the priority is to attract into treatment and maintain contact with drug takers at risk of infection. This necessarily involves a more flexible approach in setting treatment goals. The Advisory Council on the Misuse of Drugs (1988) has recommended that therapists should be willing to consider goals which fall short of abstinence, suggesting instead the adoption of a hierarchy of goals. This must necessarily take account of what one is ultimately hoping to achieve as well as what the drug taker is prepared to consider. Each hierarchy should be individually tailored. Table 35.1 shows a typical hierarchy of goals for a drug injector.

Table 35.1 Hierarchy of goals

Abstinence
Changing from injecting to oral use
Using sterile injecting equipment
Stopping sharing injecting equipment
Cleaning injecting equipment before sharing

The therapist and patient can engage in a process of negotiation to a point where agreement can be reached on an acceptable goal in the hierarchy. This must rely on the combination of the skills and subtle sensitivity of the therapist, for the patient may discontinue contact if the situation becomes pressured. When each goal is achieved a new goal, further up the hierarchy, can be negotiated. In such a process of negotiation the therapist must take care not to collude with the patient's un-willingness to give up a dangerous but pleasurable behaviour. Another important aspect of setting goals is to encourage the patient to think in the short term. Often drug takers will say 'if I got a job and a new house, I would be able to stop using [drugs]'. This may be true, but in reality it may never take place. The patient must be encouraged to focus on what can be achieved today: 'What will you do when you go home tonight?' 'What can you do this afternoon instead of buying drugs?' Alcoholics Anonymous emphasize 'one day at a time', and this makes sense in such a context.

ACHIEVING GOALS

The patient must be assisted in identifying the obstacles to achieving the appropriate identified goal and methods of overcoming the obstacles. In the early stages it may be difficult for the patient to recognize the long-term advantages of change as being preferable to the immediate discomfort which the change entails. Miller (1983) has identified therapeutic strategies which may help the patient to appraise adequately the benefits and costs of a particular course of action. Miller points out that the therapist's role is not to impose any particular view of the advantages and disadvantages, but to assist the patient to scrutinize their own uniquely personal views. This may be done by constructing a 'balance sheet'.

These views should not, however, be seen as static. The value which is attached to a particular outcome may change over time and may be subject to therapeutic intervention. The natural recovery from addiction which is observed as drug takers grow older can be viewed as evidence of this. In effect, what was once an exciting way of life may become too much effort or too risky to be worthwhile. Alternatively, other pursuits such as getting married or raising a family may become more important than taking drugs. The therapist should aim to help the patient to move through this natural process of change more quickly by encouraging the patient to reappraise the value attached to particular behaviours.

Once a goal has been achieved the patient should be helped to consolidate and maintain the achievement. Praise and encouragement are helpful, but the patient remains vulnerable to relapse. Marlatt (1985) has described a useful method whereby patients can be assisted to identify and cope with situations in which there is a danger of relapse. The rehearsal of strategies to deal with a potential relapse situation, for example working out in advance what to do if you meet a friend who offers you drugs, can protect against relapse.

CONCLUSIONS

A brief introduction of this sort can do little justice to the rapidly expanding and evolving field of therapy with drug takers. It is hoped, however, that the reader will learn to attach value to the basic interpersonal skills which are essential to successful therapy. Without such skills even the most elaborate therapeutic approaches will have little substance. Each drug taker has a unique story to tell. The therapist must learn to respond to the individual rather than the diagnosis.

REFERENCES

Advisory Council on the Misuse of Drugs (1988) *AIDS and Drug Misuse Part I*, London: HMSO.
Brown, D. and Pedder, J. (1979) *Introduction to Psychotherapy: An Outline of Psychodynamic Principles and Practice*, New York: Tavistock.
Marlatt, G.A. (1985) 'Situational determinants of relapse and skill-training interventions', in G.A. Marlatt and J.R. Gordon (eds) *Relapse Prevention: Maintenance Strategies in the Treatment of Addictive Behaviours*, New York: Guilford.
Miller, W.R. (1983) 'Motivational interviewing with problem drinkers', *Behavioral Psychotherapy* 11: 147–72.
Rogers, C.R. (1957) 'The necessary and sufficient conditions of therapeutic personality change', *Journal of Consulting Psychology* 21: 95–103.

CROSS REFERENCES

Chapter 36

Group psychotherapy for alcoholics and drug addicts

W. Falkowski

From the earliest times man has always lived in family and social groups. Many conflicts and problems created in childhood give rise to difficulties in later life and are occurring in the context of group behaviour. These issues are best explored in groups which are able to provide a fuller understanding of oneself and others. Group psychotherapy can provide a corrective experience for distorted or disrupted interpersonal relationships in early life and offer powerful support and encouragement. The aim of group psychotherapy is the promotion of psychological growth and development, emotional maturation, insight and better adjustment in relationships with others. Patients learn about themselves by feedback from the group leader and other members of the group. They can discover how their behaviour and attitudes are often self-defeating and destructive, causing themselves to be misunderstood and to misunderstand others. The group can act as a powerful support and encouragement in maintaining the patients' abstinence from alcohol and drugs.

HISTORY OF THE DEVELOPMENT OF GROUP PSYCHOTHERAPY

The systematic use of groups in the practice of psychotherapy is a relatively recent development. The Boston physician, Joseph Pratt, is usually recognized as the father of group psychotherapy. At the turn of the century he brought together patients with tuberculosis to instruct them on the medical aspects of their illness. He also promoted a group climate through which patients provided mutual support. Several years later a number of American psychiatrists incorporated Pratt's ideas into their treatment of mentally ill patients. The term 'group psychotherapy', however, was first used around 1920 by Moreno, whose main contribution was the development of psychodrama.

GROUP THERAPY FOR ALCOHOL AND DRUG ABUSERS – THEORETICAL CONSIDERATIONS

Group psychotherapy for alcoholics and drug addicts has several advantages over individual psychotherapy: it promotes interpersonal relations and mutual support among the patients (who are often emotionally isolated), increases their self-respect and enhances their motivation and expectation of successful therapy by meeting patients who are functioning well without drugs and alcohol. Since many alcoholics and drug addicts have had complex and difficult previous personal relationships, they tend to project strong feelings from the past towards the therapist. In individual therapy, such a transference by alcoholics and drug addicts towards the therapist is often difficult to deal with, while in group psychotherapy it tends to be less powerful.

In the group, dependence on the therapist is less pronounced than in individual therapy and tends to be diffused among other members of the group. The group setting allows the therapist and members of the group to observe directly and interpret the patient's interpersonal behaviour and relationship skills. Denial is a frequent defence mechanism used by alcoholics and drug addicts. Interpretation or confrontation of such denials is much more effective in a group setting with the support of other group members. Finally, group therapy is much more economical than individual therapy, as a single therapist can treat ten to twelve patients at a time.

Regrettably, group psychotherapy for alcohol and substance abusers is not always beneficial and can even be harmful. There is little research into the selection criteria for patients who are likely to respond to group therapy. Unfortunately, group leaders often have little opportunity for proper training or are trained to conduct only general groups.

THE TREATMENT STRATEGY OF GROUP PSYCHOTHERAPY FOR ALCOHOL AND DRUG ADDICTS

There is a large variety of group therapies, such as Alcoholics Anonymous and Narcotic Anonymous self-help groups. The following description is concerned with systematic group psychotherapy and is based on my experience of supervising and running group psychotherapy for alcoholics and substance abusers over many years and constitutes nothing more than a personal approach. However, I hope it will help the reader to explore further, modify and form constructive criticism of the strategies of group therapy for alcohol and drug addicts. For the sake of brevity in this paper reference is going to be made only to male patients, but the same applies to female patients.

Group psychotherapy should never be considered as invariably essential or an entirely sufficient treatment for alcoholics and drug addicts. Patients may benefit from such measures as practical advice concerning legal, accommodation and employment problems. In addition some patients may require behaviour therapy, antidepressants, vitamins or other medication. When appropriate, it is important to provide marital and sexual counselling and family therapy.

Before patients are considered for group psychotherapy, it is useful to provide them with education concerning the effects of drugs and alcohol on social functioning and the damage they produce to family, mental and physical health. This can be most economically and usefully provided through lectures. Patients also seem to benefit from an introduction to some basic concepts of transactional analysis, which is easy to understand and highly valued by many patients. It helps them to evaluate their attitudes and patterns of behaviour and forms a useful preparation for group psychotherapy.

Each group develops a specific 'group culture' of its own. It is advisable from the very beginning of the group to establish some rules and conditions which create a therapeutic social system. The patient who is referred to a group should be interviewed before joining. He may not be suitable for any group psychotherapy or may be more suitable for another group if there is more than one group available. He should be told about the purpose of the group and agree to conform to certain rules, such as complete abstinence from drugs and alcohol, punctuality, informing the therapist if he is not able to attend the group session, preserving absolute confidentiality as to the content of the session and being truthful about his problems and feelings. Since a number of patients are frightened by the prospect of being in group psychotherapy and sometimes leave the treatment after the first session, I suggest that each new patient should agree to attend four consecutive sessions before deciding to discontinue attendance. At the same time I ask the patient to give a week's notice to the group before intending to end therapy. It often happens that patients announce intention to leave the group but discover during the four sessions their real reason for wishing to leave, such as avoiding some painful issues in their therapy, and they may decide to continue in the group. In other instances, when the patient has achieved the desired goal of therapy, made satisfactory adjustments to life and is appropriately ready to leave the group, the four sessions give the patient and the group an opportunity to work through separation and to reinforce feelings of successful therapy.

Careful consideration should be given to whether or not the patient should be allowed to attend another form of therapy. For instance, a patient simultaneously in individual therapy may avoid confronting important issues, by reporting that he is dealing with these issues in individual therapy, and vice versa. Different therapists' styles and orientations may confuse the patient and sometimes even cause misunderstanding between the therapists.

EARLY STAGES OF THE GROUP

It is most important to recognize that patients may come into groups initially with a great deal of anxiety, doubts and fears. Some patients are resentful and angry or covertly hostile at having been coerced into treatment by employers or pressure from relatives. Failure to recognize these feelings and to deal with these issues may lead to excessive resistance to treatment or even discontinuation of attendance. Dealing with these feelings early in the group, when handled skilfully by the therapist, can contribute to group cohesion.

Patients who suffered trauma, deprivation and difficulties in psychological development at an earlier age will have particular difficulty in understanding and relating to the group and the therapist, and will require much tolerance and support. It is equally important to recognize that some patients may join the group with expectations of miraculous cure and may invest the therapist with great imaginary power. When the therapist fails to come up to their expectations they will feel rejected, discouraged and disillusioned.

Denial of their drink and drug problem is one of the commonest and most important defence mechanisms used by alcohol and drug addicts early in group therapy. Examples of denial include 'I can stop drinking any time I wish and therefore I have not got a drink problem', or 'being a commercial traveller, having to entertain clients and being under constant stress, I cannot cope without a drink'. The patient may deny the existence or the significance of important factors leading to drinking or taking drugs. Such factors are often strongly supported by psychological defence mechanisms which protect against intolerable anxiety and emotional pain. Thus the patient becomes a victim of his own psychological defence mechanisms. Considerable therapeutic skill is required to deal with such defences. Patients may need to be confronted. Such confrontations should be specific and based on undisputed objective evidence. For example 'you drink too much' is a personal opinion with which the patient may disagree and this may lead to unproductive and frustrating debate. It is more effective to say 'let us examine the effect your drinking has on your job and your marriage'. Confrontation must be delivered with a great deal of care and genuine concern as otherwise the patient will perceive it as an attack and become more entrenched in his position. The therapist must guard himself against expressing attitudes which are judgemental, punitive, superior or moralistic.

Ideally, interpretation or confrontation should happen when the patient's anxiety is not too high, when he feels safe in the group and when there is sufficient support and cohesion within the group. When the patient gains insight he will need a lot of support, encouragement, positive feedback, protection, concern, attention and affection.

If a patient is drinking or taking drugs, the therapist must resist at any cost the temptation to perform insight therapy, no matter how interesting the underlying psychopathological reason for drinking or taking drugs may be. Continuing to use these substances may seriously damage or even kill the patient before the cause is established. Furthermore, drink and drugs interfere with the proper ego (or 'adult ego state' in transactional analysis terminology) functioning which is necessary for progress. Abstinence from drugs or alcohol often produces amelioration in his general condition and functioning.

It is not uncommon for the patient who has given up drinking or taking drugs to face a number of problems and responsibilities which he was previously able to ignore. After recovery patients may be confronted with severe guilt which may lead to repeated relapses. Some group members are keen on adopting the 'medical model', regarding themselves as suffering from an illness. While such an attitude is helpful in diminishing the shame and stigma of being an alcoholic or a drug addict, it may lead the patient to adopt a passive role, expecting a magic cure without much effort on his part and without taking an adequate share of responsibility for his behaviour: 'It's an illness, so I can't help it'.

LATER STAGES IN GROUP THERAPY

As the group therapy progresses, discussion about drugs or alcohol should be replaced by discussions of family relationships, self-worth, problems at work, financial problems, sexual relationships and attitudes and other important topics. Extension in the social microcosm of the group leads to the development of new behaviours and attitudes which eventually generalize to healthier adaptations to the world outside the group.

CHARACTERISTICS OF THE GROUP THERAPIST IN RELATION TO THE OUTCOME OF THERAPY

There are many important factors which contribute to a successful group, possibly the main one being the therapist. It is highly desirable that the group therapist is not only trained in conducting general groups, but also specifically trained for running groups for alcoholics and drug addicts. Unfortunately only a few group leaders have the opportunity for proper training. The variability in the training and experience of group leaders contributes to the numerous methodological difficulties of research into the efficacy of group psychotherapy for alcoholics and drug addicts. Results are therefore inconclusive.

The personality of the therapist is more important than the particular type of therapy he is practising. The therapist who is able to instil cohesion and trust in the group, who is non-judgemental in his attitudes, who is a good listener and skilled communicator, who cares and who is understanding and empathic is much more likely to have a good outcome.

Conducting group therapy for alcoholics and drug addicts can be particularly exhausting and stressful for the group leaders. Regular supervision is most valuable, and meetings with other therapists facilitates the exchange of ideas and can offer important mutual support.

CONCLUSION

Group psychotherapy for alcoholics and drug addicts can be a valuable and effective treatment. A group can constitute a suitable environment to deal with patients' denial of alcoholism and drug abuse and other problems. It can act as a powerful support and encouragement in maintaining patients' abstinence from alcohol and drugs. Group psychotherapists should be experienced not only in conducting general groups but should have the opportunity to have special training to run groups for alcoholics and drug addicts. The personality of the therapist is of great importance. Regular supervision and support for therapists should be available.

SELECTED READING

Brown, S. and Yalom, I. (1977) 'Interaction group therapy with alcoholics', *Quarterly Journal of Studies on Alcohol* 38: 426–56.
Falkowski, W. (1989) 'A brief outline of transactional psychotherapy', *Postgraduate Doctor* 12: 28–34.
Flores, P.J. (1988) *Group Psychotherapy with Addicted Populations*, New York: The Haworth Press, Inc.
Lieberman, M.A., Yalom, I.D. and Miles, M.B. (1973) *Encounter Groups: First Facts*, New York: Basic Books.
Steiner, C. (1971) *Games Alcoholics Play*, New York: Grove Press.
Stewart, I. and Joines, V. (1987) *TA Today. A New Introduction to Transactional Analysis*, Nottingham and Chapel Hill: Lifespace Publishing.
Yalom, I.D. (1975) *The Theory and Practice of Group Psychotherapy* (2nd edn), New York: Basic Books.
Yalom, I.D., Black, S., Bond, G., Zimmerman, E. and Zimmerman, E. and Quall, B. (1978) 'Alcoholics in interactive group therapy: an outcome study', *Archives of General Psychiatry* 35: 419–25.

CROSS REFERENCES

Chapter 37

Family therapy for alcohol problems

Ian Bennun

The devastating impact of consistent excessive drinking on family interaction, children, employment and other social factors is well known. In this chapter, the assumption is made that in many instances, it is appropriate and viable to include the problem drinker's family network in treatment. Therapists working with addiction have come recently into the family field and, similarly, family therapists are now increasingly interested in addictive behaviours.

Family treatment interventions place problem drinkers within their family context which are often nominally intact. Originally, family interventions were restricted to including the drinker's spouse (Zweben *et al.*, 1988), illustrating the conceptual development in seeing drinking as an interaction process. Another approach was the development of couples groups for both the drinker and spouse, or groups for the partners alone. Two further variants of conjoint treatment are the inclusion of the spouse as a facilitator of change, reinforcing appropriate non-drinking behaviour (Sisson and Azrin, 1986) or a joint hospital admission based on the rationale that the drinking is related to marital conflicts and that the joint admission is a way of decreasing and containing family system disruption.

As therapists began to consider the systemic nature of drinking, other family members were included in the treatment. Family approaches take a variety of forms which can be dichotomized: drinking may be an adaptive family response, which serves a function for the family system, or family members can be included in treatments as co-agents of change (Bennun, 1988a). A more recent development, unilateral family therapy, utilizes just one member of the family in treatment, with the focus being on altering the problem-drinking patterns even if the problem drinker refuses to attend (Thomas and Santa, 1982). A similar approach has been used effectively in the treatment of drug dependence (Szapocznik *et al.*, 1983).

A SYSTEMS APPROACH TO FAMILY THERAPY

The majority of family therapists base their clinical approach within a broad systems theory framework, although the extent to which therapists adhere to a pure systems theory varies. Systems theory, as formulated within the biological sciences, implies a relationship between mutually independent units. Systems can therefore be defined as the relationship between constituent elements and their attributes (Bennun, 1988b).

Within systems theory, the family represents a functioning operational system or unit comprising a set of collected interrelated parts, which combine to determine its total functioning. Each element within the system is in a functional relationship with all of the others that comprise that particular system. This formulation, when applied to the family, places it within a social context and highlights the interdependence taking place among the elements within that context. The system can thus be activated by any constituent element. Systemic therapists invariably construct a map defining the organization, rules and roles of the families they treat. Equating the family as a system determines, among other things, how competently the whole serves each individual member.

The family system is differentiated in terms of sub-systems which are identified by shared characteristics (e.g. generation, gender) or in terms of more abstract psychological phenomena (attraction, alliances). Since each sub-system gains its identity or differentiation through boundaries, there may well be hierarchical differences within or between sub-systems defined by the boundaries between them (generations, roles). Boundaries control exchanges between the various sub-systems and determine the flow of communication and feedback. The issue of causality (aetiology) has special significance within systems therapy. The family or individual, in this case a problem drinker, does not 'cause' the problem: rather the genesis or development of family or individual problems arise from the interrelationships between various systems and sub-systems, so feedback is critical in understanding family pathology.

An important characteristic of systems and sub-systems is that a steady state is maintained throughout time. Thus, when a system is put under stress, the usual balance of forces is disturbed and it is inclined towards imbalance. The dynamic mechanism that regulates the family back on course, be it functional or dysfunctional, is that of homeostasis. Although family stability is a prerequisite for healthy family functioning, homeostasis maintains stability by counteracting disruption.

Within systems theory, presenting problems can be seen as serving an adaptive function. If alcohol problems are continually viewed as maladaptive and disruptive, then treatment invariably has to deal with elements of blame, scapegoating and guilt. It is proposed that excessive drinking may be operating at an intra-psychic level, an intra-couple level or at a level that maintains the homeostasis of the person's wider social system, in this case, the family. The goal of the therapist assessing each family should be, primarily, to uncover the adaptive functions that the problematic drinking may serve. Once these are identified, an intervention directed towards the individual, as part of the system, may be embarked upon thereby re-organizing the system and searching for a more appropriate means of maintaining the family system's homeostatis.

A second task for the systemic therapist is to construct a dynamic map that describes each family member's response and possible contribution to the maintenance of problem drinking. Often families inadvertently organize themselves in such a way that the drinking remains adaptive or is strengthened and maintained. The therapist then needs to construct a systemic hypothesis to explain the maintenance and adaptive function of drinking.

A clinical example illustrates the model: the presenting problem of a couple referred to the marital and family therapy unit was a breakdown in their sexual relationship. Since the husband was also noted to have a long-standing drink problem, it was suggested that the excessive drinking resulted in marital and sexual conflict. Indeed, there is much research evidence to support this notion of a linear relationship between drinking and sexual difficulties. However, by investigating the adaptive functioning of the drinking and the sexual difficulty, it emerged that the drinking served to make the husband unattractive to his wife and therefore her wish for a sexual relationship less apparent. This in turn allowed the husband not to fail sexually, which was his major anxiety, and drinking therefore protected him from his own fear of failure. The couple were in a sense organized so that both drinking and avoiding sex were maintained. When demands were placed on their sexual relationship and the dynamic homeostatic process, linking sex, drinking and rejection was put to good effect. Attempting to alter the drinking directly would most probably have been resisted because of its adverse consequences on the couple's sexual relationship.

This case illustrates some of the characteristics of systems theory and therapy. The treatment only involved one sub-system (the marital sub-system) but it demonstrates that the boundary differentiating each partner within the marital dyad obstructed the flow of communication about an intimate aspect of their relationship. If the whole family had been seen, then the clinician may well have suggested that just the couple attend, placing them in a hierarchical position in relation to their children and suggesting that some work had to be done with the parents alone.

A PROBLEM-SOLVING APPROACH TO FAMILY THERAPY

The problem-solving approach offers a different avenue for intervention. Although it is seen as a generic clinical approach, in its behavioural context, it is linked to more systematic control of those stimuli initiating the (drinking) response (D'Zurrila and Goldfried, 1971). One way to investigate the relationship between stimuli and their consequences is to conduct a functional analysis of the problem. The aim of the analysis is to identify those factors that operate as setting the occasion for the drinking to occur and secondly, identifying the consequences of drinking that are usually reinforcing and, by definition, strengthening the pattern of drinking. In the clinical setting, both individual behaviours and the reinforcement that follows, need to be identified so that the frequency of more adaptive behaviours, be they control or abstinence, can be increased and maladaptive behaviours decreased.

Problem-solving is a step-by-step approach to altering the contingencies operating. Family members clearly work with the therapist to generate ways of altering the family drinker's behaviour. The first step is to obtain a concrete definition of the presenting problem. In defining the problem, a focus for change needs to be made explicit, so clear descriptions are necessary. Secondly, all aspects of the problem need to be operationalized. This stage moves beyond formulations of blame and emphasizes a consistent understanding of all the elements contributing to the problem, so that any negotiation of change will not be tangential to the defined problems. The next step involves brain-storming alternative solutions to the problem with the emphasis being on quantity rather than quality. The family needs to collaborate in generating solutions and so help each other in their respective efforts towards change. Each solution then needs to be evaluated in terms of costs and outcome so that the best quality options for change can be selected. Each option needs to be evaluated so one, or a combination of alternatives, can be implemented in a coherent and consistent fashion. The role of each family member in implementing the change and altering the contingencies operating around the drinking requires careful clarification. Finally, the choice option needs to be evaluated so that the success or failure of the intervention can be assessed. The process of problem-solving requires that family members adopt a non-critical definition of the problem, thus minimizing negative attitudes. A working alliance is necessary as this maintains the collaboration between family members and between the family and the therapist which will create an environment conducive to problem-solving.

A clinical example: a referred family presented with their 23-year-old daughter who had a four-year history of excessive drinking. The defined problem was loss of control over drinking, operationalized to needing to drink in order to remain calm in larger social situations. Over time, drinking in these environments had generalized to loss of control in any social situation, including family engagements. The solutions generated with the family included:

1 hospital admission;
2 isolating the daughter from her friends and relatives;
3 social skills training;
4 forced unemployment and isolation;
5 only going out with her parents and one larger engagement per month;
6 abstinence;
7 moving the daughter away to live with a relative.

The best solution, taking into account its impact on all family members, was a combination of social skills training and only socializing with her parents. If this worked satisfactorily for three months, then a plan review entailed increasing more independent social engagements. The on-going treatment continued and was supplemented with a social skills group.

The indices against which the choice was assessed included alcohol consumption, perception of self-confidence and family tension. Apart from initial difficulties, this plan worked well. By providing a structure for the family's response to the problem, each person was aware of their responsibility and objectives. The importance of structuring a very clear plan, with each family member knowing their part in the intervention, is a pivotal aspect of family problem-solving and enables the therapist and family to assess the efficacy of the intervention.

THE FAMILY PERSPECTIVE: CONCLUSION

The two contrasting approaches have different emphases. The systemic model places the drinking in the context of a family's struggle at negotiating particular tasks, whereas the problem-solving approach identifies the drinker as having the problem and intervening as such. In neither approach is the problem treated in isolation, because the family perspective adopts the drinker's psychosocial environment as the appropriate arena for change. There are clearly different formulations and interventions within each and choices as to the most effective treatment must be left to each clinician.

REFERENCES

Bennun, I. (1988a) 'Treating the symptom or the system: an evaluation of family therapy with alcoholics', *Behavioural Psychotherapy* 16: 165–76.

— (1988b) 'Systems theory and family therapy', in E. Street and W. Dryden (eds) *Family Therapy in Britain*, Milton Keynes: Open University Press.

D'Zurrila, T. and Goldfried, M. (1971) 'Problem-solving and behaviour modification', *Journal of Abnormal Psychology* 98: 107–20.

Sisson, R. and Azrin, N. (1986) 'Family-member involvement to initiate and promote treatment of problem drinkers', *Journal of Behaviour Therapy and Experimental Psychiatry* 17: 15–21.

Szapocznik, J., Kurtines, W., Foote, F., Peres-Videl, A. and Hervis, O. (1983) 'Conjoint versus one person family therapy: some evidence for the effectiveness of conducting family therapy through one person', *Journal of Consulting and Clinical Psychology* 51: 889–99.

Thomas, E. and Santa, C. (1982) 'Unilateral family therapy for alcohol abuse: a working conception', *The American Journal of Family Therapy* 10: 49–58.

Zweben, A., Perlman, S. and Li, S. (1988) 'A comparison of brief advice and conjoint therapy in the treatment of alcohol abuse: the results of the marital systems study', *British Journal of Addiction* 83: 899–916.

CROSS REFERENCES

Chapter 38

Self-help groups

Brian Wells

The self-help movement provides non-professional support and encouragement for people in a variety of situations. Groups exist for cardiac patients, parents of twins, diabetics, widows and many other people with difficulties. Disenchantment with professionals, cost effectiveness and the sense of well-being engendered are some of the reasons why the self-help movement is a growth industry, having greatest prominence in the arena of addictions.

Groups cater for clients, families, friends, professionals with problems (doctors, lawyers), still-using addicts, those who are HIV positive and even adults who have grown up with alcoholic parents. Varied in ideology, frequency of attendance, geographical distribution and organization, self-help groups remain an important and valuable resource, freely available to all who work with problem drinkers and drug users.

Most have many features in common with the main topic of this brief chapter: the abstinence-based Twelve-Step fellowships.

HISTORY

Alcoholics Anonymous (AA) began in 1935 when Bill Wilson (Bill W.), a former alcoholic stockbroker, met Dr Robert Smith (Dr Bob), an alcoholic GP in Akron, Ohio, USA. The two men discovered that their mutual sharing of the experience strengthened their resolve to remain abstinent. Operating from Dr Bob's home, they attracted in other alcoholics and AA was born. The 'AA Big Book', the Twelve Steps and the Traditions were written by the first 100 members in a style derived from the religious Oxford movement, with which Bill had previously been involved. AA came to the notice of the medical profession, particularly following the appearance of an article in the *Saturday Evening Post* that described recovery in thousands of alcoholics who had previously been regarded as therapeutic failures. Groups spread rapidly with similar programmes being developed for the families (Al Anon, Alateen), whilst the 'illness concept' was applied to other 'behaviours' so that Gamblers Anonymous, Overeaters Anonymous, Emotions Anonymous and, significantly, Narcotics Anonymous began to appear.

Narcotics Anonymous (NA) began in California in 1953. The AA view of the 'illness of alcoholism' was broadened to that of 'addiction'. Thus persons suffering problems with or dependence upon the entire range of mind-altering chemicals (including alcohol) were also included.

AA and NA have now spread to most countries in the world. Their literature is available in many different languages and indicators suggest that current growth of NA and the recently formed Cocaine Anonymous (CA) are likely to continue.

MODUS OPERANDI

The fellowships are based on the understanding that 'alcoholism' or 'addiction' is a progressive illness for which there is no cure. Recovery is possible however if the sufferer remains completely abstinent from all mind-altering agents and applies him- or herself to the suggested programme of recovery.

To this end they provide meetings in the community and institutions (hospitals, prisons, treatment centres). They may be 'open' to non-addicts (interested friends or professionals) or 'closed', in a variety of formats (speaker meetings, step meetings, discussion meetings). Typically a member will share his or her experience of addiction and recovery, or that of a particular topic such as 'relationships'. The meeting then opens to the remaining members for identification and further sharing. Sharing is non-judgemental and supportive, often with members moving on afterwards to a nearby coffee-shop. Telephone numbers are exchanged and newcomers are encouraged to get involved, attend as many meetings as possible in early days and to allow the process of recovery to take place gradually.

The fellowships assert that individuals are not responsible for their illness but entirely responsible for recovery by following the suggested programme. Friendship, practical information and a great deal of collective wisdom are provided at meetings, cafés, dances, workshops and conventions. The newcomer is encouraged to live-in-the-day, stay close to the fellowship and discover how a life based on honesty, open-mindedness and willingness can lead to an enhancement of self-esteem and general improvement. Many members consolidate their recovery and later move on to include other activities (psychotherapy, yoga, martial arts), in the pursuit of personal growth.

THE TWELVE STEPS

1 'We admitted we were powerless over alcohol (our addiction [NA]) – that our lives had become unmanageable.'
2 'Came to believe that a Power greater than ourselves could restore us to sanity.'
3 'Made a decision to turn our will and our lives over to the care of God as we understood Him.'
4 'Made a searching and fearless moral inventory of ourselves.'
5 'Admitted to God, to ourselves, and to another human being, the exact nature of our wrongs.'
6 'Were entirely ready to have God remove all these defects of character.'
7 'Humbly asked Him to remove our shortcomings.'
8 'Made a list of all persons we had harmed, and became willing to make amends to them all.'
9 'Made direct amends to such people whenever possible, except when to do so would injure them or others.'
10 'Continued to take personal inventory and when we were wrong promptly admitted it.'
11 'Sought through prayer and meditation to improve our conscious contact with God as we understood Him, praying only for knowledge of His will for us and the power to carry that out.'

12 'Having had a spiritual awakening as the result of these steps, we tried to carry this message to alcoholics, and to practise these principles in all our affairs.'

In spite of some reference to God in six of the Steps, the programme is not religious, but has a spiritual component that is suggested. Working the Steps involves an acceptance of the need for daily abstinence (Step 1). The development of a relationship with a power greater than oneself – often the power of 'the group'. Insight is gained and restitution for damage done to others is made. Finally, the helping of still suffering alcoholics/addicts and the practice of spiritual principles in all the affairs of daily life (Step 12) are an essential part of the programme. 'We keep what we have by giving it away' (AA).

WHO ATTENDS?

'Very simply an addict is a man or woman whose life is controlled by drugs. Anyone may attend regardless of age, race, sexual identity, creed, religion or lack of religion' (NA).

In practice the meetings are attended by persons from all walks of life, their common feature being problem-related drinking and drug taking. Different groups attract different types of client and it is therefore important for newcomers to 'shop around' to find optimal identification.

HOW CAN THEY HELP US?

Self-help groups can provide powerful intensive support and after-care to clients and families able to affiliate. Group attendance may be used as part of a treatment programme. Members are often prepared to assist therapists, emergency rooms and clergymen, and more recently NA members have been providing valuable links to the drug-taking community, sometimes assisting professional 'outreach workers'.

HOW TO ENGAGE

Most clients and families do not want to attend self-help groups. Many have preconceived notions, often returning to the therapist full of complaints about 'how it's religious', 'how they're all liars', or how 'it's simply not for them'.

Many will attend and subsequently affiliate, however, if encouraged to do so, to keep an open mind (especially about 'the God bit'), to shop around and to look for similarities rather than differences. AA and NA run a 'twelve step' service whereby the client will be taken to a meeting upon request. A useful ploy is to encourage the client to telephone the relevant office during the consultation. Use can also be made of ex-clients and members with whom one has become acquainted.

Many clients benefit from a period of Twelve-Step-based treatment.

THE MINNESOTA MODEL

The most widely adopted model of treatment in the USA consists of a highly focused programme that adopts AA/NA ideology. Treatment is based around the first five of the Steps and attendance at meetings is an essential component of after-care. These centres are available on a residential or day attendance basis.

EVALUATION

Many accounts of self-help groups have been written, as have comments concerning the lack of available hard data. Such research is notoriously difficult given the nature of the 'behaviours' as well as the status and traditions of the organizations concerned.

No controlled studies on the Minnesota treatment model have yet been published. Such a study will be essential for the movement to gain credibility with the academic establishment, which in turn will have major implications for the future funding of such treatment centres.

SOME PROBLEMS

Self-help groups are not 'the answer' for everyone. Many clients (and professionals) have great difficulty with the disease model and what is seen as the religious aspect. People relapse (perhaps taking their newly found romantic partner with them) and bad advice is sometimes heard, e.g. concerning use of lithium or depot antipsychotic drugs, from fervent believers in total abstinence. Sometimes a poor opinion is expressed concerning the medical and other professions, whilst newly formed groups may be lacking in sobriety or 'clean time' (maturity).

CONCLUSION

Workers in the addiction field require an open-minded awareness of the need for a range of services to cater for client variation. Self-help groups can be valued and encouraged. Workers can learn about their usefulness, iron out difficulties and develop relationships (with fellowships and treatment centres) based upon mutual respect. Visits to 'open' AA and NA meetings are an essential component of training, whilst many professionals now regularly attend Al Anon and other groups for their own well-being and development.

FURTHER READING

Cook, C. (1988) 'The Minnesota Model in the management of drug and alcohol dependency: miracle, method or myth?', Part I: 'The philosophy and the programme', Part II: 'Evidence and conclusions' *British Journal of Addiction* 83: (Part I) 625–34; (Part II) 735–48.

Fingarette, H. (1988) *Heavy Drinking – the Myth of Alcoholism as a Disease*, London: University of California Press.

Robinson, D. (1979) *Talking Out of Alcoholism*, London: Croom Helm.

Wells, B. (1987) 'Narcotics Anonymous (NA): the phenomenal growth of an important resource', *British Journal of Addiction* 82: 581–2.

Chapter 39

Therapeutic communities

Mitchell S. Rosenthal

Modern drug-free treatment for drug abusers dates from development of the therapeutic community (TC), where the self-help concept and group process were first applied to the treatment of drug abusers. Methods that derive from this approach are now broadly employed by treatment regimens of all kinds, both drug-free and chemically-assisted.

At the TC, these methods are applied within a highly structured community that offers an established route of recovery from all forms of drug abuse. Viewing drug abuse as a disorder of the whole person, the TC provides a comprehensive response and brings a variety of resources to bear on the maladaptation of clients and on their social, educational and vocational deficits.

Treatment is directed towards the integration of clients into society as productive individuals. Thus, its goals extend beyond sustained abstinence to include changes in negative attitudes, values and behaviour (which are as much a part of the drug abuse syndrome as chemical dependency) and to the acquisition of social and vocational skills necessary to support a rewarding and drug-free lifestyle. This global view of rehabilitation is pursued through motivation, self-help and social learning within a closed community capable of providing the structure, discipline and support needed to achieve change of such magnitude.

ORIGINS OF THE TC

The TC, as we know it today, began with the formation of Synanon in the early 1960s and the subsequent appearance of similar self-help alternatives to existing forms of drug abuse treatment in the United States. The term 'therapeutic community', however, was not a new one. It had been applied almost a decade earlier to the special treatment units started by Maxwell Jones and others in Britain's psychiatric hospitals.

There are similarities between the two TC models, for both employ group process. But, although the psychiatric TC has influenced treatment methods of TCs for drug abusers in Britain, there was no such influence on the original therapeutic communities for drug abusers in the United States. There were common roots in various forms of communal healing. But the immediate antecedent of Synanon and the other early American TCs was Alcoholics Anonymous.

It is important to note that the first TCs were started by ex-abusers themselves. Although a number of medical and mental health professionals subsequently became involved in their development, the TCs operated far from the medical and mental health mainstreams.

This distance permitted the TCs freedom to innovate and form communities that permitted long-term, humanistic involvement with residents and supported a sustained environmental context for learning, change and growth. Within these communities, residents who shared a common code of behaviour and a common belief system provided a framework for social therapy capable of successfully addressing character disorder.

TC STRUCTURE

In recent years, an infinite number of residential programmes for drug and alcohol abusers have taken on the designation of 'therapeutic community'. The greatest impact on drug abuse in the US, however, has been achieved by roughly one-quarter of the programmes that use the TC nomenclature. These are programmes – like Daytop Village, Samaritan Village, Gateway Foundation, Phoenix House and others – that generally conform to the traditional TC approach, although all have substantially modified many original TC practices and have developed adaptations of the initial regimen.

There are a great many similarities in the basic programmes of these traditional therapeutic communities. Structurally, the basic treatment model remains a 24-hour-a-day residential programme with a primary treatment staff most often composed of trained former-abuser clinicians.

Although traditional programmes usually consider the optimal length of treatment to be at least 15 months, there is no longer any absolute minimum time requirement. Phoenix House, for example, now operates a special programme for employed men and women that involves only an initial three months of residential care, followed by a year of outpatient treatment.

Nevertheless, research has made clear the importance of long-term treatment for most abusers who enter therapeutic communities. Both the Drug Abuse Reporting System studies of treatment outcome (supported by the National Institute on Drug Abuse) (Simpson and Sells, 1981) and the long-term outcome studies of Phoenix House (De Leon and Andrews, 1978; De Leon, 1974) have found favourable treatment outcome directly related to time in treatment. The longer residents stay, the greater the likelihood of sustained post-treatment success.

The Phoenix studies also found significant correlation between time in treatment and psychological status. Successful clients who remained in treatment for the optimal period of time registered the greatest improvement.

To achieve changes of the magnitude they seek, TCs have developed a treatment process based (as any effective psychotherapy must be) on the existential reality of clients. Clients *choose* to enter treatment, although this decision is generally made under some form of pressure – more often external (from families, employers or the law) than intrinsic. Nevertheless, entering treatment involves a decision by clients, who must then accept the consequences of that decision. They must conform. They must follow the rules. 'Buying the whole package' is the first learning experience of the new resident, and that package includes separation from the outside world within a hierarchical social treatment system.

Although treatment – even long-term treatment – is a relatively brief episode in a client's life, it must be potent enough to overcome all the influences that preceded it and to sustain treatment changes in the face of all the influences that will follow it. To give the treatment episode this impact, the TCs believe it is necessary to distance residents from the context of their drug abuse and to shelter them within a family- like community that will encourage, support and reward positive behaviour.

Thus, the TC is best perceived as a setting designed – as society itself is *not* – to encourage and support social learning. Socially responsible attitudes are acquired by acting responsibly – at first, simply because such behaviour is required. Both TC staff and residents who have progressed in the programme serve as role models and reaffirm the resident's changing perceptions of self and society.

Self-help is the mechanism to change, achieved through the interaction of the individual and the treatment community. The intensity of this interaction and the potency of the self-help dynamic are best reflected in the extraordinary standards of revelation and honesty found within the TC and in the acceptance of confrontation as a means of eliciting honesty and self-revelation.

TC life is demanding. The daily schedule fills at least 12 hours with a variety of activities – seminars, classes, special meetings and training, as well as group therapy, work and recreation. This regimen produces an orderly environment for residents who often come into treatment from chaotic and disruptive settings. It minimizes boredom and allows few opportunities for negative associations or pre-occupation with drugs. It offers job satisfaction and increased status within the community, based upon job performance and progress in treatment. It provides emotional rewards and the guided acquisition of coping skills.

All these aspects of the therapeutic community have remained much the same as TCs adapted to changes in treatment populations. Methods conceived to treat the initial TC clients, long-term heroin addicts, have proven equally effective with abusers of other drugs and for younger abusers.

To provide an appropriate treatment setting for the growing number of adolescent TC clients, however, certain programmes have departed substantially from the classic therapeutic community format. But, in so doing, they have not departed at all from basic TC concepts and values.

Indeed, at Phoenix House we have found that, by modifying the treatment community to create the Phoenix Academies (residential high schools for adolescents in treatment), we have produced communities significantly better suited to the resocialization of youngsters and better able to reinforce motivation.

At the Phoenix Academies education shares the focus with socialization. An accelerated academic programme (able to aid the learning disabled and provide both remedial and independent studies) allows residents to recapture opportunities for further education and careers. Teachers and counsellors work together, so that social learning and academic learning occurs simultaneously. Participation of families in the treatment process (through required education programmes, family groups, and family therapy) aids retention and strengthens the family unit, providing a more stable home to which young residents can return.

SUITABILITY FOR TC TREATMENT

Most traditional therapeutic communities employ similar criteria to determine suitability for admission. These include *chronic* drug use and, more important, client conviction that drug use is an essential means for managing life situations and dealing with emotional discomfort or stress. Candidates should display some degree of psychological dependency and, while physiological dependency may also exist, detoxification is generally required before admissions (Rosenthal, 1984).

Involvement in drug-related crime or non-violent 'property' crime, as a result of drug involvement, is viewed as behaviour that can be addressed within the therapeutic community. A history of violence, sexual abuse or arson, however, is generally considered grounds for exclusion.

Candidates whose drug use has impeded the ability to sustain intimate relationships or to fulfil demands of school or the workplace are considered highly suitable for TC treatment. Signs of social dysfunction, anti-social behaviour, and dysfunctional family relationships are all indicators of suitability.

Adolescent candidates pose special problems. When assessing youngsters for admission, levels or patterns of drug use may be less significant than motivation and circumstances. For example, adolescents who invariably use drugs to cope with the stress of social situations are demonstrating characteristic signs of progression towards increasingly compulsive use.

Family ability to both set and enforce standards of behaviour must also be considered in determining the suitability of TC placement for adolescents. Where the home situation is chaotic or so disrupted that there is little parental presence or monitoring of behaviour, placement may be required. But, whenever possible, the adolescent drug abuser should not be removed from a supportive family environment.

Psychological status is often the basis for exclusion, although most TC clients are measurably depressed and anxious and have characteristically low self-esteem when they enter treatment (De Leon and Jainchill, 1981–82; De Leon *et al.*, 1973) with psychological measures tending to be in the deviant range.

Appropriate candidates for treatment generally appear impulsive and exhibit character disorder with acting out behaviour symptomatic of underdeveloped psychosocial skills. Frank clinical illness (e.g. psychosis or suicidal depression), however, is generally regarded as cause for exclusion, and candidates should be carefully screened for delusions, hallucinations, incoherence, loose associations and inappropriate affect.

FUTURE DEVELOPMENT OF THE TC

Although the therapeutic community today is primarily employed for the treatment of substance abuse, the possibility of its application to a wider range of disordered behaviour has long been recognized, for the TC treatment process addresses, not drug abuse itself, but the underlying problems that prompt and sustain it. Treatment goals are broad and include: the resumption of trust in self and in others; the assumption of responsibility; the acquisition of new, constructive ways of dealing with stress and conflict; and the ability to seek and accept help from others. The demonstrated ability of the TC to help drug abusers achieve changes of this magnitude, during the limited duration of even long-term treatment, makes the therapeutic community one of society's most potent mechanisms for change.

The young men and women who enter treatment at Phoenix House and other TCs display a considerable range of disordered behaviour. Drug abuse is but one of the ways in which they act out. During the course of treatment, all the self-destructive and anti-social manifestations of their disorder are addressed. And it is this ability to deal with both drug-abusing and non-drug-abusing behaviour that should figure most prominently in the future evolution of the therapeutic community. Indeed, there already exist TC-like programmes for criminal offenders, teen runaways, and psychiatric patients making the transition from hospitalization back to society (Rosenthal, 1989).

But broader use of the therapeutic community and application of TC methodology to other forms of disorder will depend heavily upon the acceptance and adoption of this treatment regimen by providers in other areas of human service. This will not be easy to achieve, as long as TCs (at least in the United States) continue to operate at some distance from mainstream medicine and mental health.

The kind of co-operation that widespread adoption of TC methodology would require is frustrated, in part, by its relative inaccessibility. There is no broad conceptual framework that provides a basis for understanding the therapeutic community. Indeed, there is, to date, no single, published codification of generally-accepted TC principles and practices. Although a considerable amount of work on TC theory and practice is now underway, it is the present dearth of such material that most inhibits co-operation and collaboration between TCs and other health, mental health and social service institutions.

REFERENCES

De Leon, G. (ed.) (1974) *Phoenix House: Studies in a Therapeutic Community (1968–1973)*, New York: MSS Press.

De Leon, G. and Andrews, M. (1978) 'Therapeutic community dropouts five years later: preliminary findings on self reported status', in U. Smith (ed.) *A Multi-Cultural View of Drug Abuse*, Cambridge, MA: Schenkman, pp. 369–78.

De Leon, G. and Jainchill, N. (1981–82) 'Male and female drug treatment in a therapeutic community', *American Journal of Drug and Alcohol Abuse* 8: 465–79.

De Leon, G., Skodol, A. and Rosenthal, M.S. (1973) 'The Phoenix Therapeutic Community for drug addicts', *Archives of General Psychiatry* 28: 131–5.

Rosenthal, M.S. (1984) 'Therapeutic communities: a treatment alternative for many but not all', *Journal of Substance Abuse Treatment* 1: 55–8.

— (1989) 'The therapeutic community: exploring the boundaries', *British Journal of Addiction* 84: 141–50.

Simpson, D.D. and Sells, S.B. (1981) *Highlights of the DARP Followup Research on the Evaluation of Drug Abuse Treatment Effectiveness*, NIDA Monograph Series, Washington, DC: National Institute on Drug Abuse.

CROSS REFERENCES

Chapter 40

Treatments for smokers

Petr Hajek

The majority of adult smokers would like to quit and a sizeable proportion attempt to stop smoking each year. Many succeed without any special help. However, many others do not seem to be able to quit smoking on their own, despite good motivation and repeated efforts.

A large array of methods and techniques to aid smoking cessation has been proposed. In this overview these methods are clustered (somewhat arbitrarily) into behavioural, other psychological, and pharmacological approaches. In practice, various techniques are often combined together. One section of this chapter covers interventions by general practitioners (GPs). It deserves special attention, as it can reach many more smokers than any clinic-based activities. Recommendations are given for selecting the optimal approaches to both clinic-based treatment of dependent smokers and to general-practice intervention.

TREATMENT METHODS

Behavioural methods

Aversive conditioning methods attempt to reduce the reinforcing value of smoking by pairing it with unpleasant stimuli, such as mild electric shock or cigarette smoke itself. A procedure called *rapid smoking* has attracted particular attention. It requires smokers to take a puff every 6–8 seconds until they feel sick. There were fears that this could put too much cardiovascular strain on some patients and so several milder variants of this technique were proposed, such as smoke holding, focused smoking and satiation. Although this approach has been much researched, the results are not conclusive. Rapid smoking is generally considered a worthwhile method, but not the breakthrough it was hoped it would be (Lichtenstein, 1986).

A number of *self-management techniques* have been suggested for combating cues associated with smoking, altering various reinforcers of smoking behaviour, etc. The examples are stimulus control (restricting smoking to certain places or situations only), response substitution (i.e. taking a walk after a meal instead of smoking), contingency contracting (paying fines for smoking), substitution of smoking by relaxation exercises, and self-monitoring (i.e. recording the situations and times when smoking occurs). None of these have been shown to be effective by themselves, but they are all frequently used in various multi-component packages.

Nicotine fading resembles earlier attempts to induce smoking cessation by gradually reducing the number of cigarettes smoked. With nicotine fading, smokers switch gradually to lower yielding brands. A related technique consists of providing smokers with a series of cigarette holders or filters with progressively larger ventilation holes to dilute the smoke. There is also a gadget on sale which perforates cigarettes with the same purpose in mind. No method of gradual cessation has been found very effective (Schwartz, 1987).

Currently there is growing interest in *cognitive-behavioural approaches*, especially with regard to relapse prevention. Maintenance of abstinence is the major problem in smoking as well as in other addictive behaviours. Although knowledge and understanding of relapse in smokers may be increasing, no clearly successful techniques have as yet been developed, behavioural or otherwise.

Other psychological methods

Almost any treatment providing positive expectations, structure and encouragement may have some impact, i.e. an *attention-placebo effect*. This by itself can help about 10 to 15 per cent of smokers who start treatment manage uninterrupted abstinence for the duration of one year. This is of course a worthwhile effect, especially where no other help is available. However, when considering various specific treatments, it is important to know if they have anything to offer over and above non-specific factors.

The literature on smoking cessation methods is replete with impressive 'success rates'. These are usually based on very lenient definitions of success, i.e. including only clients finishing treatment, counting reduced consumption as success, not validating claims of abstinence, and looking at smoking status 'at' one year rather than 'for a duration of' one year. The claim of a one-year success rate of 90 per cent can shrink to under 10 per cent if strict criteria are applied. Readers of smoking cessation literature, beware!

Hypnosis is a frequently commercially advertised smoking cessation method, but there is little evidence that it has any effect over and above attention-placebo factors. However, more controlled studies are needed to pass a definitive verdict.

Acupuncture can easily be evaluated in a controlled experiment by comparing its effects at the 'correct' and an incorrect or 'sham' site. Six such studies have been published (Schwartz, 1987). In only one of them was the correct site superior, while in one other the contrasting site produced better results. Acupuncture for smoking seems to work only as a placebo.

There exist a number of other rather esoteric treatments. To mention at least one of them, *restricted environmental stimulation* (REST) consists of having smokers lie motionless in a dark room or floating in a tank of body-temperature water while an anti-smoking message is broadcast into their earphones. In a controlled experiment, control subjects actually did better than floaters.

Group treatment is probably the most popular smoking cessation method. It is more economical than individual approaches, and group processes have been shown to have a significant effect on outcome. There are many types of groups for smokers using various mixtures of other techniques. As acute cigarette withdrawal lasts for about three weeks, it follows that a reasonable group programme should encourage smokers to quit as early on as possible and last long enough to see them through this period. By contrast, the Five-Day Plan and its many variants consist of meetings on 5 consecutive days, while some courses have up to 20 sessions, but only require that smokers actually stop smoking at the very end. To boost the discouraging success rates, some commercial group programmes do not insist on clients stopping smoking, but 'individualize treatment goals' and consider cutting down as success. (For a number of reasons, in dependent smokers, reduction in cigarette consumption is generally regarded as a dubious goal.)

Pharmacological methods

Nicotine chewing gum (Nicorette) is the most rigorously tested of all smoking cessation methods and there is no doubt that in clinic settings it is effective over and above placebo (Lam *et al.*, 1987). It is the most effective smoking cessation aid available to the public at the moment. In the UK until early 1991 nicotine chewing gum was available only on private prescription, which was an obstacle in programmes run by non-physicians. This hurdle has now been removed. The rationale for a nicotine substitute in the treatment of smoking is provided in Chapter 15. For the gum to be effective, some guidance in its use is essential. The client should understand its effects, use enough for a sufficient period of time, and start using the gum only after stopping smoking completely. The manufacturer and distributors of the gum provide leaflets on its use. Further practical skills can be gained in courses specified in the section on treatment recommendations.

Various other forms of nicotine replacement have been shown to alleviate tobacco withdrawal, i.e. nicotine nasal spray, nicotine skin patches, and nicotine vapour. Some of them will no doubt become available for general use in future. One form of nicotine substitute, Stoppers (advertised as lozenges containing tobacco extract), is available over-the-counter at chemist shops. It can provide nicotine levels comparable with nicotine chewing gum. Although the marketing of this product is questionable (the labelling does not mention nicotine) and it has not yet been evaluated, it probably has therapeutic potential.

Among other drugs which have been tested for their capacity to help smokers quit, the noradrenergic agonist clonidine should be mentioned. It has been shown to alleviate acute tobacco withdrawal, but the longer-term results have so far been inconsistent. A number of other preparations, including drugs with anxiolytic effects, are currently being studied.

A number of over-the-counter products compete for smokers' custom. Most have never been properly evaluated and are probably placebos. Some are based on lobeline sulphate, which has been on offer to smokers since 1936. It has been found ineffective when tested in controlled trials. Other products contain silver acetate, which spoils the taste of cigarettes. There is little evidence that this helps people stop smoking, and there is concern that various mouthwashes and pastilles containing this chemical can lead to systemic absorption of silver. Some over-the-counter aids do not give any rationale for their presumed effects at all (e.g. Nicobrevin).

TREATMENT RECOMMENDATIONS

The best treatment currently seems to be a combination of group support and nicotine chewing gum. Courses of this sort help 60 per cent to 70 per cent of clients to stop smoking by the end of treatment and 20 per cent to 30 per cent to become continuous abstainers for one year. Such results can be achieved consistently even in clinics providing the service free of charge and seeing very dependent smokers from socially disadvantaged environments. For details of one such treatment programme which focuses on helping clients overcome cigarette withdrawal, see Hajek (1989). In the UK, training in this approach is available in courses run by the Addiction Research Unit of the Institute of Psychiatry.

To conclude this review on a note of sober realism: the best current methods still have to improve considerably to replace all the unproven techniques and gadgets which proliferate at the moment. Even the most effective approaches available leave behind enough 'treatment failures' to keep the hope-giving placebos alive.

ANTI-SMOKING INTERVENTION BY GENERAL PRACTITIONERS

The efficacy of GP intervention has been demonstrated in a number of trials (Kottke *et al.*, 1988). Simple anti-smoking advice from a doctor accompanied by the offer of a prescription for nicotine chewing gum can yield up to 9 per cent long-term abstainers. Although at first glance this may seem to be a small effect, it has been argued that if all GPs in the UK applied this simple routine procedure to all their smoking patients, this collective effort could yield about one million ex-smokers a year. This is more than any other intervention (save political/economic) could hope to achieve.

The efficacy of nicotine gum has been demonstrated in clinic-based cessation programmes, but its value among GP patients has been questioned. As the gum is aimed at a voluntary behaviour rather than a symptom, its 'psychological packaging' seems to be important. Without proper explanation of its effects and usage, it may not do better than placebo, but when physicians are instructed on its use, its efficacy improves significantly.

A number of studies of GP intervention have looked at various additions to simple advice/prescription. Overall, it seems that if the GP invests more time and effort, results will improve. However, it is important to recognize that they will improve only a little, and the law of diminishing returns sets in very soon. A GP who has 50 hours allocated to smoking cessation activities could be successful with 48 patients, if a simple routine advice is given to all smokers (time per patient five minutes, expected success rate 8 per cent). However, if he or she decides to spend this time on intensive therapy (time per patient three hours, expected success rate 25 per cent), only four patients will stop smoking.

The new UK White Paper proposes remuneration to GPs for running anti-smoking clinics, which is likely to lead to greater involvement of GPs with clinic-type treatments. It would be unfortunate if this new incentive for more intensive efforts detracted GPs from simple routine interventions.

The World Health Organization and the International Union against Cancer drew up guidelines on smoking cessation for primary health care teams (Ramstrom *et al.*, 1988) and produced a booklet for GPs entitled *Help Your Patient Stop*. It promotes three essential activities: (1) asking about and recording all patients' smoking status in their notes, (2) asking all smokers to stop, and (3) offering leaflets on stopping smoking. This simple procedure, with the possible addition of a prescription for nicotine chewing gum (with the appropriate guidance on its use), is currently the optimal method for routine everyday use.

REFERENCES

Hajek, P. (1989) 'Withdrawal-oriented therapy for smokers', *British Journal of Addiction* 84: 591–8.

Kottke, T.E., Battista, R.N., DeFriese, G.H. and Brekke, M.L. (1988) 'Attributes of successful smoking cessation interventions in medical practice. A meta-analysis of 39 controlled trials', *JAMA* 259: 2883–9.

Lam, W., Sze, P.C., Sacks, H.S. and Chalmers, T.C. (1987) 'Meta-analysis of randomised controlled trials of nicotine chewing gum', *The Lancet*, July 4: 27–9.

Lichtenstein, E. (1986) 'Clinic based cessation strategies', in J.K. Ockene (ed.) *The Pharmacologic Treatment of Tobacco Dependence*, Cambridge: Harvard University.

Ramstrom, L., Raw, M. and Wood, M. (eds) (1988) *Guidelines on Smoking Cessation for the Primary Health Care Team*, Geneva: WHO and IUAC.

Schwartz, J.L. (1987) *Review and Evaluation of Smoking Cessation Methods: The United States and Canada, 1978–1985*, Washington: National Institute of Health.

CROSS REFERENCES

Chapter 41

Protecting your assets: caring for the therapist

Cheryl Brown and Deborah Brooke

This chapter is one of the most important in this book. Effective therapy cannot take place without attention being paid to the particular needs of therapists. Many of the issues discussed here might equally apply to other groups of professionals, as well as those working within the areas of medicine, nursing and social work.

It is our intention to focus on ways in which training and continuing support may help to prevent some of the pitfalls of everyday working-life, and to avoid the consequences which can result from ignoring the wellbeing of therapists.

Experienced workers in the field may already know how to take care of the team. It is common sense to encourage adequate recreation, provide an appropriate physical environment in which to work and to offer well-organized and supervised staff support groups. Ensuring that these things happen is time-consuming but they form a solid foundation for long-term success.

Throughout, substance misusers in treatment will be referred to as 'clients', in recognition of the fact that substance misuse is not simply confined to the spheres of medical and nursing practice.

TRAINING: SALIENT ISSUES

In many training programmes, heavy emphasis is placed on the acquisition of technical skills, but it is known that trainee therapists develop perceptions of their effectiveness as therapists according to the amount and quality of support received during training (Cartwright, 1980). This is relevant because therapeutic optimism has been shown to be a factor affecting the outcome of treatment (Miller, 1985).

Formal education alone is of limited value in changing attitudes. It increases students' knowledge and affects beliefs, but positive therapeutic attitudes towards clients will only develop if opportunities are made available to gain *experience* and *support*. These two factors have been found to be more important than other considerations such as the personality of the therapist, the type of working environment, and formal education in substance-related problems. Components of this support are reassurance of worth and the certainty of obtaining help from colleagues in times of crisis. Furthermore, approval from supervisors appears to protect against burnout among nurses (Constable *et al.*, 1986).

Effective training may involve constructive criticism: this requires sensitive handling. Staff appraisal is an area that exemplifies the differences between more objective measures of achievement (such as examination scores) and more subjective ones (such as personal style). Feedback of subjective issues is more problematic because they are more dependent on opinion and they may, therefore, be perceived as striking at the personalities involved.

Therapy aims to set the scene for continuing recovery, to equip clients with attitudes towards themselves that are positive and constructive. While not wishing to specify a training syllabus, it is clear that the qualities of warmth and positive regard for the client are essential tools of therapy. The team is a microcosm of the larger world. If these qualities are imitated and valued, individual members will incorporate them into their daily work. It is far more pertinent that these practices make a positive statement about the value of therapists for each other within the team.

IN-SERVICE TRAINING: MAKING THE MOST OF IT

In some respects, one can never be regarded as a fully trained therapist. There is a continuing need to refine clinical expertise. The management of a recovering addict demands fine tuning of relationships and communication skills. Recovery brings to the fore any pre-existing vulnerabilities of the client. Therapists are at the front line. This situation can challenge even the most insightful counsellor. One example is an increasing reliance on the therapist, as an alternative dependency. Such disturbed interpersonal dynamics can distort the relationship between therapist and client. This can make heavy demands on the therapist's emotional reserves, prevent effective treatment and lead to exhaustion and disillusionment. It is thus essential that regular meetings with a supervisor take place as part of the proper method of conducting treatment. These give the opportunity to review casework with an objective observer and to obtain guidelines for subsequent work. It provides a forum for understanding the interactions within the therapeutic relationship. Well-conducted supervision is an essential part of continuing training.

Discussion with other colleagues, both inside and outside one's own place of work, and attendance at conferences and seminars, help to foster new ideas. Committing staff to further training can be seen as an investment in their future and underlines the regard in which they are held by the institution. If we are to retain forward-thinking, dynamic members of staff, we must recognize the need for challenge and development within the basic job description. Individual creativity must be nurtured and interested staff should be encouraged to develop special areas of expertise. Staff destined for educational and managerial posts need specific training in looking after the needs of their team members as well as in developing administrative skills.

Institutional finances might not allow major investment in further education but other sources of funding, such as charities or corporate funds, should be approached. Every treatment facility should have a library for the use of staff with access to technical material such as textbooks, journals, audiocassettes and videotapes. Possibilities for study leave and exchange visits should be fully explored. Making these opportunities available enhances job satisfaction. Clinical work advances in partnership with academic progress: they complement each other. The client is the ultimate beneficiary of in-service training.

TROUBLE-SHOOTING: PRACTISING PREVENTION

An American judge said that he could not define pornography, but he would recognize it if he saw it. In the same way, we can recognize good management, but can we define it, teach it and implement it in our work practices?

Apart from administrative skills, a basic requirement for successful team leadership is to understand the attitudes and beliefs that team members have about themselves and about their work. A pertinent example, and one which often causes difficulty, is the 'carer's' perception that he or she inhabits a very different world from the 'cared-for'. The process of socialization into a profession may induce the sense of being different, and of denying human vulnerabilities. There are times when sick and troubled professionals require help. Strong identification with the role of 'therapist', reluctance to acknowledge personal difficulties and fear of admitting weakness, make seeking help a hazardous process for the health professional. Friends and workmates cannot provide detached, objective help. Corridor consultations and confusion of roles often lead to prolonged misery and continuation of problems.

The institution has a responsibility towards its staff. Those working in health settings should have access to an occupational welfare structure offering independent advice and counselling. Guidelines must be established, outlining the procedures for referral and treatment. Ethical issues, such as confidentiality and protection of staff members, must be considered when communicating with managers and employers.

CONCLUSION

Armed with an understanding of the difficulties that can develop, there may be strategies that managers could employ at the everyday level to facilitate early detection and intervention:

Would you be aware if there was a problem brewing?

What are the dynamics of the team? Are there sources of tension or unspoken resentments? Have conflicts arisen from practicalities such as salary scales or office space? Is there anyone likely to be less appreciated, perhaps vulnerable or different from the others in some way? Is anyone taking excessive sick leave? Is there a higher than average staff turnover?

How would you respond?

Is there a staff support group in place and does it function well, or do participants become threatened and defensive? Can you distinguish when it would be more appropriate to offer access to individual help? Are there established arrangements for the referral of more difficult problems to a specialist agency?

These are not issues of sophisticated technology, but of curiosity about and concern for the team members. These qualities are personal attributes that should be fostered by training, but are in danger of being eclipsed by an over-emphasis on knowledge.

At a time of outcome research, audit and value for money, issues of staff welfare may be neglected, being seen as an unprofitable use of resources. This is a false economy. Common sense suggests that happier people are more keen to help others and this is confirmed by research (Isen *et al.*, 1972). Working closely with clients in recovery presents us with their demands for problem-solving. The issues we have addressed here attempt to signpost the route for therapists towards competency in their work, and thereby to enjoyment. Personnel are indeed assets, and much should be invested in their training. Adequately protected, the rewards can be great.

ACKNOWLEDGEMENTS

The authors would like to thank Paul Revell for drawing the cartoons, and James McKeith for his helpful suggestions.

REFERENCES

Cartwright, A. (1980) 'The attitudes of helping agents towards the alcoholic client: the influences of experience, support, training and self-esteem', *British Journal of Addiction* 75: 413–31.

Constable, J. and Russell, D. (1986) 'The effect of social support and the work environment upon burnout among nurses', *Journal of Human Stress* 12: 20–6.

Isen, A. and Levin, P. (1972) 'Effect of feeling good on helping: cookies and kindness', *Journal of Personality and Social Psychology* 21: 384–8.

Miller, W. (1985) 'Motivation for treatment: a review with special emphasis on alcoholism', *Psychological Bulletin* 98: 84–107.

CROSS REFERENCES

Section VI

Services

Chapter 42

Service development and organization: alcohol

Bruce Ritson

Services should be accessible, non-stigmatizing and responsive to individual needs. Since the problems related to alcohol are diverse, the organization of services should reflect this diversity.

CRISIS AND OPPORTUNITY

The range of alcohol-related problems is discussed in a number of chapters in this book. As ailments, accidents, arguments and absences from work accumulate, so do the psychological, physical and financial costs.

The experience of those who drink excessively is replete with incidents and warning signs that their drinking is 'getting out of hand'. Each of the incidents has been a crisis, a source of embarrassment or despair.

Equally, each of these crises could be turned into an opportunity for change. A truly responsive network of services should be attuned to detecting these warning signs at the earliest possible stage. The sufferer should be persuaded that alcohol has been a significant ingredient in his or her recent troubles and should be advised on changes in lifestyle. This kind of appropriate responsiveness can only be achieved if primary level agencies are aware, informed and skilled at dealing with the damaging effects of injudicious drinking at the earliest possible stage.

LEVELS OF RESPONSE

Level 1

Table 42.1 illustrates one way of conceptualizing the organization of services. It places the individual drinker at the centre of level 1, which ultimately gives each person primary responsibility for monitoring their own drinking habits. In many instances the problem is surmounted at this level: the drinker adjusts his or her habit in the light of experience. The morning hangover, the headache that interferes with productivity at work, the intoxication that destroys a promising romance, exemplify the events that precipitate modification in drinking habits.

The potent influence of the family, public education campaigns, self-help groups and wider social and economic factors have been shown to produce changes in drinking behaviour to a greater or lesser degree. Health promotion policy should reinforce existing informal coping mechanisms.

Table 42.1 Levels of interventions

Level 1	The drinker	
	Friends	Family
Level 2	Bar manager	
	Workmates	Employer
	Social welfare agencies	
	Police Lawyers	Courts
Level 3	Primary Health Care (General Practitioner)	
	Social Worker	Probation Officer
	Casualty Department	Hospital
	Marriage Counsellors	Clergy
Level 4	Councils on Alcohol	
	Alcohol Treatment Units	
	Alcoholics Anonymous	

Level 2

At the second level are individuals who have no traditional responsibility for counselling. However, they are well placed to 'spot' the consequences of alcohol misuse and refer to the helping agencies. In some areas bar managers, for example, have received training for this. Other chapters in this book draw attention to the significance and value of the development of policies in the workplace and the role of the law enforcement agencies.

Level 3

This crucial, though often neglected, array of agencies does not have any particular specialist responsibility for working with problem drinkers. However, because these primary care services are accessible, widespread and less stigmatizing than many alcohol treatment units there is good evidence that people with a drinking problem tend to consult or encounter these more frequently than specialist services. Thus the family doctor, accident and emergency casualty department, general hospital out-patient departments, social worker and counselling agencies have important roles.

A major task facing those involved in service organization is to ensure that front-line agencies are trained to detect, assess, advise or refer problem drinkers. This training should take place during undergraduate, postgraduate and continuing education. The specialist services should provide training and ensure that support is readily available when clients are referred (Shaw *et al.*, 1978).

Level 4

This includes those services, be they voluntary, statutory or private, which are designated as having a special interest in alcohol-related problems.

As mentioned above, a fundamental function of a specialist service should be to support front-line workers and provide at least a minimum range of services described below. Therefore, it is disconcerting to discover that the range and quality vary from one district to another.

The service may include CATs (Community Alcohol Teams), a health component, a social work component, voluntary agencies and self-help groups.

COMMUNITY ALCOHOL TEAMS

Less than one in ten of individuals with alcohol problems are thought to be in contact with any appropriate specialist agency. If we aim to identify alcohol problems at an early stage it is clear that there will be insufficient specialists to meet this need. CATs have been established in some districts to bring appropriate skills to primary level services (Levels 2 and 3 in Table 42.1). They focus attention on the potential for intervention and advice at this level and provide education about alcohol, basic treatment strategies and client-centred consultation concerning specific cases. They also provide support and advice about the appropriate use of specialist services. It is important to recognize that this is not seen as a one-way learning process. The CAT learns at the same time about the experience and skills of primary level workers and the unique problems of the community which they serve. In this way the CAT serves as a bridge between the community including its primary level services and the specialist. The CAT can often utilize this knowledge to organize preventive programmes at a community level.

Only a few districts have developed CATs despite considerable support for the concept (Shaw *et al.*, 1978). Some of the resistance may lie in the difficulty in freeing specialist staff for this task. At first it was envisaged that a full-time social worker would be available in addition. In most cases CATs consist of nurse, psychologist, psychiatrist and social worker with specialist training. They commonly work part-time and their pattern of working has varied enormously.

Primary level workers' reluctance to work with alcohol problems amongst their clients has been shown to have its origins in anxieties about role adequacy, legitimacy in enquiring about drinking and particularly concern about role support where they have described anxiety as having nowhere to turn to for help when they are unsure of how to proceed. Most CATs have provided an educational programme addressing the first two of these concerns coupled with an offer of continued support with individual cases when needed. Clement (1987) has shown that CATs can be effective in enhancing the therapeutic commitment of primary level workers but this change was often frustrated by a lack of interest and support from their managers. The problem then resides not in the uncommitted agent but in the 'therapeutically uncommitted agency'.

The development of inter-agency and inter-disciplinary co-operation depends on a willingness to collaborate in this way. No clear guidance has been given about the lead responsibility for creating such terms, and the funding arrangements in joint ventures between social work and health are often complex. Some uncertainties about responsibility, management and accountability still need to be resolved in many areas.

Some teams have found it difficult to give priority to consultation and education while demands for direct services continue to grow. It has often appeared that some degree of direct service commitment on their part has proved necessary as a means of establishing credibility. Many unanswered questions remain about the optimal organization and pattern of work for CATs (Clement, 1987).

HEALTH COMPONENT

Specialist services in the United Kingdom have undergone many changes in the last 30 years. At this point, most districts should have a consultant (usually a psychiatrist) whose designated responsibility it is to organize a clinical service. Regional units for the treatment of alcoholism were first promoted in the sixties. Most were in-patient units in psychiatric hospitals and this service was combined with out-patient assessment and follow-up. Such an in-patient programme usually provided 8–12 weeks of intensive treatment, and group therapy was an important feature. However, following evaluation of this type of intensive package, emphasis shifted to out-patient treatment. An assorted range of therapy is on offer. While some units underline intensive in-patient programmes (a model popular in the private sector), some opt for day or community-based treatments, and some have abandoned residential services (Ettore, 1988). Domiciliary detoxification, working in collaboration with the primary health-care services, has been established in a number of areas (Stockwell, 1987).

SOCIAL WORK COMPONENT

Local authorities, like the National Health Service, should have a number of specialist social workers and probation officers who have a special interest in alcohol problems. Training, support and consultation with their students and colleagues working in primary care should be part of their remit, as should be provision of care for complex cases with evident social disorganization such as habitual drunkenness offenders.

VOLUNTARY AGENCY COMPONENT

Councils on Alcoholism, staffed by trained voluntary counsellors, provide help for problem drinkers and their families. In addition, they have active links with Alcohol in Employment Policies and promote alcohol education. A number of other voluntary agencies have taken a major responsibility for residential services for homeless problem drinkers. Individuals who have lost their social supports and are often unemployed will require supportive accommodation while they reorder their lives. Needs will include minimal basic care for those who continue drinking along with hostel and supported accommodation for those undergoing rehabilitation.

SELF-HELP

The benefits of self-help organizations are discussed at length by Brian Wells in

Chapter 38. These groups, such as Alcoholics Anonymous, Al-Anon and Al-a-Teen (support groups for friends and families of alcoholics) and Narcotics Anonymous, run without financial costs to the community and are extremely effective for many people and their families.

SPECIAL NEEDS

The homeless, the habitual drunken offender, the young, the elderly, women and ethnic minorities have particular difficulties which need to be addressed.

It is a notoriously complex business to achieve rehabilitation from a 'skidrow' environment. The homeless more often than not require the extra support of residential care from which the client may progress through various degrees of sheltered accommodation for months or even years. Voluntary and social work agencies share responsibility for this kind of long-term support.

During the seventies a few experimental detoxification and rehabilitation facilities were established for the habitual drunken offender. While this mode of treatment is still indispensable for those who are very ill or in need of social support, domiciliary detoxification is feasible for many.

Alcohol services in this country have traditionally been orientated towards middle-aged white males. Women, the young, the old and ethnic minorities were neglected. As discussed by Coupe in Chapter 25 certain services for women (such as women's therapy groups) have emerged, and current research is highlighting the barriers and limitations to women getting the help they need. Chapter 24 by Zeitlin and Swadi raises the issue of adequate service provision for adolescent substance misusers. Groups for young problem drinkers whose offences have been drink-related have proved particularly effective. The specific requirements of ethnic minorities are as yet little investigated.

THE CHALLENGE FOR THE FUTURE: EVERYONE'S RESPONSIBILITY

A national policy and local collaboration

As has been discussed, a multiplicity of agencies is involved in assisting problem drinkers. A national policy, facilitated by central government, as well as local co-ordination, is mandatory if such a network is to function effectively. Joint planning initiatives which link health, social work and voluntary services are essential. This involves research into epidemiological trends, service provision and treatment outcome. Regular monitoring is an important ingredient of any plan.

The role of the specialist

The sixties and seventies witnessed the creation of specialized treatment units and councils on alcoholism. These focused on the needs of the 'alcoholic'. Now that the emphasis has shifted to the early recognition of hazardous drinking, there is a danger that what is viewed as everyone's responsibility may be nobody's responsibility.

The specialist's role is likely to be to treat severe and complex cases, support the different services in the area, educate workers in the field, manage services, promote policies on prevention and organize research.

A combined drug and alcohol service – a question for debate

Increasingly many clients misuse both substances. Some argue that the differing legal and social status of alcohol and other drugs has implications for the therapeutic task. Others suggest that combining services would be detrimental to both services, and still others see this as potentially mutually beneficial. It is probably fair to say there is no optimum solution, but it seems reasonable to require at least some degree of joint planning. In certain situations, total fusion of services might be desirable.

CONCLUSION

Ideally, service organization at the local level must be confident of a role within a national alcohol policy. Such a policy, apart from providing a framework for development, must pay due consideration to adequate resource allocation. Without this, services will become demoralized and fragmented.

REFERENCES

Anderson, P., Wallace, P. and Jones, H. (1988) *Alcohol Problems. A Practical Guide for General Practice*, Oxford: Oxford University Press.
Clement, S. (1987) 'The Salford Experiment: an account of the community alcohol project', in T. Stockwell and S. Clement (eds) *Helping the Problem Drinker*, London: Croom Helm.
DHSS and Welsh Office (1977) *Report of the Advisory Committee on Alcoholism: The Pattern and Range of Services for Problem Drinkers*, London: HMSO.
Ettore, B. (1988) 'A follow-up study of alcoholism treatment units: exploring consolidation and change', *British Journal of Addiction* 83: 57–65.
Shaw, S., Cartwright, A., Spratley, T. and Harwin, J. (1978) *Responding to Problem Drinkers*, London: Croom Helm.
Stockwell, T. (1987) 'The Exeter home detoxification project', in T. Stockwell and S. Clement (eds) *Helping the Problem Drinker*, London: Croom Helm.

CROSS REFERENCES

Chapter 43

Service development and organization: drugs

John Strang

As we get older we get honester,
that's something.
And these objective changes correspond
like a language to me and my mutations.
If the way I see you now is not the way
in which we saw you once, if in you
what I see now is new, it was by self-discovery I found it.
I realise that my twenty years might be
less than mature: but for a reassessment:
what I said and ought not to have said,
and ought to have said and was silent.

(Yevgeny Yevtushenko, *Zima Junction*, 1956)

A silent revolution is taking place in the provision of services for drug misusers. Our understanding of the phenomenon and the organization of our health and welfare responses have changed during a decade of rapid growth of both the phenomenon and the services. A new examination, resulting from the increased awareness of the spread of HIV through sharing of contaminated needles and syringes, is now required.

HISTORICAL BACKGROUND

Up until the 1960s, drug services had been almost exclusively medical and were concerned with the management of a mere handful of opiate addicts – a few hundred in any year. Most were middle-aged or older and many came from the middle classes with predominantly stable backgrounds. Indeed, a substantial number were doctors or allied professionals who had gained access to the drugs as a result of their work.

During the 1960s, concern grew about the increase in the number of young drug users. Initially the concern revolved around the use of amphetamines, but later also around use of hallucinogens (LSD) and intravenous use of heroin and cocaine. Following the report of the Second Brain Committee (1965), the Dangerous Drugs Act (1967) was passed and heralded the birth of the specialist drug clinics in Britain.

These new drug clinics were given a dual script. They were expected to prescribe sufficient supplies of drugs to attract all the drug takers to the clinics, while at the same time exercising self-imposed constraints. Thus they were walking on a 'prescribing tight-rope' (Stimson and Oppenheimer, 1982), trying to prevent surplus supplies of prescribed drugs finding their way on to the street and perpetuating the recently established grey market. Drug clinics were required to navigate a safe passage between the Scylla and Charybdis – on the one side lay the danger of over-generous prescribing while on the other side lay the danger of failing to attract the drug taker into treatment.

The next fifteen years (1968–82) were the era of the exclusive specialist clinic. Most doctors withdrew their labour from this unpopular area, and referral to one of the new specialist clinics became an almost automatic 'disposal'. Despite increasing evidence that the clinics were not coping adequately with the drug problem, the view prevailed that only specialist drug services could deal with this particular patient group.

Specialist services also developed over the same period in the non-statutory sector. The largest development was the emergence of the long-term drug-free rehabilitation houses such as Phoenix House. Despite very different orientations and styles of work, these rehabilitation houses shared the 'exclusive specialist' ideology which served to emphasize their specialist status and to deter general non-statutory services from taking an active role.

During the 1980s, the specialist drug services relinquished their exclusive rights to those with drug problems. They now promote a system in which triage is applied – thus generic services are encouraged to deal with more straightforward drug users while specialist services work with a more difficult sub-group of this population. However, despite promotion nationally and locally of the importance of the generalist, so far there has been a mixed reception.

THE CHANGING PROBLEM

As the size of the drug-using population becomes larger, so the characteristics of many of those involved in drug use appear to become more normal. If the characteristics we observe amongst drug users are as a result of the drug itself, then there should be a steady increase in the extent of these abnormal characteristics in studies of drug users. However, if the characteristics are merely a feature of the unusual nature of the original population, then we will discover that this effect will be diluted during an 'epidemic' by the inclusion of drug users from a more normal part of the population. Thus while it is evident that the extent of opiate use has grown from a UK figure of less than 500 opiate addicts in the early 1960s through to an annual figure of approximately 100,000 by the late 1980s, it is essential that a critical gaze is cast at the nature of this more widespread drug-using population.

Technological advances and changes in the method of administration may well have contributed to the growth of illicit drug use in the UK (Strang, 1990a). During the late 1970s, developments occurred which enabled aspiring heroin users to use the drugs by routes other than injecting – initially by snorting the South West Asian powder, and subsequently by 'chasing the dragon' (Gossop et al., 1988).

Patterns of illicit drug use and route-loyalty vary considerably from one part of the country to another. Hence in 1986, in different parts of the UK, reports on the proportion of heroin users taking their drug by smoking varied from nearly 90 per cent (Parker et al., 1988), through 42 per cent (Donmall et al., 1989) to zero per cent (Robertson et al., 1986).

THE NEW MODEL OF SERVICE PROVISION

Nye Bevan was instrumental in introducing the National Health Service in the UK. Confronted with a resistance from the medical profession, he stifled their criticisms when he 'crammed their mouths with gold'. So it has been with drug services in the 1980s. During a decade of unprecedented parsimony in funding of the National Health Service, central earmarked funding has been made available for the expansion of drug services. This funding has been distributed through the NHS system of Regional and District Health Authorities, and the greater part of the expansion has occurred through the creation of locally-active services at the District level (the typical District Health Authority in England serves a catchment population of approximately one-quarter of a million). In this way, every local health authority has taken a drink from the chalice and is consequently obliged to honour its responsibility for the provision of services for local drug takers.

Drug services should be user-friendly. This can be manipulated in a number of ways. Most frequently considered is the prescribing of drugs (see Strang, 1990b). However, the service should also be local and easily approachable. The response (especially the initial response which engages the drug user) should be prompt. Stigma should be minimized – this may require location of drug services in sites other than mental hospitals and in sites which may not be immediately identifiable as drug services. Confidentiality must be observed. Like justice, it must not only be observed but must be seen to be observed. Users of illicit drugs frequently fear that information may be passed on to police/drug squads, visa departments, the Ministry of Transport, social services or other agencies; and such concern undoubtedly deters some drug users from seeking help. Edwards (1982) has described the work of the therapist as 'nudging the patient down pathways of natural recovery'; and services should recognize their responsibility to encourage flow in certain directions while not encouraging flow elsewhere.

SERVICES AT REGIONAL AND DISTRICT LEVELS

Up until the early 1980s drug services in the UK conformed to the 'specialist model' (see Figure 43.1). Not only was one agency usually responsible for the service provision, but also there was an assumption by virtually all other doctors that dealing with drug takers was outside their remit – their only role was to refer such cases on to the specialist agency.

During the 1980s, the 'specialist model' has been replaced by the 'integrated model' (see Figure 43.2). Drug dependence had come of age and was no longer to be regarded as just a bizarre interest of a small number of specialists. It now fell within the province of general health-care provision. It was but one more colour in the rich tapestry which comprised the work of the general practitioner. Those seeking help with their drug problems were to be managed in the same way as others with psychiatric problems: thus a proportion would receive help from the primary health-care team, while some would need referral on to more specialist district services. (This integrated model is similar to the layered system of provision of psychiatric care described by Goldberg and Huxley, 1980.) Only the more difficult cases would be referred on to specialist services where more labour-intensive and

Figure 43.1 The specialist model of care provision for drug-takers

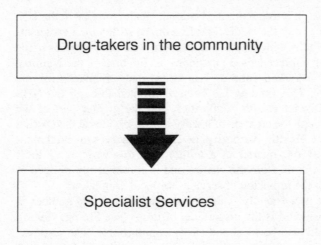

time-consuming treatments might be employed for those drug addicts with more entrenched drug habits who clearly needed more help than could be provided at the earlier levels within the triage. Thus drug services might be seen as comprising three levels of service – the primary health care team, the district service and the regional/specialist service.

Figure 43.2 The integrated model of care provision for drug-takers

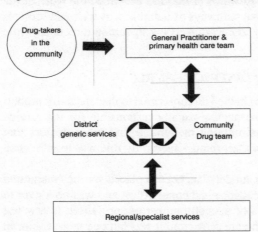

The drug taker is more likely to present initially to a member of the primary health-care team (e.g. the general practitioner). There should be a service of assessment of the nature and extent of problems at this level. Some of those who present may receive their care at this primary health-care level, but a proportion of the cases will need to be referred on through the filter to the district service. Reasons for passage through this filter might include more problematic drug use (such as chaotic use, poly-drug abuse or more long-term and hazardous use) as well as the need for more specialist treatments such as in-patient or residential care. A similar filter is seen to operate between the district and regional/specialist levels.

One approach to promotion of this district level of care was through the offer of a visiting 'satellite clinic' (Strang and Creed, 1985). The main feature of such a satellite clinic was the collaboration between visiting drug-specialist and local generic practitioners so as to assist in the application of the triage. By providing such a visiting assessment service and by taking over the care of more complicated drug users, it proved possible for general psychiatric services to manage the majority of those who present at the local level.

The new funding in the drug field enabled the adoption of a more ambitious approach at the district level. A small number of full-time drug workers were appointed to new Community Drug Teams (CDT) who served the district population. The rationale behind such appointments was to create greater confidence and competence at the district level so that all local practitioners (i.e. not just the newly appointed staff) might become more involved in the provision of care to drug users. Typically this involved the appointment of two or three full-time drug workers, e.g. one Community Psychiatric Nurse, one Social Worker and sessional medical input, whose appointment was intended to have an enabling effect on the pre-existing services. Thus, within the North Western Region of England, there is now at least one Community Drug Team in every one of the 19 Health Districts (for fuller description, see Strang, 1989; Strang et al., in press). (Services outside the NHS can be seen as existing within a similar three-level system, although the discussion in this chapter focuses on the NHS components.)

MEASURING THE CHANGES

In considering the impact of a new drug service, it is important to look beyond the immediate impact, and also consider the effect on other care providers. Thus the creation of a specialist local service (such as a Community Drug Team) might be seen as valuable assistance and support by pre-existing service-providers (e.g. general practitioners, general psychiatrists) with a resulting increase in willingness to be involved and an increase in activity; on the other hand the ambivalent care provider may see the creation of a new service as an opportunity to withdraw.

While it is commendable for the new drug service to provide new care, an examination must also be made of the total service availability in the particular geographical area, and this must include an examination of the contribution from generic care providers. Consider a total population of drug users (N); at any one time, a smaller population (n1) will be in contact with generic care-providers. What might be the impact of the introduction of a specialist service? One major change will be the introduction of a new figure in the equation (n2) comprising those drug users receiving care from the new specialist service (see Figure 43.3). However, what impact will the introduction of the new service have on the size of the generic-treated population (n1)? Consideration of total service availability involves an examination of (n1 + n2), and an examination of how this changes around the time of introduction of the new service.

Figure 43.3 Specialist and generic-treated fractions of the total drug-using population

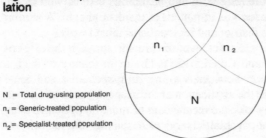

N = Total drug-using population
n₁ = Generic-treated population
n₂= Specialist-treated population

The service expansions in the North West have been studied in some detail (Donmall *et al.*, 1989). Whilst the development of a new layer of specialists at a District level has been generally welcomed, the evidence is far from convincing when the development is judged according to its capacity to fulfil a consultative function (as described in the alcohol field by Shaw *et al.*, 1978 and Spratley, 1987) and hence promote greater involvement of generalists such as general practitioners. On this point the jury appears still to be out. Analysis of activity of practitioners in three health authorities found no evidence of an increase in generic involvement in providing services to drug takers; and these findings were in accord with the self-report from practitioners themselves when interviewed (Tantam *et al.*, submitted for publication).

Figure 43.4 Annual notifications from North Western region (opiate addiction)

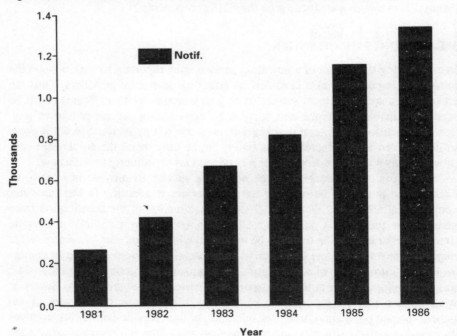

Nevertheless, despite a lack of evidence for quantitive change in the contribution from generalists during the study period, it seems that qualitative changes did occur in the direction anticipated. The regional policy was actively promoted locally and encouraged general practitioners to provide detoxification to opiate addicts with oral methadone linctus – and specifically encouraged the prescribing of one particular type of methadone linctus (BNF) as the most appropriate form. Over these years there was a steady increase in Home Office notifications from the North West. Throughout these years, there was little initial increase in the quantity of methadone prescribed followed by a disproportionately large increase (see Figure 43.5). Interestingly, this increased prescribing was in line with Regional policy with the proportion of this methadone prescribed as methadone BNF rising from 0 per cent in both 1982 and 1983 (i.e. before active promotion of this regional policy) to 3 per cent, 42 per cent and 50 per cent in 1984, 1985 and 1986 respectively (i.e. during the period of active promotion).

Figure 43.5 Methadone prescribing in North Western region (grams methadone annually)

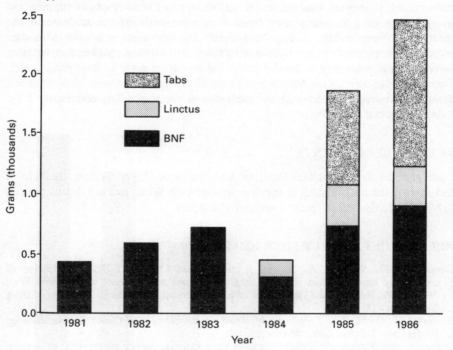

One further interesting finding from this study is the difference in extent and nature of contact by the community drug teams according to whether or not they have integrated medical input (Donmall *et al.*, 1989; Strang *et al.*, submitted for publication). When compared, community drug teams with in-built medical services (such as designated sessions from one or more general practitioners, or sessions set aside by a consultant psychiatrist) saw more new drug takers – 90 per team per year compared with 24 for teams with no designated medical input. Teams with integrated medical input saw more new heroin addicts (55 per team per year compared with 7) so that two-thirds of their case load comprised heroin addicts compared with only one-third of the case load of teams with no special medical input. The heroin addicts presenting to the teams with integrated medical input had been using heroin for a significantly shorter period of time than their counterparts in teams with no special input (averages of 2.6 years and 3.5 years respectively), and a higher proportion were taking their heroin by injecting (64 per cent and 53 per cent respectively). While it may not be possible to establish causality, it is a striking association which warrants more specific study.

CONCLUSION

The data summarized in the preceding two paragraphs indicate the need for a careful re-consideration of current policy for the development of drug services which do not include identified or specialist medical input. While it is not possible from the available data to establish whether these observed correlations represent causal connections, it appears that the initial confidence in the widespread support and co-operation of generalists may have been over-optimistic – at least in the short-term. Nevertheless it may be possible by increasing the medical and/or prescribing component of the service to increase the extent of uptake of services by heroin addicts, who may make this contact at an earlier stage in their drug career. There is surely now a case for the more critical study of these possible influences, alongside a move away from an over-reliance on the hoped-for contribution from today's reluctant generalist.

ACKNOWLEDGEMENTS

I am grateful to Dr Michael Donmall and Professor Digby Tantam for help in considering the data relating to services in the North West; and my thanks are due to Mrs Sheila Garnett for patient secretarial support.

REFERENCES AND FURTHER READING

Donmall, M.C., Webster, A., Strang, J. and Tantam, D. (1989) 'The introduction of community based services for drug misusers: impact and outcome in the North West 1982–1986', Report to the Department of Health, London: Institute for the Study of Drug Dependence (ISDD).

Edwards, G. (1982) *The Treatment of Drinking Problems – a Guide for the Helping Professions*, London: Grant MacIntyre.

Glanz, A. and Taylor, C. (1986) 'Findings of a national survey of the role of general practitioners in the treatment of opiate misuse: extent of contact with opiate misusers', *British Medical Journal* 293: 427–30.

Goldberg, D. and Huxley, P. (1980) *Mental Illness in the Community: the Pathway to Psychiatric Care*, London: Tavistock.

Gossop, M., Griffiths, P. and Strang, J. (1988) 'Chasing the dragon: characteristics of heroin chasers', *British Journal of Addiction* 83: 1159–62.

International Committee on Drug Addiction (Second Brain Committee) (1965) *Drug Addiction Second Report*, London: Her Majesty's Stationery Office.

Parker, H., Bakx, K. and Newcombe, R. (1988) *Living with Heroin*, Milton Keynes: Open University Press.

Robertson, J.R., Bucknall, A.V.B., Welsby, P.D., Roberts, J.J.K., Inglis, J.M., Peutherer, J.F. and Brettle, R.P. (1986) 'Epidemic of AIDS related virus (HTLV-III/LAV) infection among intravenous drug abusers', *British Medical Journal* 292: 527–9.

Shaw, S., Cartwright, A., Spratley, T. and Harwin, J. (1978) *Responding to Drinking Problems*, London: Croom Helm.

Spratley, T.A. (1987) 'Consultancy as part of Community Alcohol Team (CAT) work', in T. Stockwell and S. Clement (eds) *Helping the Problem Drinker: New Initiatives in Community Care*, London: Croom Helm.

Stimson, G.V. and Oppenheimer, E. (1982) *Heroin Addiction: Treatment and Control in Britain*, London: Tavistock.

Stimson, G., Alldritt, L., Dolan, K. and Donoghoe, M. (1988) 'Syringe exchange schemes for drug users in England and Scotland', *British Medical Journal* 296: 1717–19.

Stimson, G., Dolan, K., Donoghoe, M. and Alldritt, L. (1988) 'Syringe Exchange 1,' *Druglink* 3(3): 10–11.

Strang, J. (1987) 'Community initiatives in drug treatment (making the community therapeutic)', in T. Heller, M. Gott and C. Jeffery (eds) *Drug Use and Misuse – A Reader* (Open University), Chichester: John Wiley.

— (1989) 'Turning the generalist onto drugs: a model service', in S. McGregor (ed.) *Drugs and British Society*, London: Routledge.

— (1990a) 'Heroin and cocaine: new technologies, new problems', in D. Warburton (ed.) *Addiction Controversies*, London: Harwood Academic, pp. 201–11.

— (1990b) 'The roles of prescribing', in J. Strang and G. Stimson (eds) *AIDS and Drug Misuse: the Challenge for Policy and Practice in the 1990s*, London: Routledge.

Strang, J. and Creed, F.H. (1985) 'Treatment of drug dependence – the role of the satellite clinic', *Health Trends* 17: 17–18.

Strang, J., Donmall, M., Webster, A. and Tantam, D. 'Comparison between Community Drug Teams with and without in-built medical services' (submitted for publication).

Strang, J., Smith, M. and Spurrell, S. (in press) 'The community drug team: goals, methods and activity analysis', *British Journal of Addiction*.

Tantam, D., Donmall, M., Webster, A. and Strang, J. 'Drug misuse, the general practitioner and the general psychiatrist: can doctors without a special responsibility be persuaded to take a greater interest in the problem of drug misuse?' (submitted for publication).

Yevtushenko, Y. (1962) *Zima Junction*, English translation by R. Milner-Gulard and P. Levi, London: Penguin (first published in 1956).

CROSS REFERENCES

Section VII

Prevention and policy

Chapter 44

The crimes connection: alcohol

P. T. d'Orban

It is generally recognized that there is a marked association between alcohol consumption and crime. Probably most of us would readily jump to the conclusion that alcohol abuse is a direct cause of criminal behaviour: that intoxication and disinhibition caused by alcohol lead people to commit crime. Obvious examples of this 'direct cause' model are the chronic drunkenness offender, or the man who commits a drunken assault in a public bar. However, single-cause explanations based on the assumption that drinking leads to disinhibition and hence to anti-social behaviour are inadequate because even heavy intoxication does not inevitably lead to aggression, and individual and sociocultural factors have to be taken into account.

The pharmacological effects of alcohol vary with individual personality, genetic factors, the presence or absence of organic brain disorder or psychiatric illness, and also with the social and cultural setting in which drinking occurs. Expectations and attitudes surrounding drinking behaviour differ in different societies, and among different social classes within a society. Labelling particular types of behaviour as criminal also influences the crime-alcohol relationship. For example, if public drunkenness were decriminalized, this would have a substantial impact on the total number of alcohol-related offences.

Although the importance of sociocultural factors has gained increasing recognition, we should not dispense with biological explanations. They are a salutary reminder that the causation of crime is multifactorial. Thus intoxication with alcohol should not be thought of as the sole cause of a criminal act, but as one factor of relevance.

A number of strands of evidence illuminate the association between alcohol and crime. These include surveys of the prison population, studies of hospital patients treated for alcoholism, and studies of the involvement of alcohol in specific types of offences. Long-term follow up studies provide some information, and some aspects of recent genetic research are also relevant.

ALCOHOLISM IN PRISONERS

Studies of the English prison population carried out in the 1970s show a high prevalence of alcoholism and problem drinking. While the proportion of alcoholics varies with type of prison, the highest rates tend to occur among recidivist prisoners, and among those who are serving short-term sentences. For example, a study of recidivists conducted in Wandsworth Prison serving up to three-month sentences, found that two-thirds had serious drinking problems, and at least one-third were physiologically dependent on alcohol. Drunkenness offenders had the highest rates of alcoholism and other short-term prisoners also had high rates. Long-term prisoners had the lowest rates, but in this group a significant association was found between alcoholism and offences of violence.

In other countries such as Australia and the United States, studies of the prison population have shown similar findings, with just under half the prisoners suffering from alcoholism or serious problem drinking. The prevalence of alcoholism in female prisoners is lower, but few studies have been done. A survey of Holloway Women's Prison in 1967 found that a quarter of the women had a drinking problem.

The definitions of alcoholism and problem drinking may differ in these studies, but the overall conclusions seem clear: nearly half the prison population suffers from alcoholism or has a serious drinking problem. A recent study of imprisoned young male offenders found that their average self-reported weekly alcohol consumption was 58 units, compared with 28 units in a comparable normative sample (McMurran and Baldwin, 1989).

Some characteristics of short-term offenders with drinking problems emerge from these studies. They commit petty offences, mostly against property. Their offences are often committed in a state of intoxication. They are unemployed, socially isolated, suffer from personality inadequacies, and there are excess proportions of older men and men of Irish or Scottish origin among them.

CRIMINALITY IN ALCOHOLICS ADMITTED TO HOSPITAL

The studies described above are complemented by a few studies of the prevalence of criminality in alcoholics admitted to hospital. Among alcoholics admitted to four hospitals in England, 30 per cent of male and 17 per cent of female patients had criminal records, considerably higher rates than in the general population. In a Swedish study on patients admitted for sequelae of alcohol abuse, there were two distinct groups: those with serious medical complications of alcoholism but little criminality; and those with little physical damage but an extensive criminal record, including offences of drunkenness.

ALCOHOL AND TYPE OF OFFENCE

Homicide and violence

Studies of offences of violence show that the majority of the offenders, the victims, or both, had consumed alcohol prior to their offence. Offences of violence, particularly homicide, have received more attention than property offences. A recent Scottish study compared violent offenders with non-violent controls, mainly property offenders: the violent offenders more often consumed alcohol at the time of their offence than the controls, but a pattern of heavy drinking was evident in both groups. Alcohol is involved in about 50 to 60 per cent of homicide offences in the United States. In Britain, alcohol is particularly associated with homicide in the West of Scotland, where there is a tradition in urban areas of heavy drinking, especially at weekends. A study of 400 persons charged with murder found that half the male and one-third of the female accused committed their offence when intoxicated, and a high proportion of the victims were also intoxicated. In contrast to intoxication, chronic alcoholism was rare among homicide offenders, and the chronic alcoholic is not usually involved in violent crime.

Victims

The victims of violence have also been found to have high rates of alcohol consumption. A recent prospective survey of assault victims attending an Accident and Emergency department found that 74 per cent of male and 42 per cent of female victims reported drinking alcohol in the six hours prior to being assaulted. Assault victims over 25 years of age drank to excess, and this group should be a priority target for alcohol education programmes (Shepherd *et al.*, 1989).

Domestic and sexual crimes

A link with alcohol abuse has often been observed in domestic violence, but there is no simple causal relationship, and excessive alcohol consumption should not be seen as a cause of domestic violence but as a condition which co-exists with it (Smith, 1989). Indeed it has been suggested that some men deliberately get drunk to get Dutch courage to beat their wives, rather than becoming violent because of their drinking. Alcohol has also been implicated in sexual offences, especially rape, incest and indecent exposure. Here again, it plays a triggering role and is likely to be one aetiological factor among a number of others.

Public disorder

In urban areas, football hooliganism and other forms of public disorder associated with drinking problems have become a common experience. A more recent phenomenon has been the problem of 'rural' or non-metropolitan violence. In the summer of 1988 a press release by the main police organizations claimed there was

> an alarming picture of nationwide disorder in once-tranquil small towns and rural areas of England and Wales . . . Groups of usually young and often drunk people gather to fight each other, and attack police and property in a way that was a rarity even as recently as 10 years ago.
>
> (Tuck, 1989)

A survey was then commissioned by the Home Office (Tuck, 1989) which found that those involved in the disorders were young men who drink heavily (64 per cent drank more than 8 units on at least one weekend evening, and 23 per cent drank nearly every day). They were poorly educated, unemployed or in low-status jobs, and felt they had no useful role to play in society. There was also a considerable amount of under-age drinking by 16–17-year-olds, who were disproportionately likely to become involved in disorder. The survey illustrates how heavy drinking is associated with public disorder, but is not the prime 'cause' of the behaviour, which seems related to a whole host of much wider social problems.

GENETIC FACTORS

There is ample evidence that alcoholics have a disorder that is familial, and to some extent, genetically influenced. The studies of Cloninger and his colleagues (Bohman *et al.*, 1981; Cloninger *et al.*, 1981; Cloninger, 1987) have distinguished two types of alcoholism, which differ in their relationship to criminality. Type 1 is of late onset and occurs in both sexes; their alcohol problems are relatively mild and there is no special association with criminality. Type 2 occurs in men; they have an early onset of alcohol problems, a history of violence both with and without alcohol and a propensity to abuse drugs. Their biological fathers have a history of alcoholism and criminality. However, attempts to validate this theoretical framework have had equivocal results, and it is too early to draw definite conclusions about the validity of this typology (Schuckit and Irwin, 1989). One problem is that the Type 2 phenotype may be heterogenous and that a substantial subgroup of Type 2 men in fact suffer from a second and relatively independent syndrome, namely anti-social personality disorder. Further efforts to clarify the genetic relationship between alcoholism and criminality will be of great interest.

LONG TERM FOLLOW-UP STUDIES

Follow-up studies tracing the course of criminal careers and drinking careers over a long period are another interesting approach to the understanding of the crime-alcohol relationship. Criminality and alcohol abuse tend to run in parallel, as both have their peak incidence in young adults and tend to diminish with age. Those who continue with heavy drinking and petty crime into mid-life tend to become habitual drunkenness offenders.

Drunkenness offenders are a heterogenous group. A study of their criminal records showed that one-third had no offences other than drunkenness; one-third had in addition a history of convictions for (usually minor) drink-related offences; the remaining third had more serious criminal records. This latter group had a biphasic career: the serious offences, unrelated to drink, tended to occur early in their criminal careers and to cease after the age of 35, but their drunkenness offences became more frequent after that age.

DRUNKENNESS OFFENDERS

Public drunkenness has been a criminal offence since 1606, when the penalty was a fine of 5 shillings, or 6 hours in the stocks. Modern offences date from the Licensing Act 1872 and are divided into simple drunkenness (e.g. 'being found drunk in a public place') and aggravated offences (e.g. 'being drunk and disorderly', 'drunk and indecent', or 'drunk in charge of cattle'). The latest addition to simple drunkenness offences is 'being drunk in, or when entering a designated sports ground' under the Sporting Events (Control of Alcohol, etc.) Act 1985. There were 920 convictions for this in 1987.

Home Office statistics show that 83,000 persons were found guilty or cautioned for drunkenness offences in England and Wales in 1987. Because of a change in recording practice, it is difficult to make a comparison with earlier years. Nearly half the offenders (41,000) were cautioned, reflecting a new policy introduced in 1984 under which offenders are taken to a police station to sober up and are then released with an official caution. Those found guilty are nearly always fined, as imprisonment for most drunkenness offences was abolished in 1978. However, fine defaulters (850 in 1987) are still usually sent to prison on short sentences of one week or less. At any one time these offenders form a very small proportion of the prison population (there were only 20 in prison as at 30 June 1987) but because of their frequent re-admissions they cause problems quite out of proportion to their number.

Habitual drunkenness offenders are defined as persons who have been arrested for a drunkenness offence three or more times within the previous 12 months. The total number of habitual offenders is estimated to form 12 per cent of all drunkenness offenders – 7,700 in England and Wales, and 2,800 in Scotland ('Out of Court', 1989). They are usually rootless and socially isolated middle-aged men of lower socioeconomic background, often of Irish or Scottish origin. They tend to congregate in 'drinking schools' where they share alcohol, money and shelter. They seldom suffer from any major psychiatric disorder, and any abnormal personality traits may be the result rather than the cause of their chronic alcohol dependence and their increasing social deterioration. Their most common physical health problems are accidental injuries and peptic ulcer. Women account for only 7 per cent of habitual drunkenness offenders and they have high rates of cervical carcinoma and venereal disease.

FUTURE DIRECTIONS

The treatment of drunknness offenders remains the most controversial issue in the field of the alcohol-crime connection. Since the late nineteenth century, society's response has alternated between seeking medical solutions, moral and religious reform, or resorting to the criminal justice system. These changes reflect society's (and the medical profession's) ambivalent and often judgemental attitudes towards the chronic drunkenness offender, who is alternatively labelled as sick, sinful or criminal. None of these medical, moral or punitive responses have had much impact.

Within the criminal justice system, most prisons provide some treatment facilities. The available services lack central co-ordination (McMurran and Baldwin, 1989). The probation service has developed a variety of initiatives ('Out of Court', 1989). However, their help is unlikely to be utilized by habitual drunkenness offenders. Since the introduction of the cautioning system in 1984, they have become the responsibility of the police, who do not have the requisite training and resources. In 1985 the government withdrew further funding from the three designated detoxification centres that had been established. Future developments now seem to have been left to the voluntary agencies.

The decriminalization of public drunkenness is again under discussion. While this would be seen as an important statement of principle which may have some future influence on public attitudes, fears have been expressed that decriminalization would lead to an even greater neglect of the problem and that it is better for the homeless skid-row alcoholic to get temporary shelter in a police cell rather than to be ignored. Decriminalization, however desirable in principle, may have to wait until there are some alternative resources available.

REFERENCES

Bohman, M., Sigvardsson, S. and Cloninger, C. R. (1981) 'Maternal inheritance of alcohol abuse: cross-fostering analysis of adopted women', *Archives of General Psychiatry* 38: 965–9.
Cloninger, C. R. (1987) 'Neurogenetic adaptive mechanisms in alcoholism', *Science* 236: 410–16.
Cloninger, C. R., Bohman, M. and Sigvardsson, S. (1981) 'Inheritance of alcohol abuse', *Archives of General Psychiatry* 38: 861–8.
McMurran, M. and Baldwin, S. (1989) 'Services for prisoners with alcohol-related problems: a study of U.K. prisons', *British Journal of Addiction* 84: 1053–8.
'Out of Court – Alternatives for drunkenness offenders' (1989) *Drunkenness Offenders. The State of the Nation*, London: Action for Alcohol Abuse.
Schuckit, M. and Irwin, M. (1989) 'An analysis of the clinical relevance of Type 1 and Type 2 alcoholics', *British Journal of Addiction* 84: 869–76.
Shepherd, J., Irish, M., Scully, C. and Leslie, I. (1989) 'Alcohol consumption among victims of violence and among comparable U.K. populations', *British Journal of Addiction* 84: 1045–51.
Smith, L.J. (1989) *Domestic Violence: an Overview of the Literature*, Home Office Research Study No. 107, London: HMSO.
Tuck, M. (1989) *Drinking and Disorder: a Study on Non-Metropolitan Violence*, Home Office Research Study No. 108, London: HMSO.

CROSS REFERENCES

Chapter 7 The role of genetic predisposition in alcoholism
Adityanjee and Robin M. Murray
Chapter 28 Screening and early detection of alcohol problems
Morris Bernadt
Section VII
Prevention and policy

Chapter 45

Drug use and criminal behaviour

Trevor Bennett

It is widely believed that there is an association between drug use and criminal behaviour. This belief is based on the results of a substantial body of academic research which has shown that drug use and criminal behaviour are related. This belief is also based on popular wisdom as revealed in the stereotype of the drug-crazed addict who will stop at nothing to obtain drugs or money for drugs. However, the wealth of evidence supporting a drugs-crime connection belies a poverty of knowledge in our understanding of this association.

The problem can best be explained by making a distinction between a 'statistical connection' between drug use and crime and a 'causal connection'. The former concerns whether drug use and criminal behaviour are found together – either in the same place or in the same individual. The latter concerns whether drug use and criminal behaviour are related to one another in any kind of meaningful or causal way.

There is a great deal of evidence on the 'statistical connection' which is in some (but not total) agreement that there is a relationship between drug use and crime. There is much less evidence available on the 'causal connection'. Until the nature of the relationship between drug use and criminal behaviour is understood the evidence of a statistical association is of little importance and has limited policy implications.

THE STATISTICAL CONNECTION

Research on the statistical association between drug use and crime uses three main methods of investigation. The first is referred to here as studies of 'national and regional trends' which examine the relationship between broad movements in drug use and broad movements in crime. The second is referred to as studies of 'drug-using criminals' which examine drug use among samples of criminals. The third is referred to as studies of 'criminal drug users' which examine criminal behaviour among addicts and other drug users. The words 'drug' and 'drug use' are used in this chapter to refer mainly to heroin and other opioid drugs.

National and regional trends

The relationship between crime and drug use was investigated by the 'ecological school' of Chicago sociologists during the 1930s, who argued that criminal behaviour and other social problems (including drug use) tended to be concentrated in certain areas of the city. The general findings of these studies supported their theories and showed that high rates of addiction were associated with high rates of crime and delinquency. Later studies conducted in New York City in the 1950s confirmed these early findings showing that drug use was most frequently found in areas of the city which had high crime rates.

A common method of investigating the drugs–crime connection using aggregated data is to examine the relationship between the price of heroin and crime. Studies of this kind are based on a number of assumptions about the demand for heroin. First they assume that the demand for heroin is fairly inelastic and will be unaffected by price. Second, they assume that the higher the cost of heroin the greater the amount of money needed by the pool of addicts to purchase the drug.

According to this research the relationship between heroin use and criminal behaviour can be observed by monitoring what happens during a price rise in heroin. If a rise in the price of heroin is not associated with a rise in criminal behaviour it would be assumed that addicts financed their drug use through legitimate means and that there was no evidence of a drugs–crime connection. If a rise in the price of heroin is associated with a rise in crime (particularly 'income-generating' crime) it would be assumed that addicts financed their drug use through illegitimate means and that there was evidence of a drugs–crime connection. Research which has used this technique has tended to show that there is a correlation between the price of heroin and rates of 'income-generating' crimes.

Another technique of assessing the relationship between drug use and crime is to ask experts for their opinions. The findings of these studies are sometimes referred to as 'informed guesses' or 'best estimates'. The most common method used is to mail a questionnaire to a large number of 'professionals' or 'experts' working in the field of crime or drugs (senior police officers or hospital consultants) and to ask them what percentage of criminal behaviour they believe is drug-related. The findings of this research are remarkably similar to those obtained by more rigorous methods. Professionals tend to believe that between one-third and one-half of property crimes are drug-related.

Drug-using criminals

Studies of drug use among criminals are usually based on samples of prisoners or samples of arrestees.

Research conducted in prisons and other correctional institutions in the United States report a high proportion of drug users among imprisoned offenders. Some North American studies have reported that between 50 per cent and 75 per cent of all prisoners were heroin users at the time of conviction. More typical estimates are that around one-third of all prisoners have used heroin at least once in their lifetime and fewer than 20 per cent are regular users. There are no reliable figures published on drug use among British prisoners although estimates suggest that the proportions are much lower than those shown by the North American research.

Other studies which aim to determine the proportion of drug users among criminals use arrestees as their informants. The usual research method is to interview or to conduct urine tests on a consecutive sample of individuals arrested by the police. Research of this kind conducted in the United States has shown that about one-quarter of arrestees either admit to recent drug consumption or produce a drugs-positive urine test.

Criminal drug users

Another group of studies provide evidence on the drugs–crime connection by drawing on samples of known addicts and determining by various means their involvement in criminal behaviour.

The most common method of this group of studies is to determine the proportion of particular samples of addicts who have been convicted for at least one criminal offence. The aim of this type of research is to arrive at an estimate of 'prevalence' of offending – that is the percentage of the population of addicts who have at least one criminal conviction. The bulk of this research shows that the majority of regular opioid users receive at least one criminal conviction in their lifetime. Studies which compare the prevalence of conviction among opioid users and the prevalence of conviction among the general population show that opioid users are much more likely to be convicted of a criminal offence.

Another method is to determine the proportion of drug users who admit recent offending based on self-reports. These studies show, not surprisingly, that almost all addicts interviewed admit that they have committed some kind of drug offence (e.g. possession or supply) during a recent period prior to the interview. More surprisingly, these studies show that between one-third and two-thirds of addicts admit to some kind of property offence (e.g. shoplifting, theft, burglary). One study which was conducted from a 'store front'; in East and Central Harlem found that 40 per cent of the street opioid users admitted committing a burglary within the last 28 days and 60 per cent admitted committing at least one act of shoplifting (Johnson *et al.*, 1985).

The timing of the onset of drug use and the onset of criminal behaviour is important as it tells us not only about the relationship between drug use and crime but also something about the potential causal ordering of the two events. The usual method is to compare official records of first criminal conviction with either official records concerning the onset of drug use or self-reported first drug use. These studies show that a high proportion of drug users had a criminal conviction prior to drug use. A Home Office study of English addicts showed that about one-third of males had been convicted prior to first admitted drug use and about half had been convicted before first opioid use (Mott and Taylor, 1974).

Some studies look at the association between periods on and off drug use and periods on and off criminal behaviour. One method is to look at the arrest rate of opioid users when they are using drugs regularly and during periods of abstention. Most of these studies show much higher arrest rates during periods of drug consumptions than during periods of abstention.

The relationship between treatment of drug addicts and criminal behaviour is important from the point of view of treatment policy. It is hoped that addicts in treatment will not only abstain from drug taking following completion of the programme but also abstain from criminal behaviour. The results of research relevant to this problem has produced contradictory findings. Studies of this kind sometimes compare prescription groups with non-prescription groups in terms of reported criminal behaviour. The results of these studies show either that the prescription groups have lower criminal behaviour scores or that there is no difference between the two groups. Another method is to compare the criminal behaviour of users in treatment with those not in treatment or to compare the criminal behaviour of users prior to treatment with the rates for the same individuals after treatment. Research of this kind sometimes shows that treatment is associated with lowering offending rates and sometimes shows no difference in offending rates.

It is interesting to speculate on whether drug users who retire or 'mature out' of addiction also retire from crime. There are no studies to my knowledge which address this issue. Research of this kind would be useful in determining the long-term association between drug use and criminal behaviour and might provide some insights into the causal connection between the two variables.

THE CAUSAL CONNECTION

Research on the nature of the relationship between drug use and crime has focused on three kinds of association: the first is referred to here as 'drug use directly causes crime'; the second is referred to as 'drug use indirectly causes crime'; and the third is referred to as 'drug use and crime are interconnected'.

Drug use directly causes crime

There are relatively few writers who argue that drug use directly causes crime. This explanation is more common in the alcohol and crime literature which argues that alcohol use can cause disinhibition which can cause the release of anti-social tendencies.

Pharmacological explanations are rare in the drugs and crime literature. It has been argued that opioid use can lead to a destruction of the character of the user which might lead to forms of behaviour that might otherwise have been considered unacceptable by the user. It has also been argued that any kind of depressant drug can lead to the same kind of disinhibition experienced under the influence of alcohol. However, there are few convincing explanations of the way in which opioid use leads directly to the motivation to commit property crimes.

Drug use indirectly causes crime

There are many more explanations of the relationship based on the idea that drug use indirectly causes crime. The main explanation of this connection if referred to as the 'economic necessity' argument.

The economic necessity argument is that addicts are forced to commit crimes to support their drug-taking habits. It is argued that regular heroin users have to spend large sums of money (often quoted at between £50 and £100 a day) to pay for drugs on the black market. As many of these users are not in full-time or well-paid employment they must be funding their habits by illegal means.

Proponents of the 'economic necessity' argument provide evidence for their view by pointing to the disparity between estimates of addicts' incomes and the costs of financing an opioid habit. The results of this research are generally impressive in their accounting skills and tend to show marked disparities between estimated costs and estimated incomes.

The findings of some of the research already mentioned is also used to support the economic necessity argument. The research shows that addicts who receive opioids on prescription tend to report lower offending rates than those not on prescription. It also shows that addicts commit fewer offences during periods of drug use than during periods of abstinence. It is believed that these findings show that when addicts no longer need to purchase drugs on the black market they no longer need to commit property crimes.

Other research provides competing evidence. One North American study showed that addicts have a number of economic options open to them apart from theft. Some income can be raised as a result of selling drugs to other addicts. Addicts might raise funds from state benefits, from contributions from family and friends and from begging and hustling.

Research conducted in this country shows that some addicts do continue to commit offences after receiving a prescription (Bennett and Wright, 1986). Some of the addicts interviewed admitted that their reasons for offending were unrelated to financing their addiction. Another writer has argued that the 'enslavement theory' that users are forced into a life of crime in order to support their habits is too simplistic (Inciardi, 1981). He points out that many addicts are involved in crime before becoming addicted and many addicts continue offending while in receipt of free drugs or while in receipt of an income from legitimate employment.

Drug use and crime are interconnected

This argument is based on the proposition that drug taking immerses the drug taker into a deviant world on the borderline of legal and illegal activity. In order to become an addict it is necessary to have access to drugs which for most users must be through dealers and other contacts on the borderline of the criminal world. It has been argued that some prior contact with criminality is a necessary condition of drug use for many addicts.

Criminality and addiction might also be interconnected because certain psychological or sociological conditions produce a propensity towards general deviance (rather than criminality or drug use) and that this general deviant disposition might lead to a wide range of rule-breaking behaviours. Evidence for this view can be found in the research which shows that many drug users have prior criminal convictions before they begin drug use.

CONCLUSIONS

The results of this body of research show that there is some evidence of a statistical relationship between drug use and criminal behaviour. It is perhaps too strong to say that the evidence at this stage is overwhelming as the research providing this evidence is largely a hotchpotch of mainly small-scale studies with varying research designs.

The results of this body of research are less informative about the nature of the relationship (assuming that there is one). There is some evidence for the view that drug use causes a financial problem for some users which can only be resolved by criminal pursuits. There is also some evidence that drug users commit crimes for reasons unrelated to their addiction.

It is possible that drug use may lead to criminal behaviour among those who would not have otherwise committed an offence during their lifetime. It is more likely, however, that individuals who become involved in drug taking are the same individuals who become involved in criminal behaviour. At this stage the most realistic conclusion seems to be that drug use exacerbates criminal behaviour rather than creates criminals.

REFERENCES

Bennett, T.H. and Wright, R. (1986) 'The impact of prescribing on the crimes of opioid users', *British Journal of Addiction* 81: 265–73.

Inciardi, J.A. (1981) *The Drugs/Crime Connection*, Beverly Hills, CA: Sage.

Johnson, B.D., Goldstein, P.J., Preble, E., Schmeidler, J., Lipton, D.S., Sprunt, B. and Miller, T. (1985) *Taking Care of Business: The Economics of Crime by Heroin Abusers*, Lexington: Lexington Books.

Mott, J. and Taylor, M. (1974) *Delinquency Amongst Opiate Users*, Home Office Research Study No. 23, London: HMSO.

CROSS REFERENCES

Chapter 46

Interventions in the workplace

James McEwen

Many substances of addiction have been part of society for thousands of years and have been used by workers and affected those who work. In industrial societies the various substances tend to have been considered separately and this has resulted in the fragmented, ambiguous, and confused attitudes that still exist to addictive substances and their use and impact in a working environment. It is only with the recent overall commitment to health promotion and the recognition that those responsible for workplaces should not be concerned only with occupational disease that a new comprehensive interest has begun to emerge.

The three examples of alcohol, tobacco smoking and drugs will be used to illustrate this chapter. Being drunk at work has long been accepted as a cause for dismissal, but to many the executive lunch with lavish supplies of free alcohol is essential if contracts are to be won and customers treated properly. Indeed, staff see their personal ability to cope with such a working lunch a requirement for success in their careers. Illicit drugs are often not acknowledged, perhaps because they are illegal, yet screening programmes to detect use and then disciplinary action are sometimes considered without knowledge of direct deleterious effects on work. Smoking tobacco, for long considered normal and unremarkable, has become a major concern recently, with strong pressure, sometimes from management, occupational health staff or unions for the *right* to work in a smoke-free atmosphere. Not surprisingly, this has been accompanied by rearguard action by the tobacco lobby pressing for the *rights* of smokers.

Clearly, within a general approach to addictive substances in the workplace, there are many paradoxes and, despite the recent increase in concern and various programmes of action, the basic problems have not been defined well, the similarities and the differences not indicated clearly and thus the solutions are equally uncertain. In the past, with alcohol, the normal workplace approach was collusion, cover-up and finally when these failed an embarrassed dismissal. Even with newly developed alcohol policies, few are comprehensive – little general education, and the identification and caring aspects may be less than satisfactory.

While action is now being taken in many workplaces, this should not be taken to imply that the factors responsible for inappropriate use or abuse are located primarily in the workplace – merely that most people with problems are at work and that virtually all people who might in the future have problems are employed. Hence it is legitimate that the workplace should contribute through its activities to health promotion, early identification of risk, and care.

This chapter will attempt to identify a general framework for action, yet recognizes that specific additional solutions are required for specific problems and that there is the possibility of making interventions locally relevant.

A FRAMEWORK OF HEALTH FOR ALL

The World Health Organization and its work on Health For All, through its emphasis on health promotion and primary care has made a significant contribution by developing an acceptable co-ordinated approach to health. In the European context, where a series of defined targets and measurable objectives have been accepted by governments, the Faculty of Community Medicine of the Royal Colleges of Physicians of the United Kingdom has defined the tasks for different sectors of society including: national and local government, health authorities, health professionals, industry, trades unions and individuals. The following is a WHO definition of health promotion:

> At a general level, health promotion has come to represent a unifying concept for those who recognise the need for change in the ways and conditions of living, in order to promote health. Health promotion represents a mediating strategy between people and their environment, synthesising personal choice and social responsibility in health to create a healthier future.
>
> (WHO, 1984)

This indicates clearly the balance between individual and societal responsibility, the need for change, and the importance of the environment and the potential for co-ordination and co-operation.

Against this philosophy, the existing disjointed approaches seem very inadequate, and this has led to the idea of workplace health promotion policies – particularly involving smoking, alcohol, heart disease, nutrition, exercise or stress.

POLICIES

The development of workplace policies, their aims and objectives, the barriers, costs and benefits, their implementation and evaluation have been described in detail. In general they seek to produce a spectrum of concern and action – from general health education through to disciplinary action and rehabilitation. They will emphasize adverse environmental factors as well as individual behaviour and will tackle policy issues such as availability of alcohol or cigarettes on premises. Some of the main issues will be summarized.

Possible barriers

Perhaps the basic barrier is a reluctance to get involved in issues relating to personal freedom. Management or unions may not wish to admit to a problem or may not wish to grapple with a confusing matter which seems to divide all sectors at work. Some large companies that have been involved in developing alcohol policies have been accused of having a special alcohol problem, instead of being seen as having a special commitment to a normal problem. Frequently there is uncertainty over the nature and size of the problem and of the possible benefits of action – even amongst health professionals who may have generally negative views of health education and are openly pessimistic about the benefits of intervention for those involved with addictive substances. People with problems may not wish to be identified for fear of lack of confidentiality or victimization.

At a more general level, there is uncertainty over what can or should be considered as normal behaviour, this varying with substances, different cultural groups and different parts of a country. Those anxious to provide a consistent health message or to devise a personal approach based on the quality of a working environment may be challenged by entrenched commercial interests such as the Tobacco Advisory Council, who actively promulgate misleading and inaccurate information. Despite the evidence of all research studies, including a MORI poll, which show that the majority of both smokers and non-smokers support restrictions on smoking in the workplace and the rights of people who wish to work in a smoke-free environment, and the scientific evidence of an independent government committee, which showed the risks of passive smoking, the publications of the Tobacco Advisory Council proclaim that people at work do not see this as a problem, that there is no proof of the risk of passive smoking and that smoking is not an issue for management.

Potential benefits

The reduction of existing personal conflicts and misunderstandings, such as may exist with smokers and non-smokers in an open-plan office, is likely to be seen as the most important immediate benefit. Similarly, the end to cover-up and collusion in a factory unit may produce a new attitude to acceptable drinking.

For tobacco smoking, the benefits of a formal written policy have been well documented and are considerable. They include: protection for non-smokers and 'to a degree' smokers; support for smokers who want to stop; minimizing conflict between employees and a reduction in the need for management intervention in individual smoking disagreements; evidence of the organization's commitment to the health of employees; identification of a hazard, a statement of appropriate control, and a general contribution to a safe and healthy workplace. Drawn from international studies, there is evidence that a policy can lead to reduced absenteeism, improved safety performances, lower maintenance costs, lower air-conditioning and ventilation costs, increased productivity, improved morale among non-smokers, fewer accidents and a lowered risk of losing skilled employees through premature retirement or death.

While the rights of the non-smoker to work in a smoke-free environment are paramount, the policy must recognize the rights of smokers and through consultation make appropriate arrangements.

Implementation

Most policies for health begin with a firm commitment by an individual or a group to the particular problem, but if a policy is to be effective there must be commitment by management. Simply copying another organization's policy will achieve little. Each organization needs to produce its own carefully developed and agreed policy, using whatever are the normal methods of consultation and participation involving all levels and interests. A smoking policy working group should include smokers and non-smokers. An initial workforce questionnaire has been found helpful, both in identifying levels of support and local issues, and in publicizing the intention to develop a policy. For an alcohol policy, following the identification of the nature of the problem and the impact on employees and employment, the following stages may need to be addressed: preparing for a policy, the policy statements, prevention, training, resources, communicating the policy, and legal implications.

Implementation, if it is to be effective, must cover all aspects of the company and be seen to be applied to all – the shop-floor workers and the managing director must be treated equally with regard to consumption of alcohol, while in a hospital with a smoking policy the restriction must be enforced on the consultant and the porter. There is the added opportunity in most workplaces to show the strength and consistency of a policy through action in canteens, shops and areas for visitors – not selling cigarettes, or making easily available a variety of non-alcoholic drinks.

Resources

While all policies will require some resources, often quite minimal, unless special rooms have to be set aside for smokers, alcohol policies are likely to require greater staff provision and training. Staff with special skills in health promotion and counselling may be brought in from health authorities or voluntary organizations to assist with programmes and with staff training. If managers and supervisors are to feel confident in the early detection and support of those with drinking problems, there will have to be a commitment to a programme of staff training. Only large companies and organizations have currently much experience in health promotion programmes and there are limited materials suitable for the workplace. Videos, computer quizzes and management-training manuals all now exist, and lists of agencies which can help in developing and supporting policies can be obtained from existing publications or local health education departments and the appropriate agencies.

Finally, there needs to be a clear definition of responsibility. Who is going to co-ordinate the policy and be the contact person? Who is going to be responsible for training? Who is going to ensure the full spectrum of support is available? Who will monitor implementation and keep it going?

WORKPLACE AND COMMUNITY

The Health For All approach provides a co-ordinating and integrating concept. Many health authorities and local authorities have been pioneers in developing policies and through their public health and health-promoting functions are able to ensure consistent programmes throughout all ages and sectors in a community. They are supported by local and national specialized agencies and voluntary organizations, and at national levels the Health Promotion Authorities can help with integration. However, the overall picture is incomplete and falls far short of what could be attained. Much effort will be required to achieve effective participation for all – from general practitioners to hospital consultants, industry and pressure groups, statutory and voluntary organizations.

THE WAY AHEAD

While there are existing examples of good practice, few have developed from a sound basis of theory and proven practice and many of the controversial questions remain unanswered. Is industry committed to health promotion or only as far as it affects productivity? Is it interested in changing undesirable individual behaviour or is it prepared to examine the adverse factors in the working environment which contribute to it and, when they are identified, will it devote resources to reduction of stress, to providing a better physical environment and encouraging employees who seek better working practices? Are workplaces prepared to implement the policies, or are they content with tokenism and prepared to leave the policy in a drawer in the personnel manager's desk?

In interviews with people at work, few see that workplace action has contributed either to their own health behaviour or to a general health-promoting environment, yet most have an interest in health and are willing to consider change. Most policies have been related to an individual disease or problem, but there is evidence that this may be seen as either not being relevant, or so personally relevant that they are unwilling to admit an interest. It is suggested that industrial policies need to be set in a broader context of health promotion including all aspects relevant to the workplace – stress, noise, dust, as well as smoking, alcohol or drugs. Stigma and irrelevance may be reduced.

Like many new areas of endeavour, there is urgent need for monitoring and evaluation, both with regard to process evaluation and long-term outcomes of such policies. A particular challenge must be the large number of small workplaces where health policies or health promotion are never on an agenda. There is no national framework for health in the workplace. Despite the recognition of this in many reports throughout this century, little advance has been made. Addictive substances provide support for a focus for health which embraces the workplace and the wider community if there is to be a reduction in mortality and morbidity and development of health-promoting behaviour and a health-promoting environment.

BIBLIOGRAPHY

Specific references have not been identified in the text. The material in this chapter draws on papers, studies and reports which are covered in the following publications.

Confederation of British Industry (1986) *Danger Drugs at Work: An Employees' Guide to Drug Use*, London: CBI.

Cyster, R., Macklin, D. and McEwen, J. (1987) *Alcohol Policies: A Guide to Action at Work*, London: The Industrial Society.

Faculty of Community Medicine (1980) *Charter for Action*, London: FCM.
Jenkins, M., McEwen, J., Moreton, W. J., East, R., Seymour, L. and Goodin, M. (1988) *Smoking Policies at Work*, London: Health Education Authority.
The Post Office (1986) *Someone Like You* (a video-driven training package), London: The Post Office.
Roberts, R., Cyster, R. and McEwen, J. (1988) 'Alcohol consumption and the workplace: prospects for change', *Public Health* 102: 463–9.
WHO (World Health Organization) (1984) *Health Promotion: Discussion Document of the Concept and Principle*, Copenhagen: WHO.

CROSS REFERENCES

Section IV Screening and detection
Section VI Services
Section VII Prevention and policy

Chapter 47

What does a national alcohol policy look like?

Joy Moser

DEVELOPING THE CONCEPT OF A NATIONAL ALCOHOL POLICY

Over the centuries, communities and authorities have sought ways of reducing the extent and gravity of disturbances and disorders related to alcohol consumption. These problems have come to the fore particularly at times of rapid social and industrial change and by the 1980s were recognized as having serious effects on public health and welfare in large areas of the world. The spread of alcohol problems resulted partly from massive increases in commercial production and distribution of alcoholic beverages as well as in purchasing power and leisure time among populations. Traditional constraints on drinking have tended to break down and the ease of communications has led to the adoption of alien drinking patterns which have been added to the old ways rather than replacing them.

Since the early 1950s, the World Health Organization (WHO) has promoted greater consideration of these matters at national levels. The findings have been exchanged and compared through meetings, seminars and publications and have led to suggestions for more effective action (Grant, 1985; Rootman and Moser, 1984; Moser, 1980; Bruun *et al.*, 1975; Mäkelä *et al.*, 1981; 1982).

In the early 1980s, increasing concern about alcohol problems led to international discussions between delegates from more than 100 WHO Member States. Agreement was reached on the urgent need for national alcohol policies (Moser, 1985).

All these activities have helped to promote the establishment and reformulation of alcohol policies (Grant, 1985; Moser, in press).

PRESENT STATUS OF NATIONAL ALCOHOL POLICIES

It is now possible to distinguish a wide range of national responses to alcohol problems, including:

1 complete *disregard* of the fact that such problems occur;
2 attempts to turn a *blind eye* to such problems, because: alcoholic drinks are a source of revenue to governments; powerful groups make big profits out of production and sale of alcoholic beverages; the alcohol industry is a source of employment; drinking habits are part of the cultural heritage, which does not easily respond to change;
3 an awareness of drinking problems that has led to *some action*, such as: legislation against drunkenness in public; certain restrictions on availability of alcoholic beverages (e.g. places of sale, minimum drinking age); some provision of treatment for those labelled as 'alcoholics';

4   an *ambivalent* response: for instance, efforts at public and school education on the possible harmful consequences of alcohol consumption are promoted, while at the same time the availability and advertising of alcoholic beverages continue without restriction;
5   recognition by governments, in some parts of the world, that alcohol consumption is leading to problems with serious effects on the health and well-being of a considerable percentage of their population. They are aware of an urgent need to reduce the extent, gravity and duration of these problems by means of carefully *co-ordinated efforts*, including: improvement of data collection and analysis to achieve a broad understanding of the situation; review of existing preventive and treatment measures and enhancement of their efficacy and application; research into causes of alcohol problems and means of intervention, followed by application of findings; collaboration at national and local levels to establish or improve a national policy and programmes.

Such efforts may entail collaboration with other countries in an international effort.

IN WHAT FORM DO NATIONAL POLICIES EXIST?

Statement

Only a minority of governments have an official national policy which has been explicitly formulated, usually as the result of a long series of deliberations. The statement may be embedded in an alcohol law (Finland) or formulated in a Parliamentary decree (Sweden) or an edict promulgated at top party level (USSR), enshrined in the constitution (India, Switzerland) or appear as a religious injunction (Islamic countries: the Koran) (Moser, in press, table 2).

Responsible body

Even in the absence of an official statement, most countries that recognize the significance of alcohol problems have now established national structures for developing and possibly implementing at least partial alcohol policies.

In general, the main responsibility for alcohol policies and programmes devolves upon the Ministry or Department of Health and/or Social Welfare and Education, in some cases together with other ministries. Increasingly, governments are coming to recognize the need for a broad interministerial or parliamentary committee to carry out this work, with possibilities of assistance from specialized or voluntary bodies. In some cases the voluntary body is still the main co-ordinator and in others a national institute or foundation has been established to advise on policy development. A number of these bodies deal also with other drug problems (Moser, in press, table 3; Moser, 1980, table 1).

Objectives and scope (Moser, 1980; Moser, 1985; Moser, in press)

A broad objective for several national alcohol policies is to reduce the extent and duration of damage related to alcohol consumption.

Many experts and some governments are now convinced that the most effective way to achieve this end is to reduce average alcohol consumption. Member States in the WHO Region of Europe agreed on a major objective of reducing alcohol consumption by 25 per cent by the year 2000. Sweden and Norway have made this the basis of their policy statements.

Not all policy-makers are convinced of the value of such an objective. Despite evidence to the contrary, they argue that reducing average consumption will not affect the heavy drinkers, who cause the most damage. They emphasize that the main policy objective should be the widespread provision of information and education on alcohol problems and 'sensible drinking'. There is, unfortunately, little evidence that these methods, used alone, will have any impact on the extent and gravity of alcohol problems. However, it is widely admitted that public information and education are required to achieve acceptance of other aspects of an alcohol policy, such as imposition of controls.

The central control aspect of some proposed policies has met with very strong opposition from the powerful international corporations that are now largely responsible for alcohol production and trade. Other groups loath to accept the need to reduce availability are to be found in countries such as France, Spain and Portugal, where a high percentage of the population is engaged in wine production and trade. In Italy, where wine production continues to increase, home consumption has been stabilized, not as a result of a public health policy, but through a strategy of increased exportation to the United States. Similarly, in the United Kingdom, the high spirits production is largely channelled into the export market.

Certain countries, such as the Federal Republic of Germany, which has a high production and consumption of alcoholic beverages (especially beer) and no official alcohol policy statement, rely on an increase in the extent of treatment and rehabilitation facilities to reduce their heavy burden of alcohol problems.

Alcohol policies in some countries are directed at limiting the occurrence and impact of damage accompanying not only high but also more moderate but prolonged average consumption. Because of the much larger numbers of consumers in the second category, the total volume of problems among them far exceeds those seen among heavy drinkers. Among the major components of such policies are the development of both preventive and treatment measures on a broad scale.

WHAT FACTORS NEED TO BE CONSIDERED IN DEVELOPING A NATIONAL ALCOHOL POLICY?

Range, extent and costs of alcohol problems

Whereas in the past attention was focused on dealing with alcohol-dependent persons, many policy-makers now take into account a whole range of public health, social and economic problems related to alcohol consumption (Moser, 1985, tables 3–5, pp. 21–4).

Problems for the drinker include the consequences not only of acute episodes of heavy drinking but also of prolonged drinking. For the drinker's family, such problems may lead to family disruption, child neglect and increased risk of juvenile drinking and delinquency. Maternal drinking may lead to foetal damage. The community in general may be affected by involvement in drink-related violence and accidents, by the economic and manpower costs of providing services and by output losses due to inefficiency after drinking.

An alcohol policy aimed at responding adequately to such problems needs to be based on a review of the extent, severity and duration of the problems and the costs entailed. A mechanism is required for keeping these dimensions under continuous review (Moser, 1985, p. 47; Moser, in press, section 8).

Causes of alcohol problems

Although there is a dearth of widely accepted evidence on the psychobiological causes of individual alcohol problems, there is now fairly general agreement that, at a population level, alcohol-related problems tend to rise and fall in parallel with the availability and average consumption of alcoholic beverages. Most alcohol policies now reflect recognition of this situation to some extent, through legislative controls. Social and economic causes need further investigation in each country (Bruun *et al.*, 1975; Mäkelä *et al.*, 1981; 1982).

Availability and per capita consumption of alcohol (Moser, 1985, section 1; Moser, in press, section 3)

The need for stricter or more lenient controls entails examination of alcohol trade statistics in relation to the extent of problems. Such data need to be collected in a suitable form as a basis for policy development. Special epidemiological studies may have to be planned and continuous monitoring of the situation will be required.

Drinking patterns (Moser, in press, section 3; Mäkelä *et al.*, 1981; 1982)

The prevalence of certain problems may depend on the type of alcoholic beverage consumed. Policies of banning absinthe are based on a knowledge of its effects on the brain. Where spirits are the preferred beverage, rates of alcohol poisoning, alcoholic psychosis and violence are likely to be higher than elsewhere. A policy of legal reduction of the alcoholic content of beverages may be based on similar considerations, although the effect may be merely that drinkers consume larger quantities of the weaker beverages.

High total average of alcohol consumption is often seen where the general pattern of consumption is daily use of fermented beverages with meals. In other countries, week-end binge-drinking by a minority of the population and near abstinence for the rest may be the general pattern. Such patterns vary with time, age-group and area of the country and these factors have to be taken into account in policy-making.

Economic aspects (Moser, in press, section 4)

The returns to the state from the sale of alcoholic beverages, in the form of revenue, have to be balanced against the losses arising from the cost of dealing with alcohol problems. Losses in terms of suffering and disability can hardly be assessed.

Increasing the cost of drink relative to income is likely to lower consumption, even among heavy drinkers. Research has indicated that raising costs will not necessarily lead to decline in state revenues if adequate adjustments are made.

The possibility of introducing price controls may be affected by opposition from multinational corporations, the existence of large numbers of small producers and by international policies, as in the European Community.

Vulnerable and high risk groups (Moser, 1985, section 2)

An alcohol policy will need to make decisions on the population groups for priority attention. These are likely to include persons already drinking at a relatively high level, but whose incipient alcohol problems have not yet come to attention. Middle-aged men are likely to be strongly represented here. Increasing percentages of young women are taking up drinking, with risks both to themselves and to their offspring. Children of heavy drinkers are known to be at higher than average risk of suffering from alcohol problems. Young people as a whole, where they have increasingly available purchasing power and start to drink earlier than formerly, may require special attention. Specific social and occupational groups may be at high risk of drinking heavily or frequently, but this varies from country to country.

Sociocultural factors (Moser, 1980, sections 5 & 6; Mäkelä *et al.*, 1981; 1982)

Increasing pressures to drink, changing sociocultural conditions and breakdown of social controls contribute to increase in alcohol consumption, especially in situations of rapid social, cultural and economic change. Such factors need to be investigated in determining a national policy.

Availability of resources to respond to the problems

A review of available resources is an essential basis on which to develop a policy and plan services. Consideration is needed not only of official service and manpower resources for prevention, treatment and research, but also of voluntary and community provisions and their effectiveness, as well as the degree of collaboration between the various bodies. Some governments have recognized a priority need for training of a variety of professional and voluntary groups to respond adequately to alcohol problems.

Constraints (Moser, 1985, p. 46)

The development of an effective national policy involves examination of a series of constraints likely to affect its implementation. These include:

1   incomplete data on the size of the problems concerned;
2   limited knowledge of causes;
3   lack of proved effectiveness of certain preventive and treatment efforts;
4   high economic and manpower costs of services;

5 resistance against preventive measures by private and commercial interests;
6 fear of encroachment on personal liberty;
7 possible decline in state revenues;
8 difficulties in finding alternative crops and employment;
9 possible increase in use of other drugs.

WHAT ARE THE EXISTING AND POSSIBLE RESPONSES?

Prevention (Moser, 1980; Moser, 1985, section 3; Moser, in press, section 6)

Preventive efforts focus on reducing the availability of alcoholic beverages and reducing demand.

The former relies on controls on production and trade. A few countries have promoted reduction in quantities of beverages produced while improving the quality, thus maintaining economic advantages (France), some have legislated in favour of alternative use of certain agricultural products, or surplus crops (Switzerland) and some policies include directives concerning supply of alternative beverages, such as potable water. Restrictions on trade rely now in several countries on controlling prices of alcoholic beverages to keep in step with incomes and regulations on distribution and sales.

Policy measures aimed at reducing demand for alcoholic beverages underline the need to promote information, education and motivation in a wide range of education and training establishments as well as for the general public. Some policy-makers are now involving communities in studying and changing habits of hazardous alcohol intake (Rootman and Moser, 1984).

Treatment, management and rehabilitation (Moser, 1985, section 3.3; Moser, in press, section 7)

In view of the high costs and uncertain outcome of older treatment measures, many governments are now encouraging early detection and treatment of alcohol problems at primary health and welfare levels, in line with the health policies agreed upon by WHO Member States. Problems seen in the working environment and within the families of heavy drinkers are receiving increasing attention.

Data collection and research

A limited number of national alcohol policies are now based on an examination of continuously compiled data on all the topics considered above. Attention has been given in a few cases to the need for a national co-ordinating body empowered to collate and analyse such data, to improve the quality and means of collection, to propose action on the basis of the findings and, in some cases, to assess the efficacy of action taken (Moser, 1985, pp. 44, 47; Moser, 1980, section 9).

Much is still unknown with regard to the causes, prevalence and repercussions of alcohol problems and the effectiveness of responses to them in specific situations. A policy of stimulating and co-ordinating the necessary research on a national level is to be found in some countries (e.g. Australia, Canada, USA) but a policy of acting on the findings is not always evident (Moser, in press, section 8).

WHAT IS THE CONTEXT OF AN ALCOHOL POLICY? (Moser, 1985, section 4.1)

Some national alcohol policies have evolved within a context of the health and development of the population. Some are geared more towards revenue, trade and commercial interests, the argument arising on occasion that such policy aspects also affect health and well-being. The context may be religious and moral, with elements of temperance and prohibition. At the opposite extreme is a context of complete freedom to drink and be drunk regardless of consequences. The kaleidoscope of national policies reveals all these patterns.

REFERENCES

Bruun, K., Edwards, G., Lumio, M., Mäkelä, K., Osterberg, E., Pan, L., Popham, R. E., Room, R., Schmidt, W., Skog, O.J. and Sulkunen, P. (1975) *Alcohol Control Policies in Public Health Perspective*, Helsinki: Finnish Foundation for Alcohol Studies and WHO.

Grant, M. (ed.) (1985) *Alcohol Policies*, Copenhagen: WHO Regional Publications (European Series No. 18).

Mäkelä, K. *et al.* (1981; 1982) *Alcohol, Society and the State*, vol 1: *A Comparative Study of Alcohol Control*, vol 2: *The Social History of Control Policy in Seven Countries*, Toronto: Addiction Research Foundation.

Moser, J. (1980) *Prevention of Alcohol-Related Problems. International Review of Preventive Measures, Policies and Programmes*, Toronto: Addiction Research Foundation and WHO.

— (ed.) (1985) *Alcohol Policies in National Health and Development Planning*, Geneva: WHO (Offset Publication No. 89).

— (in press) *Alcohol Problems, Policies and Programmes in Europe*, Copenhagen: WHO/EURO.

Rootman, I. and Moser, J. (1984) 'Community response to alcohol-related problems, Washington, NIMH and WHO', summarized in E.B. Ritson (1985) *Community Response to Alcohol-Related Problems. Review of an International Study*, Geneva: WHO (Public Health Paper No. 81).

Chapter 48

The anti-smoking movement: national and international

David Simpson

While tobacco has been used in various forms for hundreds of years, the large majority of diseases caused by it in the industrialized nations and increasingly in other parts of the world, are the result of habitual cigarette smoking. Although cigarette use began to gain momentum towards the end of the last century, the dangers of smoking started to become apparent some fifty years later. Thus the anti-smoking movement – the epidemiology and other scientific evidence demonstrating the harmfulness of smoking, together with the development of health policy designed to reduce it – is a phenomenon of the second half of the twentieth century.

Cigarette smoking spread rapidly in Britain, as indeed it did in North America and Western Europe, during the first decades of this century. Initially smoking was a habit practised by males, but women followed men later on. By the 1950s, the average daily smoking prevalence among men in the Western world was typically over 50 per cent, with women not far behind.

'SMOKING AND HEALTH'

In 1962, the Royal College of Physicians of the United Kingdom published its famous report called 'Smoking and Health'. It received widespread publicity, not only in the UK, but worldwide. The first report on the subject by the Surgeon-General of the United States of America followed two years later. These early reports concluded that smoking was the major cause of the rapidly increasing rates of lung cancer being seen on both sides of the Atlantic, and was also a major cause of chronic obstructive-airways disease and heart disease. The steady rise in cigarette consumption was brought to a halt and, with the exception of fluctuations caused largely by temporary reductions in real price, has been declining ever since.

ACTION ON SMOKING AND HEALTH (ASH)

In 1971, the Royal College of Physicians published its second report on smoking, based on a wealth of new data generated since its first report. It reached even firmer conclusions about the dangers of smoking and its recommendations were tougher and more comprehensive. It declared that smoking was 'as important a cause of death as were the great epidemic diseases that affected previous generations' and concluded that 'action to protect the public against the damage done to so many of them by cigarette smoking would have more effect upon the public health in this country than anything else that could now be done in the whole field of preventive medicine'.

Several weeks later, the College formed a charity, Action on Smoking and Health (ASH) to concentrate on informing the public of the dangers of smoking and to press for policies which would lead to a reduction in disease, disability and premature death caused by it. ASH has grown steadily since then, funded mainly by an annual grant from the Department of Health. ASH has been joined over the years by increasing numbers of medical and health organizations frustrated by the failure of successive governments to take the tough action for which the medical profession has been calling for so long.

THE BMA, EEC, WHO AND UICC

Among the most significant developments of the last decade has been the emergence of the British Medical Association's (BMA's) campaign against smoking aimed especially at pressing the government to ban tobacco promotion. The importance of the BMA as a campaigning force stems from its role as a trade union which negotiates doctors' pay and conditions in the National Health Service: of all the organizations in the medical and health arena, it is probably the one whose views on tobacco and health the government feels obliged to take most seriously.

In recent years, the European Economic Community (EEC) has been formulating policies aimed at harmonizing the EEC's tobacco trade. These include directives on health warnings and advertising which, while not ideal, do at least hold out the prospect of enforced legislation in countries like the United Kingdom which have so far relied mainly on weak 'voluntary agreements' with the tobacco companies. For nations like Greece and Portugal, where consumption is rising rapidly but tobacco control measures have been virtually unknown, the EEC's activities will result in the imposition of a range of measures which could make a significant improvement to very serious tobacco problems.

The Royal College of Physicians, the International Union Against Cancer (UICC), the World Health Organization (WHO) and many other expert organizations which have examined the problems of tobacco and ill health, have made numerous recommendations about how tobacco should be controlled in order to reduce the disease, disability and premature death which it causes. Among the measures which are consistently recommended in their reports, such as the WHO Expert Committee Report 'Controlling the Smoking Epidemic' and the UICC's 'Guidelines for smoking control', are:

1 stopping the promotion of tobacco products;
2 raising price through taxation;
3 public education and public information programmes;
4 health warnings on packs;
5 controlling smoking in public places;
6 banning sales to children;
7 reducing emission levels of toxic components;
8 encouraging tobacco farmers to change to other crops.

TOBACCO CONTROL POLICY: AT A NATIONAL LEVEL

The most essential requirement for successful tobacco control policy is that it should be backed up by the force of law. A model policy will require good baseline data, top-level inter-disciplinary advisory groups to guide the formation and implementation of tobacco control legislation, and a strong 'watchdog' body to monitor implementation and to counteract attempts of the industry to sabotage it. The tobacco control policy should be agreed by the government as a whole, at cabinet level, to ensure that the Health Ministry is supported by other departments of government.

Adequate resources should be made available for tactical advertising to counter the tobacco industry's own activities in this area; for regular public attitude surveys; and for extensive public information and education programmes.

Sadly, even so long after the dangers of tobacco first became known, few countries have taken adequate action to ensure a continuous decline in consumption. Less than fifty have health warnings on tobacco packs and only around that number restrict or ban advertising. The latter is most energetically resisted by the manufacturers – and thus likely to be the most important.

Western countries

There have been successful and total bans on all tobacco promotion in a number of countries, notably in Scandinavia and most recently in Canada. In addition, an ingenious policy adopted by a number of Australian states has been a partial advertising ban coupled with a levy on each pack of cigarettes sold, which is diverted into a special health promotion fund. This is used to pay for health education, public information programmes, medical research and, uniquely, to replace the sponsorship of sporting and cultural events so dominated by the cigarette companies as a means of circumventing restrictions on advertising.

The developing world

Smoking is now static or declining in a number of Western countries as a result of intensive and sustained public health measures. In most developing countries and many other nations, however, smoking and other forms of tobacco use are still increasing and are encouraged by the massive promotional activities of the multinational tobacco companies. There is often little or no local knowledge about tobacco control policy and little informed or co-ordinated action by government. These trends – a decline in the West mirrored by an increase in the developing nations – are seen in both per capita consumption and tobacco production. Already many developing countries are witnessing the appearance of smoking-induced diseases which were previously more or less unknown. The tragedy is that a completely avoidable epidemic of disease will be suffered by many nations which already have more than their fair share of health problems due to malnutrition and endemic disease.

Those developing countries which manage to solve these problems of malnutrition and disease will probably do so in conjunction with, or as a result of, a general economic improvement. Ironically the rise in per capita income of their citizens will almost inevitably be associated with a rise in the consumption of tobacco. Thus, a developing country which has emerged from desperate health problems to fulfil the WHO slogan 'Health for all by the year 2000' will be just in time to start seeing coronary heart disease, lung cancer and respiratory disease of epidemic proportions.

THE TOBACCO PANDEMIC

The WHO estimates that between 1971 and 1981, cigarette consumption increased by 28 per cent in Latin America, 30 per cent in Asia and 77 per cent in Africa. In all these areas, consumption is still rising. The Food and Agricultural Organization estimates that demand for tobacco will continue to increase by some 1.9 per cent per annum at least until the end of the century, with the share of developing countries rising as that of the developed world falls. Consumption in the developing world is projected to increase from 3.6 million tons per annum in 1984–6 to 5.6 million tons by 2000.

Trends in the incidence of many forms of cancer, chest and heart disease follow and reflect trends in tobacco use in any population. These tobacco-induced diseases are already increasing rapidly in the developing world and unless present consumption trends are reversed, this increase will be maintained for many years to come. The World Health Organization has estimated that, at present, tobacco causes about 2.5 million premature deaths per annum world-wide, having risen more than tenfold since 1950, when the annual burden was around 0.2 million deaths.

Richard Peto of Oxford University has estimated that even at present rates of consumption, global annual mortality from tobacco will rise to 3 million by the year 2000, 8 million by 2025 and 12 million by 2050. With consumption projected to rise still further, the actual figures are likely to be much greater.

ACTION AT THE INTERNATIONAL LEVEL

Turning to action at the international level, the World Health Organization's programme on tobacco and health has been the subject of much disappointment and criticism among those active in the fight against tobacco. Recently, efforts have been made to encourage WHO to set up a strong and vigorous unit within its Geneva headquarters to significantly increase its activities. While the outcome is likely to fall far short of the ideal, it may nevertheless be a useful improvement and will include more useful clearing-house functions, training programmes and more pro-active encouragement of action by the governments of member states.

For more than ten years the leading anti-tobacco activity by any of the international health agencies has been the Special Programme on Tobacco and Cancer of the International Union Against Cancer. Chief among the activities of this programme has been the organization of tobacco control workshops at national, country and regional level, where a detailed examination has been made of all aspects of the local tobacco problems and the policies necessary to deal with them.

These have resulted in action being taken in a number of developing countries, but lack of resources has meant that only a few workshops have been carried out each year.

The International Union Against Tuberculosis and Lung Disease has concentrated on the medical profession in countries with active member organizations. A sub-committee on tobacco has carried out an international project aimed at alerting doctors to the extent of the tobacco problem and instructing them how to influence government leaders to take appropriate action.

In recent years, the International Organization of Consumer Unions has been playing a leading role in encouraging consumer organizations, especially in developing countries, to take up the tobacco issue locally. While many consumer organizations work closely with local medical organizations, or have local doctors and scientists as active members, the consumers often have much greater experience in tackling health problems, especially where policy issues are involved. They also tend to have experience of working together with a wide range of other professional groups.

THE TOBACCO INDUSTRY

There is no doubt that the situation today would be much less serious were it not for the fact that virtually all measures designed to reduce morbidity and mortality from tobacco are measures which will reduce tobacco consumption; and these measures meet with opposition from one of the world's largest and most powerful industries. Apart from the Soviet Union, the East European nations and the People's Republic of China, the tobacco market in virtually all the rest of the world is dominated by just six multi-national tobacco companies. Unfortunately, as these companies see their trade in the North American and Western European countries dwindling, so they are turning increasingly to the developing world for new markets.

In 1979, the WHO Expert Committee Report 'Controlling the Smoking Epidemic' stated:

It must be recognized that the tobacco industry has presented, and will continue to present, a formidable barrier to smoking control . . . and no worthwhile progress can be achieved unless governments are prepared to put the interests of public health before those of private tobacco enterprise, and to secure appropriate action by state-owned industry.

The international tobacco industry's irresponsible behaviour and its massive advertising and promotional campaigns are, in the opinion of the Committee, direct causes of a substantial number of unnecessary deaths.

While countries with their own tobacco monopolies have relatively little experience of dealing with the international tobacco industry, this is unlikely to remain the case. In a number of such countries recently, the US tobacco companies have mounted successful campaigns to break the hold of local monopolies. In China and many of the East European states, which officially claim to have no advertising, there is increasing evidence of promotion by Western companies of certain 'international' cigarette brands. As trade links multiply with the Western world, many of these countries will experience massive cigarette promotion by Western companies unless the strongest measures are taken and enforced.

The commonest tactics adopted by the tobacco industry to resist government health policy are: denying that smoking is harmful; misquoting and quoting out of context the scientific evidence about the dangers of active and passive smoking; generating false evidence and reports and setting up bogus conferences; changing the agenda in discussions in the media or with government; diverting governments from model anti-tobacco policies, to less effective measures; and always calling for more research. The industry is aggressive in presenting economic arguments, often false, as being more important than health considerations. It ruthlessly uses economic and political pressure and, where possible, legal action to fight health measures.

CONCLUSION

To ensure that health – and the government departments responsible for safeguarding it – are the winners between now and the year 2000, the tobacco industry has to be recognized as a major enemy to public health. Those who care about health have to declare war on its anti-health activities and to prepare for a long and bitter fight. At stake is the health and welfare of future generations, the most honourable cause for which it is our duty to enter battle.

CROSS REFERENCES

Chapter 49

The World Health Organization

Marcus Grant and Margaret Weir

Increases in alcohol consumption and other drug-related problems have been a striking feature of the situation in all regions of the world during the last twenty years. Concern about these trends has given rise to a search for new and more effective ways to prevent the adverse health and social consequences of drinking and drug abuse.

PROBLEMS RELATING TO ALCOHOL

Drawing together the data on the production of alcoholic beverages, total and per capita, by major geographical regions, it emerges that the total commercial production of alcohol rose by almost 50 per cent between 1965 and 1980, while production per person rose by just under 15 per cent over this period. Two-thirds of the world's production of alcohol at both dates occurred in Europe and North America. The fact that these are the very regions of the world where population growth was least rapid is an indication of the growing importance of international trade in alcoholic beverages.

The growth in consumption of alcoholic beverages in some developing countries has been much more rapid than in others, and if this trend continues for another generation they will attain or exceed the present levels of per capita alcohol consumption in the developed countries. These trends are disturbing in view of the high levels of alcohol-related problems and resultant social costs that exist in developed countries where alcohol consumption per person is high and where reporting systems are reliable. The rapid growth of alcohol consumption in developing countries is likely, after some lapse of time, to be followed by a higher incidence of alcohol-related problems. These additional problems will represent a very substantial drain on scarce economic and social resources.

Alcoholic beverage industries can develop at a very rapid pace in countries with no industrial tradition. Access to the technology of brewing, distilling and wine production is now relatively easy, the capital investment required is not large and, given a suitable agricultural base, the raw materials may be available locally in many regions of the world. The availability of alcoholic beverages is likely to continue to increase and to spread around the world, bringing concomitant increases in alcohol-related health problems and associated social costs.

PROBLEMS RELATING TO DRUG ABUSE

Drug dependence and abuse problems are in a large number of countries a major public health problem. The damage to health and social productivity as well as the fact that the abuse often concerns adolescents and young people heightens awareness and strengthens requests for action.

Patterns of drug use are not static, but present a shifting focus between countries and over time. Abuse of particular drugs or combinations of drugs can rapidly become prevalent and then, just as rapidly, be replaced by others. Differences can also occur over time and between demographic groups with respect to related factors.

Both at national and international level, the information available on the nature and extent of drug-abuse problems is far from adequate. Although the general upward trend is clear, estimates of production and consumption are uncertain and information on the prevalence of particular problems, including dependence, is very hard to obtain.

The resources and expertise of any one country are rarely enough to deal with all needs in the field of drug dependence. Some countries share common drug-abuse problems and, for geographic or cultural reasons, form natural groups for co-operative action, for example the opium-producing countries of Asia and the Middle East and the coca-using countries of the Andes.

A NATIONAL POLICY OF PREVENTION

It is possible to see the world of alcohol and drug-abuse problems as a battlefield. As far as one can see, there are casualties. They are the casualties of the damage caused or exacerbated by excessive drinking and drug abuse. They are the victims of road traffic accidents, of fires, of crimes, and victims of domestic violence, including child abuse. They are suicides, suffer from anxiety, depression and a whole range of mental health problems. Despite the severity of the condition of these casualties, there seems little sign of any abatement in the hostilities.

There is, of course, concern. But concern does not in itself presume effective action. It seems that there has been some disagreement about how best to proceed in dealing with this costly and distressing problem. Various strategies have been suggested. There are, first, the laissez-faire free-market economists whose view is that man by nature is a warlike animal; that the carnage is indeed distressing but that, given the right approach, it need not necessarily be quite so costly as seems inevitable at first sight. In such circumstances, the elasticities of demand being favourable, they see worthwhile opportunities for the state to maximize revenue. A proportion of the revenue thus generated may have to go to financing services to alleviate the suffering of the casualties.

Such a view, of course, is incompatible with the public health perspective, incompatible with a sense of common humanity and incompatible, certainly, with the aims of WHO. What then are the health options that are advanced as alternative strategic approaches? There are those who see the most urgent need as the improvement of the efficiency of the treatment systems. They argue that the first priority must be the welfare of those already damaged. They plead for better hospitals, better accident and emergency units, better psychiatric care, more staff and new technology. Then there are those who believe that the priority must be the prevention of future suffering. There are two separate camps within this group. One group argues for health promotion, while the other argues for control policies.

All of these strategies have their advantages and would, in one way or another, lead to improvements in the present intolerable state of affairs represented by the problem of alcohol and drug abuse. What is, however, immediately apparent is that, while any strategy might have some effect, all are partial. If the level of casualties is to be reduced, then the economists, the treatment agencies, the health promoters and the control policy advocates all need to be brought together. Researchers also need to be persuaded to help in forming a concerted and integrated approach to the development of a range of linked strategies that can be continuously evaluated.

PREVENTION AND CONTROL OF ALCOHOL AND DRUG ABUSE

There is a growing recognition throughout the world that alcohol and drug abuse are creating major social and health problems. These can be seen as the consequence of complex interactions involving a wide range of factors including the pharmacological and toxicological properties of the substance or combinations of substances used, the poor accessibility of appropriate health care, the nutritional habits and status of those dependent on alcohol or drugs and their level of social integration.

The analysis of trends in the frequency and severity of health problems related to drug abuse reveals their continuing increase in most countries, particularly in the developing world. Although different drugs are predominant in particular cultures, there is a general trend towards wider diffusion of drug use across national boundaries. There is an increasing tendency to multiple drug use and to drug use in conjunction with consumption of alcohol. At the same time, expressions of concern over alcohol abuse are no longer confined to countries that have traditionally recognized its presence; reports have been received from countries in all WHO regions, including those with long traditions of abstinence, indicating sharp increases in health damage, family problems, crimes and accidents in which alcohol and drugs have played a part.

Over the past few years, WHO has been able to build upon a new consensus regarding key concepts, such as the nature of dependence and the relationship between substance availability and health and social problems. WHO has collaborated with countries in implementing more comprehensive national programmes with an emphasis on prevention. In addition, techniques for early identification of individuals and groups at risk have been developed. Networks of experts and collaborating institutions have been built up, which now represent a very wide range of disciplines and experience. Increasingly, the field of psychoactive substance use is being seen as a whole, with the differences between substances being less important than their commonalities.

The health and social consequences of alcohol and drug abuse have reached dimensions that deeply affect large groups in society as well as the economy and politics of nations. Rationally based policies and actions have to take into account the substances that are abused, the groups who are at risk, and the nature of the effects. It is therefore of high priority to monitor the epidemiological trends, and to evaluate the usefulness of these data for more effective planning of national and international responses. At the same time, much more needs to be known about the factors that influence the use of licit and illicit substances as well as the relative effectiveness of measures designed to combat their abuse. In addition, dependence itself presents an important research challenge, both in terms of the biochemical mechanisms involved and the social dimensions of alcohol and drug-dependent populations.

FUTURE ACTIVITIES

At country level, WHO will co-operate in the development and application of techniques for assessing health and social problems related to the abuse of alcohol and drugs and their determinants, and in activities designed to increase awareness of the size, complexity and repercussions of these problems. Such activities will encompass the active involvement of national non-governmental organizations and voluntary groups. With their co-operation, WHO will also contribute to the formulation, on an intersectoral basis, of relevant policies and programmes concerning alcohol and drugs within the context of national development planning.

Whilst policies on alcohol, narcotic drugs and psychotropic substances are often formulated and implemented separately, the technology necessary to prevent abuse and to treat dependence has much in common. Preventive action in particular requires the active involvement of workers from many social sectors such as education, social welfare, industry, as well as health. In particular, health workers can be trained to identify alcohol and drug abuse at an early stage, when brief interventions can often be effective. Appropriate information about existing methods of diagnosis, prevention and treatment will therefore be incorporated in training curricula and learning materials for health personnel. Research on the effectiveness of different policies and programmes, including legislation, relevant to specific national needs, will be further stimulated and strengthened through the involvement of institutions in multicentre projects. Particular emphasis will be placed on the development of measures for the prevention of substance-abuse problems in the young and in families.

At regional level, WHO will promote the utilization of effective techniques for prevention, identification and treatment of alcohol and drug-dependence and the rehabilitation of those affected. In efforts directed to promotion, and, in co-operation with countries, WHO will seek collaboration with non-governmental organizations. Based on studies carried out during the Seventh General Programme of Work to identify the relative effectiveness of different approaches to prevention and treatment of alcohol and drug abuse, WHO will encourage the development of intervention programmes integrated into national strategies for health for all. Training, often on an intersectoral basis, will be an integral part of this approach.

At global level, information gathered at national and regional levels will be collated and disseminated to increase further the awareness of governments and the public about the range and severity of health problems related to alcohol and drug abuse, and about the steps that can be taken to reduce them. Particular attention will be paid to the links between injecting drug use and the spread of HIV infection. WHO will stimulate an active programme of advocacy of the public health interest, seeking to involve other sectors of government and non-governmental organizations in developing more comprehensive approaches to problems related to alcohol and drugs. Research on effective programmes of prevention and treatment will be co-ordinated and results will be used in advocacy and in co-operation with other countries, in policy formulation. Building upon policy development at national and regional levels, WHO will seek to establish and maintain more effective linkages with other United Nations bodies, particularly the United Nations International Drug Abuse Control Programme, on activities related to the prevention and control of alcohol and drug abuse.

These themes are reflected in the World Health Organization's new Programme on Substance Abuse, which has been developed in response to a number of important resolutions at World Health Assemblies.

BIBLIOGRAPHY

Grant, M. (ed.) (1985) *Alcohol Policies*, Copenhagen: World Health Organization Regional Office for Europe (WHO Regional Publications, European Series No. 18).
—— (1986) *Action in a Changing World: Developing National Responses to Health Problems Related to Drug Misuse* (Conference of Ministers of Health on Narcotic and Psychotropic Drug Misuse, London, 18–20 March 1986), Geneva: World Health Organization (unpublished document WHO/NAPD86/WP7).
Grant, M. and Gossop, M. (eds) (1990) *Preventing and Controlling Drug Abuse*, Geneva: World Health Organization (Non-Serial Publication).
Walsh, B.M. and Grant, M. (1985) 'The alcohol trade and its effects on public health', *World Health Forum* 6: 1985.
World Health Organization (1987) *Eighth General Programme of Work covering the period 1990–1995*, Geneva: World Health Organization ('Health For All' series, No. 10).

CROSS REFERENCES

Section VII Prevention and policy

Section VIII

Training

Chapter 50

Professional training in substance abuse: the UK experience

Ilana Belle Glass and John Strang

REPORTS, REPORTS

Over the last five years there have been, among others, a number of reports on substance misuse from the Royal Colleges (Royal College of Psychiatrists, 1986, 1987; Royal College of Physicians, 1987; Royal College of General Practitioners, 1986). While it was clear that training for medical personnel should be improved, guidelines for achieving this were not outlined. A mechanism for the setting up and implementation of courses in fields such as nursing, social work and psychology was not clearly addressed until the recent report on training from the Advisory Council on the Misuse of Drugs (1990).

UNDERGRADUATE MEDICAL TRAINING IN SUBSTANCE ABUSE

In recent years some clinicians and researchers (Paton, 1984; Glass, 1988) have attempted to find out what training in substance abuse is being offered in medical schools, postgraduate teaching hospitals, psychiatric hospitals and university departments to medical students, postgraduate doctors and to psychologists, nurses and social workers.

The overall results of these studies are not very encouraging. A survey carried out in 1987 showed that medical schools in the UK are providing, on average, only 14 hours of formal education (lectures, seminars, symposia) to medical students in a five or six year course (Glass, 1989). In addition, more than 50 per cent of the clinical specialists who responded to the survey did not provide opportunities for clinical exposure to substance abuse problems. Medical students were examined on these topics in only 21 per cent of departments which responded. There was little consistency, continuity and integration into the rest of the curriculum. Further evidence of inadequate training is revealed in studies that demonstrate that senior house officers and registrars take poor drinking histories (Barrison *et al.*, 1980; Farrell and David, 1988).

These results are best understood in the context of ample evidence that 25 per cent of general medical hospital beds in this country are filled in with patients with alcohol-related problems, that as many as 100,000 people are taking heroin, and that 30 per cent of the adult population are addicted to nicotine. A review of recent research is pertinent. We must remind ourselves that over the last decade important advances in the understanding and treatment of addiction problems have accumulated (Edwards, 1988, 1989). We have a responsibility to impart this information, some of it of practical value, to students. This is one way of altering attitudes, often negative, which seriously handicap involvement in the field. We must note the progress that has been made. We no longer think of addicts as a homogenous group, stereotyped as useless, destitute individuals. We have learnt that they are a diverse group which differ not only in the extent of their dependence, but also in the social, psychological, physical and neurological problems related to their dependence. We have come to realize that recognition and identification of substance misuse coupled with intervention early in the career of the misuser, can lead to better outcome (Babor *et al.*, 1986; World Health Organization, 1986). Outcome need not be inevitably hopeless even in the more severely ill (Kleber, 1989; Saunders, 1989). We now know that not all substance misusers need specialist treatment, and indeed this may not be the most appropriate type of help (Chick *et al.*, 1985; Wallace *et al.*, 1988; Pollak, 1989). Each of these realizations offers new hope and an increasingly rewarding role for the potential worker in this area.

WHAT ARE THE BARRIERS TO TRAINING?

There are a number of limitations to overcome when considering how to go about implementing a training programme. As mentioned above, negative attitudes to substance abusers is one such barrier. Response to treatment is thought to be so poor that it is hardly worth trying. In addition, those treatments which have been shown to 'work' have often emanated from non-medical disciplines. Such orientations are sometimes difficult for physicians to incorporate into a more organic or biological approach. There is a long ingrained history of ignorance – even arrogance – and so the cycle of prejudice is continually being reinforced. Moreover, as the following section will describe, there are few experts who can serve as role models, and leaders of a multi-disciplinary team, who can train a new generation of students and staff.

POSTGRADUATE TRAINING: WHO IS BEING TRAINED?

Findings from the 1987 survey on postgraduate training (Glass, unpublished data) reveal that although most of the 17 health regions in England, Wales, Scotland and Northern Ireland provide some training for a variety of professional groups, it is scattered, unco-ordinated and unapproved. Not unexpectedly, short (day) courses are far more common than longer (six months to one year) courses. There appear to be only three longer courses open to a range of disciplines: at the Paisley College of Technology, Scotland, at Canterbury, Kent, and at the Addiction Research Unit, London. At St George's Hospital Drug Dependence Unit a year-long day release course for general practitioners is underway.

The form most training takes ranges from discussion groups, work-shops, lectures, and case-studies on in-service clinical and community placements. There appears to be little link between undergraduate and postgraduate courses.

The nursing profession has developed specific training courses on substance misuse, e.g. English National Board (ENB) 612, a year-long course covering alcohol and other drugs; ENB 616, a four- to six-month course covering 'other drugs' but not alcohol; and ENB 620 which covers alcohol problems. Many professions with an important part to play in the substance misuse field seem to be virtually excluded from the training options provided. These include pharmacists, dentists, prison officers, teachers, lawyers, economists, probation officers and the clergy. Medical schools rarely provide support for community-based services and university departments in disciplines such as social work and psychology. There is a sprinkling of MSc or postgraduate courses which provide opportunities to train in research techniques.

The precise number of full-time National Health Service consultants in the substance abuse field is difficult to estimate but as a 'guestimate' it is likely that there are only about 25 full-time consultants in substance misuse, and perhaps 50 part-time consultants. Senior registrar training is likewise restricted and generally reserved for those working in places where services, expertise and research are already clustered. This is inadequate to meet the service requirements of the population and the training needs of students and workers in the field.

WHAT IS A FEASIBLE MECHANISM FOR IMPLEMENTATION OF TRAINING WITHIN AN INSTITUTION?

The general strategy should be mobilization of resources already existing within the institution. From our experience it is important to target a respected key member in the faculty or organization who is sympathetic to the need to expand education in the substance abuse area.

There is a need for some baseline information and research before initiating a new training programme. Surveying current knowledge in, for example, medical students at the beginning and at the end of their training, is one possibility.

Since it is difficult to separate training from clinical practice and research, the establishment of a teaching base should go hand in hand with maximizing existing (clinical) facilities (e.g. drug and alcohol abuse should have a higher profile on the wards in a medical school setting) and the development of a new service provision.

The programme itself should be seen as a focus of research and monitoring. Research into addiction problems by students and staff should be encouraged. Appropriate sources of funding for projects should be identified and approached.

With this and other initiatives, a group, or task force, of committed individuals can be formed. This group should be prepared to suggest a core curriculum, to train staff and students, and to monitor the effectiveness of the training package over a period of time. The development of a training course should begin in a small way, and be phasic and evolutionary.

Teaching methods should be innovative, emphasis being placed on participatory activities. Seminars where students present material should be encouraged. Visits to a range of units and voluntary agencies, on which reports are written, should be arranged.

Above all, a training programme should be organized by individual units or departments, specialized in particular areas, and as a whole. In this way students will be able to review the components in perspective.

Different institutions in the same country and in different countries clearly have widely differing priorities. Attempts should be made to train potential trainers, e.g.

senior members of staff who are likely to be permanent, as their newly acquired expertise could then act as catalyst for change.

DIPLOMA IN ADDICTION BEHAVIOUR: THE LESSONS LEARNT

One attempt to provide a one-year full-time international multi-disciplinary course in addiction behaviour has been at the Addiction Research Unit, Institute of Psychiatry, University of London (Glass, 1990). As described in the introduction to this book, students have come from all over the world with different educational, occupational, social and cultural backgrounds. The objective has been to train a cadre of professionals who could return to their professions and countries of origin to play a part in running services, formulating policy, conducting research and educating workers in the field. We hope it provides one flexible model for training the trainers. Now in its fifth year, it is an intense learning experience, a test-bed and a continuing and evolving experiment.

Students attend regular seminars which are carefully chosen to provide a theoretical basis to clinically relevant material. In large part the content of this book is based on these seminars. Seminars are run by a seminar leader whose role it is to provide a reading list, introduce the subject, facilitate discussion of papers presented by students and highlight challenging and controversial aspects.

Clinical placements in the community and hospital setting provide students with an opportunity of clerking clients, presenting case-histories and learning about the mechanics and subtleties of running a unit or treatment centre. Students are supervised at each centre, and it is of paramount importance that centres selected provide the highest quality of care. Regular tutorials allow students to discuss their academic progress, personal difficulties and future development.

Research workshops (discussed in Chapter 51 by Griffith Edwards) prepare students for the exciting possibilities of undertaking research when they return to work.

A new feature is the development of a module on training for management, leadership and education. Experienced social scientists, managers, media personalities, politicians and health professionals equip students with those skills required for service organization, developing national and international policy and training.

There is continuous assessment of students over the year during seminars and tutorials, on placements, and by means of written essays, case-books and a research proposal. There is continuous formal and informal feedback from students to the course organizer and administrator about all aspects of the course. There is an inbuilt flexibility in the structure of the course which allows for monitoring, and rapid changes if appropriate.

Final examinations – written (essay and multiple choice) and clinical – have been the source of overwhelming anxiety. Students have aspired to an almost unrealistic degree of perfection. Thus, while important and necessary, these are assessed in the total perspective of the person's performance during the year. In essence we have placed emphasis on the students' rich personal and professional experience in their own countries. We have encouraged them to bring this experience to the group at every level.

THE REGIONAL DRUG-TRAINING UNIT

Since the first allocation of ear-marked monies to the drug field in 1982 a small number of Regional Training Units have been set up with the brief of providing basic level training to generic as well as specialist workers in the Health Region. (A region typically comprises a catchment population of about four million.) Great emphasis has been placed on the importance of generic training in line with a more integrated model of health care delivery by these new training teams (such as the North West Regional Drug Training Unit, the London Boroughs Training Unit and the Training Programme at the Leeds Addiction Unit). Typically such training has been multi-disciplinary and has crossed statutory boundaries so that the same course may be given to various health-care workers, local authority and probation staff as well as workers in the non-statutory sector.

In 1987 a drug training unit serving the South East Thames Region was established at the Maudsley Hospital, with the brief to operate along similar lines to the other recently established drug training units. Thus the emphasis was to be on the provision of a basic level of training to generic workers in the region from different professional backgrounds and in different work situations. Most of this work has been undertaken through short courses or workshops (of between half a day and three days): these have either been organized by the Training Unit alone or in collaboration with local agencies with the express purpose of encouraging local self-sufficiency in the future.

The activity of the Training Unit has been examined during a 12-month period (1988/89). Four hundred and seventy-six care providers attended one or more of these courses – 133 being staff working full-time with drug users, 37 being workers in HIV/AIDS services and 306 being workers from a variety of other services which did not specialize in providing care to drug users. This latter group of 306 generic workers were drawn from both inside and outside the NHS and were spread across different occupational groups including psychiatric nurses (28), social workers (27), general nurses (23) and trainers/tutors working at a local level (18). It is notable that this approach was singularly unsuccessful at attracting general practitioners or other doctors into these multi-disciplinary training sessions – only six doctors attended during the 12-month period.

So what sort of courses have been provided by the Training Unit? The courses can be roughly grouped into 'Drugs courses' in which basic training was given on working with drug users, and 'HIV/drugs courses' in which the main emphasis was on the special problems associated with the advent of HIV and the changes necessary within local policy and clinical practice. Two hundred and ninety-two workers attended drugs courses and 184 workers attended HIV/drugs courses. A breakdown of attendance at these courses according to the background of the audience shows that most of the training to generic workers revolved around drugs training whilst the majority of drugs workers were attending HIV courses.

TRAINING – MULTI-DISCIPLINARY OR UNI-DISCIPLINARY?

Attention is increasingly paid to the chimeral nature of the drug taker. Different disciplines are seen each to be bringing a valued contribution to our understanding and response to the drug taker. Staff from different professional and practice backgrounds are encouraged to work together in a multi-disciplinary approach. How natural it is that consideration should be given to providing this training on a multi-disciplinary basis.

The main advantage of multi-disciplinary training (apart from the administrative convenience of tying everybody together and thus losing any loose ends) is that it provides an opportunity for demonstrating the strengths of the very multi-disciplinary approach which it seeks to promote. Thus contributions from the physician, the psychologist and the social worker may help us to understand the varied form of the chimera, and may help us to understand that a comprehensive response will involve input from each of the areas of expertise.

However, there are disadvantages to an exclusive reliance on a multi-disciplinary approach. For training to be effective, it must at least reach the target audience. Some professional groups (such as doctors) are either unwilling to participate in multi-disciplinary training or are deterred by the unfamiliar format. Consider the figure given above that in the 12-month activity analysis of the Training Unit there were only six doctors amongst the 476 individuals who attended one of the training sessions. There is precious little value in having an excellent course if the potential audience fails to utilize the training opportunity. Whatever the rightness or wrongness of a particular approach, it must be adapted in the light of experience so as to ensure that it has an impact on a substantial number of the target audience.

Let us reflect in more detail the low level of 'capture' of doctors into the audience. General practitioners are increasingly regarded as key figures within the delivery of care to drug takers – both with regard to early identification and also for the opportunity for community-based responses. Over the last decade there has been active promotion of the general practitioner as one of the key figures in the delivery of care (e.g. Chang, 1988; McKeganey, 1988; Martin, 1987; Neville *et al.*, 1989) and it has been estimated that each year general practitioners in the UK see around 40,000 'new' opiate addicts (Glanz and Taylor, 1986). There is anecdotal evidence of considerable success at 'capturing' doctors into the audience when the training session is set up on a uni-disciplinary basis and is organized by an existing system (e.g. the system for postgraduate medical education). This internal uni-disciplinary approach can succeed where attempts at multi-disciplinary training have failed, for despite the failure to attract doctors to multi-disciplinary training in the Manchester area, a training day was organized by one of the local postgraduate centres and succeeded in attracting 100 local general practitioners for the entire day.

Pragmatism must surely win at the end of the day, and it demands that we adopt a mixture of uni-disciplinary and multi-disciplinary formats in which the goals and methods of training will be tailored according to the composition of the audience. It may be appropriate to consider the basis on which the audience may be gathered together. They may be grouped according to the agency in which they practise, the district in which they work, their professional background, their level of experience or their declared interest in the subject.

A balanced training approach for a district or region must take account of the different needs of the various professional groups within the region, and must also adopt a realistic approach and adapt the format according to the particular needs of different groups and any resistances which may be encountered. A training approach in which there is a rigid adherence to one format may succeed in providing competent care to a small proportion of the target population, but a more versatile approach will be required in which the audience is sorted according to various functions if the training programme is to achieve a fuller impact across the region as a whole.

CONCLUSION: IMPLICATIONS

A variety of issues need to be addressed in each country and profession. Setting up a register of formal training programmes and thereby identifying gaps and co-ordinating resources would be one useful development. Forming an organization of educators in the substance abuse field, and setting up national examination and certification might be considered. This body could formulate a national policy on education in the addiction behaviour field. Its objectives and resource implications could thus be examined. The process would include identifying groups at which education would be targeted. The key roles and scope for training and management of the various professionals in a multi-disciplinary team would need clarification for this purpose. The relationship of the professional bodies in nursing, social work and medicine could thereby be brought into focus. High priority areas must remain to improve career prospects and train trainers in the addiction field.

ACKNOWLEDGEMENTS

Our thanks are due to Hussain Rassool of the Maudsley/South East Thames Regional Drug Training Unit for assistance with the section on drug training units; and to Sheila Garnett for patient secretarial support and coaxing through the process of preparing the chapter.

REFERENCES

Advisory Council on the Misuse of Drugs (1990) *Problem Drug Use: a Review of Training*. London: HMSO.

Babor, T.F., Ritson, E.B. and Hodgson, R.J. (1986) 'Alcohol-related problems in the primary health care setting: a review of early intervention strategies', *British Journal of Addiction* 81: 23–46.

Barrison, I.G., Viola, G. and Murray-Lyon, I.M. (1980) 'Do housemen take an adequate drinking history?', *British Medical Journal* 281: 1040.

Chang, J. (1988) 'The management of drug misuse in general practice', *Journal of the Royal College of General Practitioners* 38(311): 248–9.

Chick, J., Lloyd, G. and Crombie, E. (1985) 'Counselling problem drinkers in medical wards: a controlled study', *British Medical Journal* 290: 965–7.

Edwards, G. (1988) 'Which treatments work for drinking problems?', *British Medical Journal* 296: 4–5.

— (1989) 'Addictions as challenge to general psychiatry', *International Review of Psychiatry* 1: 5–8.

Farrell, M. and David, A.S. (1988) 'Do psychiatric registrars take a proper drinking history?', *British Medical Journal* ii: 469–71.

Glanz, A. and Taylor, C. (1986) 'Findings of a national survey of the role of general practitioners in the treatment of opiate misuse: extent of contact with opiate misusers', *British Medical Journal* 293: 427–30.

Glass, I.B. (1988) 'Substance abuse and professional education: a tops-down or bottoms-up approach?', *British Journal of Addiction* 83: 999–1001.

— (1989a) 'Undergraduate training in substance abuse in the United Kingdom', *British Journal of Addiction* 84: 197–202.

— (1989b) 'Psychiatric education and substance problems: a slow response to neglect', *International Review of Psychiatry* 1: 17–19.

— (1990) 'Diploma in Addiction Behaviour: update', *Drug and Alcohol Dependence* 26: 39–43.

— 'Postgraduate Training in Substance Abuse'(unpublished data).

Kleber, H.D. (1989) 'Treatment of drug dependence: what works', *International Review of Psychiatry* 1(2): 81–100.

McKeganey, N. (1988) 'Shadowland: general practitioners and treatment of opiate-abusing patients', *British Journal of Addiction* 83: 373–86.

Martin, E. (1987) 'Managing drug addiction in general practice – the reality behind the guidelines: discussion paper', *Journal of the Royal Society of Medicine* 80(5): 305–7.

Neville, R.G., McKellican, J.F. and Foster, J. (1988) 'Heroin users in general practice: ascertainment and features', *British Medical Journal* 296: 755–8.

Paton, A. (1984) 'Undergraduate survey of medical education in alcoholism' (personal communication).

Pollak, B. (1989) 'Primary health care and the addictions: where to start and where to go', *British Journal of Addiction* 84: 1425–32.

Royal College of General Practitioners (1986) *Alcohol: a Balanced View*, London: Royal College of General Practitioners.

Royal College of Physicians (1987) *A Great and Growing Evil*, London: Tavistock.

Royal College of Psychiatrists (1986) *Alcohol: Our Favourite Drug*, London: Tavistock.

— (1987) *Drug Scenes*, London: Royal College of Psychiatrists.

Saunders, J.B. (1989) 'The efficacy of treatment for drinking problems', *International Review of Psychiatry* 1/2: 121–38.

Wallace, P., Cutler, S. and Haines, A. (1988) 'Randomized controlled trial of general practitioner intervention in patients with excessive alcohol consumption', *British Medical Journal* 297: 663–8.

World Health Organization (1986) *Drug Dependence and Alcohol Related Problems: A Manual for Community Health Workers with Guidelines for Trainers*, Geneva: World Health Organization.

CROSS REFERENCES

Chapter 51

Teaching research skills

Griffith Edwards

BACKGROUND AND FOCUS

Before getting down to the task proposed by the heading to this chapter it is necessary to determine a focus. What must stand out on any inspection of research activity in the substance problems field is the sweep and diversity of the scientific disciplines which are today staking out their claims – every grouping from anthropology to molecular genetics, from behavioural psychopharmacology to economics, from sociology to neurochemistry, and many others besides. Sometimes the representatives of one discipline will work productively in their particular and isolated corners as if no other tradition existed. At other times one begins to sense that this area may become an exemplar for multi-disciplinary or inter-disciplinary endeavours which break down the rigid traditional scientific territorial boundaries.

It must also be acknowledged that there are few research skills which are the primary and unique possession of substance problems researchers. On the contrary, the skills required for work on alcohol or drug problems are, for the most part, simply a borrowing from the basic tools of the parent disciplines. Any discussion on 'teaching research skills' must therefore be sensibly tempered by an awareness of the fact that the range of basic disciplines which might rightly demand consideration is potentially overwhelming and their diverse methods quite beyond the possibilities of any synoptic treatment. Hence the need for focus. What this chapter will concentrate on is a teaching method for developing skills to tackle what might be called plain, jobbing research questions of an everyday nature. These questions largely relate to the simpler types of epidemiology and to what is today often called 'health service research'.

This choice of focus is determined by the belief that research of the kind outlined above is in the drugs and alcohol field greatly needed and often woefully scant. The call for training to enhance this type of competence is clearly and repeatedly heard from developing countries but it would be wrong to assume that even highly developed countries have as yet found ways of getting this type of research adequately in place.

In emphasizing this undramatic species of research as a priority focus it should not be thought that the task we are proposing here is unambitious. Effectively to attack a simple question requires skills and craftsmanship of a high order. At the clinical and community front-line the wider development of this kind of research competence would radically influence the capacity to deliver health care and mount effective prevention programmes at local level.

The focus which is being offered should on the other hand not be read as denigrating the importance of more complex types of research. There is a place for PhD training in high technology laboratory research and for large sample epidemiological studies with the follow-through to multivariate analysis, but in reality that type of work will largely remain the remit of advanced centres in rich countries. To expose postgraduate students from the developing world only to that vision of science and then send them home to grapple with the vastly different resources, opportunities and priorities of their own countries is a betrayal.

RESEARCH WORKSHOPS

The research workshop format has been developed in the Addiction Behaviour diploma course as a mechanism for teaching the type of practical research skills described above. Workshops take place weekly over a 6-month period. In previous sections of the course students will have engaged in seminars dealing with such issues as statistical methods, sampling, and the conduct of controlled trials. The number of students around the table has varied between 4 and 9 according to the year's enrolment. The groups are led by the same research worker (GE) throughout. Sessions usually last about 1.5 hours. The emphasis is on informality, active participation, interaction and mutual support.

The work centres around each student preparing a 'research protocol' and the detailed nature of that exercise will be described under the next heading. What must first, however, be outlined is the attitudinal as opposed to the instrumental content of the workshop experience. Here matters can perhaps be summarized in terms of three issues:

Self-confidence

Many who enrol for the Diploma in Addiction Behaviour come to this course with the handicapping belief that research is a difficult and arcane activity which should be left in the hands of research professionals. Students who are medically qualified and psychologists are in general rather more assured, but for those whose primary training is in nursing or social work the expectation that they should plan a research project often seems to provoke anxiety. These sessions provide an environment in which that feeling can be worked through and where a consensus view can be fostered that research of the kind which is being talked about here is intrinsic to the student's professional development and absolutely within his or her capacities.

Creativity and the identification of 'good questions'

The workshop carries the message that research is not a mechanistic process of just the dull application of a set of rules. It is useful therefore at one of the early sessions to ask students each to present for group discussion a number of selected papers which illustrate a range of research representing a spectrum from participant observation and simple description to more formal designs. Debate is also encouraged around the issue of 'what makes a good research question' and students begin to explore how such questions are latent and waiting to be picked up in the most ordinary clinical day's work.

Designing research which is useful to the student's home setting

Throughout the workshop students are invited to bear in mind that the research plan which they are designing must be relevant to the circumstances of their own everyday work and must illuminate and assist that work. Students are therefore constantly asked to talk about and reflect on their own clinical settings and communities, and at best an afternoon's discussion can develop an almost magical flying-carpet quality as the group seems first, say, to be visiting an African village and then moves on to a heroin 'detoxification camp' in India, or to the cocaine problems of South America.

The workshop format ensures that these three fundamental messages are not presented as abstract principles got over in one session and then all too probably forgotten or put aside, but that on the contrary they are ideas which are floated, developed, fleshed-out and given their personal meaning as week follows week of interaction.

THE RESEARCH PROTOCOL: PURPOSE AND CONTENT

Preparation of the research protocol is not an abstract academic exercise but a task directed at the detailed and practical design of a research plan which the student will be able to put into action on returning home and when the course is over. This teaching approach is based on the belief that it is unrealistic to require a student actually to conduct a study of any significance or quality during the period of an intensive one-year academic course which is packed with many other demands. Furthermore, the ethic of the course is usefully supported by a project of this type which makes a tangible link between the course and what happens when the course is over. The workshop reinforces the message that it is the student's own country and work setting which define reality.

One or more sessions will therefore be needed to explain the nature of the protocol as a work task and work through the section headings which provide the guidelines for the protocol document which each student will shortly be working towards. Those section headings are as follows:

1 *Definition of the question which is being asked and the hypothesis tested.* Once the student has identified a 'good question' which derives from some kind of front-line personal reality, that question must then be sharpened and refined so that if another participant in the workshop puts the question 'What are you *really* asking ... I don't quite see ... ', that question can be answered convincingly and without any fumbling.

2 *Description of the background and context* which leads to the selection of this particular question.

3 *Feasibility, support and resources.* A research plan will remain no more than an elegant abstraction unless the student addresses such questions as who will pay

for the interviewers or the needed secretarial hours, or find the petrol for the Land Rover which will take the research team up country.

4 *Communication and dissemination of final results.* Discussion emphasizes the need for local and national dissemination of results by multiple means – media presentations, one day meetings which a Minister may consent to address, and so on. The belief that communication uniquely or even at all necessarily means publication in international journals is discouraged.

5 *Possible lines of follow-through* and further research development.

6 *Research design.* This heading introduces a major section of the protocol. The student is encouraged to be flexible and reminded that different projects may require varied lay-out of sub-headings. A check-list is however provided on some common design issues and these include: sample selection; how subjects are to be approached and recruited; design of instruments and data collection; coding and analysis of data; limitations of the study and issues of bias, reliability, validity, generalisability; ethical considerations.

7 *A short bibliography.*

With discussion of these ground-rules completed, illustrated by example and debated, the substantive task of the workshop gets under way.

HOW THE WORKSHOPS PROCEED

The research workshop proceeds at a pace determined by its participants and much which happens is dictated by teaching opportunities which arise spontaneously. A basic sampling issue which had previously seemed remote and theoretical may suddenly for instance become real, with cross-play between two or three participants as the commonalities and diversities in the research problems they are facing surface. Questionnaire design is a recurring topic with a discovery of the craftsmanship in scripting sensible, unambiguous questions in plain language. A diversion may be needed into some further reading.

The absolutely necessary first step is then of course the identification by each student of a research topic. Some may identify a satisfactory question at first attempt but more often early ideas are refined or even discarded. The next step is for each student to start building up a protocol while coming back to the group to discuss the issues which are emerging. Finally a stage is reached where completed draft protocols are being circulated, presented in turn to the group, commented on and revised. On average each student will present a draft to the group at least twice before the protocol reaches its final and polished form.

Whatever the outward progress of the work as measured by the step-to-step movement from a good idea to a well-crafted research statement, there is of course also the inner and dynamic play in terms of the attitudes and feelings outlined in the previous section. In particular a repeated aspect of this dynamic is the move through stages of perplexity and discouragement, the often quite overtly expressed feelings of the kind 'I can't do it, too much is being asked of me', to the very good final feelings of accomplishment.

RESEARCH PROTOCOLS: SOME EXAMPLES

Among the protocols which students have submitted as material towards completion of the Diploma's requirements have been three separate proposals for studying selected populations in Zimbabwe for prevalence of alcohol problems. These populations have included workers attending factory-based clinics, patients in urban and rural hospitals and subjects attending out-patient primary-care centres.

A British community psychiatric nurse prepared a proposal to survey local GP needs and expectations relating to support from a shortly to be established community drug team. Another nurse has looked at how community prevalence of benzodiazepine problems could be estimated, while a nurse working in a hospital setting will attempt to explore reasons for early self-discharge among hospitalized drug users.

Two controlled studies have been proposed, one in an English and one in an Egyptian setting. The latter will be contributing towards doctoral work.

A German worker is looking at attitudes towards the doctor's role in responding to cigarette smoking among practice patients and another German proposal aims to carry out a descriptive follow-up of heroin users treated in a prison setting. A British probation worker is studying married couples where both are drug addicts and the related provisions for help.

This is by no means a complete inventory of the many interesting ideas which students have developed further. Proposals dealing with heroin users in India, cocaine takers in Ecuador and drinkers of banana beer in Tanzania certainly also deserve mention. Even this synoptic account of the way in which students have responded to the challenges set them may convey something of the variety, interest and relevance of what they have developed in the workshop setting.

APPRAISAL

It seems likely that most (but not all) of the students who engaged in these workshops would describe the experience as beneficial. The success of the workshop as a teaching method undoubtedly depends however on the atmosphere which can be created and the setting up of a forum in which the learning process effectively mobilizes the group itself as a key resource. Much has been learnt from feed-back sessions at the end of each course and it is certainly a method which needs further monitoring, criticism and development.

A very important measure of success will be evidence that protocols have become projects on the ground, with results having been presented and useful follow-through to action. Much work is now underway in various home locations.

A less tangible and more long-term but highly important manner in which the success of this project must ultimately be judged is the degree to which at a personal level it has acted as change agent. In ten or twenty years' time will there be a scattering of professionals around the world engaged at times in plain, jobbing research who would never otherwise have realized their capacities? And will those people succeed in carrying that enabling message to other and younger workers at front-lines far beyond the research and imagination of a Camberwell seminar room?

Training resources

Ilana Belle Glass

ORGANIZATIONS

The following institutions and organizations are an invaluable source of books, periodicals, reports, training programmes, video and audio cassettes as well as teaching packages:

Action on Smoking and Health
5-11 Mortimer Street
London W1N 7RH
United Kingdom
(Tel: 071-637-9843)

Addiction Research Foundation (ARF)
Sales and Promotion Department ST
33 Russell Street
Toronto
Ontario M5S 2S1
Canada
(Tel: 416-595-6000)

Addiction Research Unit
National Addiction Centre
Institute of Psychiatry
De Crespigny Park
London SE5 8AF
United Kingdom
(Tel: 071-703-5411)

Alcohol Concern
305 Gray's Inn Road
London WC1X 8QF
United Kingdom
(Tel: 071-833-3471)

Drug Education Centre
Western Australian Alcohol and Drug
Authority
35 Havelock Street
West Perth WA 6005
Australia
(Tel: 09-426-7272)

Institute for the Study of Drug Dependence
18 Hatton Place
Hatton Gardens
London EC1
United Kingdom
(Tel: 071-430-1961)

Mental Health Film Council
380 Harrow Road
London W9
United Kingdom
(Tel: 071-286-2346)

National Drug and Alcohol Research
Centre (NDARC)
University of New South Wales
PO Box 1
Kensington
NSW 2003
Australia
(Tel: 02-398-9333)

National Institute of Drug Abuse (NIDA)
and National Institute of Alcohol Abuse
(NIAAA)
US Department of Health and Human
Services
Public Health Service
Alcohol, Drug Abuse and Mental Health
Administration
5600 Fishers Lane
Maryland 20857
USA

Office for Substance Abuse Prevention
(OSAP)
National Clearing-house for Alcohol and
Drug Information (NCADI)
P O Box 2345
Rockville
Maryland 20852
USA
(Tel: 301-468-2600)

Turnip Video Services
193 Queens Road
Wimbledon
London SW19 8NX
United Kingdom
(Tel: 081-543-0213)

World Health Organization (WHO)
Publications
World Health Organization
Distribution and Sales
CH-1211 Geneva 27
Switzerland

The WHO will inform you of their sales
agent in your country.

BOOKS

The following books or reports are recommended. They are inexpensive and highly
readable.

The Advisory Council on the Misuse of
Drugs has published a number of reports
the most recent of which are:

Advisory Council on the Misuse of Drugs
(1990) *Problem Drug Use: A Review of
Training*, London: HMSO.
Advisory Council on the Misuse of Drugs
(1988) *AIDS and Drug Misuse: Part I*,
London: HMSO.
Advisory Council on the Misuse of Drugs
(1989) *AIDS and Drug Misuse: Part II*,
London: HMSO.
Advisory Council on the Misuse of Drugs
(1982) *Treatment and Rehabilitation*,
London: DHSS

Berridge, V. and Edwards, G. (1987)
Opium and the People, New Haven and
London: Yale.
Edwards, G. (1987) *The Treatment of
Drinking Problems*, Oxford: Blackwell.
—(ed.) (1989) *International Review of
Psychiatry* 1(1/2), Special Double Issue:
'Psychiatry and the Addictions', pp.
1–190.
Ghodse, H. (1989) *Drugs and Addiction
Behaviour. A Guide to Treatment*,
Oxford: Blackwell.

Gossop, M. (1987) *Living with Drugs*,
Aldershot: Wildwood House/Gower.
Ludwig, A. (1988) *Understanding the
Alcoholic's Mind. The Nature of Craving
and How to Control It*, New York and
Oxford: Oxford University Press.
Madden, J. S. (1984) *A Guide to Alcohol
and Drug Dependence*, Bristol: John
Wright.
Oppenheimer, E. and Stimson, G. (1982)
*Heroin Addictions: Treatment and
Control in Britain*, London: Tavistock.
Orford, J. (1985) *Excessive Appetites: a
Psychological View of Addictions*,
Chichester: John Wiley and Sons.
Royal College of Physicians (1987) *A
Great and Growing Evil: the Medical
Consequences of Alcohol Abuse*,
London: Tavistock.
Royal College of Psychiatrists (1986)
Alcohol: Our Favourite Drug, London:
Tavistock.
Royal College of Psychiatrists (1987) *Drug
Scenes*, London: Gaskell.
Secretary of Health and Human Services
(1987) *Sixth Special Report to the US
Congress on Alcohol and Health*,
Maryland: US Department of Health and
Human Services.

Stockwell, T. and Clement, S. (1987) *Helping the Problem Drinker*, London: Croom Helm.

Vaillant, G. (1983) *The Natural History of Alcoholism*, Cambridge, MA: Harvard University Press.

World Health Organization (1985) *Alcohol Policies* (ed. Marcus Grant), Geneva: World Health Organization.

World Health Organization (1986) *Drug Dependence and Alcohol-Related Problems. A Manual for Community Health Workers with Guidelines for Trainers*, Geneva: World Health Organization.

JOURNALS

Specialist journals

Addictive Behaviours
AIDS Journal
Alcohol and Alcoholism
Alcoholism: Clinical and Experimental Research
American Journal of Drug and Alcohol Abuse
British Journal of Addiction

Bulletin on Narcotics
Contemporary Drug Problems
Drug and Alcohol Dependence
Druglink
International Journal of the Addictions
Journal of Drug Education
Journal of Drug Issues
Journal of Studies on Alcohol

Generic journals (which are likely to cover addictions)

Acta Psychiatrica Scandinavica
American Journal of Psychiatry
American Journal of Psychology
American Journal of Public Health
Archives of General Psychiatry
Behaviour Research and Therapy
British Journal of Hospital Medicine
British Journal of Psychiatry
British Medical Journal

Journal of the American Medical Association
Journal of Clinical and Consulting Psychology
Lancet
New England Journal of Medicine
Psychological Bulletin
Psychological Medicine

Name index

Acker, C. 145, 146
Adams, E.H. 85
Adams, R.D. 146
Adityanjee 62
Advisory Council on the Misuse of Drugs 242, 333
Albee, A. 236
Allgulander, C. 60, 62
Alroomi, L.G. 222
al-Sabbah, Hasan Ibn 73
American Psychiatric Association 5
Andrews, M. 259
Annis, H. 209
Ashton, H. 60, 219
Atkinson and Skegg 51
Azrin, N.H. 229, 249

Babor, T.F. 334
Baer, J.S. 20
Baldwin, S. 296, 299
Ball, J.C. 130, 181
Bandura, A. 226
Barr, H.L. 38
Barrison, I.G. 333
Beatty, W.W. 147
Becker, H. 27
Becker, J.T. 147
Begleiter, H. 44
Bennett, T.H. 305
Bennun, I. 249
Benowitz, N.L. 96
Bergland, M. 142
Berlyne, N. 147
Bernadt, M.W. 153, 156, 157, 187, 188
Bevan, A. 285
Bikle, D.D. 137
Blume, S.B. 107, 108
Blumer 26, 27, 28
Bohman, M. 42, 43, 160, 298
Bolderston, H. 159
Bowden, S.C. 147
Box, S. 27
Bozarth, M.A. 19
Brandt, J. 145

Brannen, J.M. 181
Bridgewater, R. 176
Brown, D. 240
Bruun, K. 313, 316
Brzek, A. 137
Burks, B.S. 42
Bury, M.R. 28, 29
Busby, W.J. 176
Busto, U. 36–7
Butters, N. 147, 148

Cadoret, R.J. 42, 43
Carlen, P.L. 146
Cartwright, A. 269
Casswell, S. 36
Centers for Disease Control 126
Cermak, L.S. 147
Chadwick, O. 102
Chaisson, R.E. 127
Chang, J. 338
Chick, J. 142, 334
Childress, A.R. 233–4
Clausen, J.A. 26
Clement, S. 279, 280
Clifford, C.A. 41, 42
Cloninger, C.R. 43–4, 160, 298
Coid, J. 145
Collard, J. 181
Constable, J. 269
Cooke, B.R. 102
Corn, T.H. 148
Cotton, N.S. 41
Coupe, J. 281
Creed, F.H. 287
Crowley, T. 232
Cushman, P. 142
Custer, R.L. 107
Cutting, J. 143, 147

David, A.S. 333
Davies, B. 36
DAWN 173
De Leon, G. 259, 261
Dembo, R. 36

Subject index

willpower 23
wine: drinking repertoire 7; market for
    48–9; production 315; progression from
    165
withdrawal avoidance theories of addiction
    20–1, 23
withdrawal management: alcohol 207–15;
    barbiturates 219; benzodiazepines 219;
    cocaine 87–8, 220; opiate 67–8, 216–18
withdrawal symptoms: alcohol 11;
    avoidance of 7, 15, 17; barbiturates 219;
    benzodiazepines 90–4, 219; cannabis
    220; chemical treatment 216; neonatal
    91, 171; opioids 67–8; PCP 220; relief
    of 7; repeated 6–7; tobacco 98
women: alcohol services 281; drug
    complications 124; drunkenness
    offenders 299; prisoners 173, 296;
    substance abuse issues 168–74; see also
    gender effects

workplace interventions 307–11
World Health Organisation (WHO)
    326–30; alcohol dependence study 5;
    alcohol policy 313, 315, 318;
    benzodiazepines recommendation 31;
    Health For All 308, 323; ICD 152;
    smoking cessation guidelines 267, 321;
    tobacco deaths estimate 115, 323;
    tobacco programme 323, 324

xylene, 101, 102

Yage 79
young drug users 283; see also
    adolescents, children
youth issues see adolescents
Yugoslavia 127

Zimbabwe 345

THE INTERNATIONAL HANDBOOK OF ADDICTION BEHAVIOUR

'Helping people with substance problems is a difficult business. The common sense and vision which this text offers will help the helping professions make that business better informed, more effective, and a little more humane.'

Professor Griffith Edwards
in the *Foreword*

International in its scope and multidisciplinary in its approach, *The International Handbook of Addiction Behaviour* gives authoritative coverage of current issues in the addiction field in an easy reference form. It brings together the full variety of scientific approaches to addiction behaviour and provides a sound theoretical grounding to the clinical situation.

Written by experts and based on clinical and teaching experience, the *Handbook* proposes a way forward towards integrated treatment interventions. It covers a wide range of licit and illicit drugs including alcohol, nicotine, heroin and cannabis, and deals with gambling as an example of a non-drug dependence. It discusses many aspects of treatment, training, prevention and policy formation in an international perspective.

The International Handbook of Addiction Behaviour breaks new ground by highlighting the links between clinical work, training and research and sets an agenda for a new approach in the addictions field. It will be an invaluable guide for students, trainers and professionals.

Jacket design: Carole Oliver